PRAISE FOR *WHITEWASHING RACE*

"Far from writing a collection of essays, the authors of *Whitewashing Race* have collaborated to produce a brilliant, seamless book on America's deepest divide. Framed as a response to conservative analysts who claim that racial problems are essentially solved, the book provides an authoritative overview of how the nation's two principal races still remain sharply apart by every social measure."

—Andrew Hacker, author of *Two Nations: Black and White, Separate, Hostile, Unequal*

"In today's political climate, even the most well-meaning liberal tends to believe that institutional racism is a thing of the past and that we've truly achieved a color-blind society. *Whitewashing Race* makes a powerful case that racism is still with us. Relying on solid evidence rather than polemics, the authors have amassed an overwhelming body of data to show the persistence of racism in the job and housing market, education, the criminal justice system, and the political arena. If we ever have a real 'national conversation' on race, *Whitewashing Race* ought to be mandatory reading."

—Robin D. G. Kelley, author of *Freedom Dreams*

"*Whitewashing Race* is the most important social science statement on race in more than a decade. It lays bare the expressly conservative, ideological, and deeply flawed analyses of those pundits pressing for 'color-blind' social policy. With lucid prose and truly definitive scholarship, Brown, Wellman, and colleagues thoroughly debunk the reigning conservative consensus. Anyone who cares about racial justice and the fate of the American Dream should read this vitally important book."

—Lawrence D. Bobo, editor of *Prismatic Metropolis: Inequality in Los Angeles*

WHITEWASHING RACE

THE GEORGE GUND FOUNDATION
IMPRINT IN AFRICAN AMERICAN STUDIES

The George Gund Foundation has endowed
this imprint to advance understanding of
the history, culture, and current issues
of African Americans.

WHITEWASHING RACE

The Myth of a Color-Blind Society

Michael K. **Brown**
Martin **Carnoy**
Elliott **Currie**
Troy **Duster**
David B. **Oppenheimer**
Marjorie M. **Shultz**
David **Wellman**

UNIVERSITY OF CALIFORNIA PRESS
Berkeley · Los Angeles · London

University of California Press
Berkeley and Los Angeles, California
University of California Press, Ltd.
London, England
© 2003 by the Regents of the University of California
First paperback printing 2005

Library of Congress Cataloging-in-Publication Data
    Whitewashing race : the myth of a color-blind
society / Michael K. Brown ... [et al.].
        p.   cm.
    Includes bibliographical references and index.
    ISBN 0-520-24475-3 (pbk: alk. paper)
        1. Racism—United States.   2. United States—
Race relations.   3. African Americans—Civil rights.
I. Brown, Michael K.
E185.615.W465   2003
305.896'073—dc21   2002032798

Manufactured in the United States of America

13   12   11   10   09   08   07   06   05
10   9   8   7   6   5   4   3   2   1

The paper used in this publication meets the minimum
requirements of ANSI/NISO Z39.48-1992 (R 1997)
(*Permanence of Paper*).♾

Contents

List of Illustrations

Preface

We wrote this book because we were troubled about the future of racial equality in America. Coming of age in the 1950s and 1960s, we witnessed the moral and political power of the civil rights movement to mobilize Americans of all races against Jim Crow laws. The movement ushered in monumental civil rights legislation to end nearly one hundred years of visible, legal, and punishing racial segregation. For a brief period, we watched the lives of blacks and Latinos improve, we witnessed a substantial middle class take root in minority communities, and we noticed glimmers of change in the ways police treated these communities. The civil rights movement profoundly changed America, bringing a measure of racial justice and hope to people of color.

Barely forty years later, racial justice has ceased to be a priority, and, in some instances, the gains of the 1960s and 1970s have been reversed. Today optimism about the future of racial justice has been swapped for fatalism, and a sense of possibility stymied by what passes for necessity and "realism." We are in a new era, and we face new challenges if the ugly stain of racism is to be removed from American life. Yet instead of expressing alarm at the persistence of deeply rooted racial inequalities and searching for new ways to reach America's egalitarian ideals, many former advocates of racial equality proclaim the civil rights movement is over and declare victory. Racism has been defeated, they tell us. If racial inequalities in income, employment, residence, and political representation persist, they say, it is not because of white racism. Rather, the problem is the behavior of people who fail to take responsibility for their own lives. If the civil rights movement has failed, they insist, it is because of the manipulative, expedient behavior of black nationalists and the civil rights establishment.

These sentiments have migrated to the general public from the small number of conservative think tanks that spawned them, becoming the foundation of a new national consensus on race. By the late 1990s, it had become clear to us that someone must engage this emerging explanation for persistent racial inequality in America, to subject it to scholarly scrutiny and determine if it is grounded in empirical research or ideology cloaked in academic trappings. A small number of social scientists and intellectuals have criticized individual proponents of the new orthodoxy, but no one has engaged the entire body of beliefs.

Over lunch one afternoon in 1998, two of us, Michael K. Brown and David Wellman, challenged each other to take up the task. If not us, then who? As the challenge was being transformed into an actual research project, we quickly realized that the job was too large for us alone. Too many scholarly disciplines fed into the new consensus for two people to examine it seriously and thoroughly. The project had to be an interdisciplinary, collaborative effort. So we explored the idea with Troy Duster, then Director of the Institute for the Study of Social Change at the University of California, Berkeley, to see if he thought it might be an Institute project. Duster shared our enthusiasm, and the three of us began to widen the collaboration to cover the vast territory of law, education, social theory, and policy. Martin Carnoy, Elliott Currie, David Oppenheimer, and Marjorie Shultz later joined us.

Brown and Wellman then convened and chaired a series of meetings at which the seven of us discussed books written by proponents of the new consensus on race in America. Eventually, Currie suggested that each person write four pages of a possible chapter for the book. Four pages led to eight, eight to sixteen, and on until each of us had written chapter drafts, which we then discussed as a group. This book is an extension of that process.

Whitewashing Race is profoundly collaborative. Although each of us initiated drafts of specific chapters, we all participated in constructing the fundamental argument, and we all added ideas and rewrote drafts. Brown and Wellman had the additional responsibility of coordinating the effort and giving the book one voice. The book is collaborative in another sense. We are convinced that more than one perspective is necessary to understand what Du Bois called "the problem of the color line." We come to the subject from different scholarly disciplines—among us are two sociologists, two lawyers, one political scientist, one economist, and one criminologist—and with different political judgments about how to address racial inequality. (We also come from a variety of geographical locations. Brown and Carnoy traveled the most.

Brown graciously—though not without protesting now and then—made numerous 150-mile round trips on the heavily traveled corridor between Santa Cruz and Berkeley.) Despite our intellectual differences, each of us has devoted an important part of our career to the study of race and racism in America.

Something extraordinary occurred in the four-plus-year process that followed. As each of the three drafts Brown and Wellman edited was read and critically discussed by the entire group, political and interpretive differences emerged among us. No one was surprised by the existence of disagreement. But even though the room was filled with impressive records of intellectual accomplishment, there was little of the competitive verbal jousting that often accompanies collaborations of this sort. Indeed, we were all struck by the thoughtful discussions, and the deeper we delved into the material and the harder we scrutinized each other's interpretations, the more we realized how much learning was actually taking place.

We now realize that our differences, produced by the intellectual diversity of our group, were not simply obstacles to be managed, but resources. Our differences transformed simplicity into complexity, pushed us past worn-out formulations, and helped us discover new ways to explore old problems. They enabled us to scrutinize time-worn beliefs and produce a book that none of us could have written alone. This book is a testament to the virtues of intellectual collaboration and diversity.

Despite our differences, we are convinced there is overwhelming empirical evidence that racial stratification remains a serious source of inequality in U.S. society. As people who have studied these issues for a long time, we also agree that much of the conservative consensus on race is deeply flawed and based on specious interpretations of research. While we recognize there are limits to anyone's perspective, we are committed to time-honored standards of scholarly inquiry and debate and insist on holding the architects of the new consensus on race to those standards as well.

Another point about our approach in this book is in order. We focus mostly on examples of discrimination against African Americans. Some readers might think that we have unwittingly reinscribed the so-called black/white binary that permeates so many analyses of race in North America. We are fully aware that racism in America is not a two-dimensional picture of white over black. It never was. From the moment Europeans settled in the "New World" and either removed indigenous people or exterminated them, from the military occupation of Mexico to the lynching, removal, and exclusion of Asian immigrants on the West Coast, the color of race and racism has never been monochromatic.

We also know that demographic changes beginning in the last quarter of the twentieth century seriously complicate the meaning of race and racism. As large numbers of Asians and Latinos move into America's major urban areas, the politics and economics of race are no longer represented in black and white. Old alliances based on race have been replaced by new multiracial coalitions. As racial intermarriages increase, the very meaning of race has been tangled in ways that were once inconceivable. And with the development of black cultural and athletic icons, blackness has been transformed from a badge of oppression into an image that is desired and emulated. America is now a nation so racially complicated that one black person can be secretary of state, while another is racially profiled or sodomized in a New York City police station, all in the same historical moment.

So why do we focus largely on black and white? We do so because the conservative consensus on race is mostly constructed around the relationship between black and white. Thus, if we are to seriously engage and scrutinize this development, we need to address the issues it raises. This means that while we have introduced materials on Asians and Latinos in those instances where they figure in the new consensus, we have largely restricted ourselves to addressing discrimination practiced by whites against blacks. We found it quite striking that when Asians and Latinos enter the conservative consensus, it is usually to discount the impact of racism on the life-chances of blacks. Thus, Asians are presented as a "model minority" in relation to blacks, and married Latino mothers are used to prove that the reason so many black women are on welfare is because they are single.

There is another reason we focus on black and white even though we know that today race in America is not dichotomous. It is because the black/white binary persists as a feature of everyday life and is crucial to the commonsense understanding of racism. It persists, in large part, because "whiteness" has always been important in defining who is and who is not an American. The original legislation that specified who could become a naturalized American was unequivocal: naturalization was restricted to white males. To further complicate matters, whiteness in the United States has never been simply a matter of skin color. Being white is also a measure, as Lani Guinier and Gerald Torres put it, "of one's social distance from blackness."[1] In other words, whiteness in America has been ideologically constructed mostly to mean "not black."

The increasing numbers of Asians and Latinos in the United States and the development of a black middle class have not changed this ideological construction of whiteness. Even in the twenty-first century, racism in the United States continues to be defined by a dichotomy not between black and white, but between black and nonblack. A crucial example of this comes from the literature on racial segregation. Researchers have found that whites are much more likely to leave a neighborhood when blacks arrive than when Asians or Latinos move in.[2] Similarly, new racial or ethnic groups have been historically integrated into American society by promising members of these groups that they will not be treated like blacks.[3] The relationship of African Americans to whites therefore remains fundamental to any analysis of racial inequality.

A note on stylistic conventions: Throughout the book we capitalize the names of ethnic groups but not racial groups. Accordingly, we refer to African Americans, Euro Americans, and Latinos or to blacks and whites.

A project of this magnitude requires the assistance of many hands. We gratefully acknowledge the work of Zoe Sodja of the Document Publishing and Editing Center of the University of California, Santa Cruz, and Patricia Sanders of Merrill College Faculty services for their efficient help in bringing this book to publication.

Race Preferences and Race Privileges

At the turn of the last century, the African American leader and scholar W. E. B. Du Bois declared that the "problem of the twentieth century" was "the problem of the color line." Today, as a new century begins, race is still a pervasive and troubling fault line running through American life. We are not divided because we fail to "get along" as Rodney King lamented after the Los Angeles riots a decade ago. Nor is it because diehard advocates of affirmative action insist on stirring up racial discord. What divides Americans is profound disagreement over the legacy of the civil rights movement. At the core of our national debate are very different opinions about the meaning of race in contemporary America and the prospects for racial equality in the future.

The crude racial prejudice of the Jim Crow era has been discredited and replaced by a new understanding of race and racial inequality. This new understanding began with a backlash against the Great Society and took hold after the Reagan-Bush revolution in the 1980s. The current set of beliefs about race rests on three tenets held by many white Americans. First, they believe the civil rights revolution was successful, and they wholeheartedly accept the principles enshrined in civil rights laws. They assume civil rights laws ended racial inequality by striking down legal segregation and outlawing discrimination against workers and voters. They think racism has been eradicated even though racist hotheads can still be found throughout America. While potentially dangerous, racial extremists are considered a tiny minority who occupy political space only on the fringes of mainstream white America.

Second, if vestiges of racial inequality persist, they believe that is because blacks have failed to take advantage of opportunities created by the civil rights revolution. In their view, if blacks are less successful than whites, it is not because America is still a racist society. In fact, a substantial majority believe that black Americans do not try hard enough to succeed and "with the connivance of government, they take what they have not earned."[1]

Finally, most white Americans think the United States is rapidly becoming a color-blind society, and they see little need or justification for affirmative action or other color-conscious policies. Inspired by the ideals so eloquently expressed in Martin Luther King Jr.'s "I have a dream" speech, they embrace his vision of a color-blind America and look forward to the day when race will not determine one's fate, when a person is evaluated, in King's words, by the content of one's character rather than the color of one's skin.

Jim Sleeper echoes these sentiments. Author of a caustic critique of white liberals and civil rights leaders, he rejects any suggestion that Du Bois's warning is still relevant to America's racial divide. The nation's future lies in a color-blind society, he believes, and "it is America's destiny to show the world how to eliminate racial differences—culturally, morally, and even physically—as factors in human striving."[2] If Americans remain racially divided, he asserts, it is because we have abandoned "the great achievement of the civil rights era—the hopeful consensus that formed in the 1960s around King's visions of a single, shared community." Tamar Jacoby agrees. The author of a lengthy study of racial conflict in three cities, she attributes the failure to create a color-blind society to a "new" black separatism and the "condescension of well-meaning whites who think that they are advancing race relations by encouraging alienation and identity politics."[3]

On the surface at least, these beliefs about race are compelling. They appeal to widely held principles like fairness and equality of opportunity, diminishing the differences between liberals and conservatives. More important, they also resonate with the experiences of many white Americans. In an era when economic inequality is growing, when many families stand still financially despite earning two and sometimes three incomes, these beliefs provide a convenient explanation for their circumstances. Historically, class inequality has exacerbated racial inequality, and the present is no different. The idea that lazy blacks get government handouts inflames white men whose real wages barely increased during the 1990s economic boom. And for whites turned away from elite colleges and professional schools that accept African Americans, these notions provide an outlet for deep resentment.[4]

The goal of a color-blind America is an old and cherished idea. When segregation was legal and racial classification determined where one sat or drank or worked or lived or went to school, color-blindness meant abolishing the color-coded laws of southern apartheid. Color-blindness was the opposite of Jim Crow. It was liberals who championed the idea of color-blindness in the 1960s, while conservatives were ardent defenders of racial segregation.[5] Thirty-five years ago many Americans, inspired by the civil rights movement's transcendent vision of an inclusive society, passionately searched for solutions to the problem of racial inequality. While nationalists on both ends were often strident, apocalyptic, and pessimistic, the liberal architects of color-blind politics were optimistic and confident that this approach would generate greater equality between the races.

The triumph of the civil rights movement, however, exposed the limits of color-blind social policy: what good were civil rights if one was too poor to use them? As Martin Luther King Jr. told his aide Bayard Rustin after the explosion in Watts, "I worked to get these people the right to eat hamburgers, and now I've got to do something . . . to help them get the money to buy it."[6] And in a posthumously published essay, he wrote about what it would take to achieve a genuinely inclusive society. His vision went beyond color-blind civil rights laws.

> Many whites who concede that Negroes should have equal access to public facilities and the untrammeled right to vote cannot understand that we do not intend to remain in the basement of the economic structure; they cannot understand why a porter or housemaid would dare dream of a day when his work will be more useful, more remunerative and a pathway to rising opportunity. This incomprehension is a heavy burden in our efforts to win white allies for the long struggle.[7]

Too many whites in America have failed to heed Martin Luther King Jr.'s warning of what it would take to achieve a genuinely inclusive society. Writing twenty-five years after *Brown v. Board of Education* was decided, Judge Robert L. Carter, who argued the case before the Supreme Court alongside Thurgood Marshall, observed, "It was not until *Brown I* was decided that blacks were able to understand that the fundamental vice was not legally enforced *racial segregation* itself; that this was a mere by-product, a symptom of the greater and more pernicious disease—white supremacy." Unlike those who believe that the dream of integration was subverted by color-conscious policies, Carter pointed out that "white supremacy is no mere regional contamination. It infects us nationwide," he wrote, "and remains in the basic virus that has debilitated blacks' efforts to secure equality in this country."[8]

With the clarity of hindsight, we can now see that it was naïve to believe America could wipe out three hundred years of physical, legal, cultural, spiritual, and political oppression based on race in a mere thirty years. The belief, even the hope, that the nation would glide into color-blindness was foolish. Indeed, there are good reasons to believe the current goal of a color-blind society is at least as naïve as the optimism of the 1960s and conveniently masks color-coded privileges.

The conflict over color-conscious public policies poses a powerful challenge: the issue in the debate goes beyond the future of specific policies to the very meaning of racial equality and inclusion. Advocates of color-blind policies believe that the defenders of color-conscious remedies to achieve racial justice are separatists who practice "identity politics." They oppose race-conscious solutions on the grounds that racial inclusion requires only that individuals be treated similarly under the law— no more, no less.

Those of us who disagree wonder whether it would be fair, even if it were possible and desirable, to now use color-blind and race-neutral criteria when people apply for jobs, adoptions, home loans or second mortgages, and college admissions. Racial equality requires social and political changes that go beyond superficially equal access or treatment.

Today, many white Americans are concerned only with whether they are, individually, guilty of something called racism. Having examined their souls and concluded they are not personally guilty of any direct act of discrimination, many whites convince themselves that they are not racists and then wash their hands of the problem posed by persistent racial inequality. This predilection to search for personal guilt has been reinforced by a Supreme Court that analogously locates the constitutional problem of racial injustice solely in an individual's intent to discriminate.

But if Americans go no deeper than an inquiry into personal guilt, we will stumble backward into the twenty-first century, having come no closer to solving the problem of the color line. Given America's history, why should anyone be surprised to find white privilege so woven into the unexamined institutional practices, habits of mind, and received truths that Americans can barely see it? After three decades of simply admitting Asian American, Latino American, and African American individuals into institutions that remain static in terms of culture, values, and practices, the inadequacy of that solution should be obvious.

The proponents of color-blind policies and their critics have very different understandings of race and of the causes of racial inequality. People's views on these questions have become polarized, meaningful exchange is rare, and the public policy debate has stalemated. For these reasons we think it is time to get beyond the debate over affirmative action or individual guilt and try to figure out why racial inequality continues to be an intractable American problem. Toward that end, we take a careful look at the emerging public understanding of race and racism in America. By thoroughly scrutinizing this evolving perspective and then comparing it to an alternative view, we want to show what is at stake in the current American debate over racial equality and inclusion.

THE EMERGING RACIAL PARADIGM

In the past few years a number of books have appeared that elaborate and refine the new popular understanding of race and racial inequality in America. Besides Jim Sleeper's *Liberal Racism* (1997) and Tamar Jacoby's *Someone Else's House* (1998), the other books include Dinesh D'Souza's *The End of Racism* (1995), Shelby Steele's *A Dream Deferred* (1999), and, most important, Stephen and Abigail Thernstrom's *America in Black and White: One Nation Indivisible* (1997). These books are promoted as reasoned and factually informed discussions of race in America. All of the authors give this emerging understanding of race and racism the appearance of scholarly heft and intellectual legitimacy. And they represent a diverse set of political positions. Sleeper is a self-identified liberal who believes that color-conscious policies dodge the "reality of social class divisions, which are arguably more fundamental than racial divisions in perpetuating social injustice." D'Souza, Jacoby, Steele, and the Thernstroms are conservatives.[9] Yet all might be identified as "racial realists," as Alan Wolfe calls the proponents of this perspective.

Although each of these authors has written a very different book about race, all set out to demolish the claims of color-conscious policy advocates and anyone who suggests that racial discrimination is a persistent American problem. Sleeper chastises liberals, either those who protest police mistreatment of blacks or *New York Times* editorial writers that hold African Americans to lower standards of behavior and accomplishment than whites. Jacoby argues that most of the blame for the failure of integration lies with blacks. And the Thernstroms' book is a not-so-subtle rejoinder to both the Kerner Commission's national report on race in America, issued in the aftermath of the 1960s urban upheavals, and Andrew Hacker's *Two Nations: Black and White, Separate, Hostile, Unequal* (1992).

The Kerner Commission concluded that "our nation is moving

toward two societies, one black, one white—separate and unequal." Hacker updated the Kerner Commission's assessment and provided substantial data documenting the differing conditions and fates of black and white Americans. The Thernstroms wade into the debate accusing critics of the racial status quo like Hacker of polemical posturing. They claim that, by contrast, their analysis complies with standards of neutrality and is committed to factual reporting. *America in Black and White*, the Thernstroms assert, is a treatise that overcomes ideology and addresses the hard truths. Their stated aim is to move beyond dichotomies, to find more complicated options, to construct an analysis that transcends race.

Racial realists make three related claims. First, they say that America has made great progress in rectifying racial injustice in the past thirty-five years. The economic divide between whites and blacks, in their view, is exaggerated, and white Americans have been receptive to demands for racial equality. Thus, racism is a thing of the past. Sleeper accuses liberals of a "fixation on color" and says they do not want "truly to 'get beyond racism.'" As he sees it, liberals consistently ignore evidence of racial harmony, of blacks and whites working together, or of growing intermarriage between blacks and whites. Instead, they favor a portrait of America as irredeemably racist.[10]

One reason race has remained so politically and socially divisive, racial realists often say, is that ill-conceived and unnecessary race-conscious policies such as affirmative action have been adopted. They believe these policies exacerbate white animosities and do more harm than good. One recent study, in fact, claims that merely mentioning affirmative action to otherwise nonprejudiced whites "increases significantly the likelihood that they will perceive blacks as irresponsible and lazy."[11] Many opponents of affirmative action point out that were it not for these distorting and distracting policies whipping up racial consciousness, race would virtually disappear as a marker of social identity. Race remains divisive, in their view, because race-conscious agitators exploit it to demand race-conscious policies.[12]

The racial realists' second claim is that persistent racial inequalities in income, employment, residence, and political representation cannot be explained by white racism, even though a small percentage of whites remain intransigent racists. As they see it, the problem is the lethargic, incorrigible, and often pathological behavior of people who fail to take responsibility for their own lives. In D'Souza's view, persistent and deep black poverty is attributable to the moral and cultural failure of African Americans, not to discrimination.[13]

For racial realists, color-blindness means, among other things, recognizing black failure. Jacoby reports that she has a note above her desk that reads: "'If you can't call a black thug a thug, you're a racist.' It is," she says, "an idea I stand by."[14] Racial realists charge that blacks and their liberal supporters are unwilling to acknowledge the failures of black people. Sleeper calls this the sin of liberal racism. He thinks that white liberals are guilty of holding blacks to a lower standard. They set "the bar so much lower" for blacks, he writes, "that it denies them the satisfactions of equal accomplishment and opportunity."[15] It is also counterproductive. Jacoby argues that the idea that racism still matters just encourages blacks to believe the fallacy that "all responsibility for change lies with whites." Contemporary allegations of racism, the Thernstroms insist, are mainly a cover, an excuse. Blaming whites— arguing that the "white score is always zero" or that "white racism remains a constant"—simply obscures the reality of black failure, self-doubt, and lack of effort. It deflects attention from changing the values and habits of many black people to overcome the "development gap" between blacks and whites, a process Jacoby calls "acculturation."[16]

The racial realists' final assertion is that the civil rights movement's political failures are caused by the manipulative, expedient behavior of black nationalists and the civil rights establishment. Or, as Alan Wolfe puts the matter in a review of Tamar Jacoby's recent book on integration, "Those who claim to speak in the name of African Americans do not always serve the interests for those for whom they supposedly speak."[17] The real problem today is not racists like David Duke who still prey on white fears. Instead, the genuine obstacles are misguided black militants like Al Sharpton who overdramatize white racism and white apologists who have a pathological need to feel guilty. Racial realists feel that since black civil rights leaders and militants benefit from government handouts and affirmative action, they have a vested interest in denying racial progress and fomenting racial divisions. Many black politicians, according to the Thernstroms, particularly those elected to Congress, ignore the real needs of their constituents and pursue instead "the rhetoric of racial empowerment" and separatism.[18]

Although racial realists do not claim that racism has ended completely, they want race to disappear. For them, color-blindness is not simply a legal standard; it is a particular kind of social order, one where racial identity is irrelevant. They believe a color-blind society can uncouple individual behavior from group identification, allowing genuine inclusion of all people. In their view, were this allowed to happen, individuals who refused to follow common moral standards would be stig-matized as individuals, not as members of a particular group.[19]

Ironically, like some multiculturalists, racial realists assume that the real problem facing America is not racial discrimination. Instead, it is a problem of recognition and identity, of how people see themselves. Were it not for racial preferences and black hopelessness-helplessness, the Thernstroms believe, race would virtually disappear as a political and social issue in the United States. Racial realists pay only lip service to the idea that racial discrimination matters; they do not seriously investigate how and why racism persists after the dismantling of Jim Crow laws or what causes racial inequality. They would much prefer to slay the evil dragon of racial separatism. For racial realists, upholding Martin Luther King Jr.'s noble dream to transform "the jangling dis-cords of our nation into a beautiful symphony of brotherhood" requires that the words *race* (and *racism*) must disappear from our political lexicon, and, along with rights, personal responsibility (read black failure) must be acknowledged.[20]

Racial realists did not produce this new assemblage of beliefs about race and racial inequality; they have codified it. And their case against color-conscious public policies has found receptive audiences throughout the country, among both Republicans and Democrats, young and old. But their synthesis of this new set of beliefs was not, as they claim, pro-duced by nonpartisan, neutral observations of race in America. Rather, it is an offshoot of the conservative turn in American politics. Like Dinesh D'Souza and most conservatives, racial realists categorically reject biological explanations for racial inequality while subscribing to the notion that any possibility for reducing racial inequality is under-mined by black behavior and values. Like other conservatives, both D'Souza and the Thernstroms believe in a version of racial realism that assumes that government intervention only makes things worse. Racial progress, in this view, is best achieved by letting the free market work its magic. In this instance, conservative ideology, like racial realism, makes a case against color-conscious policies and represents a generation of conservative attacks on liberal social policy.[21] In an important sense, the public's new understanding of race and racism is both a cause and a con-sequence of the emergence of modern conservatism, which is the context for the rise of racial realism.

It is time to take a cold, hard look at the case for racial realism and the new understanding of racism that it synthesizes. In the following analy-sis, we assume people bear certain responsibility for the outcomes of their lives. We do not ignore or make excuses when broadly accepted moral and legal standards are violated. Nor do we attribute every problem and failure in communities of color to persistent racism. But we cannot accept the proposition that racial inequality does not matter and that racism has all but disappeared from American life. In our judgment, the new public understanding subscribes to a false dichotomy: either we have racial prejudice or we have black failure. We think this view is deeply flawed. In this book, we present an alternative perspective, one that is sustained by empirical evidence and is more consonant with the realities of race in America as the nation enters the twenty-first century.

Throughout this book we use the term *racial realists* to refer to individuals who subscribe to the new belief system. Racial realists do not agree on every tenet of the new understanding of racial inequality, and they span, as we have indicated, the political spectrum. However, many of the writers we consider are conservatives, and they combine racial realism with political conservatism. When we analyze their views, we refer to them as conservatives rather than racial realists.

THE LOGIC OF COLOR-BLIND POLICIES AND FREE MARKET RACISM

The racial realists claim that segregation was defeated and white prejudice minimized after Congress passed the 1964 Civil Rights Act and the 1965 Voting Rights Act but that these gains have been derailed by the misguided policies of the civil rights establishment and liberal politicians. They believe that the United States made greater progress in removing racial prejudice and racist behavior in this period than many liberals will acknowledge. The Thernstroms cite big changes in racial attitudes among whites since the 1940s as evidence for this assertion. White prejudice, in their estimation, started to decline much earlier than most people realize. The shift began, the Thernstroms argue, in the early 1950s. And when the civil rights movement abolished Jim Crow, white racism withered away.

Equating attitudes with institutional practices, the Thernstroms boldly assert that racial inequality substantially diminished between 1940 and 1970. This progress, they contend, accompanied economic growth and individual achievements in education, not government programs. This claim radically twists the commonly held assumption that civil rights policies were responsible for the growth of the black middle class. There is no question that since the early 1940s African Americans have made enormous strides in income, occupation, and education. But the Thernstroms claim that the black middle class made its greatest strides *prior* to affirmative action policies and government programs designed to assist African Americans. The largest income gains and the greatest reductions in poverty rates, they assert, did not come in the 1960s but in the two decades following the Great Depression. According to the Thernstroms, Lyndon Johnson's Great Society played a small role in the creation of a flourishing black middle class and the alleviation of black poverty.

This historical account enables the Thernstroms to make an inference that is vital to the new understanding of race and racism. In this reading of history, African American economic progress—narrowing the racial gaps in wages, occupation, employment, and wealth—depends almost entirely on reducing the deficit in black people's levels of education, job skills, and experience. The idea here is that individuals succeed economically when they acquire the skills and experience valued by employers. The Thernstroms, along with many of the writers and scholars on whom they depend, assume that the most important factors that determine economic achievement for blacks are growth of the economy and the opportunity for employers to rationally choose between skilled and unskilled workers in competitive labor markets, not the elimination of institutional practices that systematically privilege whites. In this view, racial differences in employment, wages, and family income will presumably disappear as blacks acquire more job-related skills and education.[22]

Not every racial realist accepts the Thernstroms' historical account of black people's economic progress. But many people believe that after the 1960s, labor market discrimination was substantially diminished or eliminated and that what matters now is education and job skills. White racism, in their view, has very little to do with black income and wages or persistently high poverty rates in the black community.[23] It clearly makes much more sense, these people think, to look at the counterproductive and antisocial choices of poor blacks—choices that lead young women to have babies out of wedlock, young men to commit crimes, and young men and women to drop out of school.

When the Thernstroms argue that labor market discrimination was relatively unimportant in the 1940s and assert that labor market discrimination is all but gone, they rely on the economic theory of discrimination. This theory assumes that in competitive economic markets, discrimination is short-lived because ruthlessly competitive entrepreneurs will take advantage of the opportunities racial exclusion provides and hire low-wage black workers instead of their high-priced white counterparts. Victims of market discrimination, therefore, will always have an option to work, because some employers will not subordinate their chance to make a profit on cheap black labor to a desire to exclude black workers. In "a world of free access to open markets," the legal scholar Richard Epstein writes, "systematic discrimination, even by a large majority, offers little peril to the isolated minority."[24] Because the theory assumes that competition drives discriminatory employers out of the market, any differences in wages or income must be attributable to differences in education, job skills, or cultural values. In this account, when de jure segregation was demolished by 1960s civil rights legislation, blacks were free to compete on a more or less equal basis with whites. As a result, race-conscious policies that guarantee employment or education are not only unnecessary but are also harmful to the free market.

For the Thernstroms, as well as for the full range of racial realists and conservatives who subscribe to this remarkable revisionist history of racism since the 1960s, the main problem facing America was *state-sponsored* racial discrimination. The difficulty with Jim Crow laws in this view was not that they institutionalized white supremacy and racial domination. The problem with *Plessy v. Ferguson* (1896), which upheld the power of state governments to segregate public facilities and transportation by race, is that it interfered with an unfettered market. According to Epstein, southern politicians were catering to the prejudices of white voters by imposing legally binding segregation throughout the South. But these misguided laws made it impossible for employers to hire blacks and pay equal wages to blacks and whites, and this then short-circuited competition in labor markets. In this vein, he is troubled because the Supreme Court did not strike down these laws on the grounds that they interfered with the "liberty of contract," as it did when it struck down minimum wage and hours laws in the North. Epstein argues that even if segregated labor markets were to emerge in a free, competitive economic market, it would be the result of voluntary choices rather than coercion and therefore "must be sharply distinguished from the system of government-mandated segregation on grounds of race."[25]

Voluntary, individual choice is crucial to the color-blind worldview one finds in racial realism and to the new understanding of racial inequality that it promotes. Although the civil rights movement demolished publicly sanctioned racist laws, racial realists do not believe civil rights laws were intended or designed to promote integration or to eliminate racial differences in economic status. Color-blindness in this view is a formal guarantee of equality before the law; it only means that government may not treat individuals unfairly or discriminate against them. But being blind to color does not mean that racial differences in income, wages, or status will disappear. According to this version of color-blindness, people will rise or fall according to their own efforts and abilities. The onus of responsibility for success is squarely on the individual.

It should not be surprising, therefore, that these proponents of color-blindness strongly believe affirmative action policies in the late 1960s twisted and distorted the goals and statutory achievements of the civil rights movement. Affirmative action, in their view, refers to any race-conscious policy that mandates racial integration in schools, the creation of black or Latino majority legislative districts, or preferences in college admissions, employment, and business contracts. In each case, critics argue that the original, laudable goals of the civil rights movement were perverted by arrogant elites—black civil rights leaders, judges, and white liberals—who insisted on imposing their agenda and subverted the dream of a color-blind society.

The Thernstroms are typical of this sentiment. Their account of school desegregation is a classic attack on race-conscious policies. Desegregation was an entirely appropriate goal in their estimation, and it could have been achieved by abolishing Jim Crow laws and constructing school district boundaries that promoted racial balance. But, unfortunately, self-aggrandizing civil rights leaders and radical white liberals replaced this sensible policy with court-ordered busing, together with other forms of forced integration, and the results were predictably bad. In their view, the same scenario was played out with race-conscious employment policies, college admissions, business set-asides, and legislative redistricting. So far as the Thernstroms are concerned, all color-conscious policies, like much governmental regulation, are wasteful, make things worse, are prone to corruption, and, in this instance, stir up the reservoirs of racial resentment. If that were not serious enough, the Thernstroms add, none of these policies provide jobs for black students or raise their cognitive abilities.

This is racial realism's intellectual framework. It is reflected in and reinforced by contemporary white American public opinion about issues triggered by race. Persistent racial inequality is accepted as normal; African Americans are thought to be "the cultural architects of their own disadvantage." Lawrence Bobo calls this "laissez-faire racism."[26]

THE PERSISTENCE OF DURABLE RACIAL INEQUALITY

This snapshot of race in America is out of focus. Racial realists pose the wrong question. The real issue, so far as they are concerned, is whether the United States has made progress in reducing racial inequality. But every serious student of contemporary racial inequality concedes there has been progress. The Thernstroms remind us repeatedly that the good news "regarding the emergence of a strong black middle class has not received the attention it deserves."[27] Good tidings, they assert, are neglected because of a volatile mixture of "black anger" and "white guilt." This is hardly true. Every gain the black middle class has made, every uptick in black employment is trumpeted from the rooftops. There is no gainsaying the progress of the black middle class, but to dwell on this amounts to celebrating economic gains while ignoring the large and persistent gaps in economic and social well-being between blacks and whites.

An abundance of evidence documents persistently large gaps between blacks and whites in family income, wages, and wealth since the economic boom of the post–World War II years and *after* the civil rights revolution. Black families have clearly gained relative to whites over the last fifty-five years, but the absolute income gap between them has widened. In 2001, the real median income of black families was 62 percent of that of whites, only 10 points higher than it was in 1947 when the ratio was 52 percent. Over the same period, however, the *absolute* real median income gap doubled, rising from $10,386 to $20,469.[28] (If one compares black family income to that of non-Hispanic whites, a more accurate measure, the ratio is 58 percent, a gap that is largely unchanged since the early 1970s.[29])

Relative to non-Hispanic white men, black men made income gains between 1972 and 2001. Their real median income rose from 60 percent to 67.5 percent of white median income. The absolute gap declined slightly over the same period, falling from $11,624 to $10,325. (Almost all of black males' income gains came during the economic boom of the late 1990s; at the beginning of the decade black male income relative to whites' was lower than it was in 1972.) The picture for black women is very different. Compared to non-Hispanic white women, black women's real median income declined from 92 percent in 1972 to a low point of 79 percent in 1988 and then rose to 94.5 percent by 2001. The absolute gap in annual income between black and white women is much smaller than the one for the men—a reflection of the wage discrimination experienced by all women.[30] Large disparities in income remain even when the comparison is restricted to full-time workers, despite a black unemployment rate that is much higher than the rate for whites.[31]

Just as important is the startling persistence of racial inequality in other areas of American life, despite laws passed to address the disparities. Housing and health care are two matters vital to the well-being of individuals and their families, and both illustrate the limits of the civil rights revolution. The 1968 Civil Rights Act outlawed housing discrimination, yet African Americans continue to be the most residentially segregated group in the United States. They are far more likely to live in segregated neighborhoods than either Asian Americans or Latinos.[32] Blacks are much less likely to own a home, and when they can get a mortgage, they receive far less favorable terms than do comparable whites. For example, between 1993 and 1998, subprime lending—loans with higher interest rates and predatory foreclosure practices—grew by thirty times in Chicago's black neighborhoods, but by only two and one-half times in white residential areas. Race, not social class, explains this difference: in 1998, subprime lenders made 53 percent of the home-equity loans in middle-income black areas but only 12 percent of the loans in middle-income white areas.[33]

Medicare and Medicaid succeeded in expanding access to health care to many people, a clear example of progress. Racial and income differences in the use of health care facilities, including hospital stays as well as visits to doctors' offices, diminished substantially after these two laws were enacted. These laws made a difference; largely because of Medicaid, black infant mortality rates dropped by half between 1960 and 1980. Yet racial differences for many health indicators remained unchanged or in some cases widened. The black infant mortality rate remained twice as high as the white rate, and by 1998 it had actually widened.[34] Moreover, one specialist on race and health care has pointed out that in 1995 "black age-adjusted mortality rates were still 1.61 times that of whites, a disparity essentially unchanged since 1950."[35] In other words, neither the civil rights revolution nor diminishing prejudice have made much difference to racial disparities in mortality, the most fundamental matter of health. Neither income nor poverty status alone can explain these racial differences.[36]

One reason for these disparities is that blacks and Latinos are still much less likely to have access to primary care physicians than whites. For example, in South Central Los Angeles, where the population is overwhelmingly African American and Latino, the ratio of primary care physicians to the population is 1 to 12,993. By comparison, in wealthy Bel Air, only a few miles away, the ratio is 1 to 214.[37] Limited access to primary care shows up in many basic health statistics. David Smith reports that "the proportion of blacks receiving adequate prenatal care, up-to-date childhood immunizations, flu shots as seniors, and cancer screenings lags significantly behind whites, even though most of the financial barriers to such preventive services have been eliminated."[38] African Americans, Latinos, and members of other minority groups account for 75 percent of active cases of tuberculosis, and the Centers for Disease Control reports that blacks are five times as likely to die of asthma as are whites.[39] Even when blacks have *equal* access to medical care, recent evidence indicates that significant racial disparities in treatment and care remain. For example, among Medicare beneficiaries of similar age, gender, and income, blacks are 25 percent less likely to have mammography screening for breast cancer and 57 percent less likely to have reduction of hip fracture.[40]

Any credible analysis of race in America at the beginning of the twenty-first century must confront and account for these durable and persistent inequalities between blacks and whites. Many proponents of racial realism as well as those Americans who subscribe to the new explanation for racial inequality fail to do this for two reasons. First, they ignore or obscure dramatic and persistent facts of racial inequality. Second, the methodological assumptions that guide their investigation of race in America lead them to ignore alternative explanations that more closely "fit" the evidence they do cite. In the following analysis, we address each of these concerns.

THE MINIMAL RELEVANCE OF INDIVIDUAL CHOICE TO DURABLE RACIAL INEQUALITY

Today the predominant approach to understanding racial stratification in American life assumes that "social life results chiefly or exclusively from the actions of self-motivated, interest-seeking persons."[41] For those promulgating this view, it is solely the stated intentions and choices of individuals that explain discrimination. It leads writers to focus on individual whites' beliefs about African Americans and civil rights. Throughout *America in Black and White*, for example, the Thernstroms focus on the positive upward spiral of individual whites' attitudes as measured by public opinion data. The positive shift in expressed attitudes is then assumed, prima facie, to be evidence of behavior. If (white) people say they are not discriminating against blacks, the Thernstroms believe them, and infer that discrimination must be diminishing. In a like manner, persistent racial inequality is attributed to blacks' individual choices of lifestyles and attitudes.

The Thernstroms' assessment of residential discrimination is a prime illustration of how individual intentions and choices are used to explain racial inequality. They do not deny that residential segregation remains very high. Instead, the Thernstroms argue that it has declined somewhat and that this is real evidence of racial progress.[42] They go on to argue, however, that housing would be even less segregated but for the choices of blacks. Public opinion surveys prove whites are quite willing to accept blacks as neighbors. The problem, they argue, is that public opinion data show blacks would prefer to live in neighborhoods that are at least 50 percent African American. Thus, they conclude that the preferences of blacks, not white racism, produces segregated housing. In other words, present-day segregation is caused by ethnic group loyalty.[43]

Just as the Thernstroms think housing segregation reflects black preferences, Sally Satel, a psychiatrist, contends that racial differences in health and well-being are due to blacks' bad lifestyle choices. Like other conservatives, Satel thinks declining individual prejudice and the elimination of de jure segregation mean that racism is largely a thing of the past. Angered that "accusations of medical bias still linger" decades after segregation has ended, Satel severely criticizes federal funding of studies on racial and ethnic disparities in health care and any suggestion there is a relationship between blacks' and Latinos' health and discrimination or powerlessness. Satel accuses the public health establishment of neglecting the vital role of individual choices in health outcomes in its rush to analyze social injustice. "Taking responsibility for one's own health comes to be virtually ignored," she complains.[44]

Satel's criticisms about the documentation of racial disparities evade fundamental questions regarding the institutional structure of health care and racially disparate outcomes. By focusing on the stated intentions and choices of individuals, conservatives like the Thernstroms and Satel ignore the systemic and routine practices of white Americans and the consequences of their behavior. Whether these actions are motivated by group values and interests or operate through private and public institutions, the inescapable results are harmful to African Americans and other people of color.

When social scientists analyze income, employment, or occupational disparities between categorical groups—blacks-whites, men-women—they assume these gaps in material well-being are due mostly to differences in education and job skills that would affect an individual's productivity and thus that person's ability to succeed in competitive labor markets. Studies of wage discrimination, for example, typically proceed by removing the effects of individual characteristics such as education or experience that might explain wage differences between men and women or between racial groups. Any remaining gap in wages is then attributed to discrimination. Yet as Ruth Milkman and Eleanor Townsley explain, "This approach ... fails to capture the depth with which gender discrimination and the norms associated with it are embedded in the economic order—in fact, they are embedded so deeply that a willful act of discrimination is not really necessary to maintain gender inequality."[45] One problem with this approach is that an individual's job experience and education may have been shaped by deeply embedded patterns of discrimination—a racially biased allocation of public resources to schools for example—which means that education is not independent of discrimination. By focusing only on individuals and the skills they bring to the labor market, moreover, analysts obscure the relationship between racial groups, a fundamental element in the development of durable racial inequality.

In this book we will show how and why the specific intentions and choices of individuals regarding racial discrimination or exclusion are frequently irrelevant to the emergence and maintenance of social and economic inequalities in the United States. One cannot assume that individuals are the only appropriate unit of analysis. By making this assumption, Satel, the Thernstroms, and other like-minded interpreters of contemporary racial inequality neglect the collective actions of groups, the role of intermediary institutions, and the cumulative effects of durable racial inequality.

GROUP HOARDING AND THE ECONOMIC THEORY OF DISCRIMINATION

As we indicated earlier, the economic theory of labor market discrimination is a theory of individual choice. This one-dimensional theory, however, is empirically flawed. Because it assumes that economic competition drives out discrimination, the theory cannot explain why racial inequality persists once education, training, and experience are taken into account. Nor can it explain historical patterns of labor market segregation in both the North and the South. And recent attempts to rescue the theory by attributing differences in the economic success of African Americans and immigrants to cultural values have failed miserably.[46]

While individuals can and do discriminate, labor market discrimination is better understood as a group phenomenon. It is an instance of what Charles Tilly calls *opportunity hoarding*. This occurs when members of a group acquire and monopolize access to valuable resources or privileges. Most people know that informal networks of family, extended kinship, friendships, and associates are the typical routes to employment. Employers commonly recruit new workers through informal ties and word-of-mouth suggestions; current employees typically identify job candidates.[47] Because workers tend to be friends and acquaintances of members of the same race and sex, a bias toward re-creating a homogeneous workforce is overwhelming. Discrimination, therefore, can be passive and unobtrusive. One need not be a racist to use one's position to benefit friends and acquaintances, even if it means awarding jobs to whites rather than blacks.[48]

But the process of labor market discrimination is not always so passive. Once members of a group acquire access to resources, they may hoard the resources by denying access to outsiders. Tilly suggests that hoarding can be found in a variety of groups, including immigrants, criminal conspiracies, and even elite military units.[49] Once a group of employees acquire the best jobs and perks, they can make it difficult for employers to hire outsiders. Insiders can harass unwanted workers by disrupting their work and reducing their value to employers, which can eventually exclude outsiders. Intimidation is a way for insiders to discourage outsiders from even applying for a job. Justifying exclusionary practices with beliefs that denigrate the work habits and skills of excluded workers is the final step in this process. For a long time white workers used the "myth of the machine"—the idea that black workers were incapable of working with machines—to exclude African American workers from skilled, higher paying work.[50]

The Thernstroms assume that changing attitudes toward blacks is the key to reducing racial inequalities in wages, income, and employment. It makes more sense, however, to examine racial labor market competition—a prime example of opportunity hoarding—to get a better handle on a critical determinant of racial inequality. Simple models of discrimination that assume that unequal rewards to otherwise identical workers are motivated by prejudice do not capture the complexity and depth of racially divided labor markets in the twentieth century. When white workers compete for jobs, they use their advantages to exclude or subordinate black or Latino workers. Two prominent labor market economists, William Darity Jr. and Samuel Myers Jr., write that discrimination is "endogenously linked to the employment needs of non-black males." Competition between black and white workers intensifies when blacks threaten the status of white workers, either because the blacks have acquired the education and job skills to be competitive or because the job opportunities for whites diminish.[51] Employers' evaluations of the skills and talents of black workers are often based on negative stereotypes of their productivity rather than on independent assessments of their work. These stereotypes are the residue of racial labor market competition and push black workers to the bottom of the employment queue.[52]

Racial labor market competition is obviously affected by the state of the economy. When economic growth is sluggish or depressed, labor markets are slack and competition for jobs unleashes white racism. Robust economic growth produces tight labor markets as demand for workers rises, and typically has a greater impact on black unemployment rates than on white unemployment rates. Similarly, as high-wage manufacturing jobs are eliminated and whites are displaced, competition intensifies between blacks and whites for low- and moderate-wage service jobs. Job competition based on race can be modified by public policies that regulate wages and access to jobs through full employment or affirmative action policies. But unless or until a third party steps in to demand or induce employers to pursue a different recruitment strategy, a homogeneous racial and gendered workforce will almost inevitably be reproduced.

INSTITUTIONS AND THE ROUTINE, ORDINARY GENERATION OF INEQUALITY

Because the realist analysis of racial inequality assumes that racism is produced exclusively by the intentions and choices of individuals, intermediate institutions that play a crucial part in generating and maintaining racial inequality are rarely analyzed. The routine practices of corporations, law firms, banks, athletic teams, labor unions, the military, and educational institutions tend to be ignored or minimized. These institutions are neither scrutinized nor analyzed unless or until they institute strategies that redress past social grievances. Accordingly, advocates of this approach to racial inequality believe that individual access to previously segregated institutions is all that is necessary to redress past racial injustice. They never discuss the ways in which these institutions might be transformed to accommodate or better engage the groups they formerly excluded.

Any analysis of racial inequality that routinely neglects organizations and practices that, intentionally or *unintentionally*, generate or maintain racial inequalities over long periods of time is incomplete and misleading. Such an analysis will be unable, for example, to detect the ways in which real estate and mortgage lending industries routinely sustain segregated housing markets and discriminate against would-be black homeowners. It will also not notice that discrimination in the criminal justice system is produced by a large number of small decisions by the police that single out young black men, the results of which then extend to their treatment in adult courts.

Nowhere is the folly of neglecting institutional practices more apparent than in the case of racial disparities in health care and mortality. Many health care institutions remain partially segregated despite the end of Jim Crow and federal laws that prohibit distribution of federal funds to institutions that discriminate. The private nursing home industry, for example, has continued to be segregated, largely because for-profit nursing homes are reluctant to accept Medicaid patients, particularly elderly blacks, and state governments have little incentive to enforce civil rights laws. Elderly blacks are therefore less likely to use private nursing homes even though they have a greater need for such care. In Pennsylvania the segregation index for nursing homes is almost as high as the indexes for housing in metropolitan areas.[53] Moreover, nonwhites are almost twice as likely as whites to be admitted to a nursing home sanctioned by state officials for serious deficiencies in care and facilities.[54]

Segregated and unequal treatment in health care is an endemic problem, though not one that is attributable to the actions of prejudiced individuals. David Barton Smith concludes his detailed assessment of racial disparities in health care by noting that

> at least some of the reported differences in rates of drug addition, sexually transmitted diseases, and possibly even infant mortality reflect differences in the screening and reporting practices of the settings in which care is provided to blacks as opposed to those catering to whites. Such screening and reporting is more likely to be a part of the standard operating procedures of the more urban clinic settings where blacks disproportionately receive their care. In effect, these differences in procedures amount to an institutionalized form of racial profiling.[55]

While there are numerous examples of how economic, educational, and governmental organizations unintentionally produce unequal racial outcomes, it is also the case that certain institutions do better than others in reducing racial inequalities. Some universities that use affirmative action policies, for example, do better at graduating black students than universities that admit students strictly on the basis of test scores. Nor do blacks with low test scores always have lower graduation rates, as is typically assumed. It makes sense to focus our attention on institutional practices that mitigate and reduce racial inequalities. These practices will not be discovered, however, when one looks for racism in individual motivations and presumes that people with good intentions will do the right thing if only government gets out of the way.

CUMULATIVE INEQUALITIES

Inequalities are cumulative, a fact adherents of the new public wisdom on race ignore in their rush to celebrate progress. The story told by the Thernstroms in *America in Black and White,* for example, is disturbingly, sometimes even stunningly, ahistorical. This may seem surprising because the book does trace race relations over time, from the early 1940s to the present, and one of the authors is a prize-winning Harvard historian. Yet the book is insensitive to the ways in which the past shapes the future. By assuming that behavioral changes are produced by changes in attitudes, the Thernstroms implicitly distinguish between past and present discrimination.[56] But if discrimination has declined, this means one cannot look to history to explain the persistence of racial inequalities. As a result, proponents of the new understanding of racial inequality are forced to focus on individual motivations. But this neglects how the past has shaped contemporary patterns of racial inequality, or how it continues to constrain the choices of African Americans and other groups. Thus, conservatives and their realist colleagues ignore how the accumulation of wealth—economic, cultural, social, and political capital— molds economic opportunities for all Americans over time, especially blacks, Latinos, and other racial minorities. Wealth matters. At the conclusion of his book on race, wealth, and social policy in the United States, Dalton Conley writes: "One may conclude that the locus of racial inequality no longer lies in the labor market, but rather in class and property relations that, in turn, affect other outcomes. While young African American men may have the opportunity to obtain the same education, income, and wealth as whites, in actuality, they are on a slippery slope, for the discrimination their parents faced in the housing and credit markets sets the stage for perpetual economic disadvantage."[57]

When the economy falters, privileged members of society are able to help themselves over the difficult bumps and fluctuations of a market economy. Their net worth, not wages, provides the necessary reserves to ride out cyclical downturns in the economy or other disasters. Although the Thernstroms acknowledge racial differences in wealth, they attribute the black deficit to age and family structure. African American families, they argue, are younger and are more likely to be headed by single parents. Both factors militate against wealth accumulation and both, not coincidentally, are characteristics about which individuals exercise some choice.[58] Differences in the accumulation of wealth between different racial groups, however, are not solely the result of age, family structure, or the inclination to save—blacks and whites save about the same proportions of their income.[59] In fact, African Americans lost much of the wealth they acquired after the Civil War to white thievery and discrimination. A recent study by the Associated Press found that more than four hundred blacks were dispossessed of more than twenty-four thousand acres of farm and timber land in the South, worth millions of dollars today, through fraud, discrimination by lenders, and other illegal means.[60]

Since inequalities accumulate over generations, an analysis of racial inequalities in the distribution of wealth explodes any distinction between past and present racism. Cumulative inequality undermines racial conservatives' efforts to restrict the effects of racism to the past. Today's racial disparities in wealth reflect the legacies of slavery, Jim Crow, and labor market discrimination.

THE ORIGINS OF DURABLE RACIAL INEQUALITY

Discussions of racial inequality commonly dwell on only one side of the color line. We talk about *black* poverty, *black* unemployment, *black* crime, and public policies for *blacks*. We rarely, however, talk about the gains whites receive from the troubles experienced by blacks. Only when the diverging fates of black and white Americans are considered together—within the same analytic framework—will it be possible to move beyond the current stale debate over how to transform the American color line.

In our view, the persistence of racial inequality stems from the long-term effects of labor market discrimination and institutional practices that have created cumulative inequalities by race. The result is a durable pattern of racial stratification. Whites have gained or *accumulated* opportunities, while African Americans and other racial groups have lost opportunities—they suffer from *disaccumulation* of the accoutrements of economic opportunity. Rather than investigating racial inequality by focusing on individual intentions and choices, we concentrate on the relationship between white accumulation and black and Latino disaccumulation.

ACCUMULATION VERSUS DISACCUMULATION

The idea of accumulation is straightforward and can be illustrated with a simple example. Investment counselors routinely explain to their clients the importance of long-term investments. For example, a young couple that set aside just forty dollars a month beginning in 1970 and simply let it sit in an account paying 5 percent interest would accumulate about $34,000, or more than double the amount invested, by the year 2000. Rolling over modest investments of capital produces an impressive accumulation. Similarly, very small economic and social advantages can have large cumulative effects over many generations.

While accumulation is relatively well understood, there is a parallel and symmetrical idea that is usually ignored. This is the idea of *dis*investment and, over time, what might be called *dis*accumulation. Just as a positive investment of forty dollars can accumulate over time, so too can a negative investment produce a downward spiral. Consider what happens if one owes the Internal Revenue Service a few hundred dollars but allows that debt to go unpaid for a decade. The amount of that debt can increase dramatically and can lead to a debt of several thousand dollars. The amount owed can increase fivefold. From the point of view of the debtor, this is negative accumulation, or for purposes of this discussion, disaccumulation. Just as economic advantages (for example access to skilled trades) can accumulate, economic disadvantages (such as exclusion from well-paying jobs) can also be compounded over time.

Home ownership is a good example of how the principle of accumulation and disaccumulation works in a racial context. Today's very large gap in median net worth between whites and African Americans is mostly due to the discrepancy in the value of the equity in their respective homes. Blacks experience more difficulty obtaining mortgage loans, and when they do purchase a house, it is usually worth less than a comparable white-owned home. White flight and residential segregation lower the value of black homes. As blacks move into a neighborhood, whites move out, fearing that property values will decline. As whites leave, the fear becomes a reality and housing prices decline. The refusal of white Americans to live in neighborhoods with more than 20 percent blacks means that white-owned housing is implicitly more highly valued than black-owned housing. Redlining completes the circle: banks refuse to underwrite mortgage loans, or they rate them as a higher risk. As a consequence, when black homeowners can get a loan, they pay higher interest rates for less valuable property. This results in disinvestment in black neighborhoods and translates into fewer amenities, abandoned buildings, and a lower property tax base. Because white communities do not suffer the consequences of residential disaccumulation, indeed they receive advantages denied to black homeowners; the value of their housing increases and they accumulate wealth. In this way interlocking patterns of racialized accumulation and disaccumulation create durable inequality.[61]

The distribution of economic wealth is central to any account of racial inequality, but it is not the only dimension of racial accumulation and disaccumulation. For example, inadequate access to health care contributes to disaccumulation in communities of color. Health is fundamental to every aspect of life: without health, a student cannot do well in school; a worker cannot hold a job, much less excel at one; a family member cannot be an effective parent or spouse. Health crises and the staggering costs they impose are critical underlying causes of poverty, homelessness, and bankruptcy. Housing, employment, and education are vital, but without health, and the care necessary to maintain it, the quality of life, indeed life itself, is uncertain. The effect is cumulative. Inadequate prenatal care results in low birth-weight babies, which in turn leads to infant mortality and to severe physical and mental disabilities among those who survive.[62] One-fifth to one-third of African American children are anemic, and they account for a disproportionate number of children exposed to lead poisoning. Both problems impair intellectual functions and school performance.[63]

Accumulation also includes cultural and social advantages—meeting "the right people" at Harvard, Yale, and Princeton (who can and often do provide a substantial boost to one's career), for example. As we will subsequently document in more depth, a symmetrical process operates in the criminal justice system, with the opposite consequences: judges frequently incarcerate black juveniles rather than sending them home because the court believes these youngsters have fewer outside resources to help them. However well intentioned, these decisions then become part of the juvenile's record, counting against him or her in future scrapes with the criminal justice system. Diverting black youth to state institutions rather than sending them home is analogous to acquiring a small debt that can be compounded. Similarly, critics of affirmative action are correct when they tell black students who have been denied admission to the University of California at Berkeley that "there is nothing wrong with attending UC Riverside." But that is only half the story. Elite institutions are saturated with an accumulated legacy of power and privilege along lines of race and gender. The advice to attend Riverside ignores that "who you meet" at Harvard, Yale, or Princeton—or at Berkeley, Ann Arbor, or Madison—is an important aspect of the accumulation of economic and social advantage.

Many Americans, but particularly conservatives, object to the idea that past discrimination matters in the present. Marianne Means, a columnist for the Hearst newspaper chain, harshly condemns growing black demands for reparations. "We should not be a party," she writes, "to whipping up a guilt trip that is a ploy to get handouts for a social evil that officially ended nearly 140 years ago."[64] Racial realists believe that the accumulation of wealth and power by white Americans over the past 360 years is irrelevant to current patterns of racial stratification, and the use of race-conscious remedies to redress past racial injustices is therefore unnecessary and unfair. As they see it, basing current policies on past practices is wallowing in the past. The main impediment to racial equality, they feel, is state-sponsored discrimination, and the civil rights movement put an end to that. Thus, past discrimination should not matter. Ironically, adherents of this point of view ignore a different form of state-sponsored racial inequality—the use of public policy to advantage whites. Racism is not simply a matter of legal segregation; it is also policies that favor whites.

THE STRANGE CAREER OF RACE PREFERENCES IN U.S. PUBLIC POLICY AND LAW

Curiously, the current debate over race-conscious remedies assumes that the sole beneficiaries of these policies are blacks and other racial minorities. If, however, affirmative action is defined as "race and gender preferences codified into law and enforced through public policy and social customs," then it is strange and peculiar, arbitrary and incorrect, to suggest that affirmative action began in the summer of 1963 when President John F. Kennedy issued Executive Order 10925. Given the above definition, routinely cited by opponents of affirmative action, the more accurate beginning date for this legal and public policy is 1641. That is when the fledgling jurisdictions that would later become the first states began to specify in law that rights to property, ownership of goods and services, and the right to vote would be restricted by race and gender. In 1790, Congress formally restricted citizenship via naturalization to "white persons," a restriction that remained in place until 1952.[65]

Understood in this way, affirmative action has been in effect for 360 years, not 39. For the first 330 years, the deck was officially and legally stacked on behalf of whites and males.[66] In *Dred Scot* (1857), Supreme Court Chief Justice Roger Taney posed the matter in remarkably candid terms: "Can a negro, whose ancestors were imported into this country, and sold as slaves, become a member of the political community, formed and brought into existence by the Constitution of the United States, and as such become entitled to all rights, and privileges, and immunities, guaranteed by that instrument to the citizen?"[67] He answered his own question in unequivocal language. "'We the people,'" wrote Justice Taney, leaving no room for doubt, was never intended to include blacks, slave or free. "Neither Dred Scott nor any other person of African descent," he ruled, "had any citizenship rights which were binding on white American society." The authority cited by Justice Taney in his 1857 Supreme Court ruling was that the Constitution, the Courts at every level, the federal government, and the states all routinely denied blacks equal access to rights of citizenship.[68]

Thus, since the inception of the United States, wealth and institutional support have been invested on the white side of the color line, leading to an accumulation of economic and social advantages among European Americans. On the black side, economic and institutional *dis*investment has been the practice, resulting in a process of disaccumulation. When President Kennedy issued Executive Order 10925 in the summer of 1963, he was therefore simply trying to open doors that had been sealed shut for more than three centuries. Now, after only four decades of "racial and gender preferences," a vigorous and partially successful attack is being waged against affirmative action programs that were instituted to reverse three hundred years of disinvestment in black communities. Yet when power and wealth were being invested and accumulated on their side of the color line, white Americans registered hardly any opposition to the arrangement.[69]

THE ORIGINS OF MODERN STATE-SPONSORED RACIAL INEQUALITY

One need not go back three hundred years to find the antecedents of contemporary white advantage. The New Deal is the most recent benchmark for the accumulation of white privilege and the generation of black disadvantage. Franklin D. Roosevelt's policies were instrumental to both the cause of racial equality and the perpetuation of racial inequality. New Deal agricultural policies paved the way for the mechanization of southern agriculture and precipitated black (and white) migration to the North and the entry of blacks into manufacturing jobs. The Wagner Act legalized unions; minimum wage laws put an economic floor under all workers; the Social Security Act gave workers a measure of security; and the Employment Act of 1946 codified the government's responsibility for aggregate employment and price levels. These policies, combined with postwar economic growth, undermined the prewar northern racial order, set in motion changes that would dismantle Jim Crow, and reduced black as well as white poverty.

African Americans benefited from New Deal policies. They gained from the growth of public employment and governmental transfers like social security and welfare. The Great Society went further, reducing racial inequality, ameliorating poverty among the black poor, and helping to build a new black middle class. But if federal social policy promoted racial equality, it also created and sustained racial hierarchies. Welfare states are as much instruments of stratification as they are of equality. The New Deal's class-based, or race-neutral, social policies did not affect blacks and whites in identical ways. Federal social policy contributed disproportionately to the prosperity of the white middle class from the 1940s on. Whites received more from the New Deal than old-age protection and insurance against the business cycle. Housing subsidies paved the way for a white exodus to the suburbs; federal tax breaks secured union-bargained health and pension benefits and lowered the cost to workers; veterans' benefits were an avenue of upward mobility for many white men. To assume that government policies benefited only blacks or were color-blind, as many white Americans commonly believe, is like looking at the world with one eye.

Three laws passed by Congress in the mid-1930s were instrumental in generating the pattern of racial stratification that emerged during the New Deal: the Social Security Act, the Wagner Act, and the Federal Housing Act. These laws contributed to the accumulation of wealth in white households, and they did more than any other combination of factors to sow and nurture the seeds of the future urban ghetto and produce a welfare system in which recipients would be disproportionately black. It is commonly assumed that the New Deal was based on broad and inclusive policies. While there is some truth to the claim that Roosevelt's New Deal was designed, as Jill Quadagno states it, to provide a "floor of protection for the industrial working class," it was riddled with discrimination. Brokered compromises over New Deal labor and social policies also reinforced racial segregation through social welfare programs, labor policy, and housing policy.[70] How and why did this happen?

Although the Social Security Act created a work-related social right to an old-age pension and unemployment compensation, Congress defied the Roosevelt administration and explicitly excluded domestic and agricultural workers from coverage. It also exempted public employees as well as workers in nonprofit, voluntary organizations. Only 53 percent of all workers, about 26 million people, were initially covered by the old-age insurance title of the Social Security Act, and less than half of all workers were covered by unemployment compensation. Congress subsequently excluded these exempt workers from the Wagner Act and the 1938 Fair Labor Standards Act as well.[71]

Congress's rejection of universal coverage was not a race-neutral decision undertaken because, as some people claimed at the time, it was difficult to collect payroll taxes from agricultural and domestic workers. As Charles Houston, Dean of the Howard University Law School, told the Senate Finance committee, "It [the Social Security bill] looks like a sieve with the holes just big enough for the majority of Negroes to fall through." Almost three-fifths of the black labor force was denied coverage. When self-employed black sharecroppers are added to the list of excluded workers, it is likely that three-quarters or more of African Americans were denied benefits and the protection of federal law. Black women, of whom 90 percent were domestic workers, were especially disadvantaged by these occupational exclusions.[72]

Agricultural and domestic workers were excluded largely because southern legislators refused to allow implementation of any national social welfare policies that included black workers. Roosevelt presided over a fragile coalition of northern industrial workers and southern whites bound to an agrarian economic order. Although blacks began to leave the party of Lincoln for the party of Roosevelt, three-quarters of the African American population still lived in the South, where they could not vote. Southerners feared that federal social policies would raise the pay of southern black workers and sharecroppers and that this in turn would undermine their system of racial apartheid. Black criticisms of the legislation were ignored as Roosevelt acquiesced to southern demands, believing he could not defy powerful southern committee chairmen and still pass needed social welfare legislation.

As black workers moved north into industrial jobs, they were eventually included under the Social Security Act, and Congress ultimately extended coverage of old-age insurance to agricultural workers in 1950 and 1954. Although the Social Security Administration made every effort to treat black and white workers equally, black workers were nevertheless severely disadvantaged by the work-related eligibility provisions of the Social Security Act. Both old-age insurance and unemployment compensation rewarded stable, long-term employment and penalized intermittent employment regardless of the reason. In the name of fiscal integrity, the architects of social insurance in the 1930s were adamant that malingerers, those on relief, or those weakly attached to the labor market be excluded from eligibility and their benefits limited. Due to labor market discrimination and the seasonal nature of agricultural labor, many blacks have not had stable, long-term employment records. Thus, they have had only limited eligibility for old-age and unemployment benefits.

The racial consequences of wage-related eligibility provisions were already apparent in the 1930s. Because labor market discrimination lowers the wages of black workers relative to white workers or denies them employment altogether, blacks receive lower benefits than whites from old-age insurance and unemployment compensation or are denied access at all. By 1939, for example, only 20 percent of white workers who worked in industries covered by social insurance and who paid payroll taxes for old-age insurance were uninsured, but more than twice as many black workers (42 percent) were uninsured.[73] From the outset, social security transferred income from African American workers to white workers. This disparity continues today. Even though most black workers are currently covered by social security, on average they still receive lower benefits than whites and pay a higher proportion of their income in social security taxes.[74] Like old-age insurance, there is little evidence of overt discrimination in unemployment compensation—eligible black workers are almost as likely as white workers are to receive benefits. But because states imposed strict eligibility requirements during the 1940s and 1950s, black workers were disproportionately excluded.[75] Social insurance is neither universal nor race-neutral.

In combination, labor market discrimination and work-related eligibility requirements excluded blacks from work and social insurance programs in the 1930s, forcing many to go on relief and later on welfare, Aid to Dependent Children (ADC). In fact, most black women were excluded from the unemployment compensation system until the late 1960s. This is because domestic workers were statutorily excluded from unemployment compensation, and as late as the 1950s more than half of all black women in the civilian labor force still worked as domestics. Unemployed black women typically had nowhere to turn but welfare, and this is exactly what they did. By 1960, African Americans accounted for two-fifths of all welfare recipients, a participation rate that did not change much even when the welfare rolls expanded in the 1960s. It is labor market discrimination and New Deal social policies, not welfare, as the conservatives believe, that has harmed black families. The problem cannot be explained by a pathological black family structure.[76]

Social insurance in the United States has operated much like a sieve, just as Charles Houston predicted, and blacks have fallen through the holes. The Wagner Act and the 1937 Housing Act compounded the problem, enlarging the holes in the sieve. Sometimes labeled the Magna Charta of the labor movement, the 1935 Wagner Act was, upon closer inspection, the Magna Charta of *white* labor. Black leaders tried to add an antidiscrimination amendment to the law, but the American Federation of Labor and the white southerners who controlled key congressional committees fought it. As a result, the final version excluded black workers. The law legalized the closed shop, which, as Roy Wilkins of the NAACP pointed out, would empower "organized labor to exclude from employment in any industry those who do not belong to a union." The law also outlawed strikebreaking, a weapon black workers had used successfully to force their way into northern industries. Preventing blacks from entering into newly protected labor unions meant that black workers were subject to the racist inclinations of white workers.[77] One of the consequences of the Wagner Act's failure to protect black workers was that union rules confined them to low-wage unskilled jobs. When these jobs were eliminated as businesses modernized after World War II, black unskilled workers were replaced by automated manufacturing technologies.[78] Thus, the current high levels of black unemployment can be traced directly to New Deal legislation that allowed white workers to deny job opportunities to blacks.

State-sponsored racial inequality was also augmented by a third set of New Deal policies: federal housing and urban renewal legislation. As we will explain in chapter 2, these policies sealed the fate of America's cities by establishing "apartheid without walls." Contrary to the commonly held notion that white flight is responsible for creating ghettos and barrios, it was actually the federal government's explicit racial policy that created these enclaves.

Each of these policies, routinely hailed as major progressive government interventions to boost the economy and place a safety net under all citizens, was instrumental in creating long-run patterns of accumulation and disaccumulation based on race. These policies, along with others, institutionalized white advantage over blacks and other people of color.

RACIAL EQUALITY AND THE POSSESSIVE INVESTMENT IN WHITENESS AFTER THE CIVIL RIGHTS REVOLUTION

In the post–civil rights era, formal equality before the law coexists with de facto white privilege and whites' resentment of race-conscious remedies. Whites' resentment reflects their "possessive investment in whiteness."[79] Historically, white Americans have accumulated advantages in housing, work, education, and security based solely on the color of their skin. Being white, as a consequence, literally has value. Though race may be a cultural and biological fiction, whiteness, like blackness, is a very real social and legal identity. Both identities are crucial in determining one's social and economic status. This is why, when Professor Andrew Hacker asked his white students how much money they would demand if they were changed from white to black, they felt it was reasonable to ask for $50 million if they were to be black for the rest of their lives, or $1 million a year for each year they were black.[80] That was the financial value they placed on being white. It was, to use W. E. B. DuBois's phrase, the dollar amount they attached to their "wages of whiteness." The idea of a possessive investment in whiteness helps to explain the structures of durable racial inequality and the color-coded community processes of accumulation and disaccumulation. The formation of racial identity, in turn, connects interests to attitudes toward public issues that have racial consequences and color-conscious remedies.

In one important, and ironic, respect, the combination of legal equality with social and economic racial inequality at the end of the civil rights movement is similar to the relationship between blacks and whites at the end of Reconstruction. *Plessy v. Ferguson,* which marked the end of Reconstruction by upholding the doctrine of "separate but equal," was the culmination of a long debate over the meaning of racial equality that began with the abolitionists' struggle against slavery. At the time, it was commonly understood that the Fourteenth Amendment guaranteed equality before the law and that political rights (like the right to serve as a juror) presumably could not be abrogated. But few believed that the Thirteenth, Fourteenth, or Fifteenth Amendments required social or economic equality between blacks and whites. Not even the defenders of a color-blind Constitution accepted this idea. Indeed, Justice John Marshall Harlan's defense of a color-blind Constitution in his dissenting opinion in *Plessy* explicitly assumed the inferiority of African Americans and distinguished between legal and social equality.[81] The stigma of slavery lingered long after "the peculiar institution" was dismantled. As de Tocqueville observed about the antebellum North, "The prejudice rejecting the Negroes seems to increase in proportion to their emancipation, and inequality cuts deep into mores as it is effaced from the laws."[82]

Americans still face the question of what racial inequality means and what the nation is obligated to do about it. The civil rights movement repudiated racial classifications as a means to subordinate racial groups, and for most Americans that is sufficient. The contemporary controversy over the civil rights policies, however, cannot be reduced, no matter how hard racial realists try, to a debate over repealing color-conscious remedies like affirmative action. The larger question facing Americans is whether equality requires a commitment to go beyond formal legal equality and to rectify three hundred years of racial oppression and subordination. Racial realists and conservatives think a color-blind Constitution means that public remedies to end social inequality between racial groups are illegitimate, the equivalent of "racial social engineering." This view sharply distinguishes between public and private spheres of action. Government should be held to a strict standard of racial neutrality, proponents argue; the use of laws (or policies) to rectify racial inequalities is wrong.

We reject this position. If America is to achieve a larger measure of racial equality, we think the government must use public policies to root out enduring racial inequality. This does not mean we think affirmative action plans are the remedy. Arguments over affirmative action do not help us understand the etiology and persistence of white privilege. Nor do they help find ways to achieve genuine racial equality. We think it makes more sense to consider carefully how labor market discrimination, private institutional practices, and public policies have generated the accumulation of economic and social advantages in white communities, and the concomitant disaccumulation of social and economic capital in communities of color. By comparing the assumptions, arguments, and evidence articulated by racial realists to an alternative framework, we think it is possible to see the major differences between these two perspectives and the remedies that follow from a theory that focuses on cumulative inequalities.

In the following chapters we address these questions by examining the main arguments made by proponents of racial realism. In chapter 1 we explore their concept of racism, the idea that racism is solely a matter of prejudiced attitudes. We show how this outdated, misleading conception of racism speaks from only one side of the color line, and we compare it to the idea that racism is a sense of group position based on the accumulation of racial advantage. Our critical analysis of the concept of prejudice enables us to develop a detailed examination of the racial realists' explanation for racial disparities in income, poverty, education, and crime—their argument that individual failure is the cause of contemporary racial inequality. In chapters 2 through 4 we show the inadequacy of this explanation and develop an analysis of racial inequalities based on the relationship between racially based accumulation and disaccumulation. In chapters 5 and 6 we turn to the conservative arguments against employment discrimination laws and the use of the Voting Rights Act to create black or Latino majority legislative districts. Racial conservatives think that government support of civil rights policies contributes to black failure and racial conflict. Arguing against this notion, chapter 5 assesses the conservative critique of employment discrimination law. Chapter 6 argues that when applied to voting rights cases, the doctrine of color-blindness is a form of color consciousness—white consciousness of lost political power. The conclusion offers suggestions for what we believe to be essential and realistic strategies to minimize and eliminate durable racial inequality.

Of Fish and Water

Perspectives on Racism and Privilege

There ain't no white man in this room that will change places with me—and I'm rich. That's how good it is to be white. There's a one-legged busboy in here right now that's going: "I don't want to change. I'm gonna ride this white thing out and see where it takes me."

Chris Rock

According to a well-known philosophical maxim, the last thing a fish notices is the water. Things that are unproblematic seem natural and tend to go unnoticed. Fish take the water they swim in for granted, just as European Americans take their race as a given, as normal. White Americans may face difficulties in life—problems having to do with money, religion, or family—but race is not one of them. White Americans can be sanguine about racial matters because their race has not been (until recently) visible to the society in which they live. They cannot see how this society produces advantages for them because these benefits seem so natural that they are taken for granted, experienced as wholly legitimate.[1] They literally do not see how race permeates America's institutions—the very rules of the game—and its distribution of opportunities and wealth.

Blacks, Latinos, and other people of color in the United States are racially visible, and everyone seems to notice their race. For them, the same culture, law, economy, institutions, and rules of the game are not so automatically comfortable and legitimate. In a white-dominated society, color brings problems.[2] And if people of color cry foul, if they call attention to the way they are treated or to racial inequality, if they try to change the distribution of advantage, if they try to adjust the rules of the game, white Americans (whose race and racial advantage are invisible) see them as asking for special privileges. They are seen as troublemakers.

What this means is that there is no such thing as a "view from nowhere"—to use Thomas Nagel's apt phrase.[3] People's perspectives on race reflect their experience on one side of the color line or the other. Whites routinely misperceive the reality of black lives. For example, even though blacks are about twice as likely as whites to hold low-paying jobs and are more than twice as likely to be unemployed, 50 percent of whites say the average black is about as well off as the average white person. (Blacks, on the other hand, tend to be more realistic and accurate in their perceptions of their economic status relative to whites.[4]) If white Americans make no effort to hear the viewpoints and see the experiences of others, their awareness of their own privileged racial status will disappear. They can convince themselves that life as they experience it on their side of the color line is simply the objective truth about race. But while this allows them to take their privileged status for granted, it also distorts their understanding. This error poses serious problems for conservatives' analysis of racial inequality.

Of course, individual views within racial groups vary. Not everyone who shares the same subjective perspective will draw the same conclusions about policy. But any perspective that is unreflectively locked inside its own experience is limited, and this is particularly so when that perspective reflects the dominant culture. Failure to understand that they take whites' racial location for granted leads racial realists to ignore the ways in which race loads the dice in favor of European Americans while simultaneously restricting African Americans' access to the gaming table. White privilege, like the water that sustains fish, is invisible in their analysis.

This chapter is about perspective, and how definition—the power to name—determines perception, and ultimately, prescription. It traces the difference it makes if one group's perspective pervades almost everything, from culture to law. Apostles of the new perspective on race insist that racism is primarily a thing of the past. They come to this conclusion because they filter their evidence and their judgment through an outdated, discredited understanding of racism as intentional, obvious, and individual. These misconceptions are not unique to any particular writer or writers. Many white Americans and American institutions, including the current Supreme Court majority, hold parallel views. Because racial conservatives ignore the variability of racial reality in America, they do not recognize that racism is lodged in the structure of society, that it permeates the workings of the economic, political, educational, and legal institutions of the United States. Without that recognition, however, we will be unable to resolve the pernicious problems of race that confront us as Americans.

CONCEPTIONS OF RACE AND RACISM AFTER THE CIVIL RIGHTS REVOLUTION

In the new conventional wisdom about race, white racism is regarded as a remnant from the past because most whites no longer express bigoted attitudes or racial hatred. The Thernstroms note that despite black riots and crime in the streets in 1968, "nowhere in the voluminous polling evidence available for these years is there any sign that whites were drifting in the direction of the virulent anti-black sentiments so prevalent in the 1940s and 1950s."[5] Indeed, the real story for most whites is that racism has almost disappeared. Marianne Means flatly asserts, "We all agree that slavery was evil. But the blood of slavery does not stain modern mainstream America."[6] The Thernstroms concur. "White racial attitudes have truly altered," they write. "Whites with a pathological hatred of African Americans can still be found, of course. But the haters have become a tiny remnant with no influence in any important sphere of American life."[7]

Racial realists conclude that racism has ended because of the massive change in white attitudes toward blacks over the past sixty years. For example, more than half of all whites once believed that blacks were intellectually inferior. In 1994, however, only 13 percent of whites believed that blacks had "less in-born ability to learn" than whites. Whites also used to favor school segregation by overwhelming majorities, but now 90 percent favor school integration. In the 1940s whites believed they should be favored in competition for jobs. Today, on the other hand, whites unanimously agree that "blacks and whites should have an equal chance to compete for jobs."[8] The Thernstroms go so far as to assert that white attitudes had already changed for the better before the civil rights movement erupted in the 1960s.[9]

To racial realists, this evidence means that the color line has been radically altered. Although many whites still accept one or more negative stereotypes about African Americans, a recent study by Paul Sniderman and Thomas Piazza asserts that only 2 percent of the population could be considered old-fashioned bigots who subscribe to a large number of racist stereotypes.[10] Consequently, it is rare today to find cases of discrimination such as the ones involving Texaco's executives calling

African Americans "black jelly beans," a member of the Dallas school board referring to African Americans as "niggers," and the "raw racism" experienced by black secret service agents in a Baltimore Denny's restaurant.

The evidence cited by racial realists indicates that they, like many whites, use a particular understanding of racism.[11] This notion assumes that racism is motivated, crude, explicitly supremacist, and typically expressed as individual bias. Racism, in short, is a form of "prejudice." Paul Sniderman and Thomas Piazza define it as "a consistent readiness to respond negatively to a member of a group by virtue of his or her membership in the group, with the proof of prejudice being thus the repetitiveness with which a person endorses negative characterization after negative characterization."[12]

Given this concept of racism and the use of opinion surveys to measure it, one should hardly be surprised that many people believe racism is a thing of the past. After all, virulent antiblack sentiments have diminished, formal barriers based on malicious intent have in large part been dismantled, and few Americans would accept publicly sanctioned racial barriers today. Were these its undisputed characteristics, one might be tempted to agree that racism is obsolete.

The law institutionalizes the American ideal of equality, and it provides remedies for those hurt by bias. Current law embraces the concept of racism as intentional individual prejudice, and also its corollary— that whites today are often unfairly accused of being racist. Evolving doctrine in racial discrimination cases reflects what Angela Harris has called an "essentially moralistic" view.[13] In several reverse discrimination lawsuits, for example, the Supreme Court has explicitly worried that affirmative action plans impose unacceptable burdens on "innocent" third parties (read whites).[14] In equal protection cases, the Court has increasingly emphasized invidious intention as a necessary element for finding actionable discrimination.

But this perspective has its critics. Twenty-five years ago, Alan Freeman documented how, after a brief period of attention to what he called a "victim perspective" in the jurisprudence of equality, the Court moved decisively to adopt a "perpetrator perspective" on issues of race.[15] Adopting the perpetrator perspective means looking at contested race issues from the vantage point of whites. The "perpetrator perspective" in law, like the conservatives' understanding of racism, is preoccupied with white guilt or innocence. It largely ignores whether people of color have suffered injury or loss of opportunity because of their race. Other critics have raised analogous arguments, paying attention to group subordination or disadvantage.[16] Ignoring these analyses, the courts have extended and deepened their attachment to the perpetrator perspective as the racial law of the land.

The Supreme Court's standard for white innocence is very low. Before the modern civil rights era, the Supreme Court often insisted that analysis of motive was inappropriate in constitutional adjudication.[17] During the past several decades, however, the Court has increasingly required that plaintiffs in equal protection discrimination cases not only may, but must, probe defendants' motives. To be successful, plaintiffs must prove specific and conscious bad intentions, the equivalent of the concept of racism as personal prejudice. Under the equal protection clause of the Fourteenth Amendment, the Court holds it is not enough to show that people would reasonably know the discriminatory consequences of their actions. Nor is it enough that actors foresaw the predictable effects of their actions and still proceeded in spite of them. To gain or sustain a remedy for racial injustice, litigants must meet a very high standard: they must show specific discriminatory purpose or malice. Reva Siegel argues on the basis of credible evidence that the Court knew this was a level of responsibility plaintiffs would "rarely be able to prove."[18]

Under congressional statutes, the role of intent is somewhat reduced. The Court has sometimes said that proof of employment discrimination may be based on a demonstration that policies have a disparate impact rather than on a showing of intent—proving, for example, that African Americans or other racial groups are more likely to be disadvantaged by an employment practice than whites.[19] Although the courts give lip service to unintentional bias in cases involving claims of discriminatory treatment, particularly in employment, most of the governing precedents require that plaintiffs prove intentional bias.[20] In 2001 the Supreme Court further extended that requirement. It held that under Title VI of the Civil Rights Act, which prohibits the discriminatory use of federal money, proving disparate impact would no longer be sufficient to win discrimination suits by private parties against federally funded contractors or institutions.[21]

The Court now requires proof of invidious intention in most cases of racial discrimination. But it does not apply this standard of intent in age discrimination cases where the relevant statutory language is identical to that in Title VII. In these cases, the courts have accepted a distinction between motive (a factor in causing action) and intent (a specifically proven state of mind) that is more favorable to plaintiffs alleging discrimination.[22] In other settings that address harms caused by others, such as personal injury law, courts assess liability and compensate victims not simply for intentional harms but also for injuries caused accidentally, that is, negligently. Plaintiffs do not have to prove malice or purpose unless they seek punitive damages.[23]

Choosing to make the specific intentions of identifiable individuals the criterion of racism is neither neutral nor appropriate. It is self-aggrandizing and misguided to judge others by their actions but ourselves only by our intentions.[24] In Supreme Court decisions and in the minds of many whites, the relevant "ourselves" are predominantly white or, in Freeman's phrase, potential "perpetrators." Many whites want to determine whether racism exists by exploring their explicit personal intentions. If we are deciding whether to put someone in jail, then assessing his intentions may be appropriate.[25] However, where disputes do not involve criminal charges but rather decisions about social, educational, welfare, or employment policy, questions of guilt, innocence, and punishment are not the issue. No one goes to jail for discrimination.[26] In discrimination litigation, the focus is on the legitimacy and fairness of the distribution of scarce opportunities and resources. To ameliorate injustice and achieve a more desirable state of civil affairs, it is more important to examine the problems of discrimination, injuries, and unfairness than to evaluate the culpability and motives of particular perpetrators.

The Court's narrow definition of discrimination, like the realists' equation of racism with prejudice, severely restricts what counts as bias or as evidence of bias. This definition tends to exonerate whites, blame blacks (by default), and naturalize (render unobjectionable) the broad realities of race-based subordination in the United States. This definition of racism, as we have already noted, is also empirically and conceptually flawed. It depends almost exclusively on attitudinal evidence uncovered by opinion polling. This poses two problems. First, even on its own terms, this interpretation of racism ignores significant research that shows how racist attitudes have persisted. In his recent book *The Ordeal of Integration*, Orlando Patterson examined a variety of evidence and concluded that "all things considered, it is reasonable to estimate that about a quarter of the Euro-American population harbors at least mildly racist feelings toward Afro-Americans and that one in five is a hard-core racist."[27] This is not a small number. If Patterson is correct, the Thernstroms' "miscreants of the night" are hardly a fringe.

Second, by relying on survey questions written in the 1950s, this research ignores possible changes in the character of racism and is, therefore, incorrectly measuring modern expressions of it. Donald Kinder and Lynn Sanders write that "a new form of prejudice has come to prominence, one that is preoccupied with matters of moral character, informed by the virtues associated with the traditions of individualism. Today, we say, prejudice is expressed in the language of American individualism."[28] Statements about individual failure, in other words, may be racially coded expressions of a derogatory stereotype.

There are also abundant survey data documenting the persistence of widespread racial prejudice forty years after the civil rights revolution. Many writers who use polling data to show the decline of racism cherry pick among these surveys and omit this evidence. Some of the most compelling evidence of tenacious prejudice comes from studies of residential discrimination. In 1992, the Detroit Area Survey found that 16 percent of whites said they would feel uncomfortable in a neighborhood where 8 percent of the residents were black, and nearly the same percentage said they were unwilling to move to such an area. If the black percentage rose to 20 percent, 40 percent of all whites indicated they would not move there, 30 percent said they would be uncomfortable, and 15 percent would try to leave the area. Were a neighborhood to be 53 percent black, 71 percent of whites would not wish to move there, 53 percent would try to leave, and 65 percent would be uncomfortable.[29] A more recent study of four cities (Atlanta, Boston, Detroit, and Los Angeles) yielded similar results. Camille Zubrinsky Charles found that more than half of whites in these four cities expressed a preference for same-race neighborhoods, while blacks expressed a strong preference for integrated neighborhoods.[30]

Contrary to the optimism of racial realists, one finds precious little evidence, even in the polling data they use, that many white Americans believe in integrated neighborhoods, especially if that means a neighborhood with more than a very few black families. Pejorative racial stereotypes are not restricted to one's choice of residence. They continue to be fundamental to (white) American culture. When the University of Chicago's National Opinion Research Center asked people to compare blacks and other ethnic groups on a number of personal traits in 1990, they discovered that 62 percent of nonblack respondents believed that blacks were lazier than other groups, 56 percent stated that they were more prone to violence, and 53 percent thought they were less intelligent.[31] Another report suggests that white Americans are still substantially opposed to intimate contact with African Americans. In one national survey conducted in 1978, 70 percent of whites rejected interracial marriage on principle.[32] This hardly represents the significant change in whites' attitudes trumpeted by the proponents of racial realism.

Both the meaning of survey data and the way they are used by these cheerleaders for racial progress are also problematic. Because the typical questions used to measure changes in racial attitudes essentially gauge how closely attitudes conform to the American creed enshrined in the Declaration of Independence, it is not surprising to find that most (white) Americans sound tolerant. This is because when prejudice and tolerance are evaluated by these criteria, the questions assess only whether people subscribe to American ideals. It is hardly a major discovery to find that racism has declined when individuals are asked whether they believe in equal job treatment and integrated schools. Because the ideals of equality and formal tolerance are central to American identity, most Americans know the "correct" answers to such questions. Thus, rather than representing a decline in racism, these polling data actually measure adherence to the principles of American society.

Because most surveys tap only surface commitment or verbal adherence to ideals, polling data may reveal more about the correlation between self-presentation and socioeconomic class than about the persistence of racism. When tolerance means verbalizing principles acquired through exposure to liberal middle-class institutions, lower- and working-class whites will appear to be more racist than middle-class whites. Surveys that find prejudice and intolerance declining among America's white middle class also link racist sentiments disproportionately to poor and working-class white Americans, or to the "lunatic fringe." This finding is not new. As long ago as 1966, Paul Sheatsley found that the highest scorers on his "pro-integration scale" shared three features in common: they attended college, their earnings were high, and they were professionals.[33] But the narrow catch of this racism net reflects only its limited definition of racism. The behavior between classes may not differ much, but, unlike well-educated middle- and upper-class whites, poorly educated working-class white people are nearly precluded from this conception of "tolerance" because they have not learned the "proper" ways to present their racial views to pollsters.

Some writers promoting the new orthodoxy on racial inequality also seem unaware that evidence based on broad changes in opinion is insufficient to assess a complex, multifaceted problem like the persistence of racism. The gap between what people tell survey researchers and what they actually do or believe is wide, and a very different picture emerges when one moves from political abstractions to routine behavior.

Discrepancies between racial attitudes and behavior are large and pervasive. White Americans overwhelmingly endorse civil rights principles. When asked, 88 percent of whites in 1978 agreed that blacks have a right to live wherever they want to, up from 76 percent in 1970. By 1980, in fact, just 5 percent of whites were willing to tell a pollster they preferred strict segregation.[34] Yet only 40 percent said they would vote for a law stating "a homeowner cannot refuse to sell to someone because of their race or skin color."[35] White Americans may support the principle of fair housing, but less than half say they are willing to act on this principle. In fact, when actual patterns of racial isolation are examined, it is clear that very few whites prefer integrated to segregated neighborhoods.

American Apartheid, an award-winning study of housing segregation by Douglas Massey and Nancy Denton, reveals just how wide the gap is between attitudes and behavior. Using demographic data about where African Americans and whites actually reside, Massey and Denton demonstrated that levels of residential segregation have hardly changed since the 1960s. Applying a sophisticated index of segregation to thirty metropolitan areas with the largest black populations between 1970 and 1980, they discovered that in northern cities, "this (segregation) index averaged over 80 percent in both 1970 and 1980."[36] The index declined a mere 4 points over the decade of the 1970s and only 2 percent during the 1980s, and most of the decline occurred in small cities with small black populations. Massey and Denton conclude that "blacks living in the heart of the ghetto are among the most isolated people on earth."[37]

The Thernstroms challenge this conclusion, arguing that Massey and Denton exaggerate the persistence of residential segregation. But they provide no counterevidence, nor do they generate demographically grounded indices of integration. Rather, they attempt to refute Massey and Denton with an analysis that is laughable. "The strongest proof that residential segregation has been declining for a generation," they write, "comes from national surveys [that] have intermittently asked blacks and whites whether members of the other race live in the same neighborhood as they do." They find the patterns "striking" and report "fully two-thirds of all African Americans at the time (1964) said that they had white neighbors." The fact, they write, "that the figure was as high as five out of six in 1994" is evidence that residential apartheid has declined.[38] The Thernstroms apparently imagine that people's beliefs about who lives in their neighborhood are a more accurate indication of residential segregation than measures of where and how people actually live.

Similar gaps between attitudes and behavior are found in most contexts where race is an issue. These gaps become especially obvious when the reality of one's everyday life is directly affected. Support for desegregation of schools was relatively free of cost so long as no busing was involved or one's own children attended private schools. On-the-job equality also had an all-American sound to it, especially when there were very few blacks in one's occupation. Upgrading blacks from unskilled to skilled work was a fine goal if one's own work was white-collar or professional. But as black enrollments in prestigious universities and professional schools increased, constitutional amendments eliminating affirmative action became the order of the day.[39] When the demands of people of color hit closer to home and directly affect middle- and upper-class whites, these traditionally color-blind Americans begin to sound distinctly less tolerant and become seriously concerned with the color of people's skin.

These empirical flaws in studies purportedly demonstrating that racism has declined are compounded by fundamental conceptual problems. By now, the prejudice approach to the study of racism has been discredited and has become almost completely obsolete. The challenge to the prejudice paradigm began as early as 1958 when sociologist Herbert Blumer first argued that racism was better understood as a sense of group position than as a collection of bigoted individual attitudes. Since Blumer's groundbreaking article, a long line of sociologists, social psychologists, and legal theorists have moved beyond the outdated notion of racism employed by most advocates of color-blind ideology.[40] Instead of locating racism in intentions, attitudes, and obviously crude supremacist expressions or in pathological individual psyches, these scholars use a more complicated conception. Their analysis assumes that racism is often unintentional, implicit, polite, and sometimes quite normal. They look for racism in behavior as well as in attitudes and find it in culturally and economically produced systems of advantage and exclusion that generate privilege for one racially defined group at the expense of another.

Using this more realistic conception of racism, it becomes apparent that those who argue racism has declined ignore critical evidence that contradicts their assumptions. Their understanding of race paints a one-sided, terribly inaccurate portrait of racism in modern America. A very different picture emerges when racism is understood as a sense of group position and as the organized accumulation of racial advantage, a system best understood by observing actual behavior.

RACIAL PRIVILEGE AND GROUP POSITION

Because it extends far beyond individual attitudes, permeating the very structure and organization of American society, race strongly determines the ways in which Americans are treated and how they fare. White Americans, whether they know it or not, benefit as individuals and as a group from the present social pecking order. The social, political, and economic benefits of being white encourage white Americans, argues George Lipsitz, to invest in whiteness as if it were a form of venture capital and to work at increasing its value. When it comes to race, white Americans' social choices are very often molded by the relationship between whiteness and accumulated racial advantages.[41]

The possessive investment in whiteness is like property. And as a kind of property, the value of whiteness, as Cheryl Harris points out, lies in "the unconstrained right to exclude" or to deny communities of color opportunity or the chance to accumulate assets.[42] Exclusion, as is evident in the case of residential segregation, is a cardinal principle of white identity. To paraphrase Harris, those who possess whiteness have, until recently, been granted the legal right to exclude others from the advantages inherent in whiteness; they have accumulated wealth, power, and opportunity at the expense of the people who have been designated as *not* white. In this sense, the experiences of white and nonwhite Americans are intimately connected. The benefits of being white are related to the costs of being nonwhite. This is why it makes more sense to analyze racism in terms of group position rather than in terms of the bigoted attitudes of individuals.

White privilege is pervasive. Most discussions of racial inequality focus on labor markets, the criminal justice system, residential segregation, and education. But race also counts in ways that are less obvious, indeed typically invisible, to white Americans. While often unrecognized, these patterns of racial disadvantage point to the insidiously pervasive power of racism in American life. Because most Americans use such a narrow conception of racism, it is not surprising that they fail to recognize these subtle expressions of racial inequality that are woven into the fabric of society.[43]

To see the pervasiveness of white privilege, consider first something as ordinary as consumer trade. As we noted in the introduction, blacks and other minorities are denied mortgages far more frequently than whites with comparable incomes.[44] But even in other situations, including those where market forces would be expected to eclipse racial factors, race plays a powerful role. Researchers studying automobile dealerships in the Chicago area found, for example, that salespeople offer significantly lower sales prices to white men than to women or blacks, even when economic factors and bargaining strategies are held constant.[45] A more recent study shows that in the 1990s blacks paid significantly more for car loans arranged through dealers than whites did, despite having comparable credit histories.[46] Similarly, clerks in retail stores are frequently more concerned with the color of shoppers' skin than with their ability to pay. Cignal Clothing, a subsidiary of Merry-Go-Round Enterprises, for example, stamped an information form on the back of personal checks. The form included a section marked "race," and shoppers were classified "W" for white, "H" for Hispanic, and "07" for black.[47] Sociologist Joe Feagin, drawing on thirty-seven in-depth interviews with middle-class blacks in several American cities, found widespread evidence that black shoppers were treated less respectfully than their middle-class white counterparts. "No matter how affluent and influential," he reports, "a black person cannot escape the stigma of being black even while relaxing or shopping."[48]

Health care is another realm where significant disparities exist between blacks and whites—disparities that often mean life itself. We have already noted the wide gaps in mortality rates and access to primary care between blacks and whites. Similar disparities cut across every aspect of health and health care, and few of these differences can be fully attributed to social class or genetics. For example, the National Cancer Institute (NCI) recently reported that cancer death rates are increasing much faster for blacks than whites, sometimes by as much as twenty to one hundred times as fast. Black women are more likely than white women to die of breast cancer, even though the incidence of the disease is lower among blacks.[49] According to the NCI report, "Black men have a cancer-death rate about 44 percent higher than that for white men."[50] In fact, African American men between the ages of fifty and seventy are nearly three times as likely to die from prostate cancer as white men, and their prostate cancer rate is more than double that of whites.[51]

Higher death rates for blacks diagnosed with cancer are a recent development. In the 1930s, blacks were only half as likely as whites to die of lung cancer. Since 1950, however, the rate of lung cancer deaths among black men has increased at three times the rate for white men, and age-adjusted figures reveal that the rate was actually 40 percent higher among black men by the 1970s.[52] An increase in smoking rates is not the likely culprit behind the change. Exposure to environmental toxins and carcinogens, which are disproportionately located in poor and minority communities, is one important reason for the racial disparities in cancer mortality rates. Differential access to screening, prevention, and treatment is another reason for the disparities. One of the chief reasons black women are more likely to die of breast cancer is that they are not diagnosed until the disease has reached an advanced and more lethal stage.[53] A study of operable non–small cell lung cancer found that the rate of surgery for black patients was 12.7 percent lower than that for whites with the same diagnosis. The authors of this study concluded that "the lower survival rate among black patients . . . is largely explained by the lower rate of surgical treatment among blacks."[54] Racial differences in mortality rates for cervical cancer remain significant even after adjusting for age and poverty, and are likely attributable to disparities in screening and diagnosis.[55]

Racial disparities in mortality rates for stroke and coronary heart disease are also significant. The black mortality rate for strokes is 80 percent higher than the white rate and the black mortality rate for coronary heart disease is 40 percent higher.[56] Racial differences in hypertension are well documented and are particularly pronounced among low-income African Americans. One study rejected the common assumption that hypertension among blacks is genetic, concluding that socioenvironmental factors like the stresses of low job status and income are responsible for the different rates of hypertension.[57]

Access to sophisticated diagnostic and treatment procedures for coronary heart disease and related ailments also accounts for significant health differences between blacks and whites. Once differences in age, sex, health care payer, income, and diagnoses for all admissions for circulatory disease or chest pains to Massachusetts hospitals had been accounted for, a 1985 study found that whites underwent significantly more angiography and coronary artery bypass grafting than blacks.[58] More recent studies confirm the results. One study, for example, found that after controlling for differences in age, gender, disease severity, comorbidity, geography, and availability of cardiac facilities, blacks were 60 percent less likely to have had coronary angioplasty or coronary bypass surgery and 50 percent less likely to have had thrombolytic therapy.[59] Similarly, researchers who investigated stroke treatments found that "white patients were approximately 50 percent more likely to receive imaging than were black patients"; they also found that of patients deemed appropriate for carotid endarterectomy, two-thirds of white patients but only half of blacks underwent the surgery.[60]

Ironically, amputation of a lower limb is the one advanced procedure that blacks receive far more often than whites.[61] African Americans are more likely to have such last-resort procedures because of inadequate treatment of hypertension and diabetes—illnesses that reflect inadequate care and treatment.[62] This is a perfect illustration of how disaccumulation works: small deficits in health care add up over time, leading to the disaccumulation of health and a perverse outcome.

Neither income nor social class adequately explains these differences in mortality rates and treatment. Rather, the burden of evidence contained in these studies indicates that race is a crucial variable. A recent National Bureau of Economic Research study, for example, found that income inequality between racial groups—not income inequality within racial groups—explains the differences in mortality rates.[63]

Race has a powerful and widespread impact on health treatment and thus health outcomes. Blacks and Latinos are less likely than whites to have access to basic health insurance.[64] Another serious obstacle to quality care for black and Latino patients is that minority doctors, who typically treat disproportionate numbers of minority patients, have greater difficulty than white physicians securing authorization for care. Nationwide, about one-third of black and Latino doctors report difficulty obtaining necessary hospital admissions, compared to one-quarter of white physicians.[65] Racial differences in infant mortality and prenatal care are also linked to a perverse version of racial profiling. Hospitals and clinics with high proportions of minority patients often conduct more systematic and intrusive screening for drug abuse and sexually transmitted disease than do those that treat white women, even though that pattern is not justified by prevailing rates of substance abuse.[66] This in turn discourages many black women from seeking needed prenatal care. Another study found that low-income African American mothers in Chicago who reported being the victims of racial discrimination were twice as likely to give birth to very low-weight babies compared to mothers reporting no discrimination.[67]

Racial bias is another important source of the differences in the ways life-threatening diseases are treated. Recent evidence suggests that racial stereotyping, and even discrimination, influence doctors' treatment recommendations for patients. K. Schulman and his colleagues asked doctors to respond to videotaped interviews with "patients" who were actually actors with identical medical histories and symptoms. Only the race and gender of the actors were different.[68] Doctors turned out to be significantly less likely to refer black women for aggressive treatment of cardiac symptoms than other categories of patients with the same symptoms. Doctors were also asked about their perceptions of patients' personal characteristics. Black male actor-patients, whose symptoms and comments were identical to white male actor-patients, were perceived to be less intelligent, less likely to participate in treatment decisions, and more likely to miss appointments. Doctors in the study thought that both black men and women would be less likely to benefit from invasive procedures than their white counterparts, less likely to comply with doctors' instructions, and more likely to come from low socioeconomic backgrounds.[69] In other words, where actor-patients were identical except for race, black patients were usually seen as low-income members of an inferior group.

Although few doctors may be intentionally racist, not very many are immune to America's racial history and the resulting cognitive bias.[70] In his pathbreaking article on unconscious racism, Charles Lawrence III has observed that "[racism] is part of our common historical experience and . . . culture. It arises from the assumptions we have learned to make about the world, ourselves, and others as well as from the patterns of our fundamental social activities."[71] Because doctors, health insurance officials who authorize treatment procedures, and grievance hearing officers exercise considerable discretion, there is ample room for cognitive bias and stereotypes to influence their decisions. Discretion arises because only a small proportion of medical treatments are scientifically validated, because experts have differences of opinion about appropriate treatment, and because approaches must be individualized for the specific characteristics of each patient.[72] Discretion is inescapable in medicine. But combined with other sources of racial bias, it accentuates differences in treatment and health care. This pattern of racially biased discretion is similar to patterns in the criminal justice system, another institution whose practitioners wield wide powers of discretion.

Sports, a third arena in which race matters, is perceived by many as one of the most meritocratic, color-blind institutions in American life. If there is any realm in which the color line should have disappeared by now, it is professional sports, where measures of achievement are supposedly obvious, numerical, and uncontested. Yet even though 79 percent of National Basketball Association (NBA) players in the 1996–97 season were black, 76 percent of the head coaches were white. By 2001, the proportion of white coaches had dropped to 66 percent, as ten NBA head coaches were black. And although 66 percent of the National Football League (NFL) players in the 1996–97 season were black, 90 percent of the head coaches were white.[73] By the 2000–2001 season, the numbers had not changed; there were still only three African American head coaches, accounting for 10 percent of NFL coaches.[74]

The situation is not much different in college sports. Sixty-one percent of Division I-A male basketball players were black in the 1996–97 season, but 81.5 percent of the head coaches were white. The numbers barely changed at the end of the 2001 season, as the proportion of white head basketball coaches decreased to 78 percent. And although 52 percent of the Division I-A football players were black during the 1999–2000 season, 92.8 percent of the coaches were white. By 2001, nearly 97 percent of the head coaching positions had gone to whites.[75]

These discrepancies are unlikely to even out anytime soon. After the 1996–97 college football season, there were twenty-five openings for head coach of Division I-A teams. Only one of those schools—New Mexico State University—even interviewed a black candidate. During the 1997 and 1998 seasons, thirteen head coaches were named in the NFL, a turnover of almost 50 percent in the thirty-team league. Not one of the replacements was black. The situation did not change much in the next three years. Although the NFL turnover rate was 75 percent between 1998 and 2001, only one African American was hired as a head coach.[76]

Can these racial discrepancies be explained by the concept of merit? Some may think these head coaches got their jobs because they had the best records. The evidence, however, does not support this explanation. There have been only four black head coaches in the history of the NFL. Each of them has either played for or coached on a Super Bowl championship team, or was a college conference coach of the year. By contrast, as of 2001 only thirteen of the twenty-seven white NFL head coaches held this distinction. An analysis of the turnover among NFL coaches at the end of the 1997–98 season makes it obvious that merit is not the sole criterion for being a head coach. The potential pool of blacks has included (to name just a very visible few) Johnny Roland, all-American running back and Pro-Bowler who has been an NFL assistant coach for twenty-two years; Art Shell, former NFL Pro-Bowler with a 56-41 record as head coach of the Raiders and currently an NFL assistant coach; and Sherman Lewis, ten-year offensive coordinator (next in line to head coach) for the Green Bay Packers and an NFL assistant coach for twenty-nine years.

Who was chosen? One thirty-four-year-old with eleven years of coaching experience, two of which were as offensive coordinator, and a forty-two-year-old with four years of experience as an NFL assistant coach and one year as a college head coach. Each of these men had been an assistant coach under Sherman Lewis, who was passed over. Also chosen as head coaches were a former head coach whose previous four years produced records of 8-8, 7-9, 7-9, and 2-6, and ten men over the age of fifty-five with an average record of 6-10. Only one member of this latter "old boys' club" had made the playoffs the season before. All were white. It appears that race matters more than merit in hiring NFL head coaches.

According to a report released in October 2002, African Americans in the NFL are the last hired as head coaches and the first fired.[77] Few of them, the report found, were involved in the interview process. Since 1920, the league has hired more than four hundred head coaches and, as of the end of the 2002 season, eight of them (2 percent) have been African American. "When you see a Denny Green fired after the record he has built and then not get a new job," said attorney Cyrus Mehri, "or Marvin Lewis coach the best defense ever, win a Super Bowl and two years later not have a head job, you know that something is wrong."[78]

A similar pattern is apparent in baseball careers. A study of lifetime pitching and batting averages by sports sociologists at Northeastern University shows that black players have to out-hit and out-pitch their white counterparts by substantial margins to win and keep their jobs. Mere journeymen can have long and profitable careers as long as they are white, but among African Americans, only stellar and above-average players will succeed.[79] Perhaps this explains why there are so few black managers in major league baseball. Baseball typically hires managers, coaches, and front office personnel from the echelon of "good but not great" players. Because most of these players just happen to be white, black ballplayers have difficulty becoming coaches.

Professional sports are not atypical in this regard. In a national project examining the hiring practices of large law firms, Harvard University legal scholar David Wilkins observed that, as in baseball, black applicants with average grades are less likely to be hired than whites with the same records. Black partners are much more likely than whites to be Harvard or Yale graduates. The "black superstar" requirement is most obvious at the most prestigious firms. As one partner at an elite Chicago firm told the researchers, his firm sets "higher standards for minority hires than for whites. If you are not from Harvard, Yale, or the University of Chicago, you are not adequate. You're not taken seriously."[80]

As these examples indicate, race counts very heavily in the ways Americans are treated. Being white, as Chris Rock's fictional one-legged busboy recognized, has its advantages, and being nonwhite has its disadvantages. The problem of race in America is not that people come in different colors; the problem is that people are treated differently according to their color. The most important feature of being white, then, is not pigment, melanin, or skin color. It is, rather, the very close connection between being white and having improved economic opportunities and life chances.

FROM WHITE ADVANTAGE TO RACIAL SUBORDINATION: THE RECIPROCAL NATURE OF RACISM

The experiences of white and nonwhite Americans are intimately connected. The benefits of being white are related to the costs of being nonwhite. White Americans are privileged because they benefit from the present social order. As individuals and as a group, they derive advantages from the ways in which race limits the lives of people of color, whether they know it or not.

Because critics of color-conscious policies measure the decline of racism by the absence of crude personal prejudice, they do not recognize or take account of these potent realities. White coaches benefit from the higher standard to which black coaches are held. White Americans' chances of receiving loans are significantly enhanced when competition from people of color is reduced. When white men can buy new cars at markups one-third to half those offered to black men and women, their advantage (estimated at a collective $150 million annually by Yale professor Ian Ayres) is underwritten by race. In an era of cost pressure and scarcity in health care, the white advantage could be said to extend to the gift of life itself.

When economic and political resources are scarce, as most are, the relationship between whites and nonwhites may be zero-sum. Many white Americans are sure their children will lose when people of color demand their fair share of admission to elite universities or professional schools. For them, simply having to compete without the hidden benefits of being white is a significant hardship. Jennifer Hochschild articulates this concern elegantly: "As the number of contestants for a fixed number of prizes increases," she writes, "the chances of winning decrease. The arithmetic is simple: As blacks gain chances, whites lose certainty."[81]

Wins and losses look quite different from opposite sides of the racial divide. They also look different depending on time frame and basis of judgment. Sometimes whites fear that an outcome is zero-sum even if it may not truly be. Access to education looks like a zero-sum game, at least in the short run, as prestigious universities allocate limited places. But in the long run, failure to include people of color will harm everyone by limiting economic growth as well as by intensifying racial strife. Wins and losses can be calculated for a large group to which one belongs (like a race), for one's subsegment of the American population (such as an occupation), or for an individual. These different ways of judging who wins and loses, along with fear and mutual suspicion, make it difficult to assess outcomes consistently. Although they may not recognize it, whites and blacks sometimes find themselves in a lose-lose relationship. No one benefits, for example, when black youths go to jail because of a failure to invest in community social support systems. And if race was recognized and its consequences assessed instead of being ignored, perhaps policies with win-win results could be forged more often.

Whatever might be possible in a better future, today's race hierarchy is a powerful force. Thus whites, aware or not, misguided or not, typically resist change because their privileged status comes with (unearned) advantages. White Americans who believe they will lose if blacks gain are prone to oppose policies designed to reduce racial inequalities. Donald Kinder and Lynn Sanders point out that "insofar as interests figure prominently in white opinion on race, it is through the threats blacks appear to pose to whites' collective well-being."[82] Perhaps this explains why so many white American men think only of their short-term group interests and therefore oppose affirmative action policies. Because affirmative action eliminates the special advantages they have enjoyed historically, many white men believe they have something to lose when these policies are adopted. They believe this even though there is little evidence that white men lose jobs due to affirmative action.

Racism is related not only to actual privilege. It also entails a commitment to maintain *relative group status*. What matters is the magnitude or degree of difference that white Americans have learned to expect and maintain in relationship to people of color. A telltale illustration of this occurred when federal officials were trying to desegregate southern hospitals in the 1960s. A southern senator convinced officials in the Office of Equal Health Opportunity to create an exception to the desegregation policy. The exemption he created allowed doctors to place white patients in segregated rooms if physicians were willing to certify that integration would be detrimental to the patient's medical condition. Although very few doctors took advantage of this opportunity, the policy was tantamount to creating a new disease that afflicted whites: racism.[83]

Housing segregation is another, more pervasive, instance of whites establishing status differentials based on race. One expert reported "Whites prefer and are willing to pay more for segregation than blacks are willing [or able] to pay for integration."[84] White people's apprehensions about living in racially mixed neighborhoods underscore this investment in relative group position. A large number of white Americans believe that property values decline as blacks move into a neighborhood. According to a *Newsday* poll, 58 percent of Long Island's whites felt this way, and another survey found that 40 percent of Detroit's white population also subscribed to this notion.[85] Because a home is viewed not only as a major investment but also as a symbol of one's worth, Massey and Denton contend "these views imply that whites perceive blacks to be a direct threat to their social status."[86] Stanley Greenberg's study of working-class white voters in Michigan confirms this interpretation. "Blacks constitute the explanation for their vulnerability," he writes, "and for almost everything that has gone wrong in their lives: not being black is what constitutes being middle class; not living with blacks is what makes a neighborhood a decent place to live."[87] Bobo and Zubrinsky provide a dramatic example of this expression of racism. Using data from a large multiethnic survey in Los Angeles, they found that, "as the affective difference that whites prefer to maintain between themselves and members of minority groups rises, so does the level of opposition to racial residential integration."[88]

THE POLITICS OF RACISTS AND NONRACISTS

Because white privilege is invisible, it is common to describe "racists" and "nonracists" as very different kinds of people. Racists are characterized by the Thernstroms and other racial realists as deeply prejudiced individuals who express "raw racism," "people who can and will do horrendous things."[89] Nonracists, on the other hand, are said to accept the principles of the civil rights movement and display few, if any, traces of prejudice. In this view, racists today are the exception and nonracists the rule. White Americans may disagree with blacks about appropriate civil rights policies—46 percent of whites, for example, think government should "ensure fair treatment of blacks," compared to 90 percent of blacks—but supposedly their opposition has nothing to do with racism.[90] Instead, as Paul Sniderman and Thomas Piazza insist, these differences are understood as a matter of principle. "The politics of race," they write, "now has a moral bite to it that it previously lacked; for it is no longer simply a matter of rejecting prejudice in favor of the [American] creed but of rejecting key elements of the creed itself."[91]

Conservatives like the Thernstroms make nonracism the norm and racism the exception. But drawing any sharp line between racists and nonracists is a slippery business. No doubt some racists are a disturbed bunch of people whose crude talk about people of color (as well as about women, Jews, and homosexuals) is repulsively frightening. What is striking, though, is the similarity between the behavior of those who voice blatantly racist sentiments and the so-called nonracist discourse and politics of self-styled conservatives and centrists. Putative nonracists often act like racists. Until recently, for example, former Senate majority leader Trent Lott (R-Miss.) and Congressman Bob Barr (R-Ga.) were closely associated with the Council of Conservative Citizens, a right-wing, prowhite political group. Before the *Washington Post* exposed this group's racist views, Lott told its members, "The people in this room stand for the right principles and the right philosophy."[92] This was not the first nor the last time Lott expressed sentiments that blurred the distinction between conservatism and not-so-subtle racist appeals. But a later statement cost him his position as Senate majority leader. "I want to say this about my state," Lott said, at a celebration of Senator Strom Thurmond's one hundredth birthday in December 2002. "[When Thurmond] ran for president we voted for him. We're proud of it. And if the rest of the country had followed our lead, we wouldn't have had all these problems over all these years, either." What was Lott so proud of and to which problems was he referring? Senator Thurmond left little to the imagination in his 1948 campaign against Harry Truman. "On the question of social intermingling of the races," Thurmond declared, "we draw the line. And all the laws of Washington and all the bayonets of the Army cannot force the Negro into our homes, into our schools, our churches and our places of recreation and amusement."[93] Lott is hardly the only respectable Senate conservative who smudges the line between racists and nonracists. Asked in 1994 by one of his Montana constituents, "How can you live back there [in Washington, D.C.] with all those niggers?" Senator Conrad Burns recalls he told the rancher it was "a hell of a challenge." Three years earlier the senator invited a group of lobbyists to join him at an auction. Asked what was being auctioned, he answered, "Slaves." Nor does one need to be white to conflate the meaning of racist and nonracist. "Supporting segregation need not be racist," black conservative Ward Connerly is quoted as saying. "One can believe in segregation and believe in equality of the races."[94]

Because politicians use coded language, the assumed differences between bigots and nonbigots are sometimes difficult to locate. It was not Klansmen who put an anti-immigrant initiative on the ballot in California. It was so-called moderate Republican men. And Republican politicians have repeatedly succumbed to the temptation to run race-baiting campaigns. It was not George Wallace who poisoned the 1988 presidential campaign with the notorious Willie Horton ads but an establishment Republican. And it was not a member of the KKK who defended the Confederacy to the *Southern Partisan*, a neo-Confederate magazine. It was John Ashcroft, the current United States Attorney General.[95] People who do not show up as bigots in attitude surveys sometimes behave like bigots.

When a theory assumes bigots and nonbigots are quite different but does not distinguish between them very well, how should one differentiate between "racists" and "nonracists"? Does one focus on the differences between racists and nonracists, or on their similarities? Does one define racism as virulent antiblack sentiments and a pathological hatred of African Americans or, to use Melanie Kaye-Kantrowitz's words, as "a system that normalizes, honors, and rewards whiteness"?[96] Does one treat racists as exceptional or normal? Does one treat "racist" accounts of white supremacy as lunacy, or merely as expressions of American self-portraiture from another era?[97] One approach finds racism in only a tiny remnant of the white population who explicitly endorse prejudiced beliefs; the other casts a wider net, finding expressions of racism among corporate executives, national politicians, and university regents.

Arguments that demonize racism and treat it as the exception lose sight of the complicated and subtle workings of being white in America. A focus on obvious bigotry, crude verbal performance, and political practices may make American "nonracists" feel better about themselves. But it also produces a false sense of security. Because it ignores culturally acceptable sophisticated forms of racism, this perspective is unable to detect the "nonracist" ways that being white works to the advantage of European Americans. Opponents of policies that undermine white people's privileges do not use Klan ideology to justify their opposition. Instead, they invoke the principles of American political beliefs. Not everyone who opposes color-conscious policies does so with the intention of defending white privilege. But one cannot assume, as all too many critics of color-conscious policies do, that opposition to affirmative action is based entirely on the principles of fair play and individual merit. Much of the opposition is based on resentment toward blacks, and this resentment is driven by a fear (conscious or not) that the interests of whites as a group are jeopardized by color-conscious policies.[98] Because color-blind policies are cast as a defense of individualism, the group interests at stake are concealed. But this move poses a more insidious problem than the raw racism of bigots. People voicing virulent antiblack sentiments are an easy target, but restricting *racism* to them leaves the institutionalized benefits of being white invisible and untouched.

RACISM AND LAW: THE MAINTENANCE OF WHITE PRIVILEGE

The law and legal institutions normalize white advantage by articulating and enforcing cultural norms, which help to maintain racial hierarchy in the United States. At first, this seems odd. After all, in the 1950s and 1960s, federal courts helped dismantle state-sanctioned racism. The courts, however, have been ineffective in addressing contemporary racial inequality because equal protection doctrine treats individual bigotry as the core of racism. The law's insistence that intention is the sine qua non of race discrimination matches the opinion of many Americans. But this search for individual blame is psychologically naïve, and it obscures the complex sources and relationships that produce racial inequality. As Angela Harris explains,

> Translated into constitutional law, this model . . . works to identify intentional wrongdoers . . . but leaves untouched unconscious racism, everyday cognitive bias and institutional structures that faithfully perpetuate patterns of racial subordination. As the legal structures that continue to disadvantage people of color become increasingly "race-neutral" in a constitutional sense, the moral model of discrimination facilitates both the denunciation of bigotry and *the maintenance of existing distributions of wealth and power.*[99] (Footnotes omitted; emphasis added.)

The face of racial subordination today is residential segregation, unequal loan policies, differential police stops, divergent medical care and schooling, variation in criminal sentencing, and disparate administration of the death penalty. Absent a smoking gun of intentionality, constitutional challenges to these forms of racial inequality are impossible.

In addition to the intention requirement, the Supreme Court's response to proposed remedies for racism poses another formidable obstacle to meaningful change. When private or public organizations set out to correct historic racial disparities, they typically institute some race-conscious remedial plan. But because such plans classify people based on race, the courts routinely strike them down. Even though these race-conscious plans aim to help subordinated groups, the courts believe they constitute reverse discrimination.[100] Under the resulting color-blind norm, lawyers rarely succeed in justifying affirmative action plans that seek to remedy actual racial disparities and societal discrimination. As Reva Siegel points out, the result is that "doctrines of heightened [judicial] scrutiny function primarily to constrain legislatures from adopting policies designed to reduce race and gender stratification, while doctrines of discriminatory purpose offer only weak constraints on the forms of facially neutral state action that continue to perpetuate the racial and gender stratification of American society."[101]

The irony is palpable: how did the Court arrive at a position where the antiracism doctrines of fifty years ago are now the barriers that protect racial inequality? Angela Harris explains it as fear and unwillingness to "contemplate large-scale projects of political, economic and cultural redistribution and the dramatic transformation of social institutions and practices that would result from a complete renunciation of American white supremacy."[102] Reva Siegel argues that the Court got into this trap because, like the proverbial generals, society always directs moral outrage at the previous forms of subordination. Tracking her thesis through the entire history of American race law, Siegel suggests that this "past-wars" approach encourages moral smugness about earlier eras while ignoring problems in the present.[103]

Siegel exposes serious inconsistencies in the Court's reasoning about race. When it strikes down race-conscious remedial plans, the Court employs what she calls a "thin" conception of race (race-as-morphological-accident, race-as-analogous-to-blood-type). Using this thin understanding of race, the Court rejects the arguments advanced by advocates of diversity and affirmative action who employ racial classification as a proxy for differences in history, culture, and experience. It sees those arguments as impermissibly stereotyping racial groups. But when minority plaintiffs challenge state policies that create or support racially disparate outcomes in housing, employment, criminal justice, and schools, this same Court uses a "thick" conception of race to justify leaving those outcomes undisturbed.[104] For example, in the *Croson* case the Court characterized the small number of minority contractors as the "natural" result of different occupational preferences among racial groups. This thick view of race allowed the Court to conclude that the differences in racial proportions were unobjectionable.[105] The Court's inconsistent use of these thick and thin conceptions of race, Siegel argues, creates a lose-lose world for advocates of racial equality.

COLOR-BLIND OR COLOR-CODED LAW?

In rejecting race-conscious classifications or remedies, the Court adheres to a jurisprudence of color-blindness that made sense in the 1950s and 1960s when segregation was legal and was based on a rigid system of racial classification. Color-blindness undermined and transformed that system. But fifty years later when state-sanctioned racial segregation is illegal and people of color have still to achieve truly equal opportunity with white Americans, the color-blind ideal actually impedes efforts necessary to eliminate racial inequality. Formal color-blindness fails to recognize or address the deeply rooted institutional practices and long-term disaccumulation that sustains racial inequality. Color-blind ideology is no longer a weapon that challenges racial inequality. Instead, it has become a powerful sword and a near-impenetrable shield, almost a civic religion, that actually promotes the unequal racial status quo.[106]

The law and legal culture remain critical tools for dismantling racial inequality. But the law today does not speak from a genuinely color-blind vantage point. Despite having completed the vital task of eliminating Jim Crow racial classifications, legal institutions still operate with a perspective that remains perceptually, analytically, and functionally color-coded. The color is white.

Some examples can illustrate how the justice system remains color coded. Taken-for-granted white privilege explains how one unusually public-spirited citizen could refuse to vote for someone she saw as an extraordinarily qualified young black attorney who was running for judge in a community whose population is more than half minority but whose sitting judges and magistrates were white. What was the citizen's reason? She feared the candidate would be "biased toward the community."[107] The fact that all the sitting judges were white was "normal" and therefore invisible to this white voter. The candidate's black skin and the majority-black community, on the other hand, were palpable.

Selection of grand jurors is another example. Law professor Ian Haney-Lopez found that even though Mexican Americans numbered one of every seven persons in Los Angeles County during the 1960s, they amounted to only one of every fifty-eight Los Angeles County grand jurors.[108] Using judges' sworn testimony about their practices for nominating grand jurors, Haney-Lopez found that "nine out of ten nominees came from within the judges' own social circles—83 percent of nominees were friends, neighbors, family members, spouses of acquaintances, or comembers of clubs, organizations, or churches, and [a few were recommended] by someone within those same circles or a fellow judge."[109] The judges emphatically denied that discriminatory intent had anything to do with their choices, and this is most likely true. Nevertheless, regardless of their intentions, the judges' unselfconscious bias produced a degree of racial apartheid in the grand juries. Superior court judges in Los Angeles County nominated 1,690 grand jurors between 1959 and 1969; only 47 of the nominees were Mexican Americans. And of the 233 nominees who were actually seated, only 4 were Mexican Americans.[110] The number of Mexican American grand jurors trebled to more than 6 percent of the total by the 1990s. By then, however, Latinos made up almost 41 percent of Los Angeles's population.[111]

Invisible white advantage also explains how a white "gum-chewing, tennis shoe wearing" clerk in an exclusive Manhattan shop could feel it was appropriate to refuse to "buzz in" an elegant African American law professor doing her Christmas shopping.[112] The editors of the journal that published the law professor's shopping story insisted on omitting all references to personal traits like skin color. Their grounds? They believed that not mentioning race (being color-blind) was necessary to being objective. The irony, of course, is that the story made no sense unless the parties' races were identified.

Other examples show that the experience, perspective, and privilege of white Americans permeate substantive law and policy. Lawyers, particularly influential lawyers, are overwhelmingly white.[113] The law these (mostly white) lawyers have created has important strengths, but it also reflects their (mostly white) perspective on the world. From criminal to constitutional law, from federalism to family law, from immigration to original intent doctrine, the law reflects and endorses the views, needs, and advantages of the "normal" white perspective.

White perspective is not the product of skin color but of culture and experience. We speak of the white perspective because it is the perspective most often held by whites and the institutions they construct and dominate. It is the perspective of the namers, the controllers, the holders of "natural" privilege and invisible power, those who can take for granted the advantages of the status quo. Through experience and disciplined reflection, some whites expand, if not escape, the perspective of whiteness. For reasons of identification or advantage, some nonwhites may embrace it. Both, however, are exceptions to the typical taken-for-granted, normal and unreflexive white perspective.

Lawyers articulate and apply concepts like *reasonableness, harm, culpability, desert,* and *merit.* While their perspectives on these important ideas are shaped in part by their experience, that experience is filtered through the lens of their white perspective. This standpoint shapes their view of what voting arrangements are fair.[114] It shapes the analysis and criteria of relevance for just administration of the death penalty.[115] It shapes the priority accorded to hate speech as compared to "fire-crying" or national security under free speech law.[116] It shapes whether accented speech undermines job qualifications.[117] These modern examples are as much a result of an unarticulated white perspective as was the historical conclusion that when a white person was mistaken for being black, a serious compensable injury had occurred, but when the opposite happened, compensation was not legally appropriate.[118]

White perspective sets the standards for *probable cause* or *reasonable suspicion.* It assesses institutional arrangements and personal behavior, deciding when confessions or consents to search are voluntary. It decides whether reasonable people feel free to refuse police requests and "go about their business."[119] White perspective weighs the appropriate responses of *reasonable persons* and the permissible latitude of *reasonable force.* It assesses the severity of crack cocaine offenses (which mostly involve poor blacks) as compared to crimes involving powder cocaine (which mostly involve middle-class whites). And it sentences offenders using crack to more time in prison than powder cocaine users, *even when they possess the same amount of cocaine.*

Some white lawyers, judges, and professors even erase race from the writing of the Constitution and the formation of the nation.[120] Some urge courts to measure constitutional rights by the "original intent" of the framers without acknowledging the founders' racism. Many of the founders, Rogers Smith has shown, understood themselves to be the "bearers of a superior culture or racial heritage [that] . . . had obvious value in preserving the supremacy of the white, propertied, European-descended but largely native born male gentry who were the chief architects of the new governments."[121] Despite this history, commentators analyzing the constitutional framework of American federalism act as if these attitudes were unimportant when the nation's so-called neutral framework of rights and power was created. They neglect the powerful shaping force of slavery and race in the very structure of our government.

A final example comes from the heart of constitutional law. Constitutional lawyers and scholars attribute the origins of the foundational principle of judicial review to the Supreme Court's decision in *Marbury v. Madison*. But as federal appellate judge John Noonan observes, "[*Marbury*] was an empty declaration. The power asserted was not used. The power asserted was not used throughout Marshall's lifetime. For the next two generations the power asserted turned out to be mere huff and puff. . . . *The first fruit of the great declaration was Dred Scott.*"[122] (Emphasis added.) The Court's decision in the *Dred Scott* case returned an escaped slave to his former owner. By upholding slavery, the Court asserted its authority to strike down federal laws, helping to precipitate the Civil War. Nevertheless, constitutional analysts downplay the role of slavery in the evolution of the principle of judicial review. Instead, they cite *Marbury*'s reputable and lofty rhetoric rather than the slavery-tainted *Dred Scott* decision—even when that means ignoring the case that first gave the doctrine some real bite.

COLOR-BLIND OR COLOR-CODED MERIT?

If racial perspective affects the law, then the process for choosing who will be lawyers is significant. Is the process that selects candidates for professional legal training color-blind? Admission to law schools claims to be based on merit. Merit, however, is not a freestanding or self-defining concept.[123] Merit must be merit in reference to something, for some purpose, based on some set of judgments and justifications. Traditionally, law schools have used Law School Admission Test (LSAT) scores and undergraduate grade point averages (GPAs) as proxies for merit. Schools choose these indicators because they correlate with law students' grades in the first year of law school.[124] Law schools use other kinds of information, but in mostly unstructured and discretionary ways. The academic indicators are by far the most decisive factors, with the LSAT playing a crucial role.[125] When merit is defined as excellence in test-taking, however, the selection process is not as color-blind as it claims to be.

Given their role as professional schools, it seems odd that law schools rely almost exclusively on academic measures of merit to choose students. Law schools train and credential lawyers. The mission of law schools is much more focused than that of colleges and universities. Law schools primarily prepare students for professional work. Only 2 to 3 percent of graduates from elite schools enter academic careers, but, ironically, law schools place more weight on academic indicators in admissions than academic departments do.[126]

Law school graduates hold jobs that require intellectual and analytic skills; they use and apply knowledge. Academic skills are important in professional performance, but they are not the only indicators of professional achievement. If legal rather than academic jobs are the aim of most law graduates, then some of the criteria of merit should measure the capacity for outstanding performance in legal work. But law schools do not even attempt to assess these capacities. There is reason to believe that this choice about how to define merit disproportionately excludes students of color.[127]

Decades ago, in *Griggs v. Duke Power*, the Supreme Court held that devices used to screen potential employees must be job related.[128] The Court recognized that where access to education was unequal, the workforce would be unnecessarily distorted by race if employers required applicants to hold academic credentials that had little or no demonstrated relevance to successful job performance. The situation of law school admissions is more subtle and complex, but it is closely related. Unlike the academic credentials required in *Griggs*, academic intellectual skills are related both to law school and to lawyering. But extending the *Griggs* reasoning, one might still ask whether academic credentials are the only ones related to being a good lawyer. Effective lawyers must also have abilities such as problem solving skills, people skills, persuasiveness, the capacity to inspire trust, communication skills, tenacity, and goal orientation. Using the approach taken by the Court in *Griggs*, then, one might object to law schools' heavy reliance on one relevant factor (academic potential) to the exclusion of others that are equally job related in determining which applicants merit admission.[129]

Seats in law schools are not jobs, but the links to jobs and *Griggs* are closer than they might first appear. Law is a state-licensed professional monopoly. The state delegates responsibility to the organized bar for certifying professional competence (through the bar exam and requirements for continuing education) and for maintaining professional discipline. These activities of the bar are important, but attaining a law school education is the pivotal step in becoming a lawyer.[130] Thus, law schools act as the primary screening device for the job of lawyer. If one applied the reasoning used in *Griggs*, it would be unjustified to focus almost exclusively on academic as opposed to job-related criteria in selecting students for this professional education.

This argument becomes compelling when the racial consequences of conventional admissions criteria are examined. Social science research shows that job success is correlated with a variety of factors. Even for jobs with significant intellectual content such as the law, "paper and pencil tests" of aptitude or achievement are not highly correlated with on-the-job success.[131] Performance on standardized academic tests does, however, correlate with race. Whites generally do better on paper and pencil tests and similar academic indicators than do blacks or Latinos. Successful performance on the job, however, is much more similar among racial groups. Therefore, reliance on paper and pencil tests will predictably create greater racial disparities in admissions than would a system that also adds in other types of predictors of successful job performance. Even though paper and pencil tests and conventional academic indicators deserve weight in measuring merit, *overuse* of those criteria and *underuse* of other important criteria produces racial disparities in selection that are disproportionate and unjustified. Christopher Jencks calls this type of racial unfairness "selection system bias."[132] Selection system bias pervades law school admissions practices. The result is that whites are advantaged at the expense of persons of color. Put another way, the processes of exclusion and inclusion used by law schools are not simply color-blind systems that measure "objective merit." Rather, law schools make choices about whom to admit on the basis of debatable criteria that are arguably color-coded. By using such limited criteria, law schools will fill their classes with white students and make it much more likely that the legal profession and the law will continue to reflect a white perspective.

BEYOND COLOR-BLINDNESS

In recent years, some whites have begun to recognize that they, too, have a race, that being white may not equal colorlessness, normality, or neutrality. Once their race becomes marked, whites will have the opportunity to observe what they could not see before: race and the pervasive patterns of stratification with which it correlates. The Thernstroms spend hundreds of pages asserting that racism is (nearly) dead, and that if only guilty whites and unreasonably angry blacks would stop ranting about race, color-blindness would be within our grasp. Yet toward the end of their book, even they admit that whites almost always notice *blackness:* "Whites are able to shed their racial identity. . . . They had all the power. . . . Part of the package of privileges that came with being white was the liberty to think in individual terms. Blacks . . . were always black."[133] The Thernstroms note that whites have been racially invisible because they have had "all the power," but they do not recommend giving blacks power as a way to equalize racial invisibility. Instead, like other racial realists, they want formal, lip-service color-blindness without any shift in power. Would racelessness have the same meanings for blacks that do not have power as it does for whites that do? Not likely. It is power that confirms and normalizes the particular perspective of white Americans. It is dominance that allows racial invisibility. The ultimate benefit of racial power is the right to make one's advantages seem simply the natural order of things.

That unacknowledged perspective of white America radiates throughout contemporary color-blind racial discourse. The racial realist seeks to transcend racial conflict by banishing blackness and the consciousness of racial inequality that accompanies it. Racial realists could transcend racial conflict by naming whiteness and the privilege that accompanies it. But this possibility remains unexamined. Acknowledging and banishing white advantage is never considered. Nor do they propose that race be made less visible by redistributing white power, by diversifying white dominance of political, social, intellectual, academic, and economic institutions. Instead, racial realists urge color-blindness, which, in effect, "whitewashes" the racial status quo.

At the center of the debate over race in America is the question of what perspective we will use to define racism and the social policies necessary to end it. From what vantage point will problems be named and solutions found? Defining racism is not a semantic or theoretical issue. Narrowing the concept to purposeful individual bigotry is highly advantageous for whites. It locates racism in America's past. It labels black anger and white guilt as equally inappropriate. It renders most whites innocent. It blocks most governmental efforts to reduce racial subordination and isolation. And, most important, it protects and naturalizes the racial status quo. Advocates of color-blind policies do not address these issues. Nor do they admit that their conclusions mainly express the white perspective that comes naturally to them and to many other Americans. They ignore the possibility that different racial perspectives could exist. Yet only by acknowledging these profound differences in perspective can one begin to address the durable racial inequality of American society. To assume that a color-blind perspective is the remedy is to be blind to color. It is to lose sight of the reality that in contemporary America, color has consequences for a person's status and well-being.

The idea that racism is simply a collection of intentionally bigoted individual attitudes is fundamentally flawed, both theoretically and empirically. It uses assumptions that are not supported by empirical evidence, it ignores the collective dimensions of racism, and its conclusions are dictated by its vantage point. We have introduced an alternative concept of racism that rests on very different assumptions and looks to different sorts of empirical evidence to assess the persistence of racism in America. With this conception in place, a very different picture emerges of the state of racism in America.

In subsequent chapters we critically analyze the increasingly popular view that racism is obsolete and that the persistence of durable racial inequality is attributable to individual failure on the part of blacks, Latinos, and other people of color. We examine the unstated "domain assumptions" that guide the questions raised by this understanding, the data used to answer them, and the claims that follow. We show that optimistic reports of racial progress are overstated and hollow. Using our alternative understanding of racism to systematically investigate the persistence of inequality in labor markets, education, the criminal justice system, and politics, we arrive at very different conclusions. While less optimistic, our analysis is more accurate and, we think, more useful for constructing policies that reduce racial inequalities and find common ground to bridge the racial worlds that still divide America.

The Bankruptcy of Virtuous Markets

Racial Inequality, Poverty, and "Individual Failure"

Almost forty years after the civil rights revolution ended, two questions bedevil most discussions of racial economic inequality: (1) Why has deep poverty endured in the black community alongside a burgeoning black middle class? (2) Why do large gaps remain in family income, wages, and employment between blacks and whites? For many people this is the paradox and the bane of the civil rights revolution. How is it, they ask, that civil rights laws ended racial discrimination and left behind an unruly black underclass and substantial racial inequality?

Most people assume that white racism cannot account for this paradox. The Thernstroms, for example, explain it with a simple but misleading account of African American economic fortunes since the Great Depression. They argue that African Americans made large income and occupational gains relative to whites during the prosperous 1950s and 1960s, long before "preferential policies were introduced." Between 1940 and 1970, poverty rates among blacks dropped precipitously, black family income grew faster than white family income, and the proportion of black workers in white-collar jobs rose from 5 percent to 22 percent. Robust economic growth following World War II lifted all boats; it was "good for [all] Americans regardless of race" and paved the way for blacks' economic gains.[1]

But the real engine pushing black economic progress, according to the Thernstroms and other writers, is "the great educational gains made by African Americans in these years [which] meant there was a growing supply of blacks who had credentials that qualified them for white-collar positions."[2] Government action was largely irrelevant to black economic progress. What really mattered was educational attainment and socially responsible choices.

Conservatives attribute persistent gaps in poverty rates and income between blacks and whites, as well as serious inequality within the black community after the 1960s, to African Americans' socially irresponsible choices regarding education, marriage, work, and crime rather than to labor market discrimination. According to the Thernstroms and other conservatives, these choices result from profound behavioral changes among African Americans since the 1960s. Because labor market discrimination has mostly disappeared in the post–Great Society era, it cannot, conservatives argue, explain the remaining gaps in wages between black and white workers. What accounts for racial disparities in wages and salaries is substantial differences between blacks and whites in pre-market factors such as schooling, work habits, and job skills. Summarizing the new orthodoxy, the Thernstroms point out that "what may look like persistent employment discrimination is better described as employers rewarding workers [who have] relatively strong cognitive skills."[3]

Similarly, it is widely accepted that high levels of black poverty persist mainly because single mothers now head most poor black families and young black men are unwilling to accept available low-wage jobs. According to proponents of this view, the dramatic increase in the number of black female-headed families is due to black women's refusal to get married and young black men's choice of crime over jobs, a choice that temporarily puts money in their pockets but also drives investors out of the inner cities and gives employers reason not to hire them.[4]

There is no question that African Americans made substantial economic gains relative to whites during and after World War II, before federal civil rights laws were enacted. Nor is there any doubt that educational gains are important. It is also quite clear that single-parent families are economically worse off than two-parent, two-earner families. And no serious scholar argues that broad changes in the American family structure are unimportant, that the decline of the so-called traditional male-breadwinner/female-homemaker family is inconsequential. Still, conservative accounts of these changes do not acknowledge the importance of public policies for *both* black economic progress and the perpetuation of racial inequality. In their glowing account of black economic progress after 1945, the Thernstroms completely ignore the impact of racism. Instead, they suggest that economic progress occurred despite labor market discrimination and in the face of virulent, although declining, white racist attitudes in the 1940s and 1950s. They assume, as do other analysts, that education overcomes labor market discrimination and that employers act rationally and hire and promote workers primarily on the basis of their education and job skills.

This interpretation is not credible. The conservative account ignores the economic advantages and disadvantages produced by racial stratification, an arrangement that structures individual behavior and determines economic opportunity. By focusing principally on the behavior of black women and young black men, conservative explanations of racialized poverty frequently ignore not only obvious economic factors—for example, the economic stagnation of the 1970s, the declining wages of male high school graduates, and the rising wage and income inequality of the 1980s—but also the structure of racial advantage and disadvantage. Uneducated black workers experience more poverty and lower wages than uneducated white workers. The very different experiences of black and white low-income workers in the 1980s call for race to be taken into account. In this chapter we offer an alternative explanation for durable racial inequality and persistently high black poverty rates. Our analysis of African American economic gains and poverty takes into account the changing patterns of racial labor market competition since the 1940s, the impact of government policies on racial stratification, and the cumulative advantages and disadvantages resulting from white control of the labor and housing markets. The picture of racial inequality and poverty that emerges from our analysis of the past half century is very different from the accounts of conservatives and even from those of more liberal writers like Sheldon Danziger and Peter Gottschalk.[5]

THE CHANGING STRUCTURE OF RACIAL INEQUALITY

In one respect, both black and white workers had similar experiences in the periods of economic growth and stagnation of the past sixty years: each group gained in real wages from 1940 to 1970, and each suffered from income stagnation and higher levels of unemployment after 1973. But in a racially stratified society, neither the gains nor the pains of economic change are distributed randomly. Because whites have historically controlled labor markets, black workers have been denied the economic benefits that white workers have received from increased education and they have been disproportionately unemployed. Between 1940 and 1970, at the same time that wages of black workers rose relative to those of whites, black employment *decreased* relative to white employment. By 1953, the unemployment rate for black men in their prime working years, twenty-five to forty-four years of age, was three times the white unemployment rate. And since then the rate has been two to two and one-half times as high. All black men, not just the unskilled or poorly educated, routinely experience more unemployment than their white male counterparts. Black unemployment is substantially higher than white unemployment regardless of education, age, occupation, or industry.[6] Even if one were to assume that black workers have the same education as white workers, black unemployment rates would still be 20 percent higher than the rates for whites.[7]

No doubt labor market discrimination has diminished in the past sixty years, and whites are clearly less prejudiced today than they were in 1940. But these developments tell us very little about contemporary patterns of racial discrimination and racial inequality. Why is it that twice as many blacks as whites are unemployed, regardless of the unemployment rate and long-run increases in black educational attainment? Reynolds Farley and Walter Allen pointed out some time ago that "if blacks had been incorporated into the economic mainstream and if racial discrimination declined, we would expect that their incomes would approach those of whites."[8] Why, then, did racial disparities in income and earnings widen over the 1980s, even though both black and white workers faced the same labor market environment: declining demand for unskilled labor, widening income and earnings inequality, and higher levels of unemployment?

Our analysis of durable racial inequality begins by considering changes in the structure of racial labor market competition over the past sixty years. As we observed earlier, labor market discrimination is best understood as a group phenomenon in which white workers seek to limit black workers' access to economic opportunities and employers base their hiring decisions on negative stereotypes and workers' racial identities. One implication of this argument is that labor market competition between black and white workers is closely related to the economic needs of white workers. Their needs, in turn, are shaped by the economic demand for labor, structural changes in the distribution of jobs (declining demand for unskilled workers, for example), and changes in the distribution of income and earnings. During periods of slow or stagnant economic growth, as competition between black and white workers intensifies, white workers will seek to protect their position and oppose practices that are beneficial to black and Latino workers. Conversely, when the economy is robust, racial rivalry decreases. Tight labor markets may diminish racial labor market competition.[9]

Accounts of black economic progress prior to the Great Society, notably the Thernstroms', overlook changes in the structure of labor market discrimination between 1940 and 1970 and the reasons why these changes occurred. Most of the relative gains in income and occupational status took place in the 1940s and the 1960s, two periods when labor markets were tight and black workers shifted from one sector of the economy to another. The large income gains in the 1940s were primarily the result of a huge shift by black workers from sharecropping and agricultural wage labor to manufacturing. Wage compression, driven by wartime policies, and postwar ideology stressing greater income equality, also contributed to these gains.[10] The rapid growth of unions helped too, especially CIO unions that actively recruited black workers. The second set of economic gains came in the late 1960s and early 1970s, when a substantial number of blacks moved into high-status white-collar positions in the professions and management.

Rising real wages in the thirty years after the New Deal clearly contributed to the economic gains made by African Americans. By itself, however, economic growth was insufficient to transform the structure of the pre-1940 racial labor markets. Nor could it fundamentally change the conditions of racial labor market competition. Changes in racial labor markets were shaped by public policies that industrialized the South and precipitated a wave of northward migration in the 1950s and 1960s, by wartime wage policies, and by the civil rights and social welfare policies of the 1960s. But if these policies made a big difference for black workers, they were equally instrumental in creating the postwar white middle class.

THE BLUE-COLLAR BREAKTHROUGH

The sectoral shift that accelerated during World War II led to a blue-collar breakthrough for black workers. It also subverted the structure of prewar racialized labor markets. Prior to World War II, black workers in the North were mostly excluded from industrial employment, and when they did get jobs, they were forced to do the hardest, dirtiest, lowest-paid work. White workers appropriated the best jobs and excluded black workers, reflecting what Warren Whatley and Gavin Wright characterize as the "accepted expectations about the quality of black workers and the types of jobs to which they would be assigned."[11] They were also systematically denied white-collar and supervisory jobs.

The shift from agriculture to manufacturing that began with the war and accelerated when southern agriculture was mechanized gave blacks a foothold in northern industries. But their move from farm to factory was not a smooth adjustment to market forces. Black workers got defense jobs only after threatening a protest march on Washington that forced Roosevelt to create a federal antidiscrimination agency—the Fair Employment Practices Commission (FEPC)—to desegregate the defense industry. It took the government's fist to crack open the northern racial order and allow the market to work.

Black workers gained access mostly to unskilled blue-collar jobs during the war. An abundance of evidence indicates that white workers and employers regarded them as unsuitable for skilled industrial and white-collar jobs. Supervisory positions were out the question. With the connivance of unions, many firms maintained segregated seniority lists that ensured that black workers would never advance beyond the lowest-paid jobs. This practice was widespread in the South where, in 1960, 48 percent of employed black men were working in manufacturing industries (only 23 percent of all manufacturing employment in the United States was in the South). Although southern blacks were concentrated in lumber and paper and pulp mills, the steel and rubber tire industries also employed substantial numbers of black workers. The southern pattern is clearly seen in the steel industry. In 1966 blacks amounted to only 13 percent of all basic steelworkers in the nation, but they held 28 percent of the industry's lowest, menial jobs. In the South, where they were 23 percent of all steelworkers, 63 percent of them worked as laborers. White workers appropriated the best jobs and kept them with segregated seniority systems that made it impossible for black workers to compete for vacancies in skilled positions.

Things were not much better in auto plants, rubber tire factories, and paper and pulp mills. One southern rubber tire company executive said, "There were . . . separate lines of progression in the plant, based upon racial considerations alone, for purposes of seniority and job bidding. There was virtually no department in which members of both races worked." All of these southern plants operated with segregated promotion systems. Northern owners of southern factories easily accommodated themselves to Jim Crow.[12] Discrimination was subtler in the northern factories. Herbert Northrup concludes his description of Pittsburgh steel mills by observing dryly that "overt discriminatory systems are few; instead, the subtle manipulation of transfer rights, promotion criteria, and type of seniority unit result in observable inequalities."[13]

Blacks did not make it into the ranks of skilled craftsmen or into white-collar employment in any of these industries. They amounted to only 3 percent of all craftsmen in the nation's auto industry. In the mid-1960s, only twelve black craftsmen worked in southern Ford and General Motors assembly plants. In other industries the proportion ranged from 2 to 6 percent. Moreover, a minuscule number of blacks worked as white-collar employees in the auto, steel, rubber tire, aerospace, and chemical industries. As Harold Baron and Bennett Hymer point out, northern labor markets were racially divided; some firms openly refused to hire blacks, and all industries, including the public sector, had in place "occupational ceilings for Negroes." The worse the job, they concluded, the greater the number of black workers.[14]

Because of job ceilings, when African Americans did make large gains in education, as they did in the 1950s, their incomes relative to whites hardly changed. In fact, the *absolute* median income gap between black and white men actually widened in the 1950s, rising from $5,000 to almost $8,000 by 1960. In comparison, among women both the relative and absolute income gaps declined as black women moved from domestic service to clerical and factory jobs.[15]

Contrary to the assumption that income always rises with increases in education, educated black workers were more vulnerable to unemployment and wage discrimination than less educated blacks. Charles Killingsworth found that black-white unemployment ratios rose with education. In 1964 the unemployment rate for blacks with four years of college was more than three times the unemployment rate of college-educated white workers; but black workers with only four years or less of education had lower unemployment rates than comparable white workers. Baron and Hymer observe that wage gaps in the 1950s were not affected by education, noting that the "gap is greater at higher levels of education." In their study of the Chicago labor market, they discovered a stunning discrepancy. Black managers and sales workers earned just 57 percent and 54 percent of what whites in their respective occupations earned. But the wages of black operatives and laborers were 80 percent and 91 percent of whites in their occupations.[16]

Blacks did not gain much ground relative to whites in the occupational hierarchy during the 1950s. The index of occupational dissimilarity, which measures the degree of occupational segregation for blacks and whites, is the best indicator of this pattern. The index reveals whether black or white workers are more likely to be concentrated in one occupation rather than another. The more concentrated workers are in one occupation, the higher the index of dissimilarity; less concentration lowers the index. This index declined sharply in the 1940s as blacks moved from farm work to industry, but during the 1950s, as white men shifted into the rapidly growing professional and managerial occupations, the absolute gap in occupational status between white and black men employed in these occupations widened. The proportion of white men employed in high-paying jobs rose from 16.6 percent in 1940 to 25.9 percent by 1960, while the proportion of black men in those jobs rose only from 3.1 to 6.8 percent. Although both white and black men made occupational gains, the absolute gap between black and white professionals or managers rose from 13 percent in 1940 to 19 percent in 1960.[17] The proportion of blacks employed as salaried workers, moreover, actually declined between 1940 and 1960, dropping from 4.6 to 3.4 percent.[18] If war and migration broke open blue-collar jobs for black workers, the discrimination educated blacks suffered indicates just how brutal racial competition was for white-collar jobs after 1945.

THE WHITE-COLLAR BREAKTHROUGH

Postwar occupational ceilings were undermined in the late 1960s and early 1970s by government policies and growing public sector employment. In this period, black workers made sharp income gains relative to white workers and significant occupational gains as they moved into professional, managerial, and technical positions. This white-collar breakthrough was due to the massive number of blacks moving into higher-ranking positions in the public sector and to the implementation of affirmative action policies that eliminated job ceilings and other exclusionary devices aimed at educated black workers. Federal policies also enabled blue-collar black workers to pull down the barriers erected by skilled white craftsmen. Segregated jobs in the South were abolished, and industries that had historically excluded black workers were opened up when antidiscrimination laws were enforced.[19]

This white-collar breakthrough indicates that one of the core conservative arguments against antidiscrimination legislation is misleading. Gains in education did not produce the growth of the African American middle class in the 1960s; rather, it was government policies—the very factor that conservatives consider irrelevant—that led to the white-collar breakthrough. Although historically blacks have been more likely to work in the public sector than whites, prior to the 1960s they were concentrated predominantly in low-level jobs in agencies like the U.S. Post Office. The growth of federal spending in the 1960s generated an enormous number of professional, managerial, and technical jobs in state and local government. As a result, until the 1970s most of the gains blacks made in high-ranking jobs were in publicly funded social welfare and education agencies.[20]

College-educated blacks were the main beneficiaries of the growth in public sector jobs. By 1970, half of all black male college graduates and three-fifths of black female college graduates worked for the government. Public employment was crucial to the wage and salary gains made by African Americans relative to white workers in the 1960s because the wage gap between black and white workers is far narrower in the public sector. There is also evidence that, unlike white workers, black public employees were paid a higher salary than their counterparts in the private sector.[21]

By the 1970s, blacks were also making job gains in the private sector. Among black male workers, the proportion working as professionals or managers rose from 6.8 percent in 1960 to 17.4 percent by 1980. These private sector gains were chiefly due to affirmative action. As we show in chapter 5, enforcement of these policies opened up employment in industries and occupations previously closed to blacks, raised the incomes of college-educated blacks, and reduced wage discrimination for both black men and black women.[22]

Blacks were not the only group to benefit from government policies in this period. The white middle class also gained, expanding after 1945 because of a variety of public programs forged in the crucibles of the depression and war. Whites' advantage in labor markets was augmented by the advantages they received from the welfare state.

WHY THERE ARE NO WHITE BOOTSTRAPS

In the words of Jonathan Rieder, middle-class whites worship "the spontaneity of the marketplace, the pluck of bootstrapping, and the sacredness of middle class advantage."[23] Bootstrapping, however, had little to do with the postdepression expansion of the white middle class. Most Americans forget that on the eve of World War II, the majority of whites were hardly middle class. In fact white poverty rates were very high. Using the federal poverty standard as a measure, in 1940 two-thirds of white Americans lived in poverty. This changed radically over the next twenty years. By 1960 less than one-fifth of whites lived in poverty, and many had acquired the accoutrements of middle-class status.[24]

In addition to dramatic occupational gains, the wages and salaries of white men rose rapidly after the war; consequently, the absolute income gap between white and black workers almost doubled between 1940 and 1960.[25] Home ownership numbers also doubled for whites, rising from 14 million to more than 30 million. By 1960 almost 65 percent of white Americans owned their homes compared to 38 percent of blacks. Even though African Americans made sensational gains in home ownership (black-owned homes rose from 778,000 to almost 2 million during the same period), the gap between white and black home ownership widened.

Like black workers, white workers rode the crest of the postwar economic boom, but they also had considerable help climbing into the middle class. Black workers were denied, or unable to take advantage of, the assistance whites received from the federal government. In combination, the benefits of these federal social policies and segregated seniority systems generated substantial advantages in income and wealth for white workers. These postwar wages of whiteness were augmented in the stock market boom of the 1980s and 1990s.

The GI Bill powered whites' upward class mobility after the war. The readjustment benefits of the GI Bill, for example, underwrote a massive shift of white men from working-class jobs into high-income professional and managerial occupations. By 1955 veterans had substantially higher incomes, more liquid assets, and were more likely to own homes than nonveterans. They also had a disproportionate share of the highest-paid, highest-status jobs, and they were more likely to be professionals, managers, or skilled workers than nonveterans. Twenty-one percent of World War II veterans were professionals and managers compared to 14 percent of nonveterans. An additional 20 percent of these veterans were skilled workers and foremen compared to 15 percent of nonveterans. Readjustment allowances in education, training, and unemployment benefits added up to half of all veterans' expenditures during the peak years between 1947 and 1951. According to the President's Commission on Veterans' Pensions (the Bradley Commission), these allowances made it possible for veterans to be upwardly mobile. For example, 31 percent of the World War II veterans who took advantage of readjustment educational and job training benefits eventually landed professional and managerial jobs. Among those who did not, only 11 percent were upwardly mobile.[26] In its final report, the Bradley Commission concluded that the "present position of World War II veterans suggests that, as a group, their earnings and progress in later life will permit them to maintain their present advantage. This will mean, among other things, that most veterans will acquire more savings and qualify for larger retirement pensions (under Old-Age Survivors Insurance [OASI] and private pension plans) than non-veterans."[27]

But unlike the experience of white veterans, readjustment benefits did not translate into high-paying, high-status jobs for African Americans. One reason blacks did not receive their fair share of veterans' benefits is that they were more likely to be rejected by the armed services than whites (48 percent of black inductees were rejected compared to only 28 percent of whites). Although African Americans who did serve in World War II were just as likely to receive readjustment benefits as white veterans, whatever advantages they gained through the veterans' education and training programs were undermined by labor market discrimination. And while black veterans lost, white veterans gained.

Black veterans were not employed at the same rate as returning white soldiers. According to the National Urban League, many black soldiers had little confidence that the Veterans' Employment Service or the United States Employment Service (USES) would find them jobs "other than the traditional Negro jobs." They had good reason to be suspicious. Manufacturing industries, for example, were able to maintain segregated occupations and job ceilings for blacks because black veterans were funneled into low-skilled jobs by the USES.[28]

Nowhere was discrimination in the distribution of veterans' benefits more apparent than in the South. Southern whites received a disproportionate share of veterans' benefits. Although only 20 percent of the veterans lived in southern states, 35 percent of all veterans' benefits went to this region. The South paid high readjustment payments, and more than half of all southern veterans were enrolled in training and educational programs. These benefits were redistributive, raising income in the South.[29] Black veterans, who made up one-third of all southern veterans, received few of these benefits. USES forced black veterans into unskilled jobs; in Mississippi, for example, white veterans got 86 percent of the professional jobs filled by USES, while blacks got 92 percent of the low-wage, unskilled jobs. Southern black veterans had great difficulty securing the veterans' unemployment benefits to which they were entitled. And they found it equally difficult to use readjustment benefits for job-training programs. A 1946 study by the Southern Regional Council found that black veterans made up just 8 percent of the people enrolled in southern on-the-job training programs. And only 4 percent of all college students enrolled under the GI Bill in 1946–47 were black veterans.[30]

Black veterans also received less payoff from veterans' educational benefits than did whites, whose veterans' benefits were key to white middle-class prosperity.[31] The incomes of black versus white college-educated veterans was less than that of black versus white high school dropouts who were also veterans. The median income of black college-educated veterans was only 65 percent of white college-educated veterans. In comparison, the ratio of incomes for black high school dropouts was 67 percent. Not surprisingly, twenty-five years after the war ended, black veterans were earning substantially less than white veterans.[32] Privilege clearly has its rewards.

The mortgage loan programs of the Federal Housing Administration (FHA) and Veterans Administration (VA) were additional boons to white workers. These two federal programs financed more than one-third of all post–World War II mortgages, accounting for more than $120 billion in new housing.[33] The FHA and VA insured home mortgages that allowed lenders to liberalize the terms and conditions of loans. VA mortgages also provided a direct subsidy to home buyers. Unlike the veterans' loans, FHA mortgages were redistributive, aiding working- and middle-class families. Both programs helped extend home ownership to millions of families who otherwise would have been unable to afford it. They also subsidized the development of postwar suburbs. Either the FHA or VA financed almost half of all suburban housing built in the 1950s and 1960s, a benefit that was typically reserved for whites.[34]

As we now know, FHA guidelines for lenders used racist criteria to assess the credit worthiness of loans. Housing expert Charles Abrams accurately concluded that the FHA policy "could well have been culled from the Nuremberg laws." Federal housing administrators were unwilling to insure mortgages in integrated neighborhoods, fearing that anything less than rigid segregation would undermine property values. The FHA underwriting manual warned lenders, "If a neighborhood is to retain stability, it is necessary that properties shall continue to be occupied by the same social and racial classes." Lenders were explicitly told to add restrictive covenants to contracts and deeds. As a consequence, FHA loans favored the suburbs. In a study of St. Louis County, Missouri, Kenneth Jackson compared how FHA loans were distributed in suburban towns with central cities in the same county. His study revealed enormous disparities between the treatment of central cities and suburban jurisdictions. St. Louis County, for example, received five times the number of mortgage loans and dollars as the city of St. Louis.[35] The upshot was that black families living in the city were denied mortgage insurance, and when they did receive a mortgage, the terms were less favorable.

African Americans received only 3 percent of all the home loans under-written by FHA and VA in 1960, a total that amounted to just 30 percent of all black mortgages. White homeowners, on the other hand, were far more dependent on government-insured and subsidized mortgages: 42 percent of white mortgages in that year were paid for by FHA and VA loans. Black veterans fared somewhat better than black clients of the FHA (African American veterans received two-thirds of all government-sponsored mortgages held by blacks in 1960), but they lagged behind white veterans. By 1950, about 5 percent of black World War II veterans took advantage of a VA loan compared to 13 percent of white veterans.[36] But of course these mortgages could be used only to purchase segregated housing.

Using federal housing policies to sustain segregation is only the best-known instance of this practice. Until the 1960s federal social policy was also integral to propping up southern segregation. Southern states used federal subsidies for public works to reinforce the color line.[37] Veterans' hospitals, for example, were rigidly segregated. Most federal grants contained "nonintervention" clauses that prevented federal officials from supervising or controlling the construction of these buildings. The 1946 Hill-Burton Act contained an explicit exception allowing separate facilities for "separate population groups" if the plan made equitable provision for services of "like quality." Hill-Burton's separate but equal provision was declared unconstitutional in 1963, but by then southerners had used $37 million in federal funds to build eighty-nine segregated medical facilities. In the process, many African Americans were denied medical care, while southern whites benefited from the best medical facilities the federal government could build.[38]

These federal policies underwrote a new pattern of white accumulation and black disaccumulation throughout the country, but especially in the South and in northern cities. White families prospered as suburban developments were constructed, while black families were left holding a losing hand. After World War II, federal housing and urban renewal policies facilitated rigidly segregated neighborhoods and disinvestment in black communities. Blanket federal redlining signaled private investors to avoid making housing or business loans in black communities. One study of Chicago demonstrated that life insurance companies withdrew mortgage money from the city in the 1950s and 1960s for the same reasons the FHA refused to underwrite loans in black neighborhoods. The consequences were severe. As Douglas Massey and Nancy Denton write, "The lack of loan capital flowing into minority areas made it impossible for owners to sell their homes, leading to steep declines in property values and a pattern of disrepair, deterioration, vacancy, and abandonment." This meant that white-owned housing was more valuable than black-owned housing and that the value of white-owned housing largely depended on public policies that created and sustained residential segregation. Compounding these color-conscious, state-sponsored advantages, whites reaped all the benefits of home owning, which, in addition to being cheaper than renting, entitled them to America's major middle-class tax subsidy: the mortgage interest deduction.[39]

The 1950s federal social policies guaranteed the members of an expanding white middle class that they would accumulate considerable wealth with government assistance. Consequently, whites today possess substantially more property and financial assets than black families. In 1993, the median net worth of white households was ten times that of black and Latino households. Blacks have less equity in their homes and fewer investments and Individual Retirement Accounts (IRAs, also known as Keogh accounts). While the ratio of black to white income is 62 percent, the ratio of black to white median net worth is just 8 percent. Perhaps more important, 61 percent of black households have no net financial assets whatsoever. In contrast, only 25 percent of white households find themselves in the same predicament. And even among households with equal incomes, blacks have substantially less wealth than whites.[40]

There is little doubt that federal housing policies, veterans' readjustment benefits, the tax write-offs these policies provided (like the mortgage interest deduction), and various forms of public and private social protection enabled newly minted white middle-class Americans to construct a financial cushion that would enable them to ride out bad times and pass on the savings to their children. The best predictor of current net worth for young black and white families is their parents' net worth, a reflection of the legacy of white privilege in labor and housing markets and access to government handouts. These advantages are currently reproduced and sustained by a variety of discriminatory practices that limit black families' access to credit, require them to pay higher interest rates on mortgage loans, and constrain business ventures.[41]

The picture we present is a much more complicated account of black and white economic fortunes in a period of mostly steady economic growth and rising wages than conservative accounts of black economic progress. The story we tell is not a tale of individual triumphs in acquiring human capital and slogging unassisted up the ladder of success.

White Americans' ability to capitalize on access to high-wage jobs depended in large part on doors opened by veterans' benefits. The job ceilings that placed limits on the mobility of educated blacks and confined black skilled blue-collar workers to unskilled jobs, moreover, did not fall under their own weight. They were cracked open when Title VII of the Civil Rights Act was implemented and the public sector expanded. But not even the Great Society and civil rights legislation were sufficient to overturn the legacies of white privilege. This would become apparent during the economic turbulence of the late 1970s and 1980s, when African Americans lost ground.

THE 1980S RACIAL BACKLASH

Blacks lost ground in the Reagan years, and some of these reversals are quite startling. They also clearly fly in the face of conservative assertions that education brings economic advancement. For example, in this period young (twenty-five to thirty-four years of age) college-educated black men's earnings dropped to 72 percent of the white median income from a high of more than 80 percent, a serious setback by any measure. Compared to white men and women in the 1980s, black men made fewer occupational gains, and they were more likely to be downwardly mobile.

Unemployment rose for all black men relative to white workers, but especially for highly educated black workers. By the end of the 1960s the ratio of unemployed college-educated black workers to similarly unemployed white workers was even, a stunning reversal of the pattern Charles Killingsworth found in the 1950s and early 1960s. By 1980, as figure 1 shows, college-educated black workers were once again at an employment disadvantage relative to college-educated whites. They were almost three times as likely to be unemployed as college-educated white workers were. While black high school dropouts also experienced high unemployment rates during the 1980s, they were just one and one-half times as likely to be unemployed as white high school dropouts.

These reversals are not explained by a failure of black workers to learn or acquire job skills. By the 1970s, the difference between the proportions of black and white youth attending secondary schools had all but disappeared. Despite this, some conservative writers insist that racial gaps in earnings and occupation result from deep differences in educational and job skills between educated blacks and whites. In other

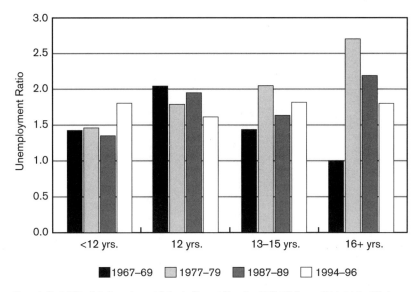

Figure 1. Black-White Male Unemployment Ratios by Years of Education, 1967–96. *Source:* Chinhui Juhn, "Black-White Employment Differential in a Tight Labor Market," in Robert Cherry and William Rodgers III, *Prosperity for All? The Economic Boom and African Americans* (New York: Russell Sage Foundation, 2000), Table 3.2, p. 93.

words, they assume that the attainments of college-educated blacks and whites are not comparable. Yet as Martin Carnoy points out, black Scholastic Aptitude Test (SAT) and Graduate Record Examination (GRE) scores *increased* relative to whites in the 1980s. Thus, the notion that college-educated blacks lost ground to whites because of an increase in the gap between so-called unmeasured educational skills is simply wrong.[42]

Nor can the widening pay gap between black and white workers be explained by the increase in wage inequality among all workers. Although both white and black workers lost jobs and income, it is usually assumed that black workers lost more ground in the shift to a service economy because they were concentrated in the high-wage manufacturing jobs that were eliminated in the 1970s and 1980s. The notion that blacks just happened to be in the wrong place at the wrong time oversimplifies matters and ignores persistent discrimination. As the President's Council of Economic Advisers (CEA) recently concluded, there is "indirect evidence that discrimination also contributed to widening pay gaps across racial groups" in the 1980s.[43]

The evidence that labor market discrimination persisted in the 1980s is even stronger than the CEA's measured statement suggests. In some cases labor market discrimination endures despite repeated efforts to regulate an industry. Certain sectors of the economy are impervious to antidiscrimination policies. For example, black workers have been consistently excluded from construction jobs that do not require high levels of education. As Roger Waldinger and Thomas Bailey conclude, "The low levels of black penetration into construction's skilled trades are prima facie evidence of continuing discrimination." They show that flagrant discrimination continues in the construction industry because white-controlled unions resist efforts to break down the color barrier.[44] Another more recent study confirms the persistence of labor market discrimination. Deirdre Royster systematically followed the experiences of an evenly divided group of fifty young black and white men searching for entry-level jobs. All of these men had graduated from a vocational high school and had similar grades, attendance records, motivation and character, and commitment to hard work. Royster found that white male students gained the inside track to jobs routinely thought to be available only because of standard interviews and institutionally certified qualifications. Skill deficits in human capital could not explain why young black men were denied blue-collar jobs.[45]

The major reason why black economic progress was reversed is that competition for jobs intensified between black and white workers in the 1980s. Like the immediate postwar years, the Reagan era was good for white upward mobility. In this period, deindustrialization and rising wage inequality reduced the middle-class jobs and incomes that were the backbone of economic progress after World War II. Although both black and white low-income workers saw their wages decline, the earnings gap between low-income, young (sixteen to twenty-four years of age) black and white male family heads widened in the 1980s. The earnings ratio of white high school dropouts to white college-educated males remained mostly stable from 1970 to 1988. In contrast, however, the earnings ratio of poorly educated young black male family heads to black college graduates sharply declined. The problem, as William Darity Jr. and Samuel Myers Jr. point out, is that if "the widening [income] gap between black and white families . . . is to be attributed to the higher representation of blacks among the less skilled and the uneducated, then why is there a widening gap between black and white family heads with the *same* low degree of educational preparation?"[46] The answer will not be found by examining who had the necessary job and educational skills. Rather one must look at how black and white workers fared in the scramble for jobs after deindustrialization. The evidence indicates that blacks lost out.

In the period after 1970 as blacks lost blue-collar jobs (mostly work as operatives because few made it into the ranks of skilled craftworkers), they found employment in white-collar sales jobs. But they also took a 13 percent pay cut. White workers who had also been pushed out of good manufacturing jobs, on the other hand, moved into well-paying sales jobs, which gave them a 36 percent pay increase. Thus, black-white income ratios in 1989 were lower for white-collar jobs (67 percent) than for blue-collar jobs (75 percent).[47] The important change during the 1980s was that black workers moved from good (high-paying) jobs to bad (low-paying) jobs. The employment rates of young black and white workers also differed depending on whether they worked in manufacturing or service industries. Employment rates for white and black youth in the manufacturing sector have been relatively equal over the past four decades. In the service industry, however, which is where nearly all the new jobs are found, whites enjoy an accumulated advantage of nearly three times the employment rate of blacks.

The problem black workers faced was that there were fewer good jobs to go around, and they lost out in the racially competitive and discriminatory labor markets of the 1980s. Convincing evidence indicates that retail establishments, one of the fastest growing sectors of the economy, are far more likely to discriminate against black youth than manufacturing firms. One group of researchers sent matched pairs of white and black high school graduates from the Newark, New Jersey, class of 1983 out in the world to seek employment. These job applicants were not faking an interest in employment. They had been screened to make sure they were actually seeking work and were matched for academic achievement. In the manufacturing sector, blacks and whites had about equal success in obtaining employment. In the service sector, however, whites were four times as likely as blacks to be fully employed.[48] In fact, in audit studies, whites or males are 5 to 20 percent more likely on the average to receive job offers than blacks or women.[49]

Although both black and white workers lost good jobs, persuasive evidence demonstrates that blacks lost a greater share of the good jobs and gained more of the bad jobs than whites. Darity and Myers report a 30 percent decline in the ratio of good jobs held by blacks compared to whites and a 1 percent increase in the ratio of bad jobs.[50] Carnoy discovered a similar pattern. He showed that the proportion of white males in low-paying jobs was mostly constant throughout the 1980s, about 31 percent, while the proportion of black and Latino males in these jobs increased sharply. The proportions of black, Latino, and white workers in midlevel jobs declined in the 1980s. Unlike white men and women, however, who made large gains in high-paying jobs, black and Latino workers were downwardly mobile.[51]

Competition between black and white workers for good jobs escalated during this period, a "classic case of protecting one's occupational turf from darker rivals," much like white workers did during the Great Depression. Declining wages and sluggish economic growth exacerbated competition over layoffs, reemployment, and job credentials. Downwardly mobile white workers in the 1980s acted just like unemployed white workers in the 1930s: they played the race card to keep or acquire good jobs.[52]

White workers were not the only culprits responsible for the exclusion of young blacks from high-paying jobs. Employers, as the matched-pairs studies of black and white youth seeking work demonstrate, are less likely to hire young blacks, particularly in service sector jobs. Indeed, some of the most powerful evidence for the persistence of labor market discrimination comes from recent studies of employers' attitudes and decisions. These studies show that many employers strongly prefer to hire white men and avoid hiring black men. Employers prefer white workers because they assume that black workers are less qualified and that there is a "lack of fit" between their own expectations and the cultural values of black employees. Faced with stiff competition, employers demand workers with more soft skills—motivation and the ability to interact with customers and other employees—to the detriment of black workers. Employers believe that black workers lack the soft skills necessary to stay competitive and frequently use negative stereotypes to characterize blacks' abilities.[53] Irate customers who complain about black workers reinforce employers' reluctance to hire them. One employer told researchers, "You do get customers coming in and they'll tell you, 'You need to hire more whites.'" Another study of employers' hiring decisions found that employers with mostly white customers were less likely to hire blacks.[54]

In their study of racial inequality in four cities, Philip Moss and Chris Tilly found that suburban employers were more likely to hire white women, Latinos, and black women than black men. The ratio of the percentage of black males hired in suburban firms to the percentage of black applicants was just .51. The ratio for whites was 1.22 and for Latinos, .87. Among central city employers the pattern was the same, though it was marginally better.[55] Other research shows that employers recruit applicants primarily in white neighborhoods to avoid potential black applicants, or advertise only in suburban or white ethnic newspapers.[56]

Many employers have cleverly taken advantage of these negative stereotypes of black workers. One study in New York City showed that as whites vacated desirable jobs, employers reclassified these well-paying jobs as low-skilled work. They did so partly for economic reasons—reclassification lowers labor costs. But they also assumed that black and Latino workers were incapable of anything but the most rudimentary of tasks. As a result, as "nonwhite New Yorkers get more jobs and have greater access to previously white occupations, [they] still find themselves locked into the [low-wage, dead-end jobs of the] secondary labor market."[57]

Blacks lost out in the 1980s for another reason. Republican policies hostile to affirmative action and labor intensified racial labor market competition. The enforcement of antidiscrimination laws was relaxed, and this was crucial in unleashing racial competition over jobs. Evaluations of affirmative action show that one of the traditional advantages whites have used to cope with economically tough times was restored when antidiscrimination laws were not strictly enforced in the 1980s (we discuss these findings in chapter 5).

This is the context that set the stage for the recent political conflict over affirmative action. Unlike the Thernstroms and other conservative critics of affirmative action, white voters clearly understand the stakes in this controversy. A 1995 poll of likely voters on California's anti–affirmative action ballot proposition (Proposition 209) discovered that white voters were more concerned about losing jobs or promotions because of affirmative action policies (45 percent) than about the potential effects of racial discrimination for blacks and Latinos (25 percent). On the other hand, 80 percent of African Americans and 54 percent of Latinos were concerned that minorities would lose out because of discrimination.[58] Whatever the reality—and there is very little evidence that whites have lost jobs to affirmative action—white workers see themselves as an embattled group whose economic well-being is seriously threatened by affirmative action.

RACE AND POVERTY

Conservatives insist that large numbers of African Americans remain mired in poverty because of flawed character and socially irresponsible choices in marriage and work. They believe the problem of the poor "is now more a moral one than an economic one" and often refer to the "pathological" behavior of poor African Americans.[59] The black poverty rate dropped from 93 percent in 1940 to 30 percent by the early 1970s, where it has remained until very recently.[60] Although it is true that high employment and rising wages between 1940 and 1973 helped drive down poverty rates, many conservatives conveniently ignore the impact of declining wages on poverty rates in the past twenty-five years. Instead, they assert that all one need know about black poverty is that more than 80 percent of poor black children grow up in fatherless families.

Consider the Thernstroms' argument, one typically advanced by today's conservatives. They begin with an obvious fact: employed married women have higher family incomes and lower poverty rates than unemployed single mothers. In 1990, 73 percent of black unemployed single mothers were poor compared to 63 percent of white unemployed single mothers. In contrast, only 6 percent of black employed married mothers were poor compared to 3 percent of similar white mothers.[61] The Thernstroms think these numbers point to an inescapable conclusion: since there are so many more black female-headed than white female-headed households, the persistently high rate of black poverty is caused by the dramatic increases in the number of black unmarried mothers since the 1960s. They point out that the poverty rate for black women between the ages of twenty-five and thirty-four was two and one-half times that of white women. Since the wage differentials between black and white women are minimal, and the unemployment rate for black women is only slightly higher than it is for white women (30 percent versus 24 percent), the large gap in poverty rates cannot be explained by labor market experience. What matters, the Thernstroms claim, is that "the poverty rate for white females is far lower chiefly because a much higher proportion of them reside with a spouse who brings in an income."[62]

According to conservatives, African Americans' poverty is intensified because the progeny of these unmarried black mothers, particularly young black men, fail to choose work and education instead of crime. Although the Thernstroms briefly nod in the direction of alternative explanations—they acknowledge there is some truth to the spatial-mismatch hypothesis, the idea that poor blacks mainly live in central cities and good jobs are found in the suburbs—like other conservatives, they dismiss this possibility. The real problem facing young black men is not the absence of jobs in the inner city but the unwillingness of black youth to take available work because the wages are too low. There is a mismatch, in other words, between black workers' expectations of what they ought to be paid and their actual worth in the labor market. In contrast, Latino and Caribbean immigrants are prospering, the Thernstroms contend, because they are willing to take the low-wage jobs blacks reject.[63]

Many conservatives believe family structure, not social class or racial discrimination, is the main cause of poverty in American society today. The income gap among African Americans is greater than the gap among whites because two-thirds of white women are married, while only one-third of all black women have husbands. If this shift in family structure has had a more pronounced effect on African Americans than whites, it is because black adult women have chosen to form families by birth, not marriage.[64] Other than gratuitous advice encouraging African Americans to change their ways, marriage is conservatives' major policy recommendation. "Marriage influences the family income of employed and unemployed alike," the Thernstroms write. "A marriage license is, in effect, an insurance policy: a spouse fired from a job will usually have someone else to depend on."[65]

Can family structure be so crucial? Marriage may (or may not) be a desirable state of being, but would it make a critical difference to African American poverty rates? The answer is no to both questions. There is no reason to believe an increase in single-parent families causes persistent high poverty rates or is responsible for continued gaps in earnings and poverty rates between blacks and whites, or between Latinos and whites. To think otherwise is to confuse cause and effect; most poor single heads of families were poor before they were parents. If anything, poverty increases the chances of out-of-wedlock births. More than 80 percent of teenagers who became single mothers were already poor. Kristin Luker likens the process of becoming a teenage mother to a sieve "filtering out the rich and successful, letting mostly the poor and discouraged through."[66]

It is true that there are more single mothers among poor, uneducated black and white women. But it is also true that the proportion of female family heads increased at *every* educational level between 1970 and 1991. Indeed, the sharpest increase in the proportion of single-parent households over this period, from 8 to 28 percent, was among black college-educated women. (The proportion of single-parent families among white college-educated women increased from 4 to 7 percent.) And although the number of female-headed families has increased sharply, the relative proportions among blacks and whites remain about the same. Family structure is not a very good explanation for changes in poverty rates, or in wages and income.[67]

WHY THE RACIAL POVERTY GAP REMAINS SO WIDE

Many conservatives are so preoccupied with attributing poverty to "bad" behavior that they neglect obvious economic causes and ignore the problem's racial dimensions. Changes in family structure are much less important than employment and wages, both of which depend on robust economic growth and viable economic opportunities. Yet because of labor market discrimination and entrenched residential segregation, poor blacks have limited access to these opportunities.

While unemployed single mothers have the highest poverty rates in the United States, it is employment, not marital status, that is the key to their high poverty rates. The poverty rates of unemployed married black or Latina mothers are almost identical to those of employed single black or Latina mothers. In 1990, about 26 percent of married black home-makers and 27 percent of married Latina homemakers were below the poverty line, compared to 10 percent of married white homemakers. Among employed single black and Latina mothers the poverty rates were 27 and 26 percent, respectively, compared to 16 percent for employed single white mothers. Clearly, as Sara McLanahan and Lynne Casper point out, "Black and Hispanic women have much less to gain economically from marriage than do white women."[68]

The comparison between black women and Latinas is vital because Latinas are much more likely to be married: 55 percent of Latinas were married compared to 34 percent of black women. Poor Latino children, in other words, are more likely to live in two-parent families. (In fact, one study found that 63 percent of poor Mexican American children were in married-couple households, while only 37 percent were in female-headed households.[69]) Yet the Latino poverty rate is almost identical to the African American rate. In 1998, about 22.7 percent of Latino families were poor compared to 23.4 percent of black families. Thus, the notion that a marriage license is the ticket out of poverty is a moral-ideological injunction, not an empirically based observation.

Changes in family structure explain only a small part of the poverty gap between blacks and whites. The President's Council of Economic Advisers estimates that had there been no change in black family structure since 1967, the poverty and income gaps would have declined by only one-fifth. "These are surprisingly modest effects," the CEA noted, "when one considers that since 1967 the proportion of female-headed families increased from 28 percent to 47 percent among black families."[70] Economic factors, mainly rising wage and income inequality and, until very recently, the relatively slack demand for labor, are far more important causes of persistently high rates of black and Latino poverty than family structure. As Sheldon Danziger and Peter Gottschalk point out, it is impossible to draw intelligent conclusions about the role of family structure in generating poverty without considering obvious economic causes such as wage inequality, which is responsible for most of the increase in poverty between 1973 and 1991.[71]

Unlike the period between 1949 and 1973 when economic growth produced rising wages and family incomes, the Reagan years were characterized by increasing poverty and rapidly rising average incomes. As a result, the economic bottom dropped out for everyone except those in the top one-fifth of the income distribution. The income share among the poorest fifth fell sharply, declining from 5.6 to 4.5 percent of total income. The middle class, defined as the second and third quintiles, also lost out. Middle-class family income was stagnant: married-couple families in the second quintile, for example, had an average income in 1989 that was only 5 percent above the 1973 mean, hardly a big increase over sixteen years.[72] Thus, rising wage inequality mostly caused increasing poverty during the Reagan years. Because wages were stagnant for all but the upper middle class, growth in Gross Domestic Product (GDP) had little effect on wages and thus reduced poverty less in the 1980s than it did in the 1960s.[73] The diminished effect of economic growth on poverty rates was not the result of demographic factors like changes in family structure, declining labor market participation among the poor (it actually rose during the 1980s), or changes in income maintenance policies. It was due to rising wage inequality.[74]

The consequences of wage stagnation for workers at the bottom of the economic order, however, were very different for whites than for blacks. Young, uneducated black single mothers (and young black men) faced a very different set of economic opportunities than whites. Darity and Myers showed that not only did the economic position of these black women deteriorate relative to young, uneducated white single mothers, but that if young, uneducated black women had been treated the same as whites, the income gap between the two groups would have declined, not increased.[75] What really matters to their economic well-being, then, is not that they are single mothers but that they are black mothers.

BIG-CITY GHETTOS AND BLACK POVERTY

If one is to fully understand why the black poverty rate remains at almost three times the white poverty rate thirty-five years after the civil rights revolution and the Great Society, the relationship between black unemployment and the enduring structure of big-city ghettos has to be analyzed. One must examine how labor market discrimination and color-coded investment and disinvestment practices produced and sustained the deep, enervating poverty experienced by large numbers of black families.

Neither impersonal economic forces—the logic of deindustrialization—nor freedom of residential choice created urban ghettos and concentrated poverty within them. And crime did not push economic enterprises out of inner cities, as conservatives like the Thernstroms assert. Deindustrialization began before urban crime rates began to rise, and there is no evidence that crime caused inner-city disinvestment. Big-city ghettos have replaced Jim Crow as the most important contemporary source of racial poverty and separation. Ghettos have become the linchpin of racialized poverty in the United States.[76]

The persistently wide gap between black and white poverty goes back to the economic instability of the 1950s. This was *before* the numbers of female-headed families increased and *prior to* the growth of transfer programs blamed by conservative commentators for promoting high levels of black poverty. Thus, the economic opportunities facing African American workers were already sharply constricted long before deindustrialization sucked most manufacturing jobs out of big cities in the 1970s, sharply changing the economic prospects for unskilled workers. As early as the 1950s, the burden of structural economic change in manufacturing industries rested largely on the shoulders of black workers. Plant closures and automation in the meatpacking, chemical, steel, tobacco, and coal industries displaced a disproportionate number of African American workers. Black employment in coal mining, an industry that historically employed large numbers of black workers, declined by 73 percent. In Detroit, automation and discrimination combined to undercut the job gains made in the 1940s. Thomas J. Sugrue found that the unemployment rate of black autoworkers was four times that of whites, a ratio more characteristic of the late 1930s than the 1950s.[77] By the early 1960s, a large group of jobless black men had emerged. Vividly portrayed by Elliot Liebow in *Tally's Corner*, they worked only when white workers were in short supply. The proportion of blacks among the urban jobless rose from 18 percent in 1950 to 28 percent in 1960. The Great Society poverty programs were unable to reverse the social and economic forces that produced urban joblessness.[78]

The problem was not that black workers were in the wrong place at the wrong time, victims of impersonal economic forces. Rather, the chronic joblessness of many black workers is the result of discriminatory, segregated seniority lists, particularly in the South, that restricted them to the jobs being mechanized and ensured they would lose their jobs. Black workers in rubber tire factories in the South, according to Herbert Northrup, lost their jobs because "jobs in which Negroes were concentrated were eliminated and the displaced Negroes were not permitted to bid into or to exercise their seniority in all-white departments." Black workers in other southern industries suffered a similar fate, as did those in northern factories, where seniority was more likely to protect whites than blacks. There too, as Sugrue points out, blacks were concentrated in "precisely those [jobs] affected by automation [and] often found that their job classifications had been eliminated altogether."[79] Consequently, as we have already indicated, black workers lost out to whites in the competition for service sector jobs when deindustrialization took a serious toll in the 1970s.

New investment in manufacturing industries in both the South and North bypassed black communities, contributing to black unemployment. Most new private investment in Alabama, for example, went to white-majority counties in the northern portion of the state rather than to black counties.[80] Japanese automotive and other industrial plants were systematically and routinely located in areas where very few black workers lived.[81] In the North, machine shops that supply screws to the auto industry, a vital ancillary part of that industry, have been concentrated in Jackson, Michigan, which is less than 20 percent black. Black unemployment also increased when American auto manufacturers decided to build new production facilities in Windsor, Ontario, an almost exclusively white city, rather than in Detroit, where African Americans are a majority of the population. Indeed, Windsor has become an industrial suburb of Detroit, where Canadian autoworkers now number an all-time high of 120,000. Blacks also lost out when new manufacturing jobs were created in Michigan's high-technology sector. One survey of Michigan's fifty largest high-tech companies revealed that not a single firm had placed manufacturing operations within the city limits of Detroit.[82]

America's emerging twentieth-century pattern of urban apartheid was consolidated in the 1950s, when whites tried to prevent, sometimes violently, African Americans from moving into previously all-white neighborhoods. And if their efforts failed, they fled to the suburbs, armed with FHA-approved loans. Empirical indices of nonwhite-white segregation in thirty northern cities show that residential segregation peaked in 1950. To arrive at a residential pattern that was considered "even" in these thirty cities, one in which all neighborhoods reflected the racial composition of a city, 88.1 percent of the blacks would have had to move. The level of segregation hardly changed in the next forty years, and there is considerable evidence that racist practices still operate in the allocation of home mortgages.[83] Contrary to conservatives' received wisdom, moreover, white flight was only one element in the deadly mixture that produced postwar big-city ghettos, leaving the black poor stranded on what amount to urban reservations. Government policies were the other crucial factor.

Public housing is usually depicted as nightmarish caverns stalked by drug dealers, pimps, and lazy women collecting welfare and producing babies, a haven for the callous, threatening underclass. In the late 1940s and early 1950s, however, public housing was considered desirable housing and was about the only housing available for southern black migrants. Because most blacks were denied FHA mortgage assistance, their only recourse in crowded post–World War II cities was public housing, which at the time was "a positive racial policy," according to Robert Weaver, who would later become Lyndon Johnson's secretary of Housing and Urban Development. By the time Dwight Eisenhower was elected president, however, public housing had been transformed into a "Jim Crow operation," much like a southern plantation where the relationship between public housing authorities and their largely black residents was based mainly on "manipulation and paternalism."[84] Contrary to popular wisdom, public housing did not fail because of the so-called bad behavior of its residents. It failed largely because politicians made explicit choices to use federally subsidized public housing to build highly contained racial ghettos. The result was an expansion of racial apartheid throughout America's big cities. Thus, if contemporary poverty is racially concentrated, it is because local public officials chose to segregate black migrants.

Public housing was transformed into an instrument of racial apartheid when downtown business interests and local politicians realized that they might use it to remove blacks from choice downtown properties slated for "renewal." Slum clearance programs financed by state and federal policies were the tools of choice for businessmen who wanted to prop up sagging postwar real estate values. They found it easy to obtain public financing and support from local politicians; the more difficult question was what to do with the mostly black residents. When urban renewal was joined at the hip with federally subsidized public housing in the 1949 Housing Act, businessmen gravitated to public housing as a ready solution to their quandary. Because whites violently resisted residential integration, public officials ruled out dispersed public housing as a solution. Housing officials responded by building government-subsidized housing in black neighborhoods, usually on sites abandoned by industry or white homeowners. In some cases, Philadelphia for example, city officials created racially segregated neighborhoods from scratch. The proportion of black census tracks in the City of Brotherly Love containing public housing rose from 40 percent in 1950 to almost 70 percent by 1980. Local officials in other big cities acted similarly, and 1960s federal housing policies gave them new tools.[85] For example, Chicago housing officials used a federal rent subsidy program to confine African American families to black neighborhoods and to subsidize elderly whites in white neighborhoods. Like racially structured mortgage financing, public housing was a crucial building block for constructing urban apartheid.[86]

Public housing never satisfied the needs it was intended to meet. Although urban renewal had destroyed 126,000 housing units by 1961, public housing replaced only 28,000 units. Many African American families found themselves crowded together in rat-infested slum housing or simply moved to stay ahead of the bulldozer.[87] Urban renewal affected inner-city communities in another way: it helped to erode the economic base of African American communities in northern cities. It is commonplace to hear people lament the absence of grocery stores, small retail shops, services, and other businesses in the inner city. It is just as commonplace to assume that these businesses were driven out by the residents' so-called bad behavior. The truth, however, is that federally funded bulldozers destroyed black businesses. In some cases, urban renewal literally plowed under black businesses. But the more important consequence was indirect: by forcing these businesses' customers out of their neighborhoods, urban renewal actually led to the demise of black communities. The early urban renewal programs evidently also contributed to the suburbanization of manufacturing and retail businesses.[88]

The effects were cumulative, leading to pervasive disinvestment not just in inner-city economies but also in needed services such as hospitals and medical clinics. As whites left the cities, doctors followed, and hospitals followed the doctors and the population. For blacks and Latinos living in central cities, this was a devastating form of disaccumulation. Urban hospitals not only provided a disproportionate share of the health care received by blacks, they were "a source of employment, a provider of last resort, and a center of the only remaining resources available to mount a struggle against a spreading plague of poverty and despair."[89] Yet hospital closings and relocations were disproportionately concentrated in black and Latino communities. In neighborhoods where more than 75 percent of the residents were black, 47 percent of the hospitals either closed or relocated between 1937 and 1977. In neighborhoods that were less than 25 percent black, only 14 percent of hospitals closed or relocated.[90]

The grip of racial apartheid tightened at the very moment good high-paying jobs were being pulled out of big cities. This not only contributed to a spatial mismatch between jobs and residential location but also intensified the consequences of poverty. Massey and Denton describe the effects of racial segregation: "Concentrated poverty is created by a pernicious interaction between a group's overall rate of poverty and its degree of segregation in society. When a highly segregated group experiences a high or rising rate of poverty, geographically concentrated poverty is the inevitable result, and from this geographic concentration of poverty follow a variety of other deleterious conditions."[91] One of the mainstays of racialized poverty in the United States is residential segregation, which by concentrating poverty accelerates disinvestment and precipitates economic decline. It segregates poor blacks from the fruits of economic growth and opportunity.

Convincing evidence demonstrates that when manufacturing declined and industry moved from the central cities to the suburbs, poor blacks suffered. James H. Johnson Jr. and Melvin Oliver conclude that central-city blacks have been "substantially disadvantaged by their lack of access to transportation and information on jobs in suburban locations." While this phenomenon is most pronounced in the declining cities of the country's former industrial belt stretching from New England through the Midwest, it is also true of the Sunbelt, which is booming economically. Blacks suffered most in cities experiencing unbalanced growth—sharply declining manufacturing work combined with jobs moving to the suburbs. But black employment was also reduced in southern and western cities that registered growth in manufacturing employment during the 1970s and 1980s.[92] In fact, most of the good jobs were out of reach to the poorest African Americans. Atlanta is a case in point. Employment there grew by 43 percent, surpassing population growth, but most of these jobs were located in Atlanta's white suburbs. Between 1970 and 1985, manufacturing employment dropped precipitously in the central city where two-thirds of all black Atlantans live. Even though the number of employed blacks rose, the African American unemployment rate actually increased slightly, while the white unemployment rate dropped.[93]

Despite this evidence, conservatives insist that the destructive consequences of racial segregation and private disinvestment have been exaggerated. There are jobs in the ghetto, they say; the problem is that poor African Americans will not take them. Poor blacks refuse to work in available jobs, at available wages. "Their refusal to lower their demands," Lawrence Mead lectures, "helps keep them jobless."[94]

The notion that poor blacks have a high reservation wage—the lowest wage at which they will accept a job—that causes them to turn down work is inaccurate. It is true that black workers report high reservation wages (but not higher than whites). However, recent studies indicate that this does not translate into refusal to work. Whatever black workers mean when say they will only work for high wages—one explanation is that self-reported reservation wages reflect self-worth—their wage demands do not affect the duration of unemployment.[95] A more compelling explanation for the persistently high levels of unemployment among young black men is that they are placed at the bottom of labor market queues by employers and are denied employment. This may explain why, when economic growth is sufficiently robust, as it was until the onset of the recent recession, employers hire workers they ordinarily shun, and poor blacks move rapidly into the labor market.

This scenario is supported by solid evidence. Studies have clearly established that employers hold extremely negative views of the quality of inner-city residents and their employability. In a survey of employers in four cities, Chris Tilly and his colleagues found that employers were concerned about crime and violence and regarded the inner-city workforce as inferior.[96] Although there were legitimate concerns about lack of skills, 33 percent of these employers said that blacks had poor motivation, about 15 percent thought they lacked appropriate communication and interpersonal skills, and 20 percent thought blacks lacked necessary education and training. Many employers used invidious racial stereotypes to describe inner-city workers: hostile, indifferent, lazy, violent, irresponsible, untrustworthy, and so forth. Black workers were invariably depicted as the denizens of crime-ridden inner cities, the progeny of welfare-dependent single mothers, and the products of inferior schools.[97] Thus, the employers' negative views of inner cities, spaces created by public officials, are then indiscriminately transferred to all workers in America's central cities regardless of their individual capabilities.

These employers' perceptions are not necessarily mindless. Many inner-city workers do lack the education and job skills sought by employers. The problem is that employers act on stereotypes instead of assessing individual capabilities. It is therefore no surprise that Moss and Tilly found that employers in all four cities hire disproportionate numbers of white workers rather than black males.[98] But there is good reason to believe that these employers' (mis)perceptions are more a function of the state of the economy than of the skills of inner-city residents. Some researchers have discovered that very tight labor markets partially reverse discriminatory employment practices. As a result, young black men were among the prime beneficiaries of the tight labor markets of the 1990s. There is also evidence that labor shortages increase employers' willingness to hire black workers, particularly black women.[99]

Regardless of employers' stereotypes of ghetto residents as a threatening underclass, inner-city workers and their families are not poor because they are social misfits, isolated from mainstream values.[100] They are poor because they are economically and politically isolated.

PUBLIC DISINVESTMENT AND SOCIAL WELFARE

The history of postwar ghettos is a history of public disinvestment. One reason racial poverty gaps persist is that poor blacks and Latinos have limited access to public resources. Most conservatives believe that welfare payments promote poverty rather than reducing it. In their view, public welfare payments induce dependency, erode self-discipline, permit (if not cause) out-of-wedlock births, foster crime, and so on. Much of the public apparently agrees and mistakenly believes that these policies benefit only black families. The problem with government policy toward the urban poor, however, is not that it has been too generous or that it contributes to antisocial behavior. The problem is that it has always been insufficient.

Urban apartheid not only diverts private investment in housing and businesses from inner cities; it also isolates African Americans politically. Historically, ethnic diversity in big cities did not preclude united political action, according to Dianne M. Pinderhughes. White ethnics lived in close enough proximity to share resources—Polish, Italian, and Jewish neighborhoods were never as segregated as black neighborhoods—and assets allocated to one group more than likely benefited other groups.

For example, Italian Americans could see themselves benefiting from schools in Polish neighborhoods or voting for Irish politicians so long as the streets were cleared of snow. But because many whites have chosen to live in racially exclusive neighborhoods instead of integrated communities, city resources that are allocated to black neighborhoods benefit only African Americans. In other words, there is no tangible basis for political coalitions between blacks and other ethnics in most big cities.[101] As a result, public resources have been drained out of inner-city communities. Because white politicians have little incentive to make new capital investments in the inner city, when big cities faced fiscal constraints beginning in the 1970s, they disproportionately applied retrenchment policies to African American and Latino neighborhoods.[102]

Federal social policies began to compensate for inner-city capital and income deficits in the 1960s. Most of the Johnson-era service programs were targeted at inner-city communities, and they actually succeeded in shifting resources to poor communities. This was mostly reversed, however, when the Nixon administration began to distribute federal funding through block grants. Block grants impose few restrictions on how local officials allocate federal aid. This made it possible to disperse federal resources to middle-class communities (the suburbs, small towns in the South) and allowed local politicians to distribute federal dollars to middle-class beneficiaries (this was particularly true of the Community Development Block Grant program and the Comprehensive Employment and Training Act [CETA]). Thus, in 1968 only 20 percent of federal aid went to cities with less than 100,000 residents; by 1976, however, the amount had increased to 30 percent. Small counties located outside metropolitan areas—read white suburbs—received much of the gain. Converting Great Society employment training programs into block grants permitted politicians to shift resources from poor blacks to unemployed aerospace workers along with other middle-class workers. As a result, fewer poor people were served by CETA's job training component than by Lyndon Johnson's Great Society training programs.[103]

Federal aid was redirected to white middle-class constituencies at the very moment when these social programs were being defunded in real terms. Consequently, fewer dollars were spread across more beneficiaries, diminishing the funds available to inner-city communities. The Reagan administration continued to combine retrenchment with block grants. After 1981, funding for Great Society service programs was sharply reduced, and the remainder was shifted into block grants. For example, at the same time that federal regulations governing the distribution of federal aid were loosened, funding for Title I of the Elementary and Secondary Education Act (ESEA), a program that provided federal aid to inner-city schools, was reduced by 17 percent. According to one estimate, federal grants to cities declined by 46 percent in real terms, effectively withdrawing resources from black and Latino communities.[104]

Local officials also turned a blind eye to urban poverty, preferring to cater to white (and increasingly to black) middle-class sensibilities. At the same time they lobbied the federal government for bailouts, many cities used tax revenues, bond issues, and other arcane and obscure fiscal devices to fund downtown redevelopment schemes—conference centers, malls, plazas, athletic stadiums—that provided few benefits that trickled down to the poor. There is hardly any evidence to show that the urban poor got many of the low-wage jobs generated by these projects.[105]

Federal social transfers to the urban poor became especially important at that time because they replaced the disinvestment of physical and human capital in inner-city communities. Contrary to conservative dogma, expanded cash welfare and in-kind benefits such as food stamps and Medicaid helped *reduce* poverty after the 1960s. They did not sustain it. As inadequate as these payments were, they became the mainstays of poor inner-city communities when other federal resources were withdrawn in the 1970s. Excluding transfers and before taxes, the 1990 African American poverty rate was 39.7 percent. In the same year, the poverty rate for white people was less than half that rate (17.7 percent). Combining cash and noncash transfers such as food stamps and deducting taxes reduces the black poverty rate to 24.3 percent and the white poverty rate to 9 percent.[106] Thus, these transfers have a larger impact on the white poor than the black poor, reducing poverty rates by almost half among whites but by slightly more than one-third among blacks. The reason is simple: blacks and whites benefit from very different kinds of transfer programs. African Americans and Latinos are much more likely to receive federal *means-tested* transfers that are available only to individuals and families whose income falls below a legal threshold. Whites, on the other hand, typically receive *universal benefits* that are available to anyone, regardless of their income. Both rich and poor receive social security, but only the poor receive welfare.

While 74 percent of all African Americans who received federal social transfers in 1988 were given means-tested benefits, only 35 percent got universal, or non-income-tested benefits. In contrast, white beneficiaries are much more likely to receive non-income-tested benefits (77 percent) rather than means-tested benefits (29 percent).[107] This difference is significant for two reasons. First, universal programs like social security have more legitimacy than means-tested programs, which most whites assume are designed for blacks and Latinos. This assumption is mistaken, of course, because until recently whites have always been a majority or near majority of the beneficiaries of means-tested assistance like welfare. Nevertheless, welfare, food stamps, and Medicaid—all means-tested programs—are racially stigmatized. Since the 1950s public discussions of welfare have been stamped with pejorative stereotypes of African American women as promiscuous and lazy. There is compelling evidence that people's view of welfare is powerfully influenced by their racial attitudes. Blacks have come to represent, at least among many whites, the undeserving poor. For example, whites who believe that African Americans are "lazy" are far more likely to favor cutting welfare spending than those who reject this stereotype.[108] Universal programs, on the other hand, not only have higher benefits, which, unlike welfare benefits, are typically indexed for inflation, but the beneficiaries are not stigmatized. Most people presume they deserve their benefits.

Second, because of labor market discrimination, income-tested and universal programs in the United States are racially bifurcated. U.S. social insurance programs are based on wage-related eligibility criteria, which means they reward full-time employment. As we have seen, however, labor market discrimination restricts the occupational mobility of blacks or lowers their wages relative to white workers. The result is that black workers receive lower benefits from these programs or their eligibility is restricted.

These consequences become apparent when we compare the ratio of median black income to median white income with respect to whether it is derived from wages, income-tested transfers, or universal payments. The wage income of all black families is about two-thirds that of all white families, and black income from property is just one-third the amount whites receive from that source. Public cash transfers raise the income of blacks relative to whites, but only marginally so in the case of social insurance. The ratio of black to white median income from welfare payments is 94 percent, almost parity. When one looks at social security, however, the ratio is 68 percent, only slightly higher than the black-white wage ratio.[109] This is because blacks receive lower wages relative to whites, a result of the wage and occupational discrimination we have documented. Moreover, because the black unemployment rate has been two to two and one-half times the white unemployment rate since the early 1950s, blacks' access to unemployment compensation and middle-class social programs has eroded, leaving AFDC and other welfare programs as their main safety net. Black unemployment rates have been at least twice the rate of whites, even during the 1990s economic boom. But despite their higher rates of unemployment, only 23 percent of the black unemployed received unemployment compensation in 1996. In comparison, 38 percent of all unemployed white workers benefited from unemployment compensation.

Despite the significant growth of the black middle class since the early 1970s, the racial stratification of American social policy has persisted.[110] Poor whites are much more likely to be lifted out of poverty by universal programs than poor blacks. Among whites in the bottom income quintile, almost two-fifths were helped by social security payments, as compared to less than one-fifth of low-income blacks. These programs have had a proportionately greater impact on reducing poverty among whites than among blacks. Universal cash transfers like social security reduce the white poverty rate by 34 percent. They lower the black poverty rate, however, by only 13 percent.[111]

Conservatives ignore the effects of public disinvestment on inner-city communities. Instead, they focus on the difference marital status makes in poverty rates between black and white women and how white women are much better off. This focus is misguided. Compared to African American women—especially black women who are single, never-married mothers—the lower poverty rates of white women have less to do with their state of matrimony than with their greater access to a broad range of public cash transfers. White single mothers are more likely to receive income from a wide array of public social transfers—including veterans' payments, unemployment compensation, and, more importantly, social security—than black single mothers, who are extraordinarily dependent on AFDC payments and other income-tested programs that provide lower benefits. Some evidence, moreover, suggests that cash transfers are more likely to lift white women and their children out of poverty than they are black women or Latinas.[112]

The 1996 welfare law that replaced AFDC with a time-limited cash transfer and stringent work requirements has deepened the racial divide at the heart of the U.S. welfare state. Although the new welfare law has changed significantly the lives of all poor women, it has had very different consequences for black and white single mothers. Racist stereotypes and the politically motivated manipulation of the issue of race and welfare underlie both the origins and implementation of welfare reform. Reliable survey evidence documents that white racial attitudes are one of the most important factors underlying white support for "get tough" welfare policies like time limited benefits and family caps, policies that deny benefits to women who become pregnant while receiving welfare. Moreover, states in which African Americans and Latinos are a high proportion of the caseload were significantly more likely to adopt stringent time limits on benefits, tough family caps, and to impose strict sanctions on recipients for violations of the new program rules.[113] And there is evidence that welfare administrators and social workers have treated black women very differently than white women: in one state black mothers were denied needed transportation assistance that was readily given to white mothers.[114] Race is obviously not the only cause of welfare reform, but it is far and away one of the most important.

Ironically, welfare reform has resulted in a program that now disproportionately serves only black and Latino women. The number of women receiving welfare has dropped precipitously since the law was enacted, but white women are leaving the welfare rolls much more quickly than black women are. As a result, in some states black women now make up a much larger proportion of women on welfare rolls than before welfare reform. While the reasons for this change are not yet clear, one can infer from available evidence that the differences have less to do with marriage rates than with the differential treatment black and white women receive from employers. Black women face substantial racial and geographical barriers to employment. They are also disproportionately subject to sanctions for violation of program rules. Blacks are far more likely to live in states that impose strict sanctions than whites, and as a result almost two-thirds of black recipients of TANF (Temporary Assistance to Needy Families) benefits in 1999 had been sanctioned compared to just half of white recipients.[115]

Welfare reform may actually contribute to public disinvestment in impoverished black and Latino inner-city communities. Because welfare reform limits federal spending and gives state and local officials substantial leeway in distributing funds through block grants, it is quite possible that poor inner-city communities, where the most poor black and Latina mothers live, will receive insufficient resources for child care, employment training, and other services just as they did during the 1970s and 1980s.[116] Welfare reform has done little to overcome the racial inequalities embedded in federal social policies and even less to remedy black poverty.

Despite what conservatives imagine, the remedy for poverty in black communities is not marriage licenses. A far more compelling explanation for deep and persistent poverty among African Americans at the beginning of the twenty-first century is the combined consequences of labor market discrimination, wage inequality, stagnant economic growth, urban apartheid, and public disinvestment in poor black communities.

THE WAGES OF DISCRIMINATION

Many racial realists and conservatives believe that white racism no longer causes racial inequality. As they see it, racial stratification is produced by the failure of individuals to work hard, go to school, get married, and stay out of trouble. In this narrative, affirmative action and other race-specific policies are not only unfair, they also interfere with market rationality. A crucial piece of evidence for this proposition is that African Americans made most of their economic progress before the civil rights revolution, not as a result of it. According to this view, it was education, not race-conscious policies, that led to black occupational and wage gains.

Our reading of history leads us to a very different conclusion. Because their evidence is weak, we are not persuaded by the conservative or racial realist explanation for durable racial inequality and persistent poverty among black Americans. Although opinion surveys indicate that racial prejudice has declined, competition between black and white workers over jobs was as important in shaping the post–World War II economic fortunes of African Americans as it was before the war. The evidence indicates that at two crucial points in this history, white workers received advantages in the labor market that substantially disadvantaged black workers. One occurred in the struggle over white-collar and skilled jobs after World War II when job ceilings and seniority rules were manipulated to restrict educated black workers to unskilled jobs. The other took place in the 1980s when black and white workers were displaced from manufacturing jobs and scrambled for new jobs. Blacks lost this contest. As a careful reading of recent American history strongly suggests, labor market discrimination is more subtle today than it was in the 1920s, when white workers openly barred black workers from factory work and businessmen played the two races off against each other. The underlying dynamics, however, are very much the same.

In addition to the advantages white workers gained on the job market, the evidence shows that being white gave them a significant edge when they sought public social benefits and subsidies. Clearly, as the white middle class climbed the social ladder in the postwar period, they were aided by various kinds of handouts from federal bureaucrats. Indeed, the white middle class has routinely been subsidized by public social policies, regardless of whether the aid is in the form of the tangible benefits of housing and veterans' policies in the 1950s, the extensive protection white workers received from employer-provided health and pension programs, or the broadly accessible non-income-tested cash transfers. These policies not only provided a safety net; they were also instrumental to the accumulation of white wealth. At the same time, limiting the access of black families to these policies in combination with public and private disinvestment in black communities, mainly big-city ghettos, has deepened the racial gap in income and wealth. In sum, the advantages received by whites from job markets and the welfare state were critical to establishing patterns of accumulation for them and of disaccumulation for blacks.

White Americans cannot see the advantages they gain from this arrangement. A widely accepted American belief that attributes white economic progress to individual success and black failure to government intervention hides white advantages in the U.S. welfare state. Many whites are therefore hostile to welfare and affirmative action because they believe these policies violate deeply held American values. They define their individualism in opposition to blacks who they presume do not share their middle-class values. This kind of self-concept "sustains whites' illusions about their own independence and obscures the advantages they receive from federal social policies by seeing blacks' ties to the welfare state as being based on 'dependence' and individual 'failure.'"[117] Optimistic talk about America being a color-blind society may provide aid and comfort to those who mouth this tale. But it has little to do with reality.

When asked how they would attack black poverty and racial inequality, most whites and many blacks immediately mention education. No one seriously denies the importance of education at a time when those without a college education languish in low-wage, dead-end jobs. Yet rather than seeking to expand opportunities in higher education for blacks and Latinos, racial realists and conservatives call for eliminating preferential admissions to college and fixing a flawed system of public education with school vouchers. We now turn to the conservative critique of race and education.

3

Keeping Blacks in Their Place

Race, Education, and Testing

Nothing in the debate over affirmative action arouses so much passion as the topic of racial preferences in college admissions. Many whites feel admissions procedures that take race into account are unfair and counterproductive. They think that admitting African Americans with mediocre SAT scores to elite schools instead of white students with superior SAT scores is obviously the result of a double standard. They also believe strongly that the policy makes no sense when a superior college education has become the major pathway to wealth and status. Students should be admitted to colleges, they feel, solely on the basis of merit as measured by test scores, regardless of the consequences. And if black and Latino student numbers at elite colleges and universities decline, then so be it.

Racial realists and conservatives are persuaded that the black-white test gap is the main obstruction to black economic progress. The test gap indicates, they argue, that the cognitive ability of many blacks is weak and is therefore the main reason their wages and income lag behind whites. Today, argues Ronald Ferguson, the "most important disparities in opportunity may occur before young people even enter the labor market—in the provision of schooling and other resources that influence skill building and the socialization of youth."[1] But how could the same educational system that was fundamental to black educational progress in the past now be failing the African American community?

Conservatives typically respond that public education currently fails to prepare the majority of African Americans for college and that attempts by colleges to compensate for this inadequacy through affirmative action are doomed to failure. What is more, conservatives believe that the failure of public education to put blacks on a competitive footing is partly the fault of white liberals and civil rights organizations that refuse to demand and implement high standards for black children and their teachers and that also push for affirmative action. As conservatives see it, this does no one any good, least of all blacks, because race-conscious admissions bring African Americans into academic situations for which they are not adequately prepared, causing them to drop out at rates far in excess of better-prepared white and Asian American students. If universities applied the same admissions standard for blacks as they do for others, many conservatives assert, they would likely reach that standard. And reaching it, they would do as well in college as whites.

This argument is seductive. And it is widely accepted among white Americans, since it squares with commonly held perceptions about merit, fairness, and individual effort in American society. It also dovetails with a set of partial truths. Black success in the post–World War II period is due partly to closing the black-white education gap. Blacks did make large relative gains in education between 1940 and 1980. And many African Americans do attend poorer schools than whites, which does explain some disparities in black-white educational performance. Blacks do have lower college graduation rates than whites, and this is due in part to the lower quality of educational preparation they receive. But these partial truths do not prove that public education has failed or that affirmative action is futile.

In *America in Black and White*, the Thernstroms summarize the argument made by conservatives such as Milton Friedman, Thomas Sowell, Charles Murray and Richard Herrnstein, Dinesh D'Souza, Shelby Steele, William Bennett, and most recently, by a group the Hoover Institution assembled to critique American public education and propose conservative alternatives.[2] But in order to make their case against public education, conservatives have to make huge leaps over stubborn facts. America is portrayed as a society in which the only remaining discrimination *favors* disadvantaged minorities. To do this, however, they ignore the past legacy of segregation and negative imagery of African Americans that is embedded in schools, colleges, and the labor market. Murray and Herrnstein, in *The Bell Curve*, and the Thernstroms, for example, claim that teenage achievement test scores, such as the SAT or achievement tests given as part of national surveys, are excellent predictors of future success. But to make this claim they have to assume that college education makes no difference to economic success. They also have to overlook the significant variability in both white and African American accomplishments across higher education institutions.

These authors' repeated misuse of empirical data is particularly troubling in this regard. It is not clear whether they really do not understand the quantitative data sufficiently or whether they misuse it intentionally because they assume their readers are statistically unsophisticated. In either case, they spin a story that appeals to stereotypes, raises the wrong questions, and provides many wrong answers.

Conservative think tanks commonly make most, if not all, of the arguments regarding public education and affirmative action. When they discuss race, conservatives seem less concerned with improving the education and incomes of disadvantaged minorities and more with weakening the "public" in public primary and secondary education and preserving access to elite universities for the (mainly white) upper middle class. These discussions discount the hostile environment faced by blacks in historically white universities, blacks' lower social class standing compared to whites attending historically white universities, and the tremendous variation in black and white academic success across classes, schools, and universities, both public and private. Many conservative critics tacitly assume that employers, universities, and other "buyers" of high school graduates agree that "better" and "worse" high school graduates can be measured by test scores and grades. This is true, they assert, because employers and universities clearly seek to maximize economic productivity, and this objective can be achieved only when high school graduates with higher test scores and grades are accepted into colleges and jobs. Implicitly, then, any effort to increase the educational attainment or earnings of blacks relative to whites is doomed unless blacks begin to do significantly better (as measured by tests) in primary and secondary schools.

But is admitting students to college strictly on the basis of a college entrance exam such as the SAT or American College Test (ACT) and high school grades likely to result in the highest graduation rates, or the best group of graduates? Will a higher education system that heavily weights the SAT or ACT tests in admissions produce citizens with a vision of a just society? Is it not possible that college itself can play an important role in transforming entering students into better economic performers and more effective citizens? The conservative answers to these questions would postpone black (and Latino) access to higher education for many years. They would shift responsibility for the educational success of African Americans from colleges to academic preparation in primary and secondary schools. No doubt, better preparation at the primary and secondary levels would increase blacks' success in institutions of higher education. But this proposal ignores a troubling reality: historically and presently, only about one-half of all students (white, black, Asian American, and Latino) who attend four-year colleges graduate. To place the primary responsibility for college success on primary and secondary schools, therefore, absolves higher education of similar institutional responsibility. If colleges are not simply to legitimize "natural selection" but rather to add value to student learning, then one would expect some colleges to do better than others in helping students succeed. Thus, it is worth asking why blacks (and whites) are so much more likely to graduate in some institutions of higher education than in others. If we regularly scrutinize the performance of primary and secondary schools, we can certainly demand the same accountability from universities.

We therefore offer an alternative and more creative approach to the question of why an education gap persists between blacks and whites. By focusing on different graduation rates between universities, we can see an alternative to the policy judgment proposed by conservatives. Even as efforts are made to improve the schools of low-income children by raising standards and improving teaching, universities can be encouraged to admit more African Americans (as well as other low-income students) and to be more accountable for their progress.

THE CONSERVATIVE CRITIQUE OF PUBLIC SCHOOLS

The conservatives' judgment of American public education is mixed. They note that black students made extraordinary gains in reading and math proficiency in the 1970s and 1980s. Yet they also point out that public education is not delivering the high-quality education it should, especially given the vast sums of taxpayers' dollars invested over the past two decades. Blacks' test scores relative to whites', moreover, retreated in the 1990s, leaving blacks considerably behind whites by the middle of the decade.[3]

According to the conservatives, public schools have failed to educate African Americans because teachers, school administrators, and politicians are wedded to a liberal ideology that is too "subjective." This ideology permits public educators and their political allies to apologize for poor performance and cater to the very stereotypes and uniqueness that African Americans (should) want to escape. Liberal educational ideology, they insist, lacks fixed (and high) standards and is devoid of the moral backbone needed to enforce those standards.

> When we say that American education in general is in trouble, we have in mind the degree to which American students lag behind their peers in other countries—which we see as the result of a misguided educational culture. That culture stresses acquiring the tools to learn rather than covering specific subject material, allowing children to explore what interests them rather than using teachers to convey knowledge. It celebrates the uniqueness of individual children and the ethnic or racial group to which they belong, such that common academic standards, standardized tests, and grades are disdained as part of a culturally biased and judgmental package.[4]

Whatever the kernel of truth in this argument, it misrepresents a more complex reality. The problem is partly empirical. The Thernstroms are unable to cite any concrete evidence that a "misguided educational culture" is to blame for poor student performance in the United States as compared to other countries. They are unable to find a source because, according to international tests, American students actually do well in the primary grades compared to students in other countries, but they fall down in math (not in science and reading) in later grades. This has less to do with a misguided culture than with teacher training in math, a superficial math curriculum, and possibly a tracking policy that precludes many American students (not just blacks) from learning any algebra and geometry in middle school.[5] Even in math, though, students in states like Iowa do as well as those in the very highest scoring countries such as Korea. Iowa does not emphasize common academic standards and standardized tests. Further, the creativity American schools emphasize (children exploring what interests them) is now the envy of the Asian school systems that focus heavily on a standardized "package of knowledge" that, conservatives think, allows students to excel on tests.

Nor do conservatives provide very convincing evidence for why African Americans' reading test scores began to fall after 1988. In the Thernstroms' estimation, for example, the main reasons were "social disorder coupled with self-esteem strategies and Afrocentric fantasies that entail low academic standards and insufficient attention to core subjects. Condescending policies masquerading as racially sensitive ones . . . have made a bad situation worse. Blacks and whites, working together, have conspired to rob black children of a fundamental civil right—access to quality education."[6]

Once again, there is some truth to these conclusions. It is the simplistic causality that is misleading. Social disorder has increased in schools since the 1980s, but mainly in high schools. The leveling off and decline in reading test scores in the early 1990s, however, occurred among nine- and thirteen-year-olds as well as seventeen-year-olds. Math scores for nine-year-olds, on the other hand, have continued to rise for both blacks and whites. Teachers do have lower expectations of black students (most teachers of black children are, indeed, white), and this undoubtedly contributes to lower learning gains for blacks. But black children begin school with much lower test scores than whites. It would take a major investment well before school starts to reduce this initial difference. Thus, even if black children were given access to exactly the same quality education as whites, significant test score differences would probably exist at the end of the schooling process.

A recent book edited by Christopher Jencks and Meredith Phillips explores some possible reasons for the difference between black and white test scores.[7] No one really knows why blacks' test performance went up as much it did in the late 1970s and in the 1980s, though declining poverty rates and substantially improved schooling for blacks in the South in the 1970s certainly contributed to the improved test scores. Nor does anyone know why blacks' test scores then stagnated or declined (depending on the age group and the test) in the *early* 1990s. In *America in Black and White*, the Thernstroms focus on lower reading scores for blacks relative to whites in the 1990s. Even though the math score gap also widened slightly in the 1990s, they ignore the fact that blacks continue to make math score gains. And they have nothing to say about the recovery of reading scores for young blacks in the middle and late 1990s.[8] Certainly, the reasons cited by the Thernstroms to explain the failure of schools to raise reading scores after 1988 should apply to math as well. It is fair to say that blacks did not make gains as rapid as whites on national tests, and that should be of great concern. Yet it is also clear that in cities where the gap has substantially diminished, school systems have invested heavily in preschool and after-school programs and smaller classes, improvements already available to many white suburban children.[9] The investment in these programs, especially in good preschool education, may also be related to improved nutrition and preventive health care, important ingredients for improved performance in school.

Conservatives see the success of Catholic schools in raising the achievement scores of low-income black students as a way of closing the test score gap. But no convincing evidence exists to justify their faith in Catholic school education. The two best-known studies of Catholic school–public school test score differences analyzed these differences for high school students who graduated in the early 1980s.[10] The same kind of longitudinal data that measure the relative differences in scores between black and white children who attend Catholic and public primary schools does not exist. Cross-section studies, however, do indicate that children attending Catholic primary schools do no better than children of similar backgrounds in public schools.[11] Therefore, one cannot make any empirical claims about the superiority of Catholic primary schools. Despite this lack of evidence, conservatives maintain that much of the test score gap would disappear if we just sent black children to Catholic-like schools at any level.

If one compares students from the same socioeconomic background, the differences in achievement gains between students in Catholic and public secondary schools are positive, although very small.[12] For students with similar achievement scores, attending a Catholic high school rather than a public high school apparently makes a much bigger difference in graduation rates and the likelihood of attending college.[13] Conservatives attribute these discrepancies to the more rigorous academic requirements in Catholic high schools. But the differences could just as well be related to the priority Catholic high schools place on getting their students into college and their ability to remove students who refuse to meet their academic requirements. A number of Catholic high schools, moreover, are explicitly selective. They try to recruit only the most committed minority students to complement their largely white middle-class and working-class clientele.

A better explanation of differences in student achievement is the quality of teaching the students receive. Researchers are finding that much of the difference in achievement among children from similar socioeconomic backgrounds occurs between different teachers' classrooms. Steven Rivkin, Eric Hanushek, and John Kain, for example, used longitudinal data on Texas pupils to show that "unobserved teacher characteristics" explain relatively large differences in student performance.[14] Also using data from Texas, Ronald F. Ferguson demonstrated that student achievement is positively related to teacher scores on recertification tests.[15] But higher test scores are not the only reason some teachers are better than others. Good teachers are essential to the learning experience, and unless the quality of teaching improves, it is difficult to imagine that children from low-income backgrounds, whether black or white or brown, will receive a good education. It is not at all certain, however, that simply testing teachers will provide the high-quality teachers that are necessary for extensively improving primary and secondary education for black and Latino students. We now have strong evidence from a longitudinal study of teachers in New York State that teachers who have higher test scores, who have attended higher-quality colleges and universities, and who have more experience teaching, mainly teach upper middle-class students, very few of whom are black and Latino.[16] This is quite likely the pattern in most states.

This may seem obvious. Conservatives might even agree. But they are so preoccupied with blaming civil rights groups, white liberals, and public education that they refuse to confront one of the toughest issues facing educators: how will better teachers (the ones who not only have higher expectations for black children but are also able to teach them effectively) be recruited into schools with high proportions of low-income black and Latino students?

Parochial schools may not be a viable model. Catholic schools pay teachers less than public schools; they also have somewhat larger class sizes. But they can also create a more teacher-friendly environment by forcing troublesome children to leave a school. So long as a relatively small proportion of American children attend Catholic schools, teachers who are willing to work for lower pay will be found because some of them are committed to Catholic education or like working in a school environment that controls the nature of the student body. Nevertheless, Catholic school principals acknowledge that it is not easy to find good teachers because of the low pay.[17] And contradicting previously flawed research, a recent study by Susanna Loeb and Marianne Page indicates that student achievement is positively related to teacher pay.[18]

Conservatives disagree, often countering that student achievement depends on qualified teachers who are tested and not permitted to teach unless they pass. In the abstract, this seems logical. Even though SAT-level verbal ability and mathematical skills tests might be inappropriate for many other jobs, they seem relevant for teachers who should be able to pass these tests if they are to teach language arts and math, even to early primary school children. This logic may be correct for new teachers. It is not true of educators with long years of classroom experience. Indeed, basic skills tests may not fairly assess experienced teachers' educational skills or their effectiveness in promoting student learning, particularly in the lower grades. And in the higher grades, it makes sense to test teachers only in the subject matter they teach.

On the other hand, requiring new teachers to pass a test may raise scores, since they will most likely prepare for it if they want to become teachers. Ronald Ferguson's analysis of Alabama's teacher certification test shows that black teachers' basic skills rose relative to those of white teachers when the test was implemented. However, while testing teachers raises basic skills, it also has economic implications that conservative critics of teacher quality are unwilling to face. Connecticut's experience reveals that increasing starting salaries substantially helps to raise the quality (as measured by average SAT scores) of the new teachers being recruited. This is particularly true in a labor market where professional women's real wages have risen substantially in the past twenty years.

Greater emphasis on standards and testing, conservatives might reply, would probably draw attention to the poor quality of education low-income students receive, and this negative publicity might improve educational delivery. But this strategy depends on strong intervention by centralized public bureaucracies. And this, of course, directly contradicts another conservative strategy for educational reform: the call for public education authorities to decentralize their operations and leave education to private and local providers.

The Texas and North Carolina cases are enlightening in this context. These two states raised test scores substantially among black and Latino students, the lowest-scoring groups in the past five years. This success is partly attributable to teaching the test, which is a plus if the main goal is to improve basic skills. But the major lesson to be learned from the Texas and North Carolina experiences is that the entire school system had to be organized around increasing test scores. An active, state-level public bureaucracy operating over a long period of time was required to manage this systemic reform.[19]

Whether this strategy will improve higher-order problem-solving skills may be another story. The results in Texas suggest that increasing scores on basic skills tests might not be transferable to learning harder subjects such as algebra, or to substantially reducing high school dropout rates. The Texas and North Carolina results also indicate that the conservatives' belief that "disciplined, tough education" can achieve large and efficient gains in schooling is much too simplistic to be useful for serious educational change.

The most obvious problem with the conservative critique of public education is that it completely ignores the most stubborn stumbling block to any serious reform. Given the historically and consistently inadequate and segregated education experienced by African Americans, why should anyone expect (white) American society to suddenly reverse its priorities and provide quality educational opportunity, particularly because any reasonably effective reform will be exceedingly expensive?

Conservatives hold American public education responsible for blacks' poor performance and point to private institutions as an alternative. But why should one believe that private education would better serve African Americans? African Americans have not previously been treated more fairly by the business sector than the public sector. The private sector has no history of demanding fairer and better treatment for African Americans, or better housing or more resources for education or health care. Something far more radical than private schooling or testing teachers is therefore necessary if the quality of education is to be improved for most African American children.

Even in states like Texas and North Carolina, where black children are doing much better at acquiring basic skills than five years ago, the next round of educational improvement for minorities will be exceedingly difficult. Although state legislatures are ready to force public schools to teach basic skills more efficiently, they hardly seem ready to seriously increase the quality of teaching for minority children if that raises educational costs. What price are conservatives willing to pay to make schools for black and Latino children as good as suburban white schools?

The conservative conception of education problems is fabricated. It has very little relation to the social and political reality faced by the majority of black, Latino, and poor white students. While conservatives and racial realists correctly point out that the educational system has disregarded minority student needs, this failure is not because of a liberal racism that excuses black failure or teacher laziness. Rather, it is deeply rooted in American politics, the same politics that allowed the Texas educational system to remain de facto segregated until the 1980s, and permitted Kentucky schools in Appalachia to underserve children until the 1990s. Promoting "tough-minded" privately run education in north Houston or eastern Kentucky may or may not be a good idea. But it will not bring about significant change in either educational practices or student performance without major changes in American political commitment to black and Latino economic opportunity.

TEST SCORES, PREFERENTIAL ADMISSIONS, AND EARNINGS

Conservative opposition to color-conscious affirmative action in higher education is widespread. Implying that this policy is widely practiced throughout the postsecondary system and rewards people who need it least, the Thernstroms' critique is typical. Black beneficiaries, they suggest, come from affluent middle-class families; they are the "pampered children of black millionaires taking college seats that ought to go the hard-working offspring of white plumbers."[20]

This assessment is misleading. The argument over race and college admissions is actually about who will attend a relatively few elite colleges and universities. The notion that affirmative action is a widespread practice in American colleges is subverted when one recognizes that most colleges (the bottom 60 percent as ranked by SAT scores) do not use race or ethnicity as a criterion of admission.[21] These are the schools that admit the vast majority of African Americans and Latinos. Only a small percentage of "disadvantaged minorities" attend upper-tier colleges and universities.

Affirmative action for blacks and Latinos in higher education is limited to the top 40 percent of colleges ranked by average SAT score. And even then, being black or Latino is an advantage at these colleges only after grades, test scores, and gender have been taken into account. The estimated advantage of affirmative action for African Americans in colleges ranked in the fourth quintile (the second-highest 20 percent) is small. For the 1982 black high school senior cohort there was about a 3-percentage-point advantage; the effect for Latinos was negligible.[22] The advantage of being black also declined sharply between 1972 and 1992 in first-tier colleges. In the 1970s, blacks with a given set of test scores and grades had a 13 percent greater likelihood of being admitted to these schools; that bonus dropped to a 5 percent greater likelihood in the 1990s.[23]

Eliminating affirmative action from college admissions largely affects students applying to upper-tier schools. Based on the admissions procedures of five selective institutions, Bowen and Bok estimated that the current number of black students would fall from 7.1 percent to 2.1 percent if color-conscious admissions policies were ended. Their estimate was close to the mark. When the regents of the University of California eliminated race from consideration in admissions decisions, the proportion of black freshmen at Berkeley fell from 6.8 percent to 2.4 percent between 1996 and 1997.[24]

Conservatives claim that by using race as a factor in admissions, affirmative action dilutes and perverts the university's academic objectives. It punishes white and Asian American students because they are denied access to top-tier universities. And, just as important, the policy hurts black students, the intended recipients of these efforts. "When colleges attempt to display their social commitment by admitting 'high risk' students from minority groups," the Thernstroms write, "it is the students who suffer when the risks don't pan out."[25] They say that the lower admissions standards highlight students' racial differences.

> As of 1994, black undergraduates were entering Stanford with a combined SAT score of 1,164—a very good score by national standards, putting them in the top sixth of all test-takers in the country. But their white classmates had been admitted with a 1,335 average, placing them in the top 3 percent of all students nationally. As Shelby Steele has argued, black students pay a heavy price for their letters of acceptance on the basis of lower academic standards. To begin with, the affirmative action programs call attention to racial differences—they heighten racial consciousness. And then, too, they reinforce the myth of black inferiority.[26]

The conservative argument against color-conscious admissions is that blacks have lower graduation rates than whites. Because African Americans at elite colleges take longer to graduate than whites, critics of affirmative action claim that blacks would be better served if they attended less selective schools rather than competing in an environment for which they are "underqualified." The Berkeley case is a favorite of affirmative action critics. In the 1980s, according to the Thernstroms, 84 percent of whites and 88 percent of Asians graduated within six years of matriculation. On the other hand, only 59 percent of blacks graduated within six years, and this, the Thernstroms claim, is logically due to "the inadequate academic skills with which African American students arrived as a result of preferential admissions."[27] The results at other elite colleges and universities are much less extreme, but they all show that blacks and Latinos have lower graduation rates than whites and Asians.

The Thernstroms infer from this evidence that graduation rates would rise for black and Latino students if they attended colleges and universities with less competitive academic environments. Since blacks and Latinos admitted under affirmative action criteria with low test scores do not "fit," they are worse off than they would have been had they enrolled at more appropriate academic settings. Society suffers as well, the Thernstroms conclude, because blacks or Latinos admitted under affirmative action take the place of white or Asian students with higher test scores who would therefore benefit more from an elite education.

The implication is obvious: African Americans attending institutions with lower average SAT scores will graduate at a faster rate than blacks admitted to elite colleges and universities, where the average test scores of whites range from almost 300 points higher (Berkeley) to 100 points higher (Harvard). But Bowen and Bok's data indicate the opposite is true. For whites who matriculated in 1989 at twenty-eight elite colleges (Berkeley was not in the sample), the average graduation rate in the six years after matriculation was 86 percent. For Latinos it was 81 percent, and for blacks it was 75 percent. The comparison with graduation rates for whites in three hundred NCAA Division I colleges and universities is instructive in this regard. Six years after matriculation, 59 percent of the whites had graduated and 40 percent of the blacks. One can infer from these data that the higher their test scores the more likely whites, blacks, and Latinos are to graduate from college. But one cannot conclude that sending blacks to lower-scoring colleges raises graduation rates. Something other than test scores is at work here. Bowen and Bok argue that "inability to do the work is often much less important than loss of motivation, dissatisfaction with campus life, changing career interests, family problems, financial difficulties, and poor health."[28]

Actually, attending selective colleges has a positive, rather than a negative, effect on graduation. Using longitudinal data from the High School and Beyond Survey of 1982 high school seniors, Thomas Kane showed that for a given test score, once race is held constant, a student is 3 percent more likely to graduate from a selective college. This flatly contradicts previous research (with the class of 1972) showing that admission to an elite college had a positive effect on white graduation rates and a negative effect on black graduation rates.[29] Kane discounts these earlier findings because the high proportion of blacks in the class of 1972 that attended less selective (lower SAT scores) historically black colleges biased the results. In the 1980s, blacks attending historically black institutions had graduation rates 17 percent higher than those of minority students with similar records in historically white schools. When graduation rates take into account attendance at historically black colleges, Kane found that attending a selective historically white institution has about the same effect on blacks and Latino students as on whites and Asians. In fact, these students were 4.5 percent more likely to graduate than those with similar test scores who attended less selective schools. This evidence means that selective colleges create an environment that is more supportive of all their students, including blacks and Latinos. Indeed, Kane's analysis demonstrates that the lower individual students' SAT scores, the greater the effect of attending a more selective school on graduation rates. In Kane's words, "Since studying at a selective college surely puts students at some competitive disadvantage relative to their classmates, this finding suggests that such colleges have offsetting advantages."[30]

Critics of affirmative action often highlight UC Berkeley's unusual dropout figures, perhaps because these data sustain their argument against color-conscious admissions policies. But, as the Thernstroms explicitly admit, Berkeley in the 1980s was not typical of selective colleges.[31] "In none of the elite schools," they write, "is dropping out a huge problem."[32] Nevertheless, despite this disclaimer, they insist that even if dropout rates are relatively low for all students at selective schools, somehow blacks are getting a bad deal because they are in over their heads. As they put it, "None of them can boast no racial gap in graduation rates.... *It is difficult to doubt that there is a connection between the academic double standards in the admission procedures of these schools and the differences in academic outcomes.*"[33] (Emphasis added.)

Once again the empirical world is much more complicated than conservatives render it. Graduation rates at selective colleges are, indeed, related to SAT scores, especially to the math SAT. Students with math scores of less than 550 graduate at about an 82 percent rate in six years of matriculation, while those with scores of 650 or more graduate at about a 93 percent rate.[34] But graduation rates for African Americans are lower than white rates at every level of math test score, and for black men there seems to be little positive relation between math SAT score and graduation rate. This is confirmed by a recent study of students entering UC Berkeley in 1988. It showed there is no correlation between eventual graduation rates of African American students and their SAT scores.[35] Also, men of both races have significantly lower graduation rates than their female counterparts at every level of SAT score.[36] It is doubtful, however, that conservatives would conclude that selective colleges should therefore admit fewer men of all races and more women because their graduation rates are higher for a given test score.

Clearly other factors play a more important role than test scores in determining graduation rates. Dalton Conley has shown that the two most important predictors of college graduation are whether a student's parents are college graduates and the net worth of the student's household.[37] Economic support is far more important in explaining college graduation rates than race. White students in virtually every American university receive far more economic support from their families than do black students attending the same institution. In the case of UC Berkeley, for example, 1996 data show that the median family income of Anglo students was about $80,000, for Asian American students it was $70,000, and for African American and Latino students it was less than $35,000.[38] Since blacks earn less than whites at every educational level, we can assume that financial support for black students throughout the higher education system is lower than for white students. Moreover, as we documented earlier, black households have substantially less wealth than white households. Home equity turns out to be the most important asset used to finance college; it is also a strong predictor of college graduation. The much lower home ownership rates for blacks, and the lower value of the homes they do own, substantially raises the barriers black families face in financing four years of college education. Compounding the problem, financial aid, particularly grants (such as Pell Grants), has been reduced substantially over the past two decades and does not make up the shortfall.[39]

In addition, historically white universities do not provide a friendly social environment for black students. Conservatives usually interpret racial tensions on campuses through ideological lenses, arguing that affirmative action causes this hostility. By placing blacks in academic contexts where they cannot compete, conservatives and racial realists contend, college admissions officers have encouraged white students to feel that blacks "don't belong here." But it would be just as convincing to argue that even competitively bright black students are not comfortable in an environment that historically has been the exclusive domain of white elites. The elite university system has only recently become accessible to people of color. The university is an institution shaped by and for a small fraction of American society. The vast majority of Americans, including the white working class, blacks, Latinos, and Asians, have traditionally been treated as outsiders at universities.

The amount of financial support and the relative hostility of particular university environments are much more important in predicting black graduation rates than the differences in black test scores relative to those of white students. The other side of this coin is rarely mentioned, namely that some colleges are more successful in graduating students, and some, such as UC Berkeley, are less. Because conservatives are so insistent on showing black failures in competitive colleges, they never ask why colleges vary in the success rates of their students. A less ideological and more creative approach to the issue of black social mobility is to ask, why are some colleges and universities so much more successful in graduating both blacks and whites than others?

THE ECONOMIC COST OF COLOR-CONSCIOUS ADMISSIONS POLICIES

The conservative argument against affirmative action in universities implicitly assumes that cognitive skills (as measured by high school test scores) are intimately connected to labor productivity. The argument is based on two propositions: First, low black test scores directly result in decreased earnings. By bumping higher-scoring whites and Asians from elite colleges, affirmative action favors less productive students over the more productive ones. This in turn creates an economic loss for the country. Second, affirmative action hurts blacks because it decreases their likelihood of graduation and therefore lowers their future earnings. Both society and African American students would thus be better off if preferential admissions were abolished.

This argument assumes that test scores are good predictors of earnings, and that these differences in earnings are important economically. In particular, conservative analysts claim that the large discrepancies in income between black and white males with the same levels of education are not produced by discrimination. Rather, they are largely attributable to racial differences in skill level. The Thernstroms summarize this conservative complaint: "Basic shifts in our economy have been placing an increased premium on cognitive skills, and scores on the best national tests given demonstrate that groups that perform better earn more. That is why racial differences in scores on tests of cognitive skills go a long way toward explaining racial differences in earnings."[40]

It is true that blacks who attend or graduate from college do not earn the same incomes as whites. It is also true that their test scores and GPAs are not equal to whites'. When socio-economic status (SES) and test score differences are accounted for, however, the earnings difference between blacks/Hispanics and whites graduating from four-year colleges disappears. Other studies confirm this relationship between test scores and income.[41] Moreover, a number of studies indicate that even when one controls for socioeconomic background, race, ethnicity, and (in the case of earnings) attained level of education, test scores are related to a greater likelihood of completing college and earning higher incomes.[42]

Because blacks score lower on standardized tests and lower scores result in lower net productivity, the Thernstroms conclude that allowing blacks to attend college under affirmative action decreases economic output. This conclusion, however, rests on several bold but dubious assumptions. The most important one is that lower earnings for blacks compared to whites actually mean that African Americans who graduate from college generate a social cost by lowering economic output. Put another way, this argument assumes that blacks admitted into select colleges under affirmative action replace white or Asian applicants who are potentially more productive and will most likely make more money than the recipients of special treatment.

The economic cost-benefit analysis of affirmative action, however, is not quite so simple as the Thernstroms assume it to be. What one really needs to know is this: compared to whites, how much do blacks attending a select college (a college in the top 20 percent of SAT scores) gain versus what they gain at a lower-tier college? Bowen and Bok's data indicate that, in absolute terms, the economic gain for black male students who complete the highest tier of select colleges versus the next lowest tier is larger than the loss incurred by white students who complete tier two compared to tier one. When one compares tier two to tier three, the numbers are reversed: there the gain for black students is less than the cost to whites.

One must not forget, however, that these numbers are based on a sample of students who attended select colleges. The sample does not include students in nonselective colleges and therefore does not include students who move up and down between selective and nonselective colleges because of affirmative action policies. To properly estimate the economic gain or loss from affirmative action, one would have to know, or be able to simulate, who is getting bumped up and down. Then it would be necessary to estimate the gain for those who are bumped up and the loss for those who are bumped down.

A second major assumption is that the impact of test scores on economic output is increasing because cognitive skills are becoming more important in explaining individual earnings. However, the empirical evidence that supports increasing effects of cognitive skills on earnings is controversial and has been strongly challenged.[43] A third assumption is that there is a strong relationship between test scores and earnings. But the estimated increase in earnings for a college graduate with elevated high school math test scores is hardly earthshaking. It is less than 8 percent for a one-standard-deviation increase in a student's test score. According to Kane, blacks' earnings increase by only 9 percent if they graduate from college and have math test scores equal to whites. Higher reading scores have little if any effect on earnings.

Nor is there much reason to believe that test scores are important predictors of labor market success. Recent empirical evidence using a large national sample of high school seniors taken in 1982 shows that when socioeconomic class, test scores, and months of labor market experience are held constant, black males earn much less than whites only among those that did not attend college.[44] So race still plays a role in the workplace. But to see the dramatic power of race in the workplace one needs to look at the relationship between test scores and labor market success for racial minorities who are not African American. If conservatives looked at Asian Americans, for example, they would find that, compared to whites, Asian Americans score somewhat higher on the SAT math test and somewhat lower on the verbal test. If test scores predict college success and labor productivity, one would expect Asian Americans to reach higher levels of schooling than whites because their test scores are higher, and the conservatives would be correct. But because of higher test scores, they would also expect Asian Americans to earn more than whites at a given level of schooling. In this instance, however, conservatives would be wrong. While Asian Americans are far more likely to attend college and are somewhat more likely to complete it, Asian American college graduates earn slightly *less* than whites.[45]

The Asian American example undercuts any argument that blacks earn less than whites because of test score differences. Empirical studies show that verbal scores have no significant effect on later earnings. If the black-white income discrepancy is attributed to differences in mathematics test scores, then how can one account for the Asian American situation? In this instance, math results correctly predict higher college attendance and college graduation by Asian Americans. But they do not predict the lower wages Asian Americans earn when compared to whites with the same level of schooling.[46]

Consider another example. Assume critics of color-conscious policies were to analyze white women's earnings relative to white men's, controlling for education and test scores. Since women test about the same as men (slightly higher on verbal tests and slightly lower on math), test score differences would presumably predict equal wages for college-educated white men and women. But this is not the case. Moreover, since women with comparable test scores to men are much more likely to complete college, one would expect colleges to admit more women than men. The fact is, however, that they do not.

Obviously then, one's level of education and test scores are not the only factors that explain college graduation and earnings. Conservatives would look foolish if they argued that colleges should admit more women than men because men have lower college graduation rates than women with comparable test scores. They would be dismissed out of hand if they claimed that women and Asian Americans are paid less than white men because of test score differences. Yet these are the explanations they put forth to explain income discrepancies between black and white Americans.

With flimsy evidence, many Americans believe that affirmative action undermines sensible college admissions and hiring policies based on standardized test score differences. This belief is widely accepted because test score differences between blacks and whites are closely related to college graduation differences and, at least for males, to earnings differences. Put differently, using test scores to measure skills makes sense because African Americans get lower test scores than whites and are less likely to attend and graduate from college; they are also likely to earn much less than whites even when they complete the same level of education. But this is not strong evidence that differences in test scores explain the relative position of black and white men in the labor force. That is because statistical estimates indicate that the gains in earnings associated with higher math test scores are very small, and there is no relationship between test scores and earnings when Asian Americans and women are compared to white males.

Table 1, for example, shows that young blacks score about one standard deviation lower than whites on the SAT math and verbal tests, and about one-half standard deviation lower than Latino males on the math SAT. Although blacks' earnings are much lower than whites' earnings, blacks' and Latinos' earnings are quite similar. On the other hand, even though white women's math NAEP scores are almost the same as white men's, and their SAT math scores are one-third of a standard deviation lower than white men's, they earn much less than men.

To understand why many Americans feel affirmative action disrupts judicious admissions and hiring policies, one must also ask why they believe affirmative action is unfair even though only a very small percentage of white and Asian American students are bumped because of racial considerations. A typical experience with parking lots illustrates how this belief gains credibility. The individual driver searching for a space in a parking lot often feels bumped when she encounters an unused space reserved for the handicapped. She believes that she would have been able to park had the space not been reserved. In fact, more likely than not, another driver would have taken it long ago. Whites' experience with color-conscious admissions policies is similar. Only a small percentage of students with low test scores enter elite universities under affirmative action policies. Very few white and Asian students are actually bumped, and many of them get into alternative elite institutions of equal stature. Even when one makes the dubious assumption that recipients of affirmative action push down the white and Asian students who are replaced and reduce their levels of productivity, the cost to the U.S.

TABLE 1. RATIOS OF MEDIAN INCOMES
AND TEST SCORE DIFFERENCES AMONG RACIAL,
ETHNIC, AND GENDER GROUPS

	Income Ratio,[a] 1997		Test Score Difference,[b] 1996		
	High School Grads	College Grads	NAEP[c] Math	SAT Math[d]	SAT Verbal[d]
Black/White Males	0.87	0.78	280/311 (−1.10)[e]	−1.07	−0.96
Latino/White Males	0.84	0.83	287/311 (−0.83)[f]	−0.58	−0.65
White Females/Males	0.76	0.78	303/305 (−.07)[g]	−0.33	−0.04
Black/White Females	0.83	0.90	—	−0.93	−0.86
Black/Latino Males	1.04	0.93	—	−0.48	−0.30
Black/Latino Females	0.96	0.91	—	−0.35	−0.12

SOURCES: Incomes: U.S. Bureau of the Census, Current Population Survey; NAEP scores: National Center for Educational Statistics (NCES), National Assessment of Educational Progress (NAEP): Mathematics Report Card (Washington, D.C.: NCES, 1997); SAT scores: Educational Testing Service, 1996 Profile of College Bound Seniors (Princeton, N.J.: Educational Testing Service, 1996), table 4.1.
a. For 25- to 34-year-old high school and college graduates.
b. For high school seniors.
c. National Assessment of Educational Progress. Scores/standard deviations.
d. Standard deviations.
e. Represents scores of black males and females compared to white males and females.
f. Scores of Latino males and females compared to white males and females.
g. All females compared to all males.

economy is minuscule. This is because affirmative action students are a very small proportion of all college graduates, and the relationship between their test scores and their earnings is minimal.

Conservatives also object to color-conscious admissions policies because they claim that blacks themselves pay an economic cost by attending these selective institutions. This cost is high because blacks never graduate, and not graduating means they earn a much lower income than they would were they to graduate from an institution more appropriate to their skills.[47] As with many of the conservatives' assertions, this one is much more complicated than their formulation suggests. For example, although the Thernstroms acknowledge that affirmative action sometimes results in higher earnings for blacks graduating from selective institutions, they also believe that blacks admitted to selective institutions have high dropout rates. Because dropouts earn 25 percent less than graduates, the Thernstroms conclude that affirmative action for blacks probably leads to negative net economic results. More recent estimates, however, show that blacks, like whites, earn more by attending selective colleges. When SAT scores, high school grades, and socioeconomic background are accounted for, according to Kane, blacks who attend selective colleges earn about 5 percent more in their early years after college than blacks who attend nonselective colleges.[48] Thus, contrary to the Thernstroms' claim that affirmative action in selective colleges is a double-edged sword, when the earnings benefits of attending these colleges are calculated, blacks gain as much as whites.

THE OLE MISS MODEL AND INSTITUTIONAL VARIATION

What do conservatives propose as alternatives to the affirmative action practiced by selective, elite universities? The Thernstroms have come up with what they call a more "down to earth" model based on policies at the University of Mississippi. The Ole Miss model epitomizes conservatives' thinking on how to increase black access to higher education.

Why Ole Miss? The sole criterion is apparently that southern universities like Ole Miss, the University of Alabama, the University of South Carolina, and the University of Georgia graduate blacks at rates that are closer to white graduation rates than at elite colleges. The University of Mississippi graduates 48 percent of blacks compared to 49 percent of whites. Graduation rates at the University of Alabama are 49 percent for blacks and 55 percent for whites, and at South Carolina 56 percent for blacks and 62 percent for whites. And at Georgia, 48 percent of blacks graduate compared to 60 percent of whites.[49] The relatively low graduation rate for both whites and blacks in these universities does not seem to faze the Thernstroms. Instead, the most important consideration for them is that blacks and whites who attend these schools have about an equal chance to graduate.

The secret to the southern "success" story, according to the Thernstroms, is that blacks and whites must achieve a minimum SAT score that is "set high enough to bar students likely to experience severe academic difficulties."[50] But this obviously does little to produce high graduation rates. And it also means that black students are severely underrepresented. At the University of Mississippi, an institution located in a state that is 36 percent African American, blacks make up only 9.4 percent of the student body. Compare this to UC Berkeley before the regents' 1996 decision to abolish preferential admissions: in a state with about a 5 percent African American population, black students constituted more than 6 percent of the student body.

The Thernstroms cite these southern universities to demonstrate that black graduation rates rise when college admission is restricted to blacks with a minimum SAT score. But they ignore a crucial question: what rate of graduation is acceptable? Is the 50 percent graduation rate at these southern schools a desirable level? Should an equal graduation rate be the principal objective of college admissions policies?

If colleges wanted to equalize graduation rates and if, as conservatives erroneously claim, test scores are the principal determinant of graduation rates, colleges would be required to set putatively color-blind minimum test scores for entrance. But this would automatically restrict the admission of African Americans to colleges until, in some vaguely defined long run, their SAT test scores became equal to whites. Because blacks currently score lower on the SAT than whites, as Kane's research demonstrates, when minimum test scores are set as the only criterion for admission to college, the proportion of blacks relative to whites is lowered.

There are three additional problems with the Ole Miss model. First, if one really wanted to equalize graduation rates by making minimum test scores an entrance requirement, colleges would need to lower the minimum test scores for women applicants. Because women's graduation rates are higher than men's for a given test score, at least at elite colleges, this would equalize graduation rates. While these differences between male-female graduation rates may not hold at Ole Miss, other colleges would have to calculate graduation rates as a function of test scores and then set one minimum test score for women and another for men in order to achieve graduation rates that are approximately equal.

This suggests a second problem. The graduation rates at Deep South, historically white universities with restrictive entrance policies are relatively low for whites and blacks. In the early 1990s, their graduation rates were lower than the rates for blacks at UC Berkeley, and much lower than the rates for blacks at the University of Virginia, a southern school conspicuously absent from the Thernstroms' list of southern universities. The proportion of black students at the University of Virginia is 9 percent, the same as at Mississippi. But Virginia's population is only 20 percent black, compared to 36 percent in Mississippi. Thus, it might be argued that the University of Virginia is potentially less selective in admitting blacks than the University of Mississippi, assuming that most applicants at both universities are in-state candidates. At Virginia, blacks' test scores are lower than whites'. Their graduation rate, however, is high, over 80 percent. From that standpoint, Virginia looks like the elite colleges in Bowen and Bok's sample. At UC Berkeley, clearly another elite university, the graduation rate for blacks in the early 1990s was lower than the white rate, and their test scores were lower than whites', about the same as at the University of Virginia.[51] The University of Virginia is therefore apparently much more successful at graduating both its black and white students than either Ole Miss or UC Berkeley.

This raises a fundamental issue. Are blacks better off at a university that restricts admissions where 50 percent graduate (close to the white graduation rate)? Or at a university with an affirmative action policy where 60, 70, or 80 percent graduate, even though this is 10 to 25 percent lower than the white graduation rate? Why would a university strive for low graduation rates and restrictive admissions unless the main objective was to be restrictive and racially exclusive? In this sense, the University of Virginia is a much more interesting model than Ole Miss. That is not because it is restrictive but because it admits a significant proportion of black students, many under affirmative action, and graduates them at almost the same rate as whites.

Now that the University of California has eliminated racial considerations in admissions and the proportion of black and Latino admissions has dropped significantly, one wonders if the black and Latino graduation rate is likely to approach the white graduation rate. Admittedly the difference in graduation rates will probably fall, but it is not likely to equalize. Why? Because unlike the other select colleges, Berkeley's new policy did not alter the original conditions responsible for low black and Latino graduation rates. With similar average test scores for entering blacks and similar test score differences between whites and blacks, the University of Virginia achieved very different results than UC Berkeley for white students and especially for blacks.

The Ole Miss model presents a third problem for conservatives because it exposes a contradiction in their analysis of kindergarten through twelfth grade (K–12) education. In that discussion, they attribute the poor educational performance of blacks in K–12 to the institution of public schooling. They claim that African Americans are denied the chance to perform at an appropriate educational level, one they are apparently capable of achieving, because the public schools as an institution do not educate black youngsters efficiently. Catholic schools do a much better job because they are private institutions unfettered by public regulation, teachers unions, and all the other institutional baggage public schools carry. The fact that institutional structure—in this case, accountability to the market rather than a morally confused bureau-cracy—can influence outcomes is allegedly the difference between the conservatism of the Thernstroms and the genetic determinism of Herrnstein and Murray. When they turn to higher education, however, the Thernstroms abandon this institutional argument in favor of one that places responsibility for differences (in college performance) largely back on individual students' test performance.

The Thernstroms might claim that they are blaming institutions for low black graduation rates because, unlike Ole Miss, misguided colleges that admit blacks under color-conscious admissions policies cause lower graduation rates. But this claim is not plausible. As Kane and Bowen and Bok have shown, and as we discussed earlier, affirmative action institutions (selective colleges) have higher graduation rates for blacks and whites.[52] This means that, on average, the UC Berkeleys do better than the Ole Misses. If the colleges that admit blacks who are academically over their heads increase their chances to graduate, this institutional argument is clearly fallacious.

So why do the Thernstroms exchange their institutional argument in favor of a Catholic school K–12 education for an individual analysis at the college level? Catholic secondary schools, the Thernstroms maintain, do better with basically the same black students (based on a measure of students' educational performance) than public schools. Even if this is correct, it is obvious that some colleges are able to do better than others in graduating black (and white) students with the same SAT scores.[53] There is wide variation in the graduation rates of black and white students at various colleges and universities that admit similarly scoring students. Not surprisingly, some colleges do better than others in graduating students, and this is not because they grade easier. They do better because they are doing other things better, for example, providing financial aid and counseling services. As we argued above, historically white colleges do not provide black students with uniformly supportive environments. They are also not consistently sensitive to the financial difficulties faced by the disproportionately high numbers of low-income black students. Perhaps conservatives want to ignore this institutional variation because it lends credence to the notion that affirmative action is consistent with broader societal goals, and that if some colleges can be especially effective in graduating students with low test scores, others can too. Certainly, conservatives would not argue that Catholic secondary schools should refuse to admit lower scoring black students even though they do a much better job graduating these students than the inefficient urban public schools.

The Thernstroms' inconsistent treatment of public versus private education reveals yet another contradiction in the conservative analysis of the relationship between affirmative action and education. Although the Thernstroms treat privately run schools (and the market) as potential saviors of K–12 education, their critique of affirmative action applies almost exclusively to *private* colleges and universities. If conservatives strongly believe that the market and the choices it encourages improve primary- and secondary-level education, it makes no sense for them to criticize market-driven private institutions of higher education for practicing affirmative action, especially since these colleges have demonstrated they can graduate more black students who have not been admitted purely on test scores than public universities in the South that rely strictly on standardized measures of potential success.[54]

Choosing Ole Miss as the model for emulation and UC Berkeley as the one to be avoided plays to the symbolism of conservative, Bible-belt South versus corrupt, 1960s free-speech, antiwar, drug-infested, liberal Berkeley. It does not matter that UC Berkeley was graduating 10 percent more of its black freshmen than Ole Miss. Nor does it seem to matter that as late as the early 1990s, Ole Miss was under court order to end antiblack discriminatory admission practices. Evidently, conservatives do not care that huge public bureaucracies practicing all the inefficiencies they blame for the failures of primary and secondary level education run both universities. What apparently matters most to the Thernstroms is that Ole Miss is run by a traditional southern bureaucracy and Cal Berkeley by a liberal northern one.[55]

Perhaps the most important reason why conservatives are more concerned with color-conscious admissions policies in colleges and universities than education in K–12 is that higher education is much more important to one's future in today's society than are primary and secondary schools. A four-year college degree is now the difference between getting a good job and getting an ordinary one. Graduating from a select four-year institution means a greater probability of getting into professional or graduate school or getting a very good job right out of college. Thus, the legal and political struggle over affirmative action at select colleges is deadly serious, but it is not about upholding "standards." It is about money, rewards, and who gets what in the future. Traditional white colleges have historically been the playgrounds for white upper- and middle-class men. It is, therefore, easy to understand why conservatives would object to these self-styled selective institutions actually playing a different role in society and being accountable to the whole society rather than to a small minority of whites.

THE HIDDEN ISSUE: WHEN SHOULD BLACK COLLEGE ENROLLMENT EXPAND?

Reading between the lines of the conservative critique of affirmative action and the Ole Miss alternative the Thernstroms propose for improving blacks' university performance, one discovers a chilling message: African Americans are not ready to close the gap between black-white four-year college graduation rates very soon. Another conservative, Tamar Jacoby, who admits to being appalled by the decline in the number of blacks and Latinos attending UC Berkeley after affirmative action was abolished, believes that restoring preferential admissions would be an admission of failure. "Social and cultural development [of blacks] is a long, slow process," she writes, "and, even under the best of circumstances, it can take several generations."[56]

For conservatives, colleges, and particularly seriously selective colleges, are for high-SAT-scoring whites and Asian Americans. The conservative word, then, is that the nation cannot afford any other enrollment pattern. Students who test high should dominate select universities and colleges, and most of the second-tier schools as well. Indeed, conservative reasoning seems to be that African Americans and Latinos should stand still and wait patiently for a more efficient privatized education system (led by the revival of Catholic schools) to improve their K–12 performance because attending colleges for which they are not prepared just victimizes them. Only when their K–12 records are enhanced can these low-test-scoring groups be legitimately admitted to academically challenging elite institutions.

This is not an optimistic future for young African Americans and Latinos. Nor, apparently, is it intended to be. For all their criticism of primary and secondary schools, conservatives evade the question of whether the vast resources necessary to really change public education will be forthcoming. The Bush administration's widely praised education law seeks to install conservative nostrums as national policy but, not surprisingly, it has failed to come up with the necessary resources.

As select (and even not-so-select) colleges have become the gateway to the most lucrative domains of the global economy, a college degree is essential to wealth and power. Since nearly everyone currently finishes secondary school, and postsecondary education is rapidly becoming universal, in and of itself a high school degree is not worth much. As a result, the struggle over scarce educational resources has shifted to colleges and universities. Conservatives know this, and they have crafted a logic that appeals to white middle-class parents whose children usually go to well-stocked suburban high schools with lots of advanced placement classes that enable them to score well on the SAT or ACT. That this logic also appeals to Asian Americans and better-educated Asian immigrants is simply an add-on.

In addition to being based on a flawed use of statistics, this logic is hopelessly defensive and will not solve the problem of educating all Americans. The legacy of American apartheid cannot be eradicated through exclusion constructed by self-serving notions of meritocracy or by privatizing public services. Despite conservative claims to the contrary, neither of these mechanisms has worked in the past, and there is no reason to believe they will work in the future.

The conservative logic is flawed in yet another way. The raceless, egalitarian society they construct turns the reality of race in America upside down. It ignores the reality of even middle-class, successful blacks who sense that they will never attain the American Dream.[57] African Americans and Latinos know that postponing admission to white-dominated institutions indefinitely, until whites deem them ready, never worked in the past, and they have little faith that the strategy will work today. They also know that the market has never been an engine for racial equality and therefore wonder why privately run education would work today.

By reducing African American and Latino access to higher education in a global and high-tech economy, conservatives will only increase racial divisions and differences in American society. The social costs of keeping large groups of lower-scoring Latinos and blacks out of postsecondary educational institutions for even one generation will be much higher than any imagined productivity differences resulting from the job market being invaded by lower average test-scoring college graduates.[58] Even if they could be accurately measured, these economic inefficiencies are definitely small compared to the economic impact of a conflict- and poverty-ridden, fraying social fabric with a shortage of college-educated labor among groups borne and bred in the United States.

Restricting economic opportunity in this way will surely compound the ongoing process of disaccumulation among African Americans and Latinos. And to the extent that it produces social disorder, it will only intensify the demand for harsher anticrime policies and Draconian prison sentences. Conservative anticrime policies have already led to the incarceration of a generation of young black and Latino men in the belief they are prone to commit crimes. Like conservatives' views of race and poverty, and race and education, their understanding of race and crime is misleading and fails to acknowledge the persistent racism in the criminal justice system and the devastating effects of these practices on African American and Latino communities. We turn now to the conservatives' analysis of race and crime.

Been in the Pen So Long

Race, Crime, and Justice

The problem of crime among urban blacks is arguably the most visceral, emotional aspect of the debate about race in America today. Probably even more than welfare or affirmative action, the question of black violence has fueled a fundamental shift in the debate that began in the late 1960s and accelerated in the 1970s and 1980s. In these decades blacks lost the moral high ground in the eyes of numerous white commentators, including many former liberals. Between the flowering of the civil rights movement and the Reagan years, the image of black youth in particular underwent an extraordinary transformation: the brave little girl walking up to the schoolhouse door in the face of jeering white crowds was replaced by fearsome young black men coming down the street ready to take your wallet or your life. The cultural transformation of black youth from victims of injustice to remorseless predators was mirrored in public policies that quietly reduced funding for programs that had historically served minority youth. At the same time, lawmakers and legal authorities visibly cracked down on young people of color through tougher sentences, "zero tolerance" strategies in the schools and on the streets, and increased treatment of juvenile offenders as adults.

Conservative social scientists and other commentators have taken the lead in constructing this cultural and intellectual shift. Their analysis of black crime and the justice system both reflects this shift and seeks to justify it through a presentation that purports to be a straightforward recital of obvious, if troubling, "facts." The main argument, advanced repeatedly by conservative authors like James Q. Wilson, John J. DiIulio, John McWhorter, and the Thernstroms in *America in Black and White*, is that there is both good news and bad news on the crime front.[1] On the one hand, crime and violence, like other "behavioral" problems, are devastatingly high in many black communities. Indeed, the lawlessness helps to explain why so many blacks remain mired in poverty. Crime causes poverty, they contend, by scaring businesses away from black communities and by giving too many black men an alternative to honest work. On the other hand, there is no longer systematic racism in the criminal justice system. There used to be, conservatives agree, but that was in the past. Today black officials in black-dominated cities run many court systems as well as police departments, so how can racism still be a factor?

It is true, these writers acknowledge, that blacks are overrepresented in the jails and prisons. But that is because of a hard reality: blacks commit more of the kinds of crimes that get people behind bars. There is no credible evidence of systematic racial bias in the institutions of justice, they claim. Instead, the justice system simply responds to existing high levels of serious crime among blacks. The black proportion of the prison population, writes John McWhorter, "neatly reflects the rate at which they commit crimes. . . . One study after another, even by scholars expecting their results to reveal racism, shows . . . when prior records, gravity of the crime, and use of weapons is taken into account, there is no sentencing bias against blacks."[2] Conservatives do not say much about the origins of those high rates of crime. But the implication is that high levels of violence stem from the same sources as the other multiple pathologies of the so-called black underclass. And whatever those sources are, according to conservatives, they are clearly not economic. Rather, they must be cultural, since research fails to show any connection between economic disadvantage and crime.

For many racial realists, the idea that racial discrimination causes crime and leads to injustice in the treatment of blacks by the criminal justice system is itself part of the problem. The fashionable tendency to excuse black criminality as an expected and even morally tolerable response to discrimination, in the view of some writers, has helped to erode the sense of personal responsibility among blacks and has thus encouraged crime. Without fear of serious consequences or moral disapproval, the realists argue, black crime has been tacitly allowed to run rampant. The journalist Jim Sleeper, for example, acknowledges that racism against black defendants in the justice system has been "a great, historic wrong," which liberal activists and others did "much to curb" in the 1950s and 1960s.

> But lately liberals have been curbing systemic racism in favor of a racism that refuses to pay blacks the compliment of holding them to the same elementary civil standards as everyone else. With stunning callousness, "civil

rights" attorneys from Kunstler to Cochran have goaded black juries into political, "send a message" acquittals of black assailants of whites, never considering that not only are such acquittals morally indistinguishable from those of white assailants of blacks in the old South, they also encourage liberals' shameful neglect of black victims killed or raped by blacks.[3]

As with other realms of social life, the realist discussion of race and crime represents itself as simply a factual account, a hardheaded and sober examination of some troubling though inescapable realities. On closer inspection, however, it is actually a highly partisan, and oddly selective, manipulation of the evidence on the roots of crime in the black community and the workings of the justice system. The argument gains some superficial credibility because racial realists often choose to focus on soft and vulnerable targets. In this instance, the soft targets are liberals and black civil rights advocates who, according to the realists, insist that the vast numbers of blacks in the courts, jails, and prisons are simply innocents caught in the snares of a racist system. Having set up this convenient straw person, these writers proceed to knock it down by showing that social science research uniformly suggests that blacks have higher rates of serious offenses (for street crimes, though not, importantly, for white-collar crimes). They then move on from that thoroughly unremarkable finding to the much more sweeping assertion that racism is irrelevant for understanding black overrepresentation in the justice system—or in the crime statistics.

There is a cautionary note here. To the extent that some people still deny that violence in many black communities is a real problem, or who argue that black overrepresentation in the correctional system is only a reflection of the racist bias of police and courts, the realist argument appears to offer a sober, research-based corrective to soft-headed liberal ideology. That argument quickly crumbles, however, when their claims are put up against a more subtle and complex analysis that recognizes both the reality of high levels of black violence and the continued salience of racism. In this view, racism is both subtle and not so subtle, both direct and indirect, in breeding violence and shaping black Americans' experiences with the criminal justice system.

What is truly startling about the conservative assertion that liberal indulgence is responsible for black crime in America is that it comes after decades of the most rapid increases in the incarceration of black Americans in our history—a time of utterly unprecedented efforts by legislators and the courts to "get tough" on crime and drugs in the inner cities. Some of the numbers that describe this stunning change are by now numbingly familiar: at the close of the twentieth century, almost one in ten black men aged twenty-five to twenty-nine was in prison, compared to one white in ninety. In California, black men are five times as likely to be in state prison as in state college. Nationally, 28 percent of black men will spend some time during the course of their lives in a state or federal prison, and between the mid-1980s and the mid-1990s, the number of black men sentenced to prison for drug offenses increased by more than 700 percent. The fastest growing segment of the imprisoned population is black women, who are incarcerated mainly for nonviolent offenses. This curious disconnect between the idea that blacks have been absolved of personal responsibility for their behavior and the reality of nearly thirty years of increasing harshness toward black offenders suggests that there must be something fundamentally amiss with the conservative argument. There is.

The conservative argument fails in two respects. First, the serious scholarly research on racial discrimination within the justice system—which is by now extensive—does not support the view that it operates in a completely race-neutral way. Indeed these studies provide consistent evidence not only that race still matters in the justice system but also that discrimination in the justice system has a rippling effect on blacks' life-chances across every other institution in American life. Second, the relationships between race, structural disadvantage, and crime—far from being irrelevant or unproven—are among the most consistent findings in the entire body of criminological research. In this chapter we analyze each of these issues in turn—paying more attention to the first one, since it is the linchpin of conservative discussions of race and crime.

HAS RACISM DISAPPEARED FROM THE JUSTICE SYSTEM?

No one seriously doubts that the level of overt discrimination in the criminal justice system has diminished since the civil rights era. But to say that racial discrimination has been expunged from the justice system—as conservatives do—provides an extremely misleading picture of what social science research really shows.[4] To understand why, some intellectual history is necessary.

In the past few decades, there have been basically three waves of social research on discrimination in the justice system. Wave 1 researchers, writing in the era before the civil rights movement had an impact on the behavior of courts and police, typically saw pervasive discrimination throughout the system, especially in the South. Blacks were found disproportionately represented at all levels of the criminal justice process, from arrest to imposition of the death penalty. Anecdotal evidence, legal research, and descriptive statistics all pointed to a pattern of systematically harsher responses to blacks, particularly if their victims were white.

In the massive study *An American Dilemma*, for example, researched in the 1930s and published during World War II, the Swedish social scientist Gunnar Myrdal and his associates validated a portrait of endemic racism in the southern justice system already sketched by a number of earlier researchers. They claimed to find less racial bias in the North, where, in Myrdal's view, blacks faced no special problem of getting justice in the courts beyond that encountered by poor people of all races (the police were another matter). But in the South, discrimination was the norm, and it worked in two ways. On the one hand, blacks were far more likely to be put under surveillance, arrested, and sentenced, especially in the lower courts, if their victims (or supposed victims) were white. According to Myrdal's collaborator, Arnold Rose, "The courts, particularly the lower courts, often seem to take for granted the guilt of the accused Negro. Negro defendants are sentenced upon scanty evidence. When the offender is a white man and the victim a Negro, a grand jury will often refuse to indict. . . . When the offender is a Negro, indictment is easily obtained." At the same time, Myrdal and his colleagues found, the southern criminal justice system treated crimes against blacks casually, whether committed by whites or by other blacks: "As long as only Negroes are concerned and no whites are disturbed, great leniency will be shown in most cases. The sentences for even major crimes are ordinarily reduced when the victim is another Negro. The Southern Negro community is not at all happy about this double standard of justice in favor of Negro offenders. . . . Leniency toward Negro defendants in cases involving crimes against other Negroes is thus actually a form of discrimination."[5]

The second wave of research appeared mainly during the 1970s and early 1980s, after the civil rights legislation of the 1960s and after a movement toward law enforcement professionalization had, presumably, substantially altered the racial character of American justice. This research painted a very different picture than the first wave. Applying more stringent social science methodology, the Wave 2 studies concluded that when other crucial factors were controlled, race was not important in shaping offenders' trajectories in the justice system, or at least not *very* important. Wave 2 researchers pointed out that most of the early findings on the pervasiveness of discrimination were based on studies that did not control for the level (or seriousness) of black offenses when explaining their disproportionate representation in the system. Instead, these researchers took the disproportion alone as an instance of discrimination. For the Wave 2 researchers, that made no sense. Any estimation of bias in the system, they argued, had to take into account things like the seriousness of the offenses blacks were committing relative to whites, the extent of their prior criminal records, and other "legally relevant" factors. When Wave 2 researchers took those factors into account, they often concluded that little, if any, of the racial disparity in sentencing was attributable to racism.

Probably the most influential piece of research in this wave was a well-known study by Alfred Blumstein of Carnegie-Mellon University. First published in 1982, this research compared black rates of arrest for violent crime with black imprisonment rates—reasoning that discrimination in sentencing would be shown only if the black rates of going to prison significantly exceeded the rates at which they were arrested. Once the high levels of black arrest for violent crimes were accounted for, Blumstein found that about 80 percent of the difference between black and white rates of imprisonment for crimes of violence disappeared. (Note, however, that even Blumstein's findings could not explain a significant 20 percent of the disparity.[6]) Similar findings appeared in several other studies.[7]

For some people, the apparent methodological sophistication of Wave 2 research settled the issue. A partial consensus emerged among some criminologists that systematic discrimination against black offenders had been eliminated. This consensus was ably summed up (and generally accepted, with important reservations) in a book by Michael Tonry of the University of Minnesota Law School in the early 1990s. "From every available data source," Tonry concluded, "the evidence seems clear that the main reason that black incarceration rates are substantially higher than those for whites is that black crime rates for imprisonable crimes are substantially higher than those for whites." Thus, it no longer made sense to try to "ferret out a willful and pervasive bias in a criminal justice system in which most officials and participants believe in racial equality and worry about the racial patterns they see every day."[8] (Importantly, Tonry made an exception for drug offenses, where discrimination seemed much clearer.)

For Tonry, who was deeply concerned about racial disparity in the prisons and jails, this meant criminologists should pay more attention to the forces that caused high levels of black crime in the first place. For many conservatives, however, whose argument rests largely on Wave 2–type research—to the extent it is based on evidence at all—this finding proves that racial discrimination no longer has much, if anything, to do with black overrepresentation in the criminal justice system. What these conservatives either do not know, however, or do not acknowledge, is that this evidence has been superseded by a newer wave of empirical research.[9]

The third wave, which has mainly emerged since the early 1990s, finds Wave 2 research too simplistic and often riddled with severe methodological flaws. This most recent wave includes careful studies by Donna Bishop and Charles Frazier at Florida State University; Darlene Conley, Robert Crutchfield, and George Bridges at the University of Washington; Darrell Steffensmier at Pennsylvania State University; and many others.[10] Wave 3 takes the connections between race, crime, and justice to a more sophisticated level, incorporating and going beyond some of the insights of both earlier waves of research. Wave 3 researchers do not deny that street crime is high in many poor black communities. Nor do they dispute that high levels of crime substantially account for the high levels of black incarceration. But this research also clearly demonstrates that racial discrimination in the justice system still exists, though it is usually more indirect and complicated than past discrimination.

Wave 2 tended to define discrimination too simply as overt racial bias. In contrast, Wave 3 is based on a much more nuanced conception of how discrimination operates. As a recent Human Rights Watch report on the enforcement of drug laws in Georgia puts it, "Contemporary racism in public institutions" is often "subtle, diffuse, and systemic, and less likely to be the result of the conscious prejudices of individual actors."[11] Indeed, the newer research clearly shows that discriminatory outcomes can be produced by actions that appear bureaucratically neutral or color-blind—sometimes even well intentioned, undertaken in response to concerns raised by minority communities. But in the world of structured racial disadvantage, these actions predictably work against blacks (and often Latinos as well). In doing so, they contribute to the larger process of cumulative disadvantage and disaccumulation discussed throughout this book. Ironically, in a truly vicious cycle, these practices may ultimately contribute significantly to the rise of black crime. (Some of this research, however, also points to the persistence of more overt racial stereotyping and animosity, especially in certain jurisdictions.[12])

The Wave 3 studies reveal several fundamental methodological problems with the Wave 2 approach. One is what is sometimes called "over-aggregation" of the data on black-white disparities in incarceration. Taking another look at Alfred Blumstein's influential comparison of black arrests and imprisonment rates for violent crimes, for example, Robert Crutchfield and his colleagues showed that Blumstein's *national-level* comparisons obscure variations in black arrest and incarceration rates between different *states*. In some states, the proportion of blacks behind bars does indeed closely match the proportion of blacks arrested for certain serious offenses. In other states (including unexpected ones, like Mississippi) blacks appear to be imprisoned at a lower rate than would be predicted by their rate of arrests (perhaps reaffirming Myrdal's finding that black offenses against black victims are often treated leniently). But in other states, blacks wind up in prison at a rate far in excess of what would be predicted on the basis of their arrest rates. High black arrest rates explained less than half of the racial imbalance in imprisonment in Massachusetts, for example, and only 40 percent in Washington State. As the researchers put it, even measured in this blunt manner, it is clear that some states "deliver justice" less equitably than others.[13] If we look only at national-level averages, we lose sight of the harsher reality blacks face in many specific jurisdictions. To date, no one has seriously challenged this key finding.

A recent study of racially disproportional prison admissions in Pennsylvania confirms and elaborates this crucial insight. Between 1991 and 1995, according to Roy L. Austin and Mark D. Allen, only 42 percent of the racial imbalance in Pennsylvania's court commitments to state prisons was explained by racial differences in arrest rates. The proportions were especially small for lower-level crimes, where discretion in criminal justice processing is presumably greater (a finding that reappears often in recent research on racial disparities in sentencing). Thus, higher black arrest rates for drug offenses explained only 26 percent of the racially disproportionate drug sentences during those years. As with other recent research, that startlingly low percentage confirms that it is virtually impossible to explain away the stunning levels of black overrepresentation for drug offenses in the prisons of many states. But even when drug offenses are removed from the count, Austin and Allen found that black arrests explained only 70 percent of black overrepresentation in prison commitments.[14]

There is, of course, another problem with the strategy of assessing discrimination in the justice system by comparing rates of imprisonment with rates of arrest: it ignores the possibility that discrimination in police practices strongly influences who will be arrested in the first place. We will return to this issue in a moment. But for now, the key point is that the Wave 3 research makes a compelling case that discrimination still operates after arrest in the stages of detaining, diverting, and sentencing offenders. Racial conservatives and realists, for the most part, have simply ignored the research on which that increasingly strong case has been made. The Thernstroms, for example, argue that discrimination does not operate in sentencing by presenting raw figures from Justice Department studies showing that, overall, blacks who are charged with adult felonies are marginally less likely than whites to actually be prosecuted and, if prosecuted, are marginally less likely to be convicted. So there is, they say, no evidence of "greater zeal to punish African-Americans," adding, the "only hint of racial disparity was to the advantage, not the disadvantage, of blacks accused of crimes." But it is not possible to assess whether these raw figures indicate bias, or the lack of it, unless one controls for a variety of other factors that may help determine whether a given defendant is prosecuted or convicted. This is a fundamental social science principle that, curiously, the Thernstroms themselves invoke elsewhere in their discussion but abandon here.

Those sophisticated controls are precisely what distinguish Wave 3 research from most earlier efforts—and that may explain why the Thernstroms and other conservatives rarely mention it. Moreover, contrary to John McWhorter's assertion that "study after study" finds no discrimination in the justice system when other relevant factors are controlled, it turns out he is wrong. The vast bulk of recent studies that do use adequate controls produce consistent evidence of continuing discrimination.

This pattern begins with the differential treatment of juvenile offenders and continues, though perhaps less glaringly, into the treatment of adults. The fact that race has an especially visible and fateful impact in the juvenile justice system is another reason why studies that look for discrimination by assessing adult sentencing patterns at one point minimize the persistence and severity of racial disadvantage. By the time young blacks reach the adult justice system, discrimination has *already* had a serious impact. As a result, it appears that adult court processing is relatively bias-free.

The bare statistics reveal that as African Americans move more and more deeply into the juvenile justice system, a pattern of cumulative overrepresentation emerges. Thus, as of the late 1990s, black youth were

- 15 percent of the general population under age eighteen
- 26 percent of juvenile arrests
- 31 percent of referrals to juvenile court
- 44 percent of referred juveniles detained in custody
- 32 percent of youth judged delinquent
- 40 percent of youth in residential placement
- 46 percent of juveniles waived to adult criminal court
- 58 percent of youth admitted to adult state prisons[15]

The question is what to make of these figures. Many conservative writers, following Wave 2 logic, argue that these progressive disparities simply reflect the reality that black youth commit more serious offenses or commit them more often or both. More sophisticated research, however, strongly shows that differential treatment of juveniles by race is pervasive, even when such "legally relevant" factors are taken into account.

This research suggests that modern discrimination is not so much a matter of overt racial prejudice but rather of more subtle yet insidious processes that tend to accumulate over time. Small disadvantages at each successive stage in the justice process result in big disparities over the long run. Exacerbating this is the larger pattern of cumulative social disinvestment in black communities that has been described throughout this book. High unemployment, few effective public social programs, and the resulting pressure on black families all work to the disadvantage of black youth in the justice system. Because authorities perceive blacks as having fewer outside resources to help them achieve a crime-free life, the system is likely to define them as poor risks and to opt for custody over release to the community. In turn, this greater likelihood of incarceration further constricts the youths' chances upon release, thus contributing to another kind of self-fueling downward cycle.

For example, recent research finds that juvenile authorities tend to institutionalize youth that come from families they think are unable to provide sufficient support or supervision for them in the community. That choice is typically defined as race-neutral. But black youth that come from single-parent homes, or homes without an employed breadwinner, are more likely to wind up in institutional custody. Similarly, there is also a well-intentioned inclination to institutionalize troubled black children because that is seen as the only way to get them services that do not exist in their communities or that their families cannot afford, like mental health intervention or drug treatment. But this gives black youth a record of prior incarceration, which will almost certainly be used against them in their next encounter with the system. This in turn increases the likelihood that they will be incarcerated again and treated even more harshly.

The new studies do not indicate that the fate of black youth in the criminal justice system is unrelated to their actual level of offending. Far from it. There is no real question that legally relevant variables like the seriousness of the offense and the youths' prior record carry the most weight. But the research shows that the relatively high level of serious crime among black youth is not the whole story. Something else happens to young blacks as they pass through the juvenile justice system, and that "something" operates independently of the extent and seriousness of the crimes they commit. Consider these examples:

- In a study of race and juvenile justice decision making in Florida, Donna Bishop and Charles Frazier found that nonwhite youth were systematically disadvantaged at "each successive stage" of the system, from intake to incarceration. As a result, the population in the system became increasingly darker the further the youth penetrated it. Nonwhite youth were 21 percent of the population aged ten to seventeen but 29 percent of those referred to intake and 44 percent of those incarcerated or transferred to adult court. When the researchers controlled for factors like the youths' prior records and the seriousness of their current offense, the disparities, unsurprisingly, were reduced, but they did not disappear. With all else accounted for, the chances of being committed to a juvenile institution or being transferred to adult court were nearly twice as high for nonwhites as for whites. Why were black youth subject to what the researchers call a "consistent pattern of unequal treatment" at every stage of the process? Interviews with juvenile justice personnel pointed to several explanations. Officials tended to define black youths' families as uncooperative or incapable of providing sufficient support or control. They also often believed that the only way to get drug treatment or mental health services to the black youth was to institutionalize them. The problem, of course, is that these decisions become self-perpetuating, a trap for minority youth. "What may begin with good intentions at an earlier stage ultimately becomes a self-fulfilling prophecy. The influence of race is [later] obscured as decisions to formally prosecute and detain in the past are used to justify more severe sanctions for youths returning to the system."[16]

. Similarly, a study of five midwestern counties by Madeline Wordes and Timothy Bynum found that black (and Latino) youth were consistently more likely to wind up in secure detention, even when such legally relevant factors as seriousness of offense, prior record, and carrying a weapon were taken into account. Moreover, the disparity in incarceration for minority youth persisted even when a number of other social factors were also considered. Other things equal, for example, youth from single-parent families were more likely to be put in detention, which worked to the disadvantage of young blacks. But even with family structure controlled, black youth were still more likely to be detained. Wordes and Bynum concluded that blacks were systematically disadvantaged indirectly, because they more often came from the social strata and family types most likely to be incarcerated, and directly, probably because stereotypes about dangerous minority youth meant they were charged with more serious offenses at the outset.[17]

. A recent study of probation officers' reports on juvenile offenders demonstrates that minority youth tend to be seen differently than whites by court authorities, even when they have committed similar offenses. George Bridges and Sara Steen found that probation officers in a western state were much more likely to attribute black youths' delinquency to internal problems—negative attitudes and personality traits. On the other hand, they were more likely to stress the influence of external, environmental pressures as causes for white youths to break the law. As a consequence, the probation officers were apt to conclude that the black youth were more dangerous and more likely to reoffend, which in turn influenced their sentencing recommendations.[18]

. Interestingly, one recent study, by Michael Leiber and Jayne Stairs, found that black youth in a midwestern state were both more likely to be detained by juvenile justice authorities than were whites and less likely to receive some sort of structured diversion program. The black youth, that is, were more likely to be sent on for tougher punishment and to be simply let go. The system apparently did not offer supportive intervention, outside custody, to black youth in trouble.[19] This raises, once again, an important, though inadequately examined, issue: racial discrimination in the justice system may be obscured, as it was in the segregation era, because the system's response to black offenders conflates both harshness (under certain conditions) and neglect (under others), depending on the nature of the offense and the race of the victim.

Differential treatment as juveniles propels blacks disproportionately into the adult criminal justice system. It also helps hide the way race works to shape the color of the adult prison population. Even at the level of adult sentencing, several recent studies have found persistent racial disparities that cannot be explained away by the frequency or seriousness of offenses or any other legally relevant factors. This is especially true for drug offenses, and—strikingly—it remains true despite the adoption by the federal system and a number of states of elaborate sentencing guidelines designed specifically to eliminate discretion. For example, a recent study by Christopher Hebert of federal sentencing of drug offenders found there was no clear pattern of racial bias in sentencing for drug offenses generally.[20] But for cocaine specifically (and to a lesser degree opiates) the disparities in sentencing, controlling for a host of other factors, were stark. Being black, other things equal, not only doubled the chance of going to federal prison for a cocaine-related offense but added, on average, forty months to the sentence. Celesta Albonetti, in another study of sentencing under federal guidelines, found that both blacks and Latinos were disadvantaged in sentencing decisions, relative to whites, when it came to drug offenses. These disparities were apparently produced by the differential use of what the federal system calls "departures" from the guidelines, especially those providing more lenient sentencing for offenders who furnish "substantial assistance" to prosecutors and who accept responsibility for their crimes. To the degree that federal sentencing guidelines allowed considerable discretion in the justice system, in other words, the discretionary possibilities typically disadvantaged minority defendants.

This pattern can be found at the state level as well. A Human Rights Watch study of Georgia drug enforcement found that black defendants were far more likely than whites to receive the harshest sanctions for drug offenses. During some periods, for example, Georgia drug laws allowed a potential life sentence for the second or subsequent drug offense, even if both offenses were minor ones. Between 1990 and 1995, of the 573 offenders given a life sentence under these Draconian laws, *only 13 were white*. The disparity was reduced, but not eliminated, when the researchers controlled for the proportions in each race who were eligible for this harsh sentence under the state law because of the specific nature of their offense and their prior record. Three percent of whites who were convicted of a "qualifying" drug offense received a life sentence versus 15 percent of blacks. Thus "life-eligible" blacks were five times as likely to actually get a life sentence as "life-eligible" whites were.[21] Charles Crawford, Ted Chiricos, and Gary Kleck found a similar situation in a study of racial patterns in sentencing under a "habitual offender" statute in Florida in the early 1990s. Of nearly ten thousand offenders eligible to be sentenced as habitual offenders in 1992–93—which meant serving a much longer sentence than others—only about 20 percent were actually given that disposition. But with all else controlled, eligible blacks were between 36 and 69 percent more likely to be declared habitual offenders than eligible whites.[22]

Though drug offenses provide the most visible disparities, racial differences in sentencing are not confined to drugs. Crawford, Chiricos, and Kleck found that race also played a critical role in sentencing for property offenses. And in a study of race and incarceration in New York State, James Nelson discovered that—after controlling for the seriousness of the offense, county of jurisdiction, and other factors—roughly one in three blacks sentenced to jail would have received a more lenient sentence had they been treated the same as comparable white offenders.[23] Every year in the state, four thousand black defendants went to jail who would not have gone behind bars had they been treated the same as similarly situated whites. The disparity was less stark for admission to prisons, as opposed to local jails. Still, three hundred blacks went to state prison in New York annually who would not have gone to prison had they been white.

These disparities are, perhaps unsurprisingly, even greater when age and gender are combined with race. Because most studies lump all ages (and usually genders as well) together, comparisons of racial patterns in sentencing typically obscure the especially harsh outcomes for *young black men*. How much so is apparent in Darrell Steffensmier and colleagues' study of adult sentencing in Pennsylvania, a state with a system of sentencing guidelines that again, other things equal, should reduce the effects of legally irrelevant factors like race on sentences. The study found, as have others, that the severity of the offense and the defendants' prior records carried the most weight in determining whether they went to prison, and for how long. But with all else controlled, the odds of imprisonment for white men aged eighteen to twenty-nine were 38 percent less than those for black men the same age. And the prison sentences for white men, when they received them, were shorter by an average of almost three months. The racial disparities decreased at older ages, as both black and white men became less likely, other things being equal, to be sent to prison, making the odds for black and white men over fifty roughly similar. But putting race and age together changes the picture dramatically: the odds of going to prison for black men eighteen to twenty-nine were more than four times those of white men over fifty. Thus "the influence of race in the sentencing of males depends on the defendant's age."[24]

Why do younger black men so predictably get the toughest sanctions? On the basis of interviews with Pennsylvania judges, the researchers suggest that older offenders and women were often seen as more likely to be supporting a family and more likely to be holding down a steady job "now or in the future." Young black men, on the other hand, were not seen to have those stabilizing social bonds. They were also generally regarded as more dangerous to public safety, less reformable, and less likely to have suffered mitigating victimization of their own, like being coerced into crime at the hands of men or suffering from some psychological disorder. Some of the judges, moreover, "were reluctant to send white offenders to state prisons (whose populations were more than 65 percent black) for fear that whites would be victimized by black inmates." As the researchers point out, when one ignores how race, gender, and age interact to shape the fate of offenders in the justice system, we seriously underestimate the "high cost of being black, young, and male" specifically, and thus the "continuing significance of race in American society."[25]

Many of these studies are quite sophisticated, and they go a long way beyond the superficially convincing Wave 2 platitudes on which the conservative argument depends. Like their analysis of race and sentencing, the conservative discussion of race and the death penalty also neglects or misrepresents pivotal research findings. The Thernstroms, for example, spend considerable time analyzing a well-known study by David Baldus of the University of Iowa and his colleagues, which famously found that killers of whites were four times as likely to get the death penalty as killers of blacks were.[26] They counter these conclusions by pointing out that the findings surely must depend on the kind of murder involved. Killing a police officer, for example, is more likely to be a capital offense.

Since more police officers are white than black, they reason, it is only logical that people get the death penalty more often for killing whites. Thus, there is no racial bias involved. Except for a minor comment late in the discussion, one would never know that Baldus and his colleagues did control for the factors (over two hundred) that differentiated between murders. And they found that, with nearly every possible variable controlled, killers are still more likely to be sentenced to death, all else equal, if they kill a white person. One would also never know that there have been numerous other studies in several other states since Baldus's research that show approximately the same thing. These studies are not obscure. The U.S. General Accounting Office recently surveyed them in a review.[27] A more up-to-date Philadelphia study by Baldus and colleagues showed, moreover, that at least in the City of Brotherly Love, an offender's race also strongly shapes the likelihood of a death sentence. Other things controlled, they found blacks far more likely than whites to be sentenced to death for potentially capital offenses.[28]

RACE, POLICE PRACTICES, AND THE "VICIOUS CIRCLE"

The best research now available, in short, confirms—repeatedly—that race still influences whether someone who comes before a court will be sent behind bars, and for how long. It is not the only factor that matters, nor even the most important variable. But race remains a significant issue. And because going behind bars has such an enormous impact on future chances for a good job and a stable life, the powerful role race plays in funneling defendants deeply into the criminal justice system is obviously a significant part of the accumulated adversities that perpetuate racial disparities throughout every other realm of life.

Moreover, the exclusive focus on what happens *after* arrest understates these adverse effects because it ignores the issue of how and why so many people of color wind up getting arrested in the first place. Much of Wave 2 research was about sentencing. But a great deal, of course, happens before sentencing that shapes someone's chances of entering the system and, once in it, their progress to the sentencing stage. This is clearly a problem in studies like Blumstein's that measure the presence or absence of racial bias by comparing imprisonment rates with arrest rates. When those rates matched up reasonably well, that was taken as evidence that the justice system was not biased. (In fact, the rates did not match up all that well, even in Blumstein's study. The high black arrest rates for violent crime still left unexplained 20 percent of the black-white disparity in imprisonment across the country.) But that kind of conclusion is deeply flawed because it ignores the possible effect of discriminatory practices in creating the initial disparity in black and white arrest rates.

Conservatives downplay this possibility. Dinesh D'Souza, for example, along with the Thernstroms and others, invokes the findings of the victim surveys carried out regularly by the U.S. Department of Justice. These surveys ask samples of the general population about their experience of victimization by crime and, among other things, ask them about the race of the people who committed the crimes. Those studies do indeed show that victims of violent crime, including black victims, describe the perpetrators as black in proportions that far outweigh the black proportion of the population as a whole. And since the results of these surveys do not depend on the behavior of authorities, as do arrest statistics, they are often said to be free of racial bias. Following several Wave 2 researchers, many conservatives suggest that these findings demonstrate conclusively that racism has nothing to do with the disproportionate number of black arrests.

The point is an important one if it is not taken too far. But some Wave 2 researchers did take it too far, and so do some conservative writers. Though the victim surveys can offer at best only a very crude estimate of the prevalence of offenders in a given population, it is certainly true that they generally support the uncontroversial point that blacks commit a disproportionate amount of street crime. But these surveys cannot legitimately be used as evidence that the criminal justice system is free of bias because they tell us nothing about how blacks who encounter the justice system are actually treated. National-level survey data, for example, cannot get around the overaggregation problem we mentioned above. Thus, the fact that blacks are a high proportion of offenders nationwide obviously cannot be used as evidence that the police in Los Angeles or New York do not engage in discriminatory street tactics. Nor can the victim survey findings tell us anything about the extent of discrimination in the way police handle most drug offenses, which are, in a sense, "victimless" and as such do not figure in the surveys. Because the number of black men sentenced to prison for drug offenses increased by more than 700 percent from 1985 to 1995 alone—and blacks constitute 80 percent or more of incarcerated drug offenders in seven states—that is, to say the least, a significant limitation.[29]

Some recent research makes it abundantly clear that aggressive police behavior toward minorities *cannot* be explained away simply as the natural result of higher levels of crime among them. A study of police stops of civilians in New York City, for example, done for the New York State attorney general's office, found that over a fifteen-month period in 1998 and 1999, blacks were stopped by police six times as often as whites were, and Latinos, four times as often. Blacks made up about 25 percent of the city's general population but 50 percent of people stopped by the police. Whites made up 43 percent of the general population but just 13 percent of civilians stopped by police. As with the studies of differential sentencing, the researchers did find that a substantial part of this disparity could be attributed to higher levels of offenses by blacks and Latinos—as measured by the frequency with which the stops were followed by an actual arrest—but by no means all of it. Blacks were stopped considerably more often than they were arrested, whites less so; blacks endured 1.5 stops for every arrest versus 1.2 for whites.[30]

And in fact the social science evidence on patterns of discrimination in police practices, though not extensive, is nevertheless both consistent and long-standing. Evidence from a variety of sources has shown for decades that such discrimination is systemic and widespread, even in police departments that are generally considered to be highly professional. Indeed, those discriminatory practices are not only tolerated but also frequently justified as good police work, in "color-blind" terms, by police themselves. Those practices, however, are often the first steps in a cumulative process through which people of color, and minority youth in particular, are funneled disproportionately into the criminal justice system.

In a classic and careful observational study of police responses to juveniles in a midwestern city in the 1960s, for example, Irving Piliavin and Scott Briar found starkly different treatment for black youth, even in a department widely noted for "the honesty and superior quality of its personnel."[31] Especially when it came to relatively minor offenses, where officers had a great deal of discretion in deciding what to do with a youth, the police were much more likely to give blacks the tougher dispositions (from an official reprimand to arrest and citation to juvenile court) and less likely to release them outright. Piliavin and Briar discovered that the officers' decisions were heavily based on cues that "emerged from the interaction between the officer and the youth [and] from which the officer inferred the youth's character": "Older youths, members of known delinquent gangs, Negroes, youths with well-oiled hair, black jackets, and soiled denims or jeans . . . and boys who in their interactions with officers did not manifest what were considered to be appropriate signs of respect tended to receive the most severe dispositions."[32]

These cues were so significant in determining police decisions that blacks and those otherwise fitting the delinquent stereotype were more likely to be stopped and interrogated "often even in the absence of evidence that an offense had been committed." And if offenses were found, they typically received "more severe dispositions [than] for the same violations" committed by whites. The fact that black youths were greatly overrepresented among those who had to be released for lack of evidence corroborated the researchers' observations.

Piliavin and Briar found that the police often based these racially targeted responses on departmental statistics showing higher rates of offenses among black youth. The police "justified their selective treatment" on "epidemiological lines"; they concentrated their attention on "those youths whom they believed were most likely to commit delinquent acts." As one officer put it to the researchers, "our delinquency problem is largely found in the Negro community and it is these youths toward whom we are sensitized." Indeed, Piliavin and Briar found these assumptions meant that the police targeted their surveillance "in areas frequented or inhabited by Negroes" in the first place, thus assuring that black youth would be more likely to be stopped by officers. But the obvious problem with this "epidemiological" approach to policing, the researchers pointed out, was that it "may well have self-fulfilling consequences." Black youth routinely stopped by the police might become hostile toward law enforcement and display the wrong kind of demeanor in encounters with them, thus vindicating the officers' prejudices and spurring more arrests. This, in turn, might lead "to closer surveillance of Negro districts, more frequent encounters with Negro youths, and so on in a vicious circle."[33]

More recent work by Darlene Conley and others suggests that similar patterns prevail today, even after another three decades of efforts in some jurisdictions to improve the racial record of the police. The newer research reconfirms that black (and Latino) neighborhoods are more likely to be the focus of heavy police monitoring and surveillance to begin with and that black and Latino youth are more likely to be defined by police as threatening or insubordinate, more likely to be stopped more often under various pretexts, more likely to get arrested than to receive a warning, and less likely to have charges dropped by police.[34]

Some recent research suggests that police are well aware of these racially structured practices but that they often defend them on one or both of two related grounds. On the one hand, just as Piliavin and Briar found in the 1960s, police still operate with an epidemiological or "actuarial" attitude toward their surveillance of young people. Since minority youth are statistically more likely to be carrying weapons or dealing drugs on the street, why would police not concentrate their limited time and resources on them? Why, realistically, would they spend as much time patrolling middle-class white suburbs looking for armed gang members? (As a police officer in a southern state put it to one of us recently, "I could spend my time jacking up elderly Asian ladies, but why would I?") Moreover, as Human Rights Watch found in their study of the racially bifurcated enforcement of drug laws in Georgia, the police most often operate as a reactive agency that responds to public outcry over crime and drugs, and that outcry is louder in the inner-city ghettoes and barrios where the worst open drug dealing and gang presence are found on the streets.[35] So that is where they go. How can it be called "racist," police often ask, to respond to the concerns of the law-abiding citizens in minority communities? (Especially since the police doing the responding may be minority too?)

But the result of this "actuarial" reasoning, of course, is to exacerbate the very differences that are invoked to justify the racially targeted practices in the first place. This in turn helps to cement the public's image, and the police's image, of the gun-toting gangster or drug dealer as black or Latino. And this confirms the validity of the police focus on youth of color, which then goes around and around in the same kind of vicious circle Piliavin and Briar described a generation ago.

The New Jersey attorney general's report on racial profiling by the state police provides some clear contemporary evidence of how this particularly insidious variety of circular reasoning works in practice. The New Jersey authorities discovered that the vast numbers of motorists subjected to traffic stops on the state's turnpikes were almost 60 percent white. A tiny minority of all stops—less than 1 percent—resulted in a vehicle search. But of those searched, "the overwhelming majority" (77 percent) were of minority motorists. Blacks in particular were 27 percent of those stopped but 53 percent of those searched and 62 percent of those subsequently arrested. In seeking to explain these disparities, the report notes that they probably result, in part, from "willful misconduct" on the part of a relatively few troopers, but much more often from "the tautological use of statistics to tacitly validate pre-existing stereotypes."[36] The state police, in other words, search the vehicles of blacks and Latinos on the grounds that they are more likely to be carrying drugs or weapons, as determined by who has already been arrested and imprisoned for those offenses. By largely confining these searches to blacks and Latinos, they ensure that most of the people arrested for transporting guns or drugs on the freeways are black or Latino. This, of course, further validates the disproportionate scrutiny of minority drivers. "To the extent that law enforcement agencies arrest minority motorists more frequently based on stereotypes," the report concludes, they continue to "generate statistics that confirm higher crime rates among minorities which, in turn, reinforces the underpinnings of the very stereotypes that gave rise to the initial arrests."[37]

The vicious circle of intensified surveillance, the generation of statistics that support stereotypical conceptions of race and offenses, and on to still more heightened surveillance has arguably worsened in recent years because of the increasing adoption of aggressive, often paramilitary police responses to drugs and gangs in the cities. These strategies escalated in the 1990s with such practices as antigang injunctions that allowed police to target youths labeled, often vaguely, as gang members if they so much as stop to talk with a friend on the street. These practices have surely ratcheted up the role of the police in shunting minority youth into the criminal justice system in disproportionate numbers. Elliott Currie's research in one California county widely known for its extensive *white* drug-using counterculture found that 93 percent of youth sent to juvenile court for the offense of "possession of narcotics or controlled substances for sale" in the 1990s were Latino.[38] Of youth and adults arrested in 1998 in California for the recently enacted offense of "participating in a street gang," only 13 percent were white and non-Latino; almost 67 percent were Latino alone.[39]

It is abundantly clear, then, that race still helps to determine who will enter the formal justice system in the first place and thus powerfully shapes what will happen thereafter. And what the research shows clearly is how persistent racial stereotyping meshes with the effect of long-term structural disadvantages to ensure that blacks wind up more often in the criminal justice system. A legacy of adverse structural conditions causes blacks to have higher rates of offenses to begin with. The higher rates of offenses are then used to justify decisions by police to monitor blacks more intensively and by courts to sentence them more severely. Their greater levels of incarceration contribute to difficulties in getting steady jobs and maintaining stable families, which increases their risks of offending, which . . . and so on, in a tragic downward spiral.

Racial conservatives fail to acknowledge the destructive effects of that cycle, in part because they do not acknowledge that there are structural reasons for high black crime rates—an issue to which we will now turn.

DISCONNECTING CRIME AND DISADVANTAGE

One of the most uncomfortable facts about race in America today is that intolerable levels of crime and violence wrack many black communities. And, as we have seen, no one now seriously doubts that this is what most leads to the overrepresentation of black Americans in the criminal justice system. But where do those high rates of crime come from? A recurrent theme in much conservative writing on race is that high black crime rates cannot be caused by racism or by the structural conditions like poverty and extreme inequality that disproportionally afflict blacks. Instead, conservatives argue, high rates of crime, like many other inner-city ills, are produced by some kind of cultural or behavioral deficiencies internal to much of the black community.

In a 1998 issue of the *American Enterprise* magazine devoted to "Fresh Thinking on Race in America," for example, Karl Zinsmeister sums up this view: "Dangerous streets," he argues, like the rest of "our urban underclass problems, [are] not caused by race. They are caused by dysfunctional families and personal behaviors." In *America in Black and White*, the Thernstroms provide the clearest statement of this conservative argument. They never provide a detailed alternative to the argument that high levels of ghetto violence have something to do with many generations of structural disadvantage. Rather, they suggest that, like other ills of the underclass, crime is a problem blacks have brought upon themselves—with, perhaps, the perverse help of the wrongheaded ideas of guilty white liberals and black demagogues. Ultimately, they suggest that, after all, crime is an individual failing, and one that, repeated over and over again, helps to doom the black underclass to economic stagnation.

This argument is never very clearly articulated, nor is it supported by carefully assembled social science evidence. It is usually presented mostly as unsupported assertions, sometimes backed by rather simplistic historical arguments about the trajectory of crime rates among black Americans. Dinesh D'Souza, for example, argues that there can be no significant connection between racism and high crime rates among blacks because racism has generally declined since the 1950s, while black crime rates have generally gone up. The Thernstroms, similarly, resurrect the shopworn argument (James Q. Wilson used it as far back as the 1960s) that crime cannot be connected to poverty (or unemployment) because crime fell during the depression, when millions of Americans descended into the ranks of the poor, and rose in the prosperous 1960s. That paradox (as Wilson used to put it) is offered as proof that the roots of crime are individual and cultural, not structural.[40]

The fallacy of the conservative argument is not their assertion that high rates of crime in some black communities reflect cultural or behavioral problems. That is true virtually by definition (indeed, the idea that crime is "caused" by "personal behavior" is essentially tautological; crime *is* personal behavior). The problem with this argument is that conservatives tend to detach cultural or behavioral troubles from the larger social context in which they are generated. The conservative position makes a sharp distinction between structural or systemic factors and cultural or behavioral ones. But the most compelling research shows that this distinction is simplistic and misleading.

Consider first the Thernstroms' argument that poverty and crime are not linked. Once again, they radically oversimplify what has been a subtle and complex discussion about the connections between crime and economic disadvantage. Criminologists have rarely argued that crime is caused simply by a lack of money. Instead, the bulk of criminological thought about the links between crime and poverty has run in one of two other directions, or sometimes in both.

The first is that crime is related more to relative than to absolute deprivation. Crime is most likely to grow, as in the so-called strain theories of social scientists like Robert Merton or Richard Cloward, when some people are doing very well while others, for a variety of reasons beyond their control, are left out of that prosperity. Thus, it is not very surprising that crime rose in the 1960s, when the economic fortunes of young unskilled men in the ghettos were plummeting relative to the fates of many other Americans, both white and black. A number of recent studies confirm this long-standing theoretical point. Gary LaFree and Kriss Drass of the University of New Mexico, for example, have shown that rising rates of violent crime among blacks since the 1950s were closely associated with the growth of economic inequality within the black population.[41] Studying a more recent period, Richard Fowles and Mary Merva of the University of Utah have demonstrated that rising rates of murder and assault in the 1980s closely track the growth of wage inequality among men during the same period.[42]

The second important line of criminological thought suggests that poverty and crime are closely linked, but the link is mainly indirect rather than direct. It involves the destructive impact of long-term deprivation and economic marginality on the stability and supportive capacity of institutions like families and local communities. This helps explain why crime could be worse among poor people in the 1960s than in the depression—and why crime among blacks could be worse today than in the 1950s, when there was more overt racism in America. Among other things, the black poor in the 1930s, especially migrants to the cities, had lost some of the supportive network of extended families and stable communities that sustained them, to some extent, in the face of the deep rural poverty of earlier decades. By the 1960s, that kind of social impoverishment had worked its cumulative ill effects on the lives of several generations of the urban black poor. Once again, social science evidence points to the powerful effects of a long-term process of disaccumulation that has shaped the current problems in inner-city communities, a process that conservatives seem not to comprehend.

This perspective also helps to explain the link between family disruption and crime, a link that conservative writers often invoke as an alternative to a more structural explanation. For many years criminologists have noted the impact family disruption has had in increasing the rate of crime in black communities. But a substantial body of research by Edward Shihadeh, Robert Sampson, Graham Ousey, and others confirms the unsurprising point that family disruption is itself often generated by structural forces, notably high levels of long-term joblessness.[43] Similarly, it is clear that, even more than to family structure, violent crime is also related to some problems of family *functioning*. But once again, economic insecurity and disadvantage strongly predict whether, and how badly, families will be afflicted by these problems. Severe child abuse and neglect, for example, is one of the most potent sources of later violent offending. The risk of severe abuse and neglect, however, is much greater in communities suffering from endemic joblessness and dire poverty.[44] Inadequate supervision of children by parents or other adults is also a fairly good predictor of delinquency. But poor supervision in turn is more likely when parents are forced into long hours of low-wage work to make ends meet and when few public or private community institutions are available to help take care of their children.[45]

The evidence for the relationship between crime and structural conditions, then, is both far stronger and far more sophisticated than conservatives suggest. The best criminological research on these issues makes it clear that the frequent conservative distinction between individual or cultural factors on the one hand and structural or economic ones on the other—between bad attitudes and externally imposed disadvantages as explanations of crime—is much too simplistic. This research confirms the fundamental sociological insight that the effects of social structure on people's behavior are cumulative and mutually reinforcing. These studies do not suggest that black people never behave badly—that is another straw person. They do tell us that bad behavior among black people, just as among white people, is more likely to occur when they are living under extremely adverse conditions, especially if they are caught in those conditions for generations. In short, subject people—white or black—to impoverished, limited, and stressful conditions for a long time, and they may begin to act in destructive or self-destructive ways. They may have trouble staying married, might beat their children or their wives, might use drugs heavily or drink too much, or might become depressed and find it difficult to cope or to parent well. Not all of them will respond in these ways, even under the worst social conditions. But the risks that some will are much greater. Over time, these responses may even crystallize and be passed on across the generations. It would be silly to deny that these things happen or that the risks of troubling behavior are very high in some black communities. Those risks, however, cannot be divorced from their roots in the corrosive impact of generations of hardship, segregation, community disinvestment, and restricted opportunities.

Again, it is not just a few pieces of recent research that make these links between deprivation (or joblessness) and crime. By now, most serious criminologists agree that these links are undeniable and enormously important. Acknowledging the complex and sometimes indirect quality of these connections does not diminish their importance. If anything, it is the opposite. Understanding that years of not having a job, and having no hope of getting one, may have the power to wreck one's personal relationships, for example, is powerful corroboration that economic forces can have a potent impact on personality and on human relationships.

The recent trajectory of crime rates in the United States, moreover, suggests that this process can be turned around: that the spiral of disadvantage, social exclusion, and violence can be reversed under more favorable economic conditions. Culture is real. But it is not set in stone. Rates of violence among black youth, for example, fell strongly after the early 1990s, in tandem with the long economic boom of the 1990s and the decline in unemployment and subemployment among the inner-city young. Research by Jared Bernstein and Ellen Houston of the Economic Policy Institute showed that crime among minority youth indeed fell fastest in those regions where opportunities for steady work for low-income young people grew the most. Just as there is powerful evidence that the loss of entry-level jobs through the 1980s helped drive violent crime rates higher, so there is now evidence that the extraordinary growth in new kinds of employment during the boom years helped to bring those rates down by pulling young men off the street corner and into the legitimate labor force.[46] There is no guarantee that these benign effects will endure: at this writing, violent crime rates have stabilized and in some places risen along with the economic downturn in the first years of the twenty-first century. They do, however, provide one more impressive indication of the capacity of structural forces to affect the behavior of people who are often described by conservatives as hopelessly mired in a "self-defeating culture."

There are other ways in which racial discrimination may affect the crime rate that, even though there is less research on them, clearly need mentioning. First is the impact of racially structured disinvestment in the public institutions that could intervene with people once they have a problem or begin to get in trouble. Discriminatory disinvestment in the public sector in minority communities—in such services as mental health care, child protection, or drug treatment—means that the kinds of problems that make people more vulnerable to crime and violence will be more widespread. It also means that people of color who are at risk will get less help. In other words, to the extent that public sector disinvestment is structured by race, the black youth with a potentially troublesome problem is going to have less chance of getting help than a white youth. The black child at risk of severe mistreatment by her parents is much less likely to get effective attention from stressed and underfunded child protective systems. The black mother suffering from chronic depression and unable to handle her kids is less likely to get help from the crumbling public mental health system than her white counterpart who can afford a good therapist. All of this substantially increases the chances that those children will become involved with delinquency and crime in a serious way.

Second, the discriminatory processes within the criminal justice system outlined above also contribute to the high crime levels in many black communities. That has probably always been true, but it is becoming increasingly so as the level of black incarceration has skyrocketed in recent years, utterly transforming poor black neighborhoods in the process.[47] Although it is not easy to quantify, there is little doubt that crime in the black community today has increasingly become an iatrogenic malady that reflects, in part, the destructive impact of mass incarceration on individual life chances, the family, and the local community. As Dina Rose and Todd Clear have shown, there is a point beyond which the removal of so many workers, parents, uncles, and other adults from the hardest-hit communities weakens their capacity to exert what sociologists call informal social control, thus countering any crime-reducing effect of high rates of imprisonment.[48] The enormous rise in incarceration has blocked a good part of several generations of black men from attaining steady work and has accordingly hindered the formation of stable families and increased the attraction of illegal ways to make a living.[49] The sociologist Bruce Western has found that the experience of incarceration as a juvenile reduces employment by about 9 percent among black youth. Being incarcerated as a juvenile is even more detrimental to black youths' future employment prospects than is dropping out of high school.[50] The still-faster rise in the incarceration of black women has fractured families even more and left large numbers of children effectively without parents.

The growth of Draconian ancillary punishments for drug offenses in particular, like losing public assistance benefits and housing subsidies for life, has deepened the economic subordination and social impoverishment experienced by great numbers of black Americans. Voting restrictions for ex-felons have disenfranchised many others, rendering them less able to challenge adverse social and economic conditions through legitimate political action. An estimated 13 percent of adult black men are disenfranchised under these provisions. In ten states, as of the late 1990s, the number was more than 20 percent, and in Alabama and Florida 31 percent of all black men had permanently lost the right to vote.[51] Over the long run, all of these adversities contribute to high crime in black communities across the United States, and, barring changes in American criminal justice practices, will probably do so increasingly in the future.

More generally, there is a crucial sense in which the increasingly repressive responses to inner-city crime and drug abuse have been the flip side of the cumulative disinvestment in more positive strategies to reconstruct poor communities. Especially in these fiscally conservative times when there is limited scope for public investment, the diversion of billions of scarce public dollars to prisons and jails means that there will be that much less money available for child protection, dropout prevention programs, public colleges accessible to low-income young people, and a host of other public institutions that could operate as the front line in preventing crime. Since the early 1980s, the already meager and declining public investment in the social infrastructure of poor communities of color has been further eroded by the diversion of billions of dollars in scarce public spending to prisons and jails. Thus the incarceration boom has helped, in a truly vicious cycle, to aggravate the steady depletion of public and social capital available in communities already disabled by a heritage of poverty and segregation and abandoned by several decades of deindustrialization. It is not accidental that the 1980s and 1990s were decades of both crumbling schools and bulging prisons (from the mid-1980s to the late 1990s, the state of California built twenty-two prisons and one college). Americans are now paying a steep price for that choice of priorities—in high rates of violence as well as of illiteracy, preventable disease, drug abuse, and other ills. And a sustained economic downturn could intensify that destructive tradeoff.

RACE, CRIME, AND DISACCUMULATION: IDEOLOGY AND THE POLITICS OF SOCIAL POLICY

The conservative argument, then, distorts the reality of the black experience with crime and punishment in two ways, both of which impede our understanding of the causes of social troubles in the black community and hinder efforts to develop effective strategies to do something about them.

First, conservatives have diverted attention from the more subtle and complex, yet nevertheless quite destructive, problem of continuing racism in the institutions of justice. They have accomplished this by mischaracterizing the liberal view as one that sees the overrepresentation of blacks in the criminal justice system as *only* a reflection of racist police, prosecutors, and judges. This enables them to ignore a pervasive set of interlocking processes that not only help to explain the black predominance in the jails and prisons but also put all too many black Americans on a downward trajectory in every other realm of social life. For while there is a sense in which it is true that crime causes poverty, as conservatives often argue, it is also true that *imprisonment* causes poverty—indeed the whole host of difficulties such as joblessness or family problems that conservatives and racial realists often dismiss as behavioral ones. Discrimination in the justice system is not the only source of the crippling overrepresentation of black Americans in the prisons and jails. But it remains an important one, and one whose impact on black communities is pervasive and fateful.

Second, the conservative move to deny the links between black crime and black economic and social disadvantage flies in the face of decades of criminological research. It therefore leaves Americans without meaningful guidance on how, realistically, to combat the violence and drug abuse that continue to devastate poor communities of whatever color. Disconnecting these very genuine problems from their structural roots enables conservative ideologists to salvage their central idea that black problems in post–Jim Crow America simply reflect behavioral or cultural deficiencies and have little or no connection with discrimination, past or present. Thus the denial contributes to the belief that well-intentioned intervention by government is unlikely to help, and might hinder, black advancement. That argument cannot, however, stand even modest scrutiny. The evidence is overwhelming that high rates of crime and violence are one of the costs of a legacy of discrimination and of systematic disinvestment in black communities. And it suggests that Americans will not make enduring strides to minimize crime among African Americans unless and until that legacy is confronted more seriously and creatively than has been done so far.

Civil Rights and Racial Equality

Employment Discrimination Law, Affirmative Action, and Quotas

For conservatives, affirmative action and other color-conscious policies betray the original goals of the Civil Rights Act and the Voting Rights Act. The promise of a color-blind society was perverted, as they see it, by a succession of liberal political elites and civil rights activists who demanded race-conscious remedies, and by Supreme Court decisions that distorted the original legislation. School busing, affirmative action in employment and college admissions, and the creation of black or Latino majority legislative districts, conservatives argue, are the result of judicial fiat. All these policies were, therefore, imposed undemocratically, and it is no wonder that they are deeply resented.

The way conservatives and other critics tell it, the recent history of civil rights law is a story about how a color-blind policy of antidiscrimination was transformed into a policy of compensatory justice.[1] Initially, Congress and the courts responded to the evils of Jim Crow—segregated schools, denial of voting rights, and employment discrimination—with measured policies. These policies were narrowly crafted to outlaw intentional discrimination and replace public racial classifications with color-blind laws. But under pressure from civil rights activists, goes the narrative, federal agencies charged with implementing the new laws moved to broaden the scope and impact of the policies, transforming the law in the process. The Supreme Court then ratified the new interpretation and legitimized the new doctrine of racial justice. Whether one is talking about school desegregation, employment discrimination law, or voting rights, the result is the same: the policy shifts from outlawing racial classifications or prohibiting intentional discrimination to legalizing race-conscious policies.

Conservatives (and some racial realists) seem intent to portray the recent history of civil rights law as a fall from grace, a descent from a color-blind Garden of Eden to a sinful state of color consciousness. There is no question that the Supreme Court's interpretation of the Civil Rights Act, the Voting Rights Act, and its ruling in *Brown v. Board of Education* (1954) evolved in response to black demands for racial justice and white resistance in the 1960s. But to explain these changes as betraying clearly stated color-blind policy misleads.

Consider school desegregation. The Thernstroms, among others, argue that *Brown v. Board of Education* required school districts to use only race-neutral criteria when assigning children to school districts. Until the Supreme Court said otherwise in *Green v. School Board of New Kent County* (1968), they argue, national school desegregation policy was color-blind and did not mandate racial integration.[2] The notion that *Brown* required only desegregation is not found in the Supreme Court's decision. Instead, it comes from a district court ruling, *Briggs v. Elliot* (1955), which held that the "Constitution . . . does not require integration. It merely forbids discrimination. It does not forbid such discrimination as occurs as the result of voluntary action."[3]

The author of the opinion was Judge John Parker, a South Carolinian appointed to the appeals court by Herbert Hoover. Parker was described by one of his colleagues as "an extremely able judge who knows the law, and follows the law, but quite unwillingly, in the Southern country."[4] As Richard Kluger points out in his authoritative study of *Brown*, southern courts used the "Parker Doctrine" to "approve a variety of maneuvers designed to deflect the impact of *Brown* in those states and school districts that did not turn to outright defiance of the Court."[5] When the Supreme Court took up the issue of school desegregation in *Green*, it was mainly in response to southern school districts that were using so-called freedom of choice plans to subvert desegregation. Justice Brennan's opinion in *Green*, that "racially identifiable schools were a vestige of segregation and must be eliminated," is fully consistent with the Court's goal in *Brown* for a "transition to a racially nondiscriminatory school system."

The conservative reading of *Green* is a flawed interpretation of the development of civil rights law. It misreads the key court decisions and exaggerates their consequences. And it depends upon a particular view of the ends and underlying principles of antidiscrimination law. The conservatives' view that the Court's decision in *Green* and other cases was an ominous "doctrinal shift that had large and worrisome implications" is based on the belief that civil rights laws only have the narrow purpose of eradicating racial classifications, while restricting remedies to *specific* acts of intentional discrimination.[6] This interpretation can be traced to the assumption that the primary evil of Jim Crow was using state power to racially classify individuals, and outside of striking down such laws, society has no other obligation. Critics of color-conscious policies take their inspiration from Justice John Harlan's famous dissent in *Plessy v. Ferguson* (1896), which said that "Our constitution is color-blind, and neither knows nor tolerates classes among citizens." The conservatives' version of legal changes during the civil rights era presumes that Congress and the courts could choose only between racial classifications and the color-blind ideal. Any other construction of the law represented an unwarranted expansion of governmental power.

This is a gross oversimplification of the tumultuous history of civil rights legislation from *Brown* to the assassination of Dr. Martin Luther King Jr. More important, the idea that Jim Crow was evil because it distinguished among individuals on the basis of race trivializes an early and harsh form of apartheid. The defining feature of Jim Crow was the subordination and oppression of African Americans, the conscious use of political and economic power to impose upon them the badge of inferiority and to establish white supremacy. Racial classifications were not incidental, simply a way for whites to avoid unpleasant contacts, as the Supreme Court wrote in *Plessy*. To the contrary, de jure segregation was instrumental in creating and maintaining a deeply rooted system of pervasive white privilege that extended to the North. Whites in both regions of the country maintained these privileges by law, by conscious acts of discrimination, and by racial violence. As this book has documented repeatedly, racial inequality is not limited to overt acts of discrimination. Rather, it depends on facially neutral institutional practices and public policies and on the historical legacy of white accumulation and black disaccumulation.[7]

Conservatives incorrectly assume that the civil rights laws were confined to abolishing racial classifications and that the meaning of discrimination was limited to bigoted behavior. The development of civil rights law did not betray a color-blind principle. It was an effort to remedy the deeply rooted complexities of white racism. In this chapter and the next we examine the conservative critique of civil rights laws: in this chapter we focus on employment discrimination law; in chapter 6, on the Voting Rights Act of 1965.

THE CONSERVATIVE CRITIQUE OF EMPLOYMENT DISCRIMINATION LAW

One of the chief objectives of the early civil rights movement was to enact an employment discrimination law. The campaign to end job discrimination actually began in 1941 when A. Philip Randolph threatened to stage a massive demonstration in Washington, D.C., to protest discrimination in war industries. To avoid this potentially embarrassing event, President Franklin D. Roosevelt created the Fair Employment Practices Commission (FEPC), and in the 1950s and early 1960s many states followed suit. The struggle to create a national employment discrimination law culminated with the passage of the 1964 Civil Rights Act, which includes, in Title VII, a ban on racial discrimination by employers.

At the time, conservatives strongly opposed any federal law prohibiting private employers from discriminating. Robert Bork, for example, dismissed the notion that government could prohibit private discrimination as "unsurpassed ugliness."[8] Many conservatives continue to regard the idea of such a law suspiciously. Richard Epstein, an ardent critic of employment discrimination laws, has called for the repeal of Title VII, and Clint Bolick, the influential chief counsel of the Institute for Justice, a conservative Washington, D.C., public interest law firm and think tank, believes that the statute violates employers' constitutional freedom of contract.[9] Others, including the Thernstroms, claim to support a ban on intentional employment discrimination but argue that Title VII goes too far because it regulates unintentional discrimination as well.

Conservatives vehemently criticize the first Supreme Court decision to interpret Title VII, *Griggs v. Duke Power*. Epstein calls it a "travesty of statutory interpretation," while the Thernstroms see it as prima facie evidence of judicial usurpation and liberal intentions run amok. *Griggs,* they write, was an "audacious rewriting" of the law that altered it "beyond recognition."[10] The case is taken by conservatives to represent a remarkable shift from a narrowly framed law that banned only intentional acts of discrimination—different treatment of equally qualified individuals—to a law that requires "racial balancing" in the workplace and forces employers to use racial quotas. In this view, *Griggs* opened the door to affirmative action policies and proportional representation in the workplace.

Griggs v. Duke Power posed the question of whether requiring workers to possess a high school diploma or pass an aptitude test in order to be hired or promoted was discrimination when substantially more black workers than whites were disqualified as a result. The Court held that high school graduation and test requirements constituted unintentional discrimination and violated Title VII unless the employer could prove that the policies were job related and necessary to the operation of the business.[11] Conservatives level two criticisms against this decision. First, they argue the Court wrongly overturned Congress' clear decision to limit Title VII to "intentional discrimination."[12] Second, *Griggs* induces reverse discrimination. Because the Court expanded Title VII to cover "unintentional discrimination," which would be measured by statistical imbalances in a firm's workforce, conservatives argued that employers would be forced to use racial quotas and discriminate against whites to avoid being sued.[13] A southern critic of the law, Senator Absalom Robertson (D-Va.), first voiced what became a key conservative criticism of *Griggs*. Robertson said that the law as written "means that a man could be required to have a quota or he would be discriminating."[14] Echoing Robertson, the Thernstroms contend the Court's decision has rendered intentional discrimination cases a "rare bird." Congress compounded the problem in the 1991 Civil Rights Act, they add, by permitting victims of intentional discrimination to sue for damages. This too, the Thernstroms claim, forces employers to "hire by quota."[15]

This account of employment discrimination law and affirmative action rests on a series of false premises as well as misinterpretations of *Griggs* and other Supreme Court decisions. Instead of being a "travesty of interpretation," the Court acted properly when it decided that the Civil Rights Act prohibited certain forms of unintentional discrimination. Moreover, conservatives exaggerate *Griggs*'s impact in order to taint all employment discrimination law. In fact, the courts have applied the *Griggs* principle narrowly. Most employment discrimination cases allege intentional discrimination, the kind of discrimination that many conservatives, including Bolick and the Thernstroms, claim to oppose. Unintentional discrimination cases, not cases of intentional discrimination, have become the "rare bird." Although employers may reasonably fear wrongful firing suits brought by both older white men and racial minorities, they have little reason to worry about hiring suits brought by rejected black job applicants.

Conservatives are interested in more than just removing unintentional discrimination from the government's civil rights arsenal. Underlying their criticisms of *Griggs* and affirmative action is an attack on virtually all employment discrimination law. Conservatives assume that any employment discrimination law will threaten the presumption of color-blindness. The Thernstroms, for example, argue that the victims of intentional discrimination should be denied the right to sue for damages because these suits encourage employers to discriminate against whites and hire by quota. In their view, even laws against intentional discrimination are harmful, a judgment they share with other conservative opponents of civil rights laws like Richard Epstein and Clint Bolick. Epstein argues that enforcing laws against intentional discrimination is very costly and that the laws, like any other form of regulation, leave employers and employees "worse off with the regulation than they were in its absence."[16]

If adopted, the conservative civil rights agenda would eliminate all legal remedies for victims of on-the-job discrimination, whether it was intentional or not. Conservatives would shed no tears, however, because they believe that employment discrimination laws are unnecessary. They assume that racial discrimination is irrational in a competitive economy and that once state-imposed racial classifications like Jim Crow are struck down, the market, left to its own devices, will minimize discrimination. In fact, most conservatives, as we have pointed out, think that labor market discrimination is a thing of the past and that any remaining racial differences in earnings are the result of differences in job skills and ability. As we explained earlier, that argument is unconvincing. We will demonstrate in the following pages that, contrary to conservative assertions, the *Griggs* case has not led to widespread quota hiring or discrimination against whites. In fact, employment discrimination law and affirmative action have been vital to black economic advancement.

UNDERSTANDING AND MISUNDERSTANDING *GRIGGS V. DUKE POWER*

Critics of *Griggs v. Duke Power* claim the Supreme Court ignored the text of the law and evaded the intent of Congress when it held that Title VII prohibited unintentional discrimination under some circumstances. Congress, they argue, clearly intended to prohibit only intentional discrimination. The Court's ruling in *Griggs*, Gary Bryner writes, "conflicts with the working and legislative history of Title VII. . . . The Court seems to be primarily concerned with consistency in discrimination cases rather than adherence to legislative intent."[17]

To understand the *Griggs* decision, and the conservative misinterpretation of it, one must look at the actual language of the statute. Title VII prohibits two kinds of conduct: simple discrimination in hiring, firing, and so forth, and classification of employees in a way that disadvantages them based on race or other protected categories. The statute states that it is unlawful for an employer

1. To fail or refuse to hire or to discharge any individual, or otherwise to discriminate against any individual with respect to his compensation, terms, conditions, or privileges of employment, because of such individual's race, color, religion, sex, or national origin; or

2. To limit, segregate, or classify his employees or applicants for employment in any way which would deprive or tend to deprive any individual of employment opportunities or otherwise adversely affect his status as an employee, because of such individual's race, color, religion, sex, or national origin.[18]

The law also prohibited labor unions from excluding or expelling from their membership, or discriminating against, "any individual because of his race, color, religion, sex, or national origin."[19]

Labor market discrimination, as we have pointed out, is not always intentional and obvious; it can be passive and unobtrusive. Three important examples of employer policies and practices, two of which figured in *Griggs*, illustrate what is meant by unintentional discrimination. The first is nepotism. In the 1960s, many employers gave preferences to relatives of their employees. Some employers actually required referrals from current employees for job applicants, and numerous unions limited membership to the families of employees. Since many jobs and membership in many unions had been reserved exclusively (and at least until the 1940s legally) for whites, these nepotism policies institutionalized the racial status quo. While these policies could have been adopted purposely to exclude nonwhites (which would make them an act of intentional discrimination), there were rational, neutral, and nonobjectionable reasons for employers and unions to practice nepotism. But regardless of the employers' and unions' motives, many fully qualified blacks were excluded from union membership and work. If this kind of unintentional discrimination was lawful, antidiscrimination laws could not eliminate barriers facing qualified black job seekers, which was a clear objective of the law.

Second, many employers required educational achievements unrelated to the skills necessary for job performance.[20] Blacks were disproportionately excluded from many jobs because whites, on average, completed more school than they did. For example, in a community where numerous whites but few blacks graduated from high school, requiring that all applicants for laborer positions hold high school diplomas would exclude potential black workers, even though these black workers might be as capable of performing the jobs as white high school graduates. Although segregation, discriminatory school funding, and other government policies typically denied blacks a high school diploma, the requirement of a diploma could have been adopted for racially neutral reasons rather than to intentionally exclude blacks. But regardless of the reason, blacks would have been excluded.

Third, in the postwar period a large number of employers began to use intelligence tests or aptitude tests to select workers. Like high school diplomas, these tests were often unrelated to actual job performance and could not predict who would be a good worker. And like the requirements for high school diplomas, there was a significant racial disparity in the test scores of job applicants. White applicants scored substantially higher than black applicants did, even though the test's predictive value was highly suspect.[21] Like high school degree requirements and nepotism policies, these tests could be used either as a subterfuge for intentional racial discrimination or adopted for reasons that were unrelated to race. The result, however, would be the same: blacks were not hired.

The problem the Court faced in *Griggs* was that if any degree requirement or test used was lawful, blacks would be unintentionally excluded and the antidiscrimination laws would be unable to address a significant problem facing qualified black job seekers. In fact, even before the *Griggs* decision, some employers were reevaluating their degree requirements and testing policies because they were concerned that these practices might be an unwarranted obstacle to employment of blacks.[22]

Employers and legislators had good reason to be concerned about these practices. By 1966, few African American blue-collar workers had broken into the ranks of the skilled crafts, which were the highest-paid blue-collar jobs. In the auto industry, for example, blacks constituted 22 percent of all laborers but only 3 percent of the skilled crafts workers. This was also true in the steel industry, where there were virtually no black trades workers or apprentices; the rubber and tire industry (where 1.5 percent of skilled crafts workers were black); and the aerospace industry (where 5.4 percent of skilled crafts workers were black). A major impediment to bringing more black workers into apprenticeship programs was their lower scores on company-administered math tests.[23] Intentional discrimination accounted for part of these discrepancies, but high school diploma and test score requirements also played a significant role in creating the imbalance.[24] Union opposition to black membership was another important reason for exclusion.[25] Although many of these policies and practices were created without discriminatory intent, they resulted in systemic barriers that prevented black workers from job advancement. In other words, these seemingly neutral policies and practices were classifications that "would deprive or tend to deprive individual[s] of employment opportunities or otherwise adversely affect [their] status as an employee."[26]

The *Griggs* case directly addressed two of these problems: testing and education barriers. Thirteen black employees of the Duke Power Company brought the case. Prior to the Civil Rights Act, blacks were permitted to work only in the lowest-paying department in one of the company's power plants. The company changed its policy on July 2, 1965, the day the act took effect. The new policy allowed black employees to transfer into higher-paying departments if they held a high school diploma or could score average or above on two "general intelligence tests." New employees were required to pass the tests and hold a high school diploma. The lower courts found that the tests and diploma requirements disqualified a "markedly disproportionate number" of blacks.[27] But the courts also ruled that the requirements were not adopted for a discriminatory purpose. The Supreme Court held that the question of intent was not dispositive. If the diploma requirement and the test had an exclusionary effect, and if the employer could not show they were job related and necessary to its business, they were discriminatory.

Conservatives contend that in this decision the Court usurped Congress' power and redefined the scope and meaning of Title VII. There are several reasons why they are mistaken. Some critics insist the law explicitly outlawed only intentional discrimination. As evidence, they point to an amendment to the law proposed by Senator Everett B. Dirksen (R-Ill.). Dirksen's amendment inserted language into the law that limited the power of courts to order remedies by requiring a finding "that the respondent has intentionally engaged in or is intentionally engaging in an unlawful employment practice."[28] Hugh Davis Graham charges the Court with interpreting the "Dirksen amendment on intent into meaninglessness."[29]

This is a dubious criticism. Dirksen said his amendment would prevent charges of discrimination when an employer's acts were "accidental, inadvertent, heedless, unintended," an opinion echoed by Hubert Humphrey (D-Minn.), who said the amendment was a "clarifying change" that did not involve "any substantive change in the title."[30] The issue in *Griggs* is not whether the employer intends to violate the law but whether the employer intends to commit an unlawful employment practice. The Dirksen amendment makes it clear that for an employer's acts to constitute an unlawful employment practice, they must be intentional acts, not accidents. Thus, a black employee who received a termination notice by mistake could not sue for discrimination.[31] The definition of unlawful employment practice, and thus the language defining discrimination, is found in an entirely different part of the statute, Section 703, not Section 706.

In drafting Section 703, Congress was undoubtedly aware that the question of whether unintentional discrimination would be considered an unlawful employment practice would be raised. By the time Congress took up the civil rights bill, state courts had already begun to consider whether unintentional discrimination was a form of illegal discrimination. Yet other than require that any discriminatory act must be knowingly committed, Congress did not explicitly require proof of intent to prove discrimination, except when seniority and merit systems were challenged. Otherwise, the act is silent on the question of whether discrimination must be intentional to be illegal.[32]

The primary question the Court had to decide in *Griggs* was what Congress meant by the term *discrimination*. There was virtually no discussion of the meaning of the word *discrimination* in congressional debates nor was it defined in the statute. The record does indicate, however, that Congress intended to use existing state discrimination laws to define the term.[33] What the term *discrimination* meant under state law in 1964 is therefore useful in determining what it means under Title VII. By the spring of 1964, many states had begun to include unintentional discrimination within the definition of discrimination.[34]

Significantly, just prior to the passage of the 1964 act, state fair employment commissions in New York and Illinois ruled discrimination was not limited to intentional discrimination. In both employment discrimination cases, the New York and Illinois FEPCs held that discrimination resulting from a race-neutral policy was illegal. Both cases were important and well publicized, and the Illinois case figured prominently in the Senate debate of Title VII. Moreover, at the moment the Senate was debating the Civil Rights Act, the decision in the New York case was handed down and reported as a major legal development. In that case, the Commission for Human Rights ruled that a union's nepotism policy discriminated against black apprenticeship applicants because all of the union's members were white.[35] Although the commission found that the policy was motivated by racial animus, it ruled the policy was discriminatory even if there were no intent to discriminate because it disproportionately excluded black workers. The case attracted widespread attention. It was the subject of front-page stories in the *New York Times* on March 5, 1964, and again on March 24, 1964.[36] On the twenty-fourth, the Senate was in session, listening to southern senators filibuster the Civil Rights Act.[37]

The Illinois case concerned a black applicant at Motorola who applied for a job for which he was qualified but for which he had failed to pass a preemployment "general intelligence test." He filed a complaint with the Illinois Fair Employment Commission, which ruled that any test that disproportionately excluded blacks was discriminatory, regardless of intent or whether it measured job qualifications. Since the Motorola Company's standardized test had a disproportionate impact on blacks, it violated the Illinois fair employment law.[38] The rule announced by the commission was unyielding, providing no exception for tests or other selection devices necessary for the operation of business.

Thus, when Congress debated the Civil Rights Act there was already considerable legal support for the proposition that unintentional discrimination was an unlawful employment practice. Moreover, Congress explicitly provided in Title VII that under certain limited circumstances, proof of intent is required. Section 703(h) of the act states:

> It shall not be an unlawful employment practice for an employer to apply different standards of compensation, or different terms, conditions or privileges of employment pursuant to a bona fide seniority or merit system, or a system which measures earnings by quantity or quality of production or to employees who work in different locations, provided that such differences are not the result of an intention to discriminate because of race, color, religion, sex, or national origin, nor shall it be an unlawful employment practice for an employer to give and to act upon the results of any professionally developed ability test provided that such test, its administration or action upon the results is not designed, intended, or used to discriminate because of race, color, religion, sex, or national origin.[39]

The inclusion of this section indicates that the drafters of the law were aware that Title VII could be interpreted to prohibit unintentional discrimination. Otherwise, they would not have required proof of intent in certain limited kinds of cases. The drafters obviously felt they needed to explicitly provide a requirement of intent where they wanted one imposed, and they knew how to do so.

A close examination of the Senate debates confirms this interpretation. The *Motorola* decision provoked a vigorous debate in the Senate and resulted in language permitting testing in some circumstances.

Opponents of Title VII—mainly southern Democrats and western and plains states Republicans—argued that since the *Motorola* decision would apply nationally, passing any employment discrimination law would eliminate all employment testing. When the bill's floor managers, Senators Clifford Case (R-N.J.) and Joseph Clark (D-Pa.), insisted the bill would not affect tests that measured legitimate job qualifications, Senator John Tower (R-Tex.) responded with an amendment that allowed businesses to use professionally developed ability tests. This amendment was defeated by a coalition of northern Democrats and northeastern Republicans, who worried that its language could be interpreted to allow these tests under all circumstances. Senator Case told his colleagues, "If this amendment were enacted, it could be an absolute bar and would give an absolute right to an employer to state as a fact that he had given a test to all applicants, whether it was a good test or not, so long as it was professionally designed. Discrimination could actually exist under the guise of the statute."[40] Tower then came up with a compromise amendment, one that permitted professionally developed ability tests so long as they were not "designed, intended or used to discriminate." The revised amendment easily passed the Senate after Hubert Humphrey (D-Minn.) said that he and others found the new language "to be in accord with the intent and purpose of the [legislation]."[41]

Although Section 703(h) protects professionally developed tests—as well as seniority, merit, and productivity systems unless they are designed, intended, or used to discriminate—it does not offer similar protection for other requirements of employment such as high school diplomas (as required by the Duke Power Company) or nepotism systems (like the union membership rule the New York Commission for Human Rights found to be discriminatory). The section simply does not cover such systems. Thus, these arrangements violate Title VII if they are found to "deprive any individual of employment opportunities . . . because of such individual's race."[42]

When the *Griggs* case reached the Supreme Court, the Court looked at the language of the statute and the debates in the Senate to determine whether Congress intended to prohibit only intentional discrimination. The Court found no such limitation and ruled that the high school diploma requirement was clearly discriminatory if it was not job related. The justices' decision focused on aptitude tests because, although Congress had done nothing to exempt discriminatory educational requirements from the act, it had provided an exemption for certain professionally developed tests.

In deciding whether a professionally designed test adopted by an employer violated the law, the Court considered four possible approaches. First, it could hold that the test violated Title VII per se because it had a discriminatory effect. This was the Illinois rule, set forth in the *Motorola* case. Second, it could hold that a professionally developed test was always permitted under Title VII. This is the rule proposed by Senator Tower in the initial version of 703(h) but rejected by the Senate. Third, it could hold that a professionally developed test was permitted under 703(h) unless it was adopted for a discriminatory purpose. This is the interpretation of Epstein and the Thernstroms. Fourth, it could hold that a professionally developed test was permitted under 703(h) so long as it was both necessary and bona fide—the test must actually measure criteria related to job performance. This is the position the Court adopted.

Except for seniority, the Court concluded that unless an employer could show a practice was job related and necessary to the operation of business, a practice or policy that unintentionally produced discrimination violated Title VII.[43] Claiming that the *Griggs* decision "perverted both the language and legislative history of the act," Richard Epstein insists the Court "overstated the intention of the statute by insisting that it was designed to allow all persons to compete equally in the workplace regardless of differences in their prior training." Epstein and other critics construe the purposes of Title VII narrowly, arguing that it forbids only bigoted acts and otherwise "lets the chips fall where they may." According to Epstein, tests are illegal only if they were "designed, intended or used to discriminate." He argues the word "used" must mean "intentionally used."[44] Another critic of the decision, Herman Belz, bases his argument on the premise that proof of intentional discrimination was required under state laws before Title VII.[45]

Belz is simply wrong in claiming that state law required proof that discrimination was intentional. The Illinois *Motorola* case rejected an intent requirement, prompting the Senate debate on unintentional discrimination that led to the adoption of Section 703(h). Unlike Belz, Epstein does recognize that Section 703(h) was placed in Title VII in response to the *Motorola* case. In a dubious reading of legislative history, however, he argues that the section, which protects "bona fide qualification tests," protects any test used in good faith even if it does not actually test "bona fide qualifications."[46] Epstein also insists that the Court "does not choose to mention, let alone discuss, the controversial Motorola incident, which prompted the specific statutory language of

703(h)."[47] Epstein is just plain wrong about this. The Court explicitly addressed the *Motorola* case in a footnote, pointing out that "the decision was taken to mean that such tests could never be justified even if the needs of the business required them. A number of Senators feared that Title VII might produce a similar result."[48] The Court's understanding was that tests were specifically permitted by the law but, given the debate over the amendment, only in those cases where they were justified by business necessity. Although critics claim that the words "business necessity" appear nowhere in the law or in the legislative debates, Senator Case's objection to the first version of the Tower amendment clearly indicates that the majority was aware that allowing the use of any test an employer might select would be discriminatory.

Conservative critics of *Griggs* also ignore the New York nepotism case *Lefkowitz v. Farrell*.[49] The principle announced in this case established that nepotism by all-white organizations like unions and apprenticeship committees is a form of illegal employment discrimination. This, of course, is the very principle professed by the Supreme Court in *Griggs*. In the 1960s, many jobs controlled by unions or employee associations (skilled crafts and construction jobs as well as police, firefighter, and other civil service jobs) were often exclusively white. As the Farrell decision recognized, racial animus was not necessary to retain racial homogeneity in these workplaces. All that was required was a race-neutral policy that preferred the family, or family and friends, of employees. To argue, as do Belz, Epstein, and the Thernstroms, that Title VII was intended only to prohibit intentional discrimination, is to argue that it was not expected to confront problems like nepotism in all-white jobs.[50] This is not a plausible interpretation of the act. Critics of *Griggs* ignore the language of the law that prohibits employers from limiting, segregating, or classifying employees because of their race.

If critics of *Griggs* are correct that Congress had intended to prohibit only intentional discrimination, one could have expected Congress to repudiate the *Griggs* decision. It had the opportunity in 1972 when Title VII was extended to include public employment.[51] Not only did Congress refuse to change the language of Section 703(h) or the *Griggs* decision, it gave the Equal Employment Opportunity Commission (EEOC) the authority to bring lawsuits for violations of the act. Congress had refused to give the EEOC such power when it initially passed the act.

In 1989, however, a much more conservative Supreme Court reaffirmed one portion of *Griggs* while reversing another part.[52] The Court held that tests and other neutral policies that caused a discriminatory effect did violate Title VII. Thus it affirmed the essence of *Griggs*. But the Court also shifted the burden of proof to the plaintiffs and lowered the standard that businesses needed to meet in order to use a test. The Court discarded the "business necessity" standard and said that an employer could defend the choice of tests or policies if it could prove they were job related. As the Court put it, if the employer could show there was a "legitimate business reason" for its test or other selection device, it met the criteria required by Title VII.[53]

Congress responded swiftly by passing a Civil Rights Restoration Act that fully restored the standard of business necessity established in *Griggs*. When President Bush vetoed it, Congress refused to back down and passed a new Civil Rights Restoration Act that was more moderate in some respects but that retained the *Griggs* business necessity standard.[54] This time President Bush signed the law. Congress' consistent refusal to overturn or dilute the *Griggs* principle plainly undercuts the assertion by Epstein, the Thernstroms, and other critics that the Court ignored congressional intent.

Critics often say the Court's decision was radical. But that description does not square with the group of justices who decided *Griggs*. They were an ideologically balanced group of cautious moderates. At the time, the Court was divided equally among Democrats and Republicans, and nearly equally among conservatives, moderates, and liberals.[55] Even Justice Harlan, who was profoundly conservative in civil rights cases and known to "urge his colleagues to refrain from extending any group or cause special protection simply out of a well-meaning but shortsighted desire to do 'justice,'" joined the majority.[56] It therefore strains credulity to argue, as conservatives do, that this cautious and moderate group of justices unanimously adopted a radical interpretation of the Civil Rights Act.

Far from being radical, the Court's decision that the act prohibited both unintentional discrimination and intentional discrimination has deep roots in legal history. Since the early nineteenth century, Anglo-American courts in the field of tort law (personal injury law), have held that people are legally responsible for negligently caused injuries regardless of their intent.[57] The *Griggs* case extended this long-standing principle to discrimination law. In doing so, the *Griggs* case engaged an important problem Congress faced in 1964: even in the absence of racial hatred, bigotry, or intentional discrimination, business as usual frequently excluded black Americans from the workplace. The *Griggs* decision, like the statute it applies and interprets, was a necessary response to systemic, if unintended, racial discrimination.

Critics insist that *Griggs* is the first in a long line of cases that establish equality of results as the underlying standard of civil rights law. In this view, the Court mandated racial balancing in the workplace and endorsed preferential hiring to overcome statistical discrepancies between black and white workers in a particular firm. To say that *Griggs* mandates equality of results is a gross exaggeration. Nowhere in the opinion does the Supreme Court say the law requires preferential hiring or that statistical discrepancies in the racial composition of the workforce would justify preferential hiring.[58] Nor does it endorse, even implicitly, equality of results. The decision prescribes no particular set of results; it simply says that the use of tests must be justified. "Congress has not commanded," the Court said, "that the less qualified be preferred over the better qualified simply because of minority origins."

What one can say about the Court's decision is that it is based on a broad conception of equality of opportunity. The Court understood what its critics do not: Congress was concerned not just with discrete acts of discrimination but with barriers to economic opportunity. Indeed, the Court's opinion underscores a central argument of this book: racism need not be intentional. We could hardly state it better than the justices did in their opinion: "Good intent or absence of discriminatory intent does not redeem employment procedures or testing mechanisms that operate as 'built-in headwinds' for minority groups."

The final word on whether the *Griggs* decision was intemperate, unjustified, or an "audacious rewriting" will not be established by arguments between legal historians and polemicists alone. Rather, it can be found in the Court's own words (see sidebar).

THE IMPACT OF *GRIGGS*: CONSERVATIVE ILLUSIONS AND LEGAL REALITIES

For conservatives, *Griggs* is the harbinger of racial quotas and affirmative action. They argue that "disparate impact" cases (as cases based on *Griggs* are often called) dominate the field of employment discrimination law, while intentional discrimination (or "disparate treatment") cases have all but disappeared.[59] And they argue that *Griggs* induces employers to use racial quotas or discriminate against whites to avoid being sued. Conservatives are wrong on both counts.

The irony of *Griggs*, which conservative critics completely ignore, is that disparate impact cases are so expensive to bring that they are rarely filed. Such cases require an army of expert witnesses—including statisticians, psychologists, and economists—and can be funded only by the

GRIGGS ET AL. V. DUKE POWER COMPANY
Mr. Chief Justice Burger delivered the opinion of the Court.

The objective of Congress in the enactment of Title VII is plain from the language of the statute. It was to achieve equality of employment opportunities and remove barriers that have operated in the past to favor an identifiable group of white employees over other employees. Under the Act, practices, procedures, or tests neutral on their face, and even neutral in terms of intent, cannot be maintained if they operate to "freeze" the status quo of prior discriminatory employment practices. What is required by Congress is the removal of artificial, arbitrary, and unnecessary barriers to employment when the barriers operate invidiously to discriminate on the basis of racial or other impermissible classification.

The Act proscribes not only overt discrimination but also practices that are fair in form, but discriminatory in operation. The touchstone is business necessity. If an employment practice which operates to exclude Negroes cannot be shown to be related to job performance, the practice is prohibited.

On the record before us, neither the high school completion requirement nor the general intelligence test is shown to bear a demonstrable relationship to successful performance of the jobs for which it was used. Both were adopted, as the Court of Appeals noted, without meaningful study of their relationship to job-performance ability.

Good intent or absence of discriminatory intent does not redeem employment procedures or testing mechanisms that operate as "built-in headwinds" for minority groups and are unrelated to measuring job capability. Congress directed the thrust of the Act to the consequences of employment practices, not simply the motivation. More than that, Congress has placed on the employer the burden of showing that any given requirement must have a manifest relationship to the employment in question.

The facts of this case demonstrate the inadequacy of broad and general testing devices as well as the infirmity of using diplomas or degrees as fixed measures of capability. History is filled with examples of men and women who rendered highly effective performance without the conventional badges of accomplishment in terms of certificates, diplomas, or degrees. Diplomas and tests are useful servants, but Congress has mandated the commonsense proposition that they are not to become masters of reality.

The Company contends that its general intelligence tests are specifically permitted by Section 703(h) of the Act. That section authorizes the use of any professionally developed ability test that is not designed, intended or used to discriminate because of race. . . .

Nothing in the Act precludes the use of testing or measuring procedures; obviously they are useful. What Congress has forbidden is giving these devices and mechanisms controlling force unless they are demonstrably a reasonable measure of job performance. Congress has not commanded that the less qualified be preferred over the better qualified simply because of minority origins. Far from disparaging job qualifications as such, Congress has made such qualifications the controlling factor, so that race, religion, nationality, and sex become irrelevant. What Congress has commanded is that any tests used must measure the person for the job and not the person in the abstract.

(*Griggs v. Duke Power*, 401 U.S. 424 (1971) 424 (edited).

government, which rarely brings them, or by a few well-funded civil rights law firms. Moreover, plaintiffs who win disparate impact cases are awarded no damages other than back pay and attorneys fees (and the law on attorneys' fees increasingly works against civil rights lawyers). Consequently, most employment discrimination cases claim intentional discrimination.

There is an abundance of empirical evidence proving this point. Three recent empirical studies examined whether employment discrimination cases that rely on the *Griggs* theory of disparate impact, or unintentional discrimination, make up a large proportion of federal discrimination cases. Each one finds that they are only a small part of the caseload. John Donohue III and Peter Siegelman report that 7,613 employment discrimination cases were filed in the federal courts during fiscal year 1988–89. They estimate that 101 of these cases were brought under the *Griggs* theory—a mere 1.3 percent.[60] Siegelman conducted a second study that examined in detail over a thousand employment discrimination cases filed in federal court between January 1, 1985, and March 31, 1987. He found that in the 1,029 cases where the nature of the complaint could be determined, only 19, or 1.84 percent, were based on claims of disparate impact.[61] The third study focused on a nationwide sample of 1,247 employment discrimination cases. It found that between 1972 and 1973, soon after the *Griggs* decision was announced, disparate impact cases climbed to 8.7 percent of all employment discrimination cases filed. By 1986–87, however, these cases accounted for only 3.7 percent of an increasing number of employment discrimination cases.[62]

These studies provide clear-cut evidence that it is the disparate impact cases filed under *Griggs* that are quite rare. Moreover, most of the 7,500-plus individual actions filed in federal court in fiscal year 1989 were claims of discriminatory *firing*, not discriminatory hiring.[63] While the Thernstroms would have us believe the typical employment discrimination case is a broad challenge to employers' hiring policies, in truth the typical case today is brought by an individual employee who claims that his or her termination was the result of intentional discrimination.

An empirical study comparing age discrimination cases to other discrimination cases confirms the finding that relatively few cases allege hiring discrimination.[64] This study reveals that only 227 (23 percent) of 981 non–age discrimination cases surveyed involved hiring claims. By contrast, 610 (62 percent) alleged termination, 439 (45 percent) pertained to conditions of employment, 383 (39 percent) involved demotion or promotion, and 240 (24 percent) had to do with unequal pay.[65]

Despite the claims of conservative critics, it is very difficult for plaintiffs to win employment discrimination cases. The Supreme Court, like conservative critics, demands unambiguous evidence of intent to discriminate in most cases. Consider the Court's recent decision regarding proof of intentional discrimination, the 1993 case of *St. Mary's Honor Society v. Hicks*.[66] A black man, Melvin Hicks, was hired by St. Mary's (a halfway house) as a correctional officer in 1978. He was promoted to shift commander in 1980. He had a satisfactory employment record until 1984, when a new chief of custody and a new superintendent, both white men, were appointed. Within a few months he was suspended, demoted, fired, and replaced by a white man. He brought a Title VII suit in the United States District Court, claiming intentional racial discrimination.

At trial, St. Mary's claimed that Hicks had been fired for disciplinary offenses as well as for threatening John Powell, the new chief of custody. Sitting without a jury, the district court judge rejected St. Mary's assertions. The judge found that in comparable and more serious cases, St. Mary's had been more lenient with white employees. Powell, the judge ruled, had provoked Hicks to have an excuse for firing him. The federal district court found that Hicks had established that there was "a crusade to terminate him" and that the putative reasons St. Mary's gave for the crusade were untrue. In fact, the district court rejected every explanation St. Mary's offered, leaving no legitimate reason for firing Hicks. Despite these findings, the Supreme Court held they were not necessarily sufficient to prove intentional discrimination. The Court ruled that the judge was permitted to find discrimination based on these facts if he chose to, but he was not required to find discrimination. The trial judge decided that the new white supervisors disliked Hicks not because of his race but because they just did not like him. Even though the supervisors never claimed to dislike Hicks, the district court concluded that this was their motive, handing St. Mary's a complete victory. The *Hicks* decision established a very difficult standard for proof of intentionality.

By ignoring the difficulties of proving intent and misstating the extent to which proof of intent is required, conservatives misrepresent and downplay the realities of employment discrimination litigation. Conservatives also exaggerate the impact *Griggs* has on employers. They assert that because of *Griggs,* employers commonly hire by quota and practice reverse discrimination to avoid lawsuits by disgruntled job applicants. Conservatives assume that a rational employer will resort to "quota hiring" and discriminate against whites to avert potential legal liability from Title VII and *Griggs*.[67] They provide no evidence that employers actually behave this way, simply claiming, as the Thernstroms do, that it is "the obvious way to keep litigators at bay."[68]

Despite conservatives' claims of what rational employers ought to do, there are no empirical studies showing widespread employment discrimination against whites. In fact, given what we know about discrimination litigation, a rational employer would be foolish to discriminate against white job applicants. The Supreme Court made this clear in *McDonald v. Santa Fe Trail Transportation Company,* a case decided soon after the *Griggs* decision. In the *McDonald* case the Supreme Court decided that the 1964 Civil Rights Act (Title VII) and the 1866 Civil Rights Act (section 1981) prohibited all race discrimination. Discrimination against whites was just as illegal as discrimination against blacks.[69] In that case, three employees—two white, one black—had been accused of theft. Santa Fe fired the two white employees and retained the black employee. The Court ruled that the white employees had established a prima facie case of intentional discrimination, and required the employer to articulate a nondiscriminatory justification for its action. In response, the employers argued that isolated cases of discrimination against whites were permissible because Title VII was intended to help blacks, not whites. The Supreme Court rejected this contention.[70]

In 1979, to permit bona fide affirmative action plans, the Court carved out a narrow exception to the rule prohibiting discrimination against whites.[71] But to justify an affirmative action plan using racial preferences in hiring, the court held that a private employer had to meet five criteria. First, employers had to establish that there was a manifest racial imbalance in their workforces, showing substantial underrepresentation in a traditionally segregated job category. Second, employers had to certify that the purpose of the plan was to open employment opportunities for blacks. The third criterion is particularly relevant to the issue of whether civil rights legislation promotes discrimination against whites. It requires employers to demonstrate that the plan did not require the discharge of white employees or otherwise substantially interfere with any legitimate career expectations established prior to the plan. The final two criteria also speak to the possibility of disadvantaging whites. The fourth criterion states that employers had to show that the plan was not an absolute bar to hiring white job applicants, and the fifth, that it was temporary and would end when its objectives were met. For public employers, the Court added some additional requirements. The Court demanded that public employers provide convincing evidence that any racial imbalance was caused by intentional discrimination engaged in or condoned by the employer, that the purpose of the plan was to remedy the prior intentional discrimination, and that the plan was narrowly focused to remedy the prior discrimination.[72]

These are difficult requirements to meet. And although many employers have outreach, recruitment, and mentoring affirmative action plans, very few use plans that give black applicants preferential treatment. Given these restrictions, it makes no sense to say *Griggs* or affirmative action plans induce employers to discriminate against white workers.

The argument that employers discriminate against whites and hire by racial quota to avoid litigation assumes that employers are more concerned with being sued for failing to hire blacks than they are for firing previously hired black employees.[73] But current research points in the opposite direction: there are many more wrongful termination cases than failure to hire cases.[74] If their conduct is affected by the fear of Title VII lawsuits at all, rational employers should therefore be far more afraid to fire blacks than they are to refuse to hire them. This is particularly true when the employer views the black applicant as unqualified or marginally qualified. The rational employer would ask: "Why should I take a chance on an arguably unqualified applicant who is not likely to sue me if I do not hire him or her, but who may sue me if I hire and have to fire him or her?" Moreover, a rational employer would reason that if sued, he or she would rather be sued for not hiring someone believed to be unqualified than for firing (or demoting) someone initially viewed as qualified. In the failure-to-hire case the employer has a ready defense: "In my judgment, he or she was not the best qualified." This is a far easier defense than a termination case: "Initially, I thought this was the best-qualified applicant, but the person turned out to be incompetent." Ironically, litigation over Title VII may give employers seeking to avoid discrimination liability incentives to be overly cautious about hiring minority employees rather than discriminating in their favor. There is no evidence, however, that Title VII has discouraged employers from hiring racial minorities.

If *Griggs* causes employers to use quotas and discriminate against whites, one would also expect to see evidence of that in studies of discrimination litigation. To determine who files discrimination lawsuits, Alfred Blumrosen, a Rutgers University law professor, surveyed every federal court employment discrimination case based on race or sex reported in the national reporter system between 1990 and 1994, a total of over three thousand cases.[75] Blumrosen found that less than one hundred, or under 4 percent, involved claims of racial or sexual discrimination by white men. Similarly, a survey by the American Bar Foundation found that, with the exception of age discrimination cases, white men filed fewer than 5 percent of the employment discrimination cases in federal court.[76]

Why do so few white men sue for racial discrimination? Is it because they have less information about where and how to file complaints about discrimination? The data on age discrimination complaints demonstrate that this is not the case. White men *do* complain about discrimination, but not about racial and sexual discrimination. Instead white men typically complain about age discrimination. Indeed, they are among the primary users of antidiscrimination laws. One survey of discrimination claims by the federal antidiscrimination agency, the EEOC, found that one-quarter of all EEOC claims, and half of all dollars recovered, come from age discrimination cases. In those cases where the sole basis of the alleged discrimination was age discrimination, white men filed almost three-quarters of the cases.[77] Clearly, then, white men do complain about employment discrimination when they believe they have been victimized.

One reason white men file discrimination cases based on age rather than race or sex is that they are more likely to win these cases and the awards are substantially higher. Reverse discrimination cases are typically dismissed or unsuccessful. The EEOC found only twenty-eight credible cases of reverse discrimination out of seven thousand complaints in 1994, and federal courts dismissed most reverse discrimination complaints between 1990 and 1994.[78] In a study of all employment discrimination cases taken to trial between 1978 and 1985, Theodore Eisenberg found that 22.2 percent resulted in plaintiff verdicts (compared with 50.0 percent of all tort cases). And he discovered that the odds of winning are far higher in age discrimination cases (25.0 percent) than in other discrimination cases (4.5 percent).[79] Settlements in age discrimination cases are far more lucrative as well, and because white men are prone to file age discrimination suits, they gain more financially from antidiscrimination laws than do women and racial minorities. Table 2 compares the results of age discrimination complaints with race and sex discrimination complaints. It shows clearly that age discrimination claimants were more likely to prevail and were awarded more money than plaintiffs in non-age discrimination cases. The average recovery in age discrimination cases, where white men make up the vast majority of plaintiffs, is almost $84,000, compared to $12,000 for racial and sexual discrimination. For class action suits, age discrimination average awards are seventeen times the awards for race discrimination cases.[80]

TABLE 2. SURVEY OF FEDERAL COURT DISCRIMINATION
CLAIM OUTCOMES BY TYPE OF CASE

	Age Discrimination Cases[a] (white men = 74%)	Non–Age Discrimination[a] Cases (white men <5%)
Settled	58.0%	46.5%
Plaintiff Wins	6.4%	2.2%
Defendant Wins	26.3%	47.0%
Average Recovery	$68,785	$11,517

SOURCE: American Bar Foundation survey, published in George Rutherglen, "From Race to Age: The Expanding Scope of Employment Discrimination Law," *Journal of Legal Studies* 24 (1995), p. 512, table 6.

a. Totals do not add up to 100 percent because dropped cases were excluded.

There is very little evidence to suggest that *Griggs* or executive orders requiring affirmative action plans have produced widespread quota hiring or reverse discrimination. This is not surprising because employers cannot defend themselves from lawsuits under Title VII merely by creating a workforce that has the "right" numbers of racial minorities. The Court has consistently said that *Griggs* does not impose hiring preferences on employers. It looks at the process through which hiring decisions are made, eschewing any concern for *who* gets hired in favor of *how* individuals are selected. In *Connecticut v. Teal* the Court ruled that racial balancing would not protect employers from a Title VII challenge.[81]

Statistical studies of enforcement of Title VII and affirmative action provide no evidence that they lead to racial balancing or reverse discrimination. If an employer refused to hire perfectly competent whites in favor of incompetent blacks, the firm's productivity would decline. If there was evidence that firms were hiring less productive black or female workers and raising their wages relative to more productive white males, we might conclude that Title VII has caused reverse discrimination. But the research on this hypothesis shows otherwise. Using data from EEO files, Jonathan Leonard estimated the impact of affirmative action and Title VII on the productivity of firms hiring racial minorities and women. He found no evidence of reverse discrimination or a decline in productivity. On the contrary, he found that the productivity of black workers actually increased between 1966 and 1977.[82] Thus, there is no evidence for the conservatives' contention that the legacy of *Griggs* is quota hiring and reverse discrimination.

WHY EMPLOYMENT DISCRIMINATION LAW MATTERS TO RACIAL EQUALITY

If they were able to, conservatives would eliminate all government affirmative action programs and repeal Title VII. They got off to good start in this direction after the 1980 election. The Reagan administration more or less gutted the federal government's contract compliance program. Started in 1965 with an executive order issued by President Lyndon B. Johnson, the federal contract compliance program mandates that all government contractors with contracts in excess of $50,000 and with fifty or more employees institute affirmative action plans. The order prohibits discrimination by contractors and requires contracting firms to take "affirmative action to ensure that applicants are employed and employees are treated during employment without regard to their race, color, religion, sex or national origin."[83] Under this controversial program, the federal government monitored the racial composition of contractors' workforces and asked that firms set goals to remedy deficiencies.

After Ronald Reagan's election, his administration sharply cut the budget of the Office of Federal Contract Compliance Programs (OFCCP), reducing enforcement of the contract compliance program. As Jonathan Leonard notes, "fewer administrative complaints were filed, back-pay awards were phased out, and the already rare penalty of debarment became an endangered species."[84] For example, about 500 back-pay awards were granted in fiscal year 1986 compared to 4,336 during the last year of the Carter administration.[85]

Many conservatives would go further. Richard Epstein wants to repeal Title VII in its entirety and let market competition regulate discrimination. Clint Bolick agrees. He thinks that Title VII interferes with private employers' constitutional right to form contracts without governmental interference.[86] The Thernstroms' position is more complicated but no less hostile to the enforcement of any employment discrimination law. On the one hand, they say they oppose affirmative action and laws that prohibit *unintentional* discrimination, but they favor making *intentional* discrimination illegal. On the other hand, they oppose provisions in the Civil Rights Restoration Act of 1991 that permit plaintiffs to collect damages in intentional discrimination cases: "The act allowed damages and compensation, including nontaxable backpay, for intentional discrimination, which increased the exposure of employers and thus gave them more of an incentive to hire by quota."[87] The implication of this criticism of the 1991 act is that damages should never be awarded, even when employers intentionally discriminate.

The 1991 Civil Rights Act permits compensatory damages (in an amount no greater than $300,000) for future financial losses, pain and suffering, and emotional distress. This provision is explicitly limited to acts of "intentional discrimination"; it also permits punitive damages (subject to the $300,000 limit), but only when the defendant acts with both intent and malice.[88] The Thernstroms, like many conservatives, object to this provision because, they claim, it encourages employers to "hire by quota," even though they provide no evidence for this assertion. If they object to awarding damages even in cases where discrimination is intentional, their objections to banning unintentional discrimination ring hollow. As we have demonstrated, employers have little to fear from blacks filing Title VII hiring suits. Black plaintiffs succeed in only a handful of these cases, and when they do succeed, they typically receive small judgments. Most Title VII cases are for harassment, termination, demotion, or refusal to promote; very few are for failure to hire. If the Thernstroms object to the enforcement of Title VII even in cases where the employer has intentionally refused to hire minorities, it is fair to say they have no interest in enforcing any civil rights laws.

Were the conservatives' agenda for employment discrimination law to be adopted, victims of discrimination would be left with very little protection. Most conservatives are not concerned about this prospect because they think labor market discrimination has mostly disappeared and that the costs of enforcing Title VII outweigh the benefits. These arguments ignore substantial evidence of persistent labor market discrimination, especially the ways in which racial stereotypes and same-race identification affect employers' decisions. They also neglect how effective Title VII has been in diminishing racial inequality.

Earlier we examined changes in the structure of labor market discrimination, arguing that racial differences in employment and earnings are partly due to racial competition in labor markets. We also examined some of the recent qualitative evidence of racial bias in hiring decisions. These data, especially the studies of employers' hidden preferences and stereotypes, indicate why discrimination need not be intentional to be illegal.[89] Employers influenced by stereotypes and same-race identification may easily view black job applicants as less qualified than equally qualified whites not out of bigotry but out of blindness. This is not color-blindness; it is racism-blindness, a consequence that follows from white-washing the significance of race. As long as whites hold these stereo-typical views of blacks and identify with other whites, employment discrimination will continue. And so long as whites maintain their privileged position in labor markets, Title VII and federal affirmative action policies will be needed.

Contrary to received wisdom, affirmative action policies are aimed less at rectifying past injustices than at minimizing or removing white advantages in the labor market. These policies have successfully opened up employment and promotion opportunities for African Americans and reduced wage differentials between racial groups as well as between men and women. This is true regardless of whether the intent is to advance minorities to managerial positions or, equally important, to open up to them blue-collar jobs in the skilled crafts, police work, and fire fighting. Deregulation of racial labor market competition restores white advantages, and in the 1980s it was a prime cause of the widening wage gap between black and white workers. There is strong evidence for these claims.

Federal affirmative action policies increased black employment relative to whites among federal contractors. Jonathan Leonard found that in the late 1970s employment of black men grew 0.82 percent faster than white employment in firms that had contracts with the federal government compared to firms without federal contracts. Enforcement of Title VII was responsible for about 7 percent of the employment gains of black workers in manufacturing firms.[90] Taken together, these policies helped reduce the earnings difference between blacks and nonblacks from 40 percent to 15 percent—a significant change by any measure.[91]

Studies of employer decisions are consistent with these findings, showing that the level of white male employment among federal contractors is 10 to 15 percent lower than in noncontracting firms. Black men and white women gain employment as a result. The overall employment level of white men, according to these studies, is not declining, it is just growing more slowly in contracting firms. However, Leonard found that white men disproportionately absorbed layoffs in a group of federal contractors in the mid-1970s. This is "striking evidence," as he puts it, "of the impact of affirmative action."[92]

Federal antidiscrimination policy not only shifted the demand for black workers relative to whites; it resulted in significant occupational gains. Leonard estimates that almost one-third of the occupational advances of black workers in the 1970s are the result of antidiscrimination policies. This was a boon for black workers from all walks of life. Middle-class blacks made substantial gains as skilled white-collar jobs opened up, as did skilled blue-collar workers, who were able to gain access to skilled crafts jobs, one of the key occupations closed off to blacks in the 1950s and 1960s.[93] Antidiscrimination policy also benefited low-income and unskilled black workers. Title VII was instrumental in raising black wages and tearing down the walls of southern segregated workplaces, and when Title VII was applied to state and local governments in 1972, it pried open police and fire departments across the country—among the most notorious public bastions of white privilege—for working-class African Americans.

When the Reagan administration halted enforcement of federal affirmative action in the 1980s, blacks lost out. Prior to 1980, black male employment grew 17 percent among federal contractors compared to 12 percent among noncontractors. After 1981, when Reagan took office, the difference between contractors and noncontractors disappeared—the rate of growth was about 10 percent in each type of firm.[94] Wage differentials also widened. And these differentials cannot be explained solely by differences in education and job skills. The changing demand for skilled versus unskilled labor was detrimental to black employment and wages, but that is not the whole story. Leonard estimates that the black-white wage gap grew by 2.5 percent and the wage gap for Native Americans by 4.5 percent. Yet changes in wage gaps varied greatly between cities, which dispels the notion that a common lack of education or job skills explains the increase in racial wage gaps.[95]

Antidiscrimation policies have knocked a few holes in the edifice of white labor market privilege. The gains we have documented are not extraordinarily large, but they matter. Economic opportunities for blacks, Latinos, Native Americans, and females would be greatly diminished today were it not for antidiscrimination laws. The costs of enforcement, moreover, are not burdensome. Black employment gains are "modest in the aggregate," but there is no unambiguous evidence that affirmative action or enforcement of Title VII leads to losses in productive efficiency. After an exhaustive review of empirical studies of antidiscrimination policies in employment, federal contracting, and education, Harry Holzer and David Neumark concluded that the evidence is "most consistent with the view that affirmative action offers significant redistribution toward women and minorities with relatively small efficiency consequences."[96] The conservative case against employment discrimination law is not just overblown; it ignores the obvious benefits.

Conservatives have had their day in court, and so far they have not been able to completely undo federal affirmative action policy. But in two recent cases deciding the legality of minority contracting programs— *Richmond v. J. A. Croson Company* and *Adarand Constructors v. Pena*—

the Supreme Court severely limited the scope of government-sponsored affirmative action. These two cases make it harder for the government to justify taking race into account in contracting and, in all likelihood, in employment decisions. These cases do not, however, ban affirmative action. In the *Croson* case, the Court restricted affirmative action plans in state and local governments, while the *Adarand* case extended the *Croson* decision to the federal government. Taken together, *Croson* and *Adarand* subject all racial classifications used in government contracting, including affirmative action plans, to strict scrutiny—a test ordinarily fatal to any classification. The Court decided that racial classification is constitutional only if it serves a compelling governmental interest and is narrowly tailored to further that interest. Underrepresentation of minority-owned businesses among government contractors will not justify giving them preferential treatment unless there is additional evidence of discriminatory exclusion.

By any measure, *Croson* and *Adarand* were serious setbacks for black Americans. Prior to *Croson*, equal protection cases focused on whether a government policy or practice disadvantaged a "suspect class"—a discreet and insular minority that has little political influence and thus needs protection from the majority. Blacks were the paradigmatic suspect class. But in *Croson* the Court held that the focus should be on the way government classifies individuals, not suspect classes, in the law. And because race was now a suspect classification (instead of blacks being a suspect class), whites were entitled to equal protection as if they were a minority, rendering laws, policies, and practices intended to help blacks presumptively unconstitutional. After *Croson*, laws intended to benefit veterans or farmers are permitted under the Fourteenth Amendment, since the way these laws classify individuals is not suspect, while laws intended to help black Americans are presumptively forbidden. As Jed Rubenfeld points out, the great irony of *Croson* is that even though the Fourteenth Amendment was adopted to enable Congress to pass special laws to help blacks, those are the only kind of laws it now prohibits. Under this interpretation of the Fourteenth Amendment, Congress would be prevented from passing any law that allocates benefits on the basis of race.[97]

Nonetheless, the Court did not rule in either decision that all racial classifications are unconstitutional. As Justice O'Connor (author of both majority opinions) explained, "The unhappy persistence of both the practice and the lingering effects of racial discrimination against minority groups in this country is an unfortunate reality, and government is not disqualified from acting in response to it."[98] A city, she wrote, "has legislative authority over its procurement policies, and can use its spending powers to remedy private discrimination, if it identifies that discrimination with the particularity required by the Fourteenth Amendment."[99] If a state or local government "could show that it had essentially become a 'passive participant' in a system of racial exclusion practiced by elements of the local construction industry, we think it clear that the city [or other state or local government entity] could take affirmative steps to dismantle such a system. It is beyond dispute that any public entity, state or federal, has a compelling interest in assuring that public dollars, drawn from the tax contributions of all citizens, do not serve to finance the evil of private prejudice."[100] In other words, the Court ruled that government affirmative action is harder to justify than private affirmative action, but given the requisite proof, it is permissible.

These two decisions will limit the business opportunities of black-owned businesses and affect black employment, since black-owned businesses tend to hire more minority employees than other firms.[101] In the wake of the *Croson* decision, many cities and counties abandoned programs that gave preferential treatment to women and minority-owned firms. In Atlanta, contracts with women and minority-owned businesses were reduced from 37 to 24 percent of the total; in Richmond, Virginia, the numbers fell from 32 to 11 percent; and in Philadelphia, city contracts held by minority-owned firms declined from 25 to a mere 3.5 percent. In Tampa, Florida, the use of minority-owned firms as city contractors virtually ended.[102] But other cities and counties conducted "*Croson* studies" to determine whether their affirmative action programs should be scrapped, or whether they could be justified based on evidence of prior discrimination, or the city's "passive participation" in discrimination against minority-owned businesses. Not surprisingly, some studies found significant evidence of discrimination, and based on these findings some post-*Croson* affirmative action plans were approved.[103]

The Clinton administration responded to the *Adarand* ruling by asking the Justice Department and various federal agencies to assess their policies and practices and determine whether federal affirmative action programs met the strict scrutiny standard. The Thernstroms characterize this decision as "rationalization, denial, and deception" because, like many conservatives, they would like to use *Adarand* to justify an immediate end to all affirmative action policies. But the Court did not hold that affirmative action plans were illegitimate. These decisions were more of an alarm bell than a death knell. The Clinton administration's response was entirely appropriate, and by the end of the review, they had "eliminated or altered" seventeen affirmative action programs, which "led to sharp decreases in the amount of Federal contracts awarded to companies owned by minorities or women."[104] Where it decided to retain programs, the Bush administration has defended the Clinton administration's decision.

THE POLITICS OF AFFIRMATIVE ACTION: SYMBOLS AND REALITIES

The 1960s antidiscrimination policies are not the failure conservatives and critics make them out to be. On the contrary, these policies are very cautious but partial remedies for a long history of exploitation and racial discrimination. Conservatives are wrong: the Supreme Court did not audaciously rewrite the 1964 Civil Rights Act in *Griggs v. Duke Power* and replace discrimination against African Americans with discrimination against whites by extending Title VII to unintentional discrimination. Instead, the Court recognized what many of its critics refuse to see: Congress intended Title VII not just to outlaw racial discrimination in labor markets but also to open up economic opportunities for African Americans and other people of color. If Title VII had been narrowly restricted to specific acts of intentional discrimination as conservatives would like, it would not have reached so-called race-neutral practices like nepotism and would not have been effective.

Enforcement of Title VII and the federal government's contract compliance program opened up jobs and a better life to many African Americans, from unskilled black textile workers in the South to college-educated black women. Just as important, these laws helped transform labor markets by breaking down distinctions between "white work" and "black work" while eliminating the most egregious discriminatory employment practices. The evidence also suggests that these changes did not, as conservatives argue, lead to reverse discrimination or impose large disadvantages on white workers. The 1960s antidiscrimination policies are controversial because they minimized the advantage whites brought to labor markets and thus devalued whiteness. On the other hand, diminished enforcement of Title VII in the 1980s was one of the reasons African Americans lost ground to white workers in racially competitive labor markets. While labor market discrimination is less apparent today, an abundance of evidence—drawn from audit studies, surveys of employers, and studies of job displacement in the racially competitive labor markets during the 1980s—indicates that it persists.

Despite this evidence, conservatives and racial realists still assume that racial differences in wages or income stem from premarket factors, the skills and education workers bring to the job, not from labor market discrimination. For example, James Heckman regards civil rights policies as a symbolic anachronism: "The goal of achieving black economic progress is better served by policies that promote skill formation, like improving family environments, schools and neighborhoods, [rather than] strengthening the content and enforcement of civil rights laws—the solution to the problem of an earlier era."[105]

The distinction between premarket and within-market factors is artificial and unworkable. It fails for two reasons. First, the distinction presumes that discrimination is entirely attributable to prejudiced individuals—employers treating otherwise equally qualified job applicants unequally. However, as we have shown, simple models of individual discrimination do not adequately describe or explain changes in twentieth-century labor market discrimination and exploitation. In our view, dicrimination is better understood as a group phenomenon or as opportunity hoarding by one group to the detriment of another. Whites are advantaged in labor markets when they are able to rig the rules of the game and control access to jobs and promotions by defining required credentials, limiting access to training or education, or otherwise closing off access to blacks or other groups. As we have indicated in previous chapters, this often takes the form of defending dubious criteria of merit or assuming that minor differences in test scores are evidence of massive differences in qualifications. Opportunity hoarding, as we showed in chapter 2, has long-run consequences. Segregated seniority lists, for example, restricted blacks to unskilled jobs that were subsequently eliminated when manufacturers replaced workers with machines. Because opportunity hoarding often restricts the access of blacks and Latinos to jobs even before they apply, simple distinctions between premarket and within-market discrimination obscure more than they clarify.[106]

The second reason why the distinction breaks down is that premarket institutions themselves have been shaped by the history of racial inequality and oppression. In crafting policies to improve educational, family, and neighborhood environments, there is no escaping the role that racial discrimination has played in segregating neighborhoods and schools, undermining the economic basis of African American and Latino communities in the inner city, and influencing the distribution of social benefits. The black experience in premarket institutions that conservatives and racial realists want to change is produced by racially biased processes of accumulation in white communities and disaccumulation in black communities. Inadequate inner-city schools, crime-ridden neighborhoods, and concentrated racial poverty can only be altered by confronting the white privileges that sustain them. Unless the conservatives and racial realists who believe that affirmative action is unfair, counterproductive, and unnecessary are willing to confront the legacy of white accumulation and black disaccumulation, and to make the necessary investments in African American and Latino communities, affirmative action is the only alternative and is, at best, a cheap palliative.

Employment discrimination laws will be necessary for some time and will have to be combined with policies that reverse decades of disaccumulation in black and Latino communities. The authors of the 1965 Voting Rights Act assumed that the social changes necessary to dismantle centuries of legal segregation would not be possible unless equality in political representation and influence was guaranteed. The Voting Rights Act set off a political revolution in the South and remains, like employment discrimination law, one of the pillars of the civil rights revolution. But conservatives believe efforts to ensure that blacks' Fifteenth Amendment right to vote is not abridged have, like employment discrimination law, been perverted by advocates of color-conscious policies. We now consider the conservative critique of voting rights law.

6

Color-Blindness as Color Consciousness

Voting Rights and Political Equality

When the Supreme Court ruled in *Shaw v. Reno,* the 1993 North Carolina redistricting case, that it may be unconstitutional to create black or Latino majority legislative districts, the Court cut short a political revolution ignited by the 1965 Voting Rights Act (VRA). The counterrevolution continued as the Court went on to strike down several new black-majority congressional districts created by the 1990 redistricting process. When state legislators began to redraw district boundaries, many conservatives applauded the Court's halt to race-conscious redistricting. Although the Court insisted it was upholding a color-blind Constitution, its decisions actually hollowed out the principles of political equality established after the Civil War by the Fourteenth and Fifteenth Amendments to the Constitution. The Court's so-called color-blind redistricting standard undermines equal representation for racial minorities and upholds political advantages enjoyed by America's white majority. Consequently, the Court's new standard for representation limits black Americans' capacity to accumulate political capital.

The Voting Rights Act had unleashed a dramatic surge in black registration and voting by dismantling the various devices southerners had put in place to disenfranchise black voters. Disenfranchisement started during Reconstruction. Soon after the Fifteenth Amendment was ratified, white southerners began devising ways to prevent African Americans from voting. They used racial gerrymanders—drawing legislative districts so that African Americans could never be a majority—literacy tests and various registration requirements, and poll taxes to disenfranchise African Americans while pretending to uphold the Fifteenth Amendment's guarantee that voting rights could not be denied because of race. White southerners also restricted primary elections to whites in order to deprive the few African Americans who did manage to register of their right to vote and used physical intimidation to enforce these laws. Southern blacks were ruthlessly disenfranchised. Thus, before the VRA was passed, registered white voters in the South outnumbered blacks by seven to one.[1]

By banning discriminatory voting requirements and mandating federal examiners to monitor southern compliance, the Voting Rights Act dramatically changed black registration rates and voting and substantially diminished whites' advantage in voter registration.[2] In the ten years after the VRA was passed, black voters mobilized and elected black officeholders in the South for the first time since Reconstruction. Some of the most important gains in political representation came when congressional districts were reapportioned after the 1990 census. Redistricting raised the number of black members of Congress from twenty-five to forty-one, thirteen of whom were elected from new black-majority districts in the South. Before these new districts were added, only three African American members of Congress came from the South, where 45 percent of all blacks lived in 1990.

Many people thought this expansion of black representation in Congress vindicated the 1982 amendments to the VRA that permitted state legislatures to create majority-minority districts as a remedy for violations of the law. *Shaw v. Reno,* however, called this voting rights strategy into question. It opened the door to successful challenges from disgruntled white voters and office seekers who believed their right to participate in a color-blind electoral process had been trampled on by the creation of black-majority legislative districts. The plaintiffs challenged two newly drawn black-majority congressional districts in North Carolina, a state in which no African American had been elected to Congress since Reconstruction. One of the districts, created after the U.S. attorney general objected to the state legislature's decision to create only one black-majority district, narrowly wound its way along an interstate highway for 160 miles. Writing for the majority, Justice Sandra Day O'Connor said the snakelike Twelfth Congressional District raised the question of whether voters had been unconstitutionally classified by race. Although Justice O'Connor was careful to state that the Court was not prohibiting the use of race in redistricting, she wrote, "We believe that reapportionment is one area in which appearances do matter. A reapportionment plan that includes in one district individuals who belong to the same race, but who are otherwise widely separated by geographical and political boundaries, and who may have little in common with one another but the color of their skin, bears an uncomfortable resemblance to political apartheid."[3]

In a subsequent case, *Miller v. Johnson*, the Court dismantled two black-majority districts in Georgia and went beyond *Shaw* to insist that where race serves as the predominant criterion (or motivation) in redistricting, it is unconstitutional. Justice Anthony Kennedy said, "Shape is relevant not because bizarreness is a necessary element of the constitutional wrong or a threshold requirement of proof, but because it may be persuasive circumstantial evidence that race for its own sake . . . was the legislature's dominant and controlling rationale in drawing its district lines."[4]

To critics of race-conscious policies, the Court's redistricting decisions marked a return to common sense and an end to a perverted interpretation of the VRA. In their estimation, once the Voting Rights Act dismantled barriers to the voting booth, African Americans were no longer politically underrepresented or marginalized. These critics believe that just as Title VII of the Civil Rights Act outlawed only intentional discrimination, the sole purpose of the Voting Rights Act was to implement the Fifteenth Amendment. It did that, and thus the question of representation has been settled. According to the Thernstroms, the VRA was turned into a tool to expand African American and Latino political representation by an unholy alliance between the U.S. Department of Justice, under both Democratic and Republican administrations, and civil rights lawyers and activists bent on balkanizing American politics. "With the tremendous number of blacks holding office, in the 1990s, racial *exclusion* from the political arena may no longer be the main problem," the Thernstroms write. "Racial and ethnic fragmentation, driven in part by racial districting and other public policies, was perhaps the greater danger."[5]

This is a very dubious interpretation of the history of redistricting and the VRA. It also begs the question of what minority political representation means in a society with a history of racial gerrymandering. Contrary to what critics of the VRA think, equal representation is not attained once equal access to the voting booth is guaranteed. The real question is how to protect the political rights of a group of citizens who are subject, as Justice Harlan Stone wrote in a famous footnote, to "prejudice . . . which tends to seriously curtail the operation of those political processes ordinarily to be relied upon to protect minorities."[6] Guaranteeing the right to vote is surely necessary to protect minority rights and interests from majority oppression. However, it is not sufficient, especially in a racially divided society where power and privilege are associated with skin color. The authors of the Fourteenth Amendment understood this when they wrote the equal protection clause. So did Congress when it amended the VRA in 1982 to explicitly outlaw vote dilution schemes and to permit appropriate remedies, including the creation of black and Latino majority legislative districts.

Conservatives presume that such protections are neither necessary nor desirable. All that is needed, they think, is a color-blind voting process. They base this claim on two related arguments. Critics like the Thernstroms and the justices in the majority in *Shaw v. Reno* believe that equality of representation is achieved when individual rights to the franchise are protected. They also believe that race-conscious redistricting is merely another step toward creating group rights or entitlements at the expense of individual rights. Thus, it is no different than any other form of affirmative action.

Some writers critical of the Court's decision in *Shaw v. Reno* argue that the Court incorrectly abandoned the voting rights law that came out of the reapportionment cases of the early 1960s. The Court, they believe, wrongly tried to apply the equal protection principles that govern job discrimination to matters of representation and vote dilution. This view presumes that voting rights are only individual rights and that these rights are violated whenever race is used in the redistricting process. But Pamela Karlan and Daryl Levinson point out that the alternative to race-conscious redistricting is not a remedy that treats "citizens as individuals," as there might be in an employment discrimination case. The alternative to considering an individual's race in the hiring process could be an individual's test score. In redistricting there is no individual alternative. This is because political representation really pertains to the representation of *groups*, not individuals.[7]

Unless they can produce lots of cash, individuals are unimportant to politicians. What matters to politicians is identifiable groups of voters, whether they are defined by party affiliation or by more discrete but tangible indicators of political interest: religion, income, sexual orientation, and, of course, race. In a geographically based system of representation such as the United States, one might say that politicians try to pick their constituents, not the reverse. And they pick them according to politically defined demographic characteristics. Voters may walk into the voting booth by themselves, but their vote matters to politicians only when they share preferences and beliefs. If voters have any influence, it is as members of a group.

Redistricting and other decisions to change electoral rules therefore influence which groups get represented and which do not. This applies to all social groups. Consider the shift from district elections to at-large elections in many cities at the turn of the twentieth century. Justified as a way to enhance the public interest, reformers were actually more interested in using at-large elections to dilute the political influence of working-class immigrants. Irish immigrants, a distinct minority, could be forgiven for thinking that their interests would not be well served by a city council composed entirely of WASPs.[8] Similarly, when the suffrage of African Americans in the South was restricted under Jim Crow at the turn of the century, *all* African Americans were underrepresented, even those who managed to vote. This exposes the unreality, as Morgan Kousser points out, of any "distinction between group and individual rights," because the "value of an individual's right[s] depends on how her group is treated."[9]

Even when they admit that social groups matter to redistricting, the conservative critics of the VRA (and some members of the Court) deny that blacks are such a group and that African Americans' political interests can be defined by race. In this view, race-conscious redistricting falsely assumes blacks (or Latinos) have common interests. The conservatives complain that it denies the palpable economic heterogeneity, or class differences, among African Americans produced by the dismantling of de jure segregation and the diminution of discrimination. Why presume middle-class blacks and lower-class blacks have common political interests, conservatives ask? This does not mean that conservatives assume that groups are unimportant in redistricting decisions. Rather, they insist that *race* is an ignominious category that should be expunged from the law and redistricting. For America to be a color-blind society, there can be no racial classifications whatsoever.[10] As they see it, race continues to be a politically divisive subject only because black politicians elected from safe districts continue to fan the flames of racial discontent. The real function of voting rights law, the Thernstroms believe, is to protect black politicians from white competition.

To ban race from redistricting decisions as conservatives advocate—the Court has not ruled in any of the recent voting rights cases that any consideration of race is illegal—would hardly mean politicians would then ignore it. As anyone who has looked at recent election returns knows, racial groups do matter in politics. Racial groups, including whites, have identifiable political interests (as much as any other social group in society) and racially polarized voting has not disappeared. Paradoxically, the idea that the electoral process should be color-blind is in fact a very *color-conscious* notion. The redistricting cases are saturated with an awareness of racial identity, just not the identity of "discrete and insular" racial minorities. Whites who insist on color-blind redistricting are really demanding an electoral system that acknowledges *their* majority status. Their objection is to districts where they are not the majority, where they might have to relinquish the privileges of their racial status.

The redistricting cases pose a critical question for American politics in the twenty-first century: can racial minorities obtain equal and meaningful representation in a society where the rules favor a white majority and where mere access to the ballot box is insufficient to counter white control of the electoral system? Instead of addressing this question, the conservative argument against black and Latino majority legislative districts substitutes a flawed history of the Voting Rights Act and a misleading interpretation of the role of race in elections and redistricting. In the following analysis of the conservatives' interpretation of the VRA and recent Supreme Court decisions, we document the inadequacy of their interpretation and the color consciousness of color-blind logic.

VOTING RIGHTS AND THE POLITICS OF RACE

The political struggle over the Voting Rights Act was never simply about access. It has always been a fight to ensure that the formal right to participate was more than a mere formality and that black votes counted. The fear that legally guaranteed access to the ballot box could be undermined by changes in electoral laws was not provoked by political maneuvering over implementation of the Voting Rights Act. Nor was it, as the Thernstroms think, a scheme to surreptitiously treat voting rights as a form of affirmative action. After the Justice Department drafted the legislation in 1965, Attorney General Nicholas Katzenbach told Congress, "We recognized that increased black voting strength might encourage a shift in the tactics of discrimination. Once significant numbers of blacks could vote, communities could still throw up obstacles to discourage those voters or make it difficult for a black to win elective office." To prevent this, section 5 of the act required Justice Department approval of any changes in electoral systems in effect at the time the law was implemented. It prohibited any discriminatory "standard, practice, or procedure with respect to voting."[11] Congress clearly intended the act to regulate changes in electoral laws and procedures that might perpetuate discrimination by "diluting" the votes of newly enfranchised African Americans.

Vote dilution is conventionally defined as "the practice of reducing the potential effectiveness of a group's voting strength by limiting its ability to translate that strength into the control of or at least influence with elected public officials."[12] Most of the early vote dilution cases focused on state and local electoral systems and tried to prevent state and local governments from diluting the black votes with at-large elections or multimember legislative districts. Since Reconstruction, southerners had used at-large elections "to guard against the possibility of the election of black city officials."[13] For example, in a city where African Americans made up 40 percent of the electorate, and the electorate was racially polarized, instituting an at-large electoral system would make it nearly impossible for black voters to ever elect anyone of *their* choice.

As a form of racial gerrymandering, at-large elections dilute the black vote by spreading it across one large multimember electoral district. Single-member districts, on the other hand, are racially gerrymandered by spreading the black electorate thinly across several districts so that black voters never make up more than, say, one-third of the voters of any one district. This is often called "cracking" the black vote. Vote dilution can also occur in a system of single-member districts by "packing" the black vote into one district and thinly spreading it across the remaining districts. Racial gerrymandering has a long history in the United States; it flourished during and after Reconstruction in the South.[14] Civil rights lawyers and the Justice Department did not invent it.

In a 1969 case, *Allen v. State Board of Education*, the Supreme Court ratified Congress' intent to apply the VRA to changes in electoral systems. The dispute in this case turned on the meaning of section 5 of the VRA. Mississippi officials argued to the Court that the law covered only those changes pertaining to voter registration, not "rules relating to the qualification of candidates or to state decisions as to which offices shall be elective." The Court rejected this narrow interpretation and said the act was "aimed at the subtle, as well as the obvious, state regulations which have the effect of denying citizens their right to vote because of their race."[15] The Court thus decided that the VRA covered vote dilution. Cases after *Allen* have dealt mainly with the question of how vote dilution could be demonstrated.

Most conservatives construe the VRA narrowly. They accept, in so many words, Mississippi's view of the law that the intent of the VRA is to guarantee access to the ballot box, nothing more. Although the Thernstroms think that the *Allen* decision served a limited purpose in protecting blacks against "the manipulation of an electoral system for racist ends," they believe it now poses a clear danger and should be overturned. Section 5 has been perverted into a device to "ensure that black votes had value—had the power, that is, to elect blacks."[16] Lawsuits alleging vote dilution are designed to establish some form of proportional representation (the Thernstroms use the term vaguely). Thus, the Thernstroms draw an explicit parallel between affirmative action in labor markets and voting—they use the term *disparate impact* to describe an "entitlement" to proportional representation. The site of original sin is *Allen:* "When a municipality annexed a suburb, it might have added more white voters than black to the city's voting rolls, but such an effect would not be a sure clue to its purpose. In 1969 the Court had suddenly applied the prohibition of section 5 to all changes that might have a disparate racial impact, whether intended or not. A districting plan that was racially neutral in intent could nevertheless be found discriminatory in effect."[17] Thus, the Thernstroms understand the VRA to protect only access to the voting booth and to prohibit only intentional, purposive efforts at exclusion. Goaded by the civil rights establishment, Republican Justice Departments perverted the intent of the law, they assert, by refusing to accept state redistricting plans unless they maximized the number of black-majority or minority-majority districts.

This account is misleading. It also ignores conflicting evidence. Not only did Congress explicitly mandate that changes in electoral systems be subject to federal scrutiny, but neither Congress nor the Supreme Court has backed away from the Court's decision in *Allen.*[18] The Thernstroms' description of annexation is egregiously misleading. It is based on an outdated model of racism, which, as we pointed out earlier, limits legal remedies for discrimination to discrete acts of intentional bias. Thus, an annexation plan that transformed a black majority into a minority would violate the VRA only if one could prove it was explicitly intended to add white voters to the city. This notion of prejudice is oblivious to contemporary manifestations of racism, and this account of annexation does not confront recent cases in which whites used racial gerrymanders to deny blacks electoral majorities.

The most notorious racial gerrymanders were color-blind changes in electoral laws that intentionally blocked African American and Latino candidates from elected political office. For example, faced with a growing black electorate in the late 1950s, whites in Memphis fashioned legislation to outlaw "single-shot" voting, or voting for a single candidate in a multimember district. This law was designed explicitly to prevent blacks from electing an African American by voting for a single candidate. Whites were not shy about admitting this. They championed at-large city council elections in the early 1960s for the same reasons. As Morgan Kousser comments, "No civically conscious Memphian after 1962 could be ignorant of the racial implications of the choice between district and at-large elections."[19]

The conservative claim that a band of civil rights lawyers and Justice Department officials hijacked the VRA should not be taken seriously. It ignores the explicit language of the 1982 amendments to the VRA. While stipulating that the VRA did not guarantee proportional representation (which is well-nigh impossible in a system of single-member districts with plurality elections anyway), Congress said that any political process or law in which "members have less opportunity than other members to participate in the political process and to elect representatives of their choice" was a violation of the law.[20] And Congress explicitly permitted a results test to determine whether a violation had occurred.[21] This discredits any notion that the Justice Department somehow corrupted section 5.

Many conservatives also object to the litigation of vote dilution cases. They do not believe it is necessary because blacks are actually well represented, even though African Americans occupy just a little over 1 percent of all elected offices. The Thernstroms claim this figure is misleading because it incorrectly measures the racial gap in political representation. With no justification, they insist that relative differences in the proportions of black and white officeholders should be measured only within the Democratic Party, presumably because most blacks vote Democratic. Using this standard, blacks are equally represented; they are 14 percent of Democratic primary voters and have 14 percent of House Democratic seats. The Thernstroms maintain, moreover, that if representation is low—and they believe it should not be proportional—this is because blacks are concentrated in urban areas and in the North where there are fewer political offices compared to rural areas and the South. In other words, the low level of political representation is not explained by vote dilution. Just as the income gap between black and white workers is attributable to the individual failings of blacks rather than labor market discrimination, the reasons why more African Americans are not elected to political office are geographic, not racial.[22]

Racial redistricting, according to the conservative scenario, is not necessary because race no longer really matters in elections. Both racial realists and conservatives think that racial bloc voting is a thing of the past. Increasing numbers of whites vote for blacks, especially in state and local elections. The real problem, according to the Thernstroms, is that blacks will not vote for whites—a dubious claim since white politicians, not blacks, represent most African Americans.[23] Some conservatives also believe that race-baiting political campaigns are no longer tolerated. The evidence the Thernstroms cite for this assertion is changes in George Wallace's campaigns in the 1980s and Strom Thurmond's putative turnabout toward black voters in South Carolina. Although they acknowledge that the first Bush campaign in 1988 inflamed racial hostilities with the Willy Horton ads, the Thernstroms insist that the ads raised a valid issue: the wisdom of prison furloughs for prisoners.

The Thernstroms' claim that blacks are adequately represented is based on arbitrary assumptions and ignores evidence that contradicts it. The Thernstroms never explain why one should assume that representation within a political party counts more than that in the electorate. It is also absurd. Given this reasoning, blacks would improve their political representation if the Democrats *lost* seats in an election. Since black representatives are disproportionately Democrats, blacks would gain a greater share of Democratic Party representatives if the party lost seats.[24] Rather than research the matter, the Thernstroms simply assume that whites will vote for blacks. Thirty years after the VRA was passed, however, blacks had won only 35 of all House elections in white-majority districts (a total of 6,667 elections). Almost one-third of those black victories are the result of Ron Dellums being reelected time and time again by an unusually liberal constituency in Berkeley and Oakland, California.[25]

Conservatives also ignore the question of whether black representation has been diminished by the dilution of African American votes. There is considerable evidence that it has. After the VRA passed, for example, many southern cities either retained at-large elections or switched from ward-based to at-large elections, either of which had serious repercussions for the possibility of electing African Americans to local offices. In southern majority-white cities that retained at-large elections and where blacks were 10 to 30 percent of the population, blacks gained only 1 to 3 percent in representation. In majority-white cities with a black population of 30 to 50 percent, the gain in offices was not much better: 4 percent. But in those southern majority-white cities that changed from at-large elections to single-member districts, and where blacks made up 10 to 30 percent of the population, black officeholding went up 23 percent. In similar cities where blacks were 30 to 50 percent of the population, the gain was even larger: the number of offices held by blacks increased by 34 percent.[26] Given this evidence, it makes no sense to insist that the low level of black representation is the result of extraneous, nonracial factors and that race does not count in elections.

Many conservatives believe that the VRA, as interpreted by civil rights lawyers, has exacerbated race-based politics since the 1960s. Their core objection to the VRA was stated publicly by Justice Clarence Thomas in his concurring opinion in *Holder v. Hall.* Thomas questioned the Court's decision in *Allen,* noting that the Court "converted the Act into a device for regulating, rationing, and apportioning political power among racial and ethnic groups." Thomas went on to argue:

> Far more pernicious has been the Court's willingness to accept the one underlying premise that must inform every minority vote dilution claim: the assumption that the group asserting dilution is not merely a racial or ethnic group, but a group having distinct political interests as well. Of necessity, in resolving vote dilution actions we have given credence to the view that race defines political interest. We have acted on the assumption that members of racial and ethnic groups must . . . have their own "minority preferred" representatives holding seats in elected bodies if they are to be considered represented at all.[27]

If racial groups have distinct political interests, conservatives believe it is because black political leaders have emphasized a "race-conscious" political agenda. They assume the growth of the black middle class since the 1960s and the resulting schism between middle-class and lower-class African Americans undermined any possibility for a coherent black political agenda—or it should have. In *Shaw v. Reno,* Justice O'Connor labeled the notion of a black political agenda an "impermissible racial stereotype." Race-conscious redistricting, she observed, "reinforces the perception that members of the same racial group—regardless of their age, education, economic status, or the community in which they live— think alike, share the same political interests, and will prefer the same candidates at the polls."[28] Today's race-conscious politics is the legacy, according to conservatives, of 1960s black nationalists who went out of their way to antagonize whites. Civil rights leaders who agitate for black-majority legislative districts and black politicians who racially polarize elections perpetuate such intemperate behavior.

Conservative critics draw an invidious distinction between black leaders who appeal to whites and those who emphasize racial issues. For example, the Thernstroms criticize the Congressional Black Caucus for advocating a "race-conscious" agenda and believe this occurs because members of the caucus represent safe districts. With no fear of electoral retaliation, black officeholders are able to stir up issues like whether the

United States should intervene in Haiti, an issue, they assume, that does not resonate with their constituents. Just as the agenda of the 1960s black nationalists was out of step with most African Americans, the Thernstroms believe that most black representatives behave cynically toward their constituents. The political views of blacks, which the Thernstroms agree are substantially to the left of most white voters on economic and social welfare issues, derive from "the pull of African-American politicians who run in settings in which racial and economic militancy pays off politically. Or in which, in any case, candidates are free to engage in the rhetoric of racial and economic justice."[29] In their estimation, black voters do not know their own interests; manipulative black politicians produce their opinions.

On the other hand, the Thernstroms claim, black mayors must pursue a color-blind agenda because they have to compete for white votes. In other words, black politicians who represent predominantly white constituencies are more likely to be politically moderate, if not conservative. Thus, the Thernstroms believe there would be more black elected officials if blacks would run for office in white-majority districts. Black politicians do not, however, because of fear they would lose. The reason few blacks are elected to political office in such districts is that black politicians refuse to move to the center, not that white voters decline to vote for them. The Thernstroms come full circle here: black politicians should have to play by the same rules as white politicians and trim their ideological and policy views to attract their (white) constituents. This is the implicit rule of color-blind politics—like the water that fish cannot see, whiteness is the invisible prevailing norm. Race-conscious redistricting, racial conservatives therefore conclude, will only perpetuate the most invidious features of African American politics.

WHITE CONSCIOUSNESS AND RACIAL POLITICS

It is hard to know whether to take this argument seriously. Since most members of Congress are elected from safe districts, why do the Thernstroms condemn only black elected officials? Why assume that only black elected officials behave irresponsibly and manipulate their constituents? If one is to denounce black representatives for demanding intervention in Haiti, why not criticize Jewish representatives who demand unequivocal support for Israel? The Thernstroms might reply that the survival of Israel concerns their constituents. But why presume that democracy in Haiti is not salient to African American voters? The

Thernstroms' portrayal of black voters hardly squares with their belief in the value of individual voters. Yet this portrayal is based on the false and misguided idea that neither blacks nor any other racial group can have common political interests.

As a group, African Americans display a coherent and distinctive set of political beliefs. This is not particularly remarkable, it is not an artifact of an "impermissible racial stereotype," and black political leaders do not create these beliefs. Two decades of survey research demonstrate that African Americans are far more liberal than whites on matters of economic redistribution, social welfare, and racial inequality. By wide margins they are more likely to favor government aid to help the poor, guarantee jobs, and provide health insurance. On the other hand, blacks diverge far less from whites on matters of foreign policy.[30] Compared to whites, divisions along class lines are far less salient in shaping African Americans' political beliefs. White voters, however, are sharply divided on questions of redistribution, and their differences vary by socio-economic status: wealthy white Republicans are far less enamored of spending money on the poor than white Democrats who live paycheck to paycheck. In stark contrast, affluent, educated blacks are more pro-redistributive than low-income, working-class whites. Remarkably, the views of white Democrats about social welfare are closer to Republicans (an almost entirely white party) than to black Democrats. For example, while 84 percent of black Democrats believe that the government has an obligation to assure the working poor a minimum income, only 54 percent of white Democrats do, and a mere 36 percent of Republicans accept this proposition.[31]

The class schism in the black community—the widening divide between the black middle class and the black poor that underpins the conservative critique of black politics—has not significantly altered black political opinion. The emergence of black conservatism in the 1980s did not substantially change things either. In particular, some evidence indicates that the higher the level of racial consciousness, the more likely African Americans will be to favor comprehensive and redistributive social policies. Michael Dawson suggests that this stems from a strong belief among African Americans that they share a common fate—a belief that their individual lives depend on how all African Americans are treated. This belief "acts as a constraint on class divisions," and, Dawson goes on to say, "regardless of economic status, the stronger the perceived link, the more likely one is to support policies of economic redistribution."[32] In other words, African Americans subscribe to shared beliefs that override class divisions and stem from a common history of slavery, Jim Crow, and contemporary racism.[33]

Conservatives who are hostile to race-conscious redistricting are clearly wrong when they assume that blacks have no substantive interests that could be served by an increased number of African American representatives in Congress and state legislatures. Actually, some of the conservative animus toward black politicians has as much to do with conservatives' antipathy to black support for the welfare state as to their hostility to race-conscious redistricting. The Thernstroms, for example, prefer color-blind redistricting because they assume it will advance a conservative political agenda. The welfare state cannot be dismantled, they assume, because of race-conscious agitators like the Congressional Black Caucus (CBC), which, they point out, "may be the only place on Capitol Hill where entitlements are still spoken of with reverence."[34] Thus, the election of more blacks means adding more left-wing politicians to Congress. Yet defending social welfare entitlements like food stamps or Medicare, which benefit both low-income blacks and whites, can hardly be construed as a race-conscious political agenda. The Thernstroms can make this inference only because they know that blacks are, on average, more liberal than whites.[35]

The conservative assertion that racially polarized elections have virtually disappeared, that whites are ready to vote for black candidates is also incorrect. The impressive body of evidence on racial bloc voting demonstrates that very few blacks are elected from congressional districts in which blacks are less than 40 percent of the population. Only when blacks make up 50 percent of a district's population does the probability of electing a black become better than even (it is 60 percent for black-majority districts). These odds change when the proportion of Latinos increases in a district. David Lublin calculates that there is a 28 percent chance of a black representative being elected in a district that is 45 percent black. The chances rise to 59 percent if that same district is at least 20 percent Latino.[36] Racial bloc voting was routine throughout the South in the 1970s and 1980s. In the eleven southern states of the Confederacy, a minuscule number of blacks were elected to state legislatures, substantially below what would be expected if elections had been truly color-blind. During the 1980s, just 1 percent of the 1,144 white-majority southern state legislative districts elected a black representative. In contrast, 77 percent of black-majority districts did so. And not one white-majority congressional district elected a black representative.[37] "The simple truth," Grofman, Handley, and Niemi conclude, "is that at

the congressional and state legislative level, at least in the South, blacks
are very unlikely to be elected from any districts that are not majority
minority."[38]

Is this evidence of racial hostility to blacks or does it indicate that
black candidates are too liberal for most white voters? It seems that
southern white voters have behaved like white railroaders at the turn of
the twentieth century. The railroad workers refused to allow black workers into their union even though they knew that inclusion would give
them an upper hand with their employers. Responding to the prospect of
admitting black railroaders, one Texas fireman said, "We would rather
be absolute slaves of capital than to take the negro into our lodges as an
equal and brother."[39] This is how low-income white voters acted when
the Voting Rights Act was passed. They opted to vote their racial privileges rather than their class interests. Class voting among whites—measured as the gap between the proportions of working-class and middle-
class whites voting for Democratic presidential candidates—declined
sharply after the civil rights movement and all but disappeared by the
Reagan years. At the same time, racial voting—measured as the difference in the proportions of blacks and whites voting for Democratic presidential candidates—skyrocketed, and by 1984 the gap between the two
was above 50 percent. As the Democratic Party mobilized black voters,
and as they became a significant part of the Democratic Party coalition,
low-income and working-class whites deserted the party. Using exit polls
from the 1984 election, Robert Huckfeldt and Carol Kohfeld show that
in states where blacks accounted for only a small number of Democratic
voters, low-income whites disproportionately voted Democratic. As the
number of blacks increased, however, Democratic voting among low-
income whites decreased.[40]

Huckfeldt and Kohfeld also examined the voting patterns among
blacks and whites in low-income and high-income precincts in southern
cities between 1952 and 1972. Democratic margins of almost 60 percent
in low-income white precincts in 1952 dropped to about 20 percent by
1968–72. The drop-off in high-income white precincts is similar though
not as dramatic, since these voters were more likely to vote Republican.[41]
By the same token, loyal white working-class Democrats in northern
cities usually defected when it looked like a black mayor might be elected.
The 1983 mayoral election in Chicago is a case in point. In a city where
the Democratic nomination was tantamount to election, Harold
Washington, the first black to win the Democratic nomination, received
only 8 percent of the eligible white vote. In contrast, his white Republican

opponent, Bernard Epton, got 59 percent of the eligible white vote, and 33 percent did not vote at all. Only 20 percent of white Chicago Democrats who voted, most of them well-educated liberals, cast their ballots for Washington. Among white blue-collar Catholics, the bedrock of the Chicago Democratic Party, just 10 percent voted for Washington. (Washington did best among Irish working-class Catholics, picking up 18 percent of their vote; he did worst among Italian blue-collar Catholics, most of whom voted for Epton.) Clearly Washington's race was the issue in this election.[42]

Conventional wisdom suggests that this election was an aberration, largely explained by the Windy City's history of segregation. Perhaps Harold Washington was too radical for white Chicagoans and a more typical case is Wilson Goode's election as Philadelphia's first black mayor, also in the spring of 1983. At the time, it was commonly thought that racial polarization played no part in the Philadelphia election. Goode was presumably the sort of black mayor the Thernstroms think can succeed when facing white voters, one who wisely moderates his policy stances. As Paul Kleppner shows, however, this is a wildly misleading impression. Goode won the election by taking 98 percent of a highly mobilized black vote. He got 24 percent of the actual white vote, only marginally more than Washington received. Like the Chicago election, white blue-collar Catholic voters turned against the Democratic Party candidate by an overwhelming margin—Goode received only 12 percent of white blue-collar Catholic votes.[43]

The Chicago and Philadelphia elections are not atypical. A study of twenty-six large cities reveals that when black candidates entered the race, black and white voter turnouts increased and the outcomes were racially polarized.[44] Not surprisingly, successful black candidates depended on large numbers of black voters. And the pattern continued into the 1990s. In mayoral elections in Los Angeles and New York, an Asian American Democrat, Michael Woo, and an incumbent black mayor, David Dinkins, were defeated. Both Woo and Dinkins lost badly among white moderates, and both of their opponents benefited when middle-class whites were mobilized. While both candidates had some obvious liabilities, the fact remains, as Raphael Sonenshein observes, "The winning candidate's electoral coalition was overwhelmingly white in each case and the communities were racially polarized."[45] Thus, contrary to conservative assertions, racially polarized elections and racial bloc voting remain a critical feature of American politics.[46]

The reason lower-class whites defect from the Democratic Party in national elections is not because their nonracial political interests are different than blacks'. When Democratic voters in low-income precincts are compared with blacks who have similar political interests, racial voting persists, overriding social class. Low-income whites and blacks have common political interests. "It is the *presence* of blacks in the Democratic coalition," Huckfeldt and Kohfeld say, "to which lower-status whites object."[47]

Racially polarized voting is due in part to white voters' fear and mistrust of black candidates. In an imaginative study, Keith Reeves showed that despite white voters' reluctance to reveal their racial prejudices to pollsters, their views of blacks are directly linked to their feelings about black candidates. In an experimental survey Reeves devised, he presented white voters with descriptions of two candidates who differed only in their positions regarding two issues, environmental policy and affirmative action. For one group of white voters, both candidates were white; for the other group, one candidate was black. When faced with the black candidate, whom Reeves called Hammond, many whites changed their vote to the undecided category rather than saying they would vote against the black candidate. Reeves showed that these voters were quite hostile to blacks and expressed common negative racial stereotypes. The evidence, he concluded, is tantamount to a "smoking gun," an "obscure but nevertheless strong disinclination on the part of some whites to support the black Hammond candidate who is of [similar] standing [to the] white candidate."[48] Another study found that even when all voters have similar evaluations of city services, white voters express far greater disapproval of a black mayor than do black voters.[49] Voters are plainly not color-blind.

The increasing significance of the Latino vote in big cities and in key states such as California, Texas, and Florida complicates this picture of racial polarization. Many elections no longer turn on the divide between black and white voters. But this does not mean that race is irrelevant to policy debates or elections. In fact, whites and nonwhites remain divided on key issues. For example, blacks, Latinos, and Asian Americans all express strong support for color-conscious policies compared to whites, who disproportionately oppose such policies.[50] All three groups disproportionately voted for the Democratic presidential ticket in the 2000 election. In the South, racially polarized voting continues to be the norm. Al Gore received only one-quarter of the white southern vote.[51]

Racially polarized elections persist for two reasons. The most obvious one is that white candidates often play the race card. Reeves's study, as well as other data, shows that simply identifying an opponent as black easily sways white voters, as will racially coded campaign appeals to stir up racial resentment among white voters. Since 1964 the Republicans have used the race card extensively to attract the most disaffected elements of the Democratic Party coalition: white southerners and northern working-class whites. In mimicking a long-standing southern tradition of race-baiting campaigns, these politicians have cleaned up only the language. As the civil rights movement succeeded in passing legislation, southern campaign techniques were refined and exported to the North. Beginning with George Wallace's forays into the North in 1964 and Barry Goldwater's decision to appeal to southern whites by hunting "where the ducks are," racially coded language has become a mainstay in national elections over the past forty years. More than any other recent political figure, Wallace nationalized a language of racial conservatism or opposition to racial equality and changed the political discourse of racism. His genius was that he appealed to white voters' fear of racial equality by cloaking racist animosities in pungent homilies about overweening and tyrannical judges, oppressive bureaucrats, and threats to the freedoms of ordinary people. Wallace's language was picked up by Republican candidates—Ronald Reagan in his 1966 gubernatorial campaign and, of course, Richard Nixon, who in 1968 courted white voters with racially coded campaign appeals to "freedom of choice" as an alternative to school busing.[52]

Edward Carmines and James Stimson show that by 1972, "race had become 'nationalized' as a central issue in American politics, giving shape and form to many voters' political belief systems."[53] The Republican and Democratic parties were now sharply distinguished in the minds of voters and party activists by their positions on racial issues. These issues were especially salient for Republicans in the 1972 and 1980 presidential elections, as party activists used racially coded appeals to peel off white voters from the Democrats.[54] The Republican Party had become, at least implicitly, an antiblack party, a safe haven for those white voters intent on preserving their racial advantages and whose identity was threatened by the presence of blacks.

Playing the race card has paid off for the Republicans. This is best demonstrated by studies of the Willy Horton ads during the 1988 presidential campaign. These ads were intentionally deployed to "blow up Dukakis," as one of George H. W. Bush's campaign aides described the strategy, and they successfully provoked racial resentment among a significant portion of the white electorate. The Horton ads succeeded precisely because they were framed as messages about crime that conveyed implicit racial messages to voters. This enabled the Bush campaign to appeal to those Democrats and Independents hostile to African Americans.[55] Tali Mendelberg shows that the racial resentment aroused by the implicit message of the Horton ads had a "larger impact on candidate preference than did Republican identification." In the wake of the Bush campaign's success in playing the race card, Republican candidates throughout the 1990s thrived on racially coded campaign ads.[56]

Racially coded campaign slogans have also undermined efforts by moderate black candidates to appeal to white voters. One study demonstrated that in the 1982 California gubernatorial election, where the Republican candidate, George Deukmejian, defeated Tom Bradley, a moderate black Democrat, voters' negative feelings toward blacks and hostility toward governmental efforts to remedy racial inequality overrode Bradley's personal popularity. "Antiblack feelings," the authors conclude, "pushed one toward Republican candidates, even if one were registered as a Democrat."[57]

Nevertheless, the Thernstroms correctly point out that whites will, under certain circumstances, vote for black candidates. White voters did elect Gary Franks and J. C. Watts, both black Republicans, to Congress and elected Norman Rice as Mayor of Seattle. But these elections are not typical. All three candidates were elected from congressional districts or states with minuscule numbers of black residents. This suggests that the relationship between the size of the black constituency and white voting is more important than the question of whether whites will vote for blacks. As V. O. Key Jr. observed long ago in his classic study of southern politics, whites' political behavior is closely related to the size of the black population. He found that as the proportion of blacks in southern counties rose, the turnout of white voters increased. And this was in the 1940s, when most blacks could not vote and were only challenging their disenfranchisement.[58] In legislative districts or cities with few blacks, whites are not concerned that black representatives will respond to racial issues or disadvantage whites.

Just as there is a tipping point in neighborhoods—as the number of black families moving into a largely white neighborhood increases, whites are more likely to say they will move out—there is a tipping point in elections. There is "a great deal of historical and contemporary evidence," Pamela Karlan writes, that "suggests the presence of an influence 'tipping point': blacks are more likely to occupy a pivotal position when they are a relatively small share of the electorate, because white voters are then less likely to perceive them as a threat."[59] The tipping phenomenon explains why blacks have little chance of being elected to office in white-majority districts until the black population reaches at least 45 or 50 percent. The Gary Frankses and J. C. Wattses of this world are very rare.

It is often said, mostly by conservatives, that the reelection of two Southern black representatives in Georgia in 1996, after the Supreme Court ruled their black-majority districts unconstitutional, proves that blacks can be elected from white-majority districts. It is not clear what the victories mean, however, and their reelection may be better explained by the advantages of incumbency. One of the two candidates, Cynthia McKinney, received barely one-third of the white vote, not an insignificant number but insufficient for victory had there not been a substantial black turnout. A recent analysis of congressional elections in the South indicates that in order to be elected for the first time, black candidates must run in black-majority districts or for an open seat in a district in which at least 37 percent of the voting-age population is African American.[60] Besides, one or two elections is hardly conclusive evidence that racially polarized elections have ended.

Racially polarized elections over the past thirty years strongly suggest that racism in America is rooted in a sense of group position rather than in a collection of bigoted attitudes. This history also indicates that most white Americans will not accept black electoral majorities. That is because the stakes in any contest between a white and black candidate go deeper than differences over public policy or struggles for material advantage. The relative status of blacks and whites is also at stake. Electoral competition between blacks and whites and the mobilizing of black voters undermines the taken-for-granted political order, which assumes that whites will be in control and blacks will accede to the arrangement. For blacks, electing an African American legislator promises political influence and signifies that the rules of the old racial order no longer operate. For whites, on the other hand, it disrupts racial hierarchies, threatens their perceived superiority, and undermines the normality of whiteness. It is no wonder then that many whites will vote to maintain the racial status quo even when it works against their political interests.

SHAW V. RENO AND THE BANKRUPTCY OF COLOR-BLIND IDEOLOGY

The creation of black-majority legislative districts evokes the same atavistic fears white voters express when confronted with a growing and politically mobilized black population. Opposition to race-conscious redistricting stems from a perceived threat to white racial prerogatives rather than from commitment to the principle of racial neutrality or a belief in a color-blind political order. As one congressional staff person said to a political analyst, "Nobody questioned the ability of Lindy Boggs [the white Democrat who formerly represented a black-majority district in New Orleans for seventeen years] to represent blacks. She did it wonderfully. Now that a black member represents the district all of a sudden the whites see themselves as disenfranchised. Black voters never assumed they were disenfranchised because they were represented by Lindy Boggs."[61] Similarly, the Supreme Court's redistricting decisions suggest the Court is preoccupied with protecting the political racial status quo or, one might say, with maintaining a political order that assumes white majorities are the norm.

Beginning with *Shaw v. Reno*, the redistricting cases are ordinarily understood as another, more radical, step by the Supreme Court to limit the use of racial classifications for remedies to discrimination or the effects of discrimination. In *Regents of the University of California v. Bakke*, the Court struck down the use of racial quotas but permitted the use of race to allocate places in college classes so long it was only one of several criteria used by decision makers and the costs for nonminorities were not excessive.[62] *Bakke* was something of a halfway house. In the late 1980s, however, the Court began to back away from this standard. In *City of Richmond v. J. A. Croson*, the Court struck down a program that required white-owned construction companies to make a good-faith effort to subcontract some of their work to minority-owned businesses.[63] *Croson* prohibited the government from using even remedial racial classifications in all but the narrowest of circumstances.

Some observers of the Court think that the ostensible question raised by *Shaw*—whether noncompact legislative districts drawn to remedy vote dilution are constitutional—could have been decided on grounds that did not question the creation of black or Latino majority districts. Bernard Grofman points out that there were any number of nonracial arguments the Court could have used to decide the case but did not.[64] Why then did the Court choose to unsettle a more or less settled area of the law in *Shaw* and subsequent cases? In one interpretation, the Court, or at least Justice Sandra Day O'Connor, was concerned about the "excessive" use of race, just as Justice Lewis Powell was in *Bakke*. Samuel Isacharoff understands the *Shaw* ruling to have said "yes but not too much" to the question of racial distinctions.[65] Another interpretation places *Shaw* and its progeny squarely in line with *Croson*. What *Shaw* represents in this view was a "misguided" attempt to apply equal protection law to voting rights, thus ignoring the uniqueness of voting rights law as it has developed from the reapportionment cases.[66]

Although there is some truth to each of these views, what has to be explained is the radical character of the redistricting cases. The decisions in these cases are substantial departures from previous cases involving racial gerrymandering, and they threaten to undo the hard-fought political gains won under the Voting Rights Act. Justice John Paul Stevens posed the obvious question in his dissent in *Shaw*. Noting that the Court permitted legislators to draw district boundaries in order to represent rural voters, union members, Polish Americans, or Hasidic Jews, Stevens asked "whether otherwise permissible redistricting to benefit an underrepresented minority group becomes impermissible when the minority group *is defined by race*."[67] (Emphasis added.)

It seems clear that the majority was prepared to read race out of the redistricting lexicon. Even though Justice O'Connor explicitly indicated that it was not necessarily unconstitutional to consider race in redistricting, the burden of these cases indicates that race should somehow be expunged from the process. *Shaw* encouraged white voters to challenge racial gerrymandering. The Court's decision in *Miller v. Johnson* went even further. By ruling that any district in which race was a "predominant motive" would be subjected to strict scrutiny, the Court questioned practically all the districts into which racial minorities had been placed, or where race had been used as a measure of voters' intentions.[68] The counterrevolution ground to a halt only when the conservative majority split in a Texas case, *Bush v. Vera*. When the smoke had cleared, Justices Kennedy, Thomas, and Scalia would either ban majority-minority districts altogether or at least require that states minimize them. Justices O'Connor and Rehnquist equivocated, meaning it is not entirely clear when they would permit racial classifications to be used in redistricting.[69] Even if the Court has not accepted the full-blown conservative critique of the VRA, the majority is clearly sympathetic to that critique and seems prepared to strike down black or Latino majority districts at will.

But race cannot be read out of every conceivable redistricting decision in the United States. And the Court is clearly aware of this fact. So long as racial divisions matter to elections, so long as African American, Latino, and white votes matter to partisan divisions and policy debates, politicians will factor race into their redistricting calculations. Even though the Court recognizes this, it nonetheless denies that blacks or

Latinos can have racially defined political interests that may be permissibly taken into account in any redistricting process. This is an odd stand, as we indicated earlier, particularly for people who promote the legitimacy of individual preferences. The majority's logic in the redistricting cases is tantamount to saying that the law does not recognize that black voters may have common racial interests that matter.[70] Yet it is also obvious from an analysis of redistricting decisions that the majority, far from banning any consideration of race from redistricting, actually displayed an undue solicitude for *white* voters' prerogatives. While Justice Kennedy argued for a standard of racial neutrality in *Miller*, impartiality is one characteristic of judicial deliberation that is absent in these cases. Underlying the majority's color-blind logic is a concern for the privileged status of white voters.

Some readers may think it is preposterous to suggest that the Court has been preoccupied with protecting whites. But consider this: just as one can say there is a tipping point when white voters feel threatened, there also appears to be a tipping point when black representation becomes a threat to white voters. Our argument rests on an analysis of two claims the Court made in the redistricting cases: that race-conscious redistricting results in a constitutional injury to voters; and that redistricting should be governed by standards of compactness and contiguity. In both instances the Court was receptive to the idea that majority-minority districts harm whites, and it consistently applied a racial double standard.

The first element of our argument turns on the following question: what was the constitutional injury the majority purportedly addressed? The plaintiffs in *Shaw* argued that voters had a right to participate in a color-blind electoral process; an "impression of injustice" resulted, they said, from race-conscious redistricting. This meant, they alleged, that blacks could now elect a representative of their own choice who would presumably see her duty as the "representation of blacks" and nothing more. An amicus brief filed by the Washington Legal Foundation and joined by Senator Jesse Helms and other conservative organizations went further. It argued that white voters living in black-majority districts had been "effectively disenfranchised."[71] The Court rejected the white plaintiffs' claim that their vote had been diluted, but it still insisted that the creation of black-majority districts injured white voters.

Justice O'Connor defined the injury created by black-majority districts as a "lasting harm to our society [that] white voters (or voters of any other race)" could assert. The injury to society was the racial classification itself. The use of race in redistricting, O'Connor said, "reinforces the perception that members of the same racial groups . . . think alike, share the same political interests, and will prefer the same candidates at the polls; may exacerbate the very patterns of racial bloc voting that majority-minority districting is sometimes said to counteract; [and leads] elected officials . . . to believe that their primary obligation is to represent only the members of that group, rather than their constituency as a whole."[72] O'Connor's claim that white voters were injured by the racial classification was not based on any findings of fact; nor was there any evidence for her assertions in North Carolina. What the Court really asserted, according to Karlan and Levinson, was an abstract, hypothetical injury based on an "irrebuttable normative theory." In other words, black-majority districts result in "representational harm."[73] The decision in *Miller* made clear that the mere use of racial classification, absent any adverse effect on plaintiffs, is injurious.

What does it mean to say that racial classification constitutes an injury? Some analysts refer to the injury in the redistricting cases as an "expressive" harm, a term Morgan Kousser derisively labels as a "pure social construction."[74] As many commentators have pointed out, wide application of this standard would threaten numerous governmental activities and jeopardize the boundaries of most congressional districts. If whites in a black-majority district could claim they were injured, surely African Americans, most of whom live in white-majority districts, could plausibly claim they were subject to an unconstitutional racial classification. In fact, the Court's majority sought, by narrowing the scope of their decision, to avoid the unpalatable consequences of declaring that any conceivable use of race rendered redistricting suspect. They did this by claiming that only districts with an untoward appearance (*Shaw*) or cases where race was a "dominant and controlling rationale" (*Miller*) were suspect.[75]

The Court's language suggests that any use of a racial classification is stigmatizing and stereotypes individuals. But the Court has selectively applied the idea that the use of race constitutes an "expressive" harm. Judging by the majority's reasoning, it is not the racial classification by itself that matters. It matters only when it is used to advance nonwhite political representation. The majority was willing to find evidence of injury to whites while ignoring fundamental questions about equality of political representation. For example, Justice Kennedy argued in *Miller* that those individuals injured by wrongful redistricting were injured because the act of dividing them into different districts along racial lines was tantamount to publicly sanctioned segregation. This kind of districting excluded people. But Karlan and Levinson pointedly observe that the plaintiffs in *Miller* "were protesting the *inclusion* of too many nonwhite voters in the district to which they were assigned."[76]

The constitutional injury in *Shaw* and *Miller* might well be called the "tipping injury" because white voters are "injured" by their integration into black-majority districts (most of the new districts were 55 to 60 percent black and thus far more integrated than the typical white-majority district). As Justice Stevens pointed out in his dissent to *Shaw II*, the plaintiffs suffered "from the integrative rather than the segregative effects of the State's redistricting plan."[77] So when is the use of race excessive in redistricting? Apparently, only when it offends whites. At least this is the burden of the Court's reasoning in the redistricting cases.

The Court used the tipping injury to deal with white *filler people,* as they are called, when black- or Latino-majority districts are created. *Filler people* are the individuals added to a district to equalize the population and meet the constitutional requirement of one-person, one-vote. As a set of political choices designed to advance partisan ends, redistricting always favors some groups over others—Republicans seek districts with a majority of well-to-do suburbanites; Democrats favor districts composed largely of union members and racial minorities. Filler people are typically people with no desired political attributes (for example, Republicans added to a largely Democratic district), and thus they are a minority. The recent history of racial gerrymandering by whites can best be understood as a practice that treats black voters exclusively as filler people. Cracking the black vote, for example, means using black voters as filler people across a wide number of districts. Some filler people are unavoidable in any redistricting plan in order to prevent legislators from packing the vote—the law requires that filler people cannot be members of a district's majority group.[78] What this means in practice, of course, is that any black-majority district must include some white voters. Otherwise, the plan could be challenged on grounds of packing the black vote.

In a case decided prior to *Shaw, United Jewish Organizations v. Carey,* the Court concluded that filler people were not denied any rights under the Constitution because they were "virtually represented."[79] In that case, the Hasidic community of Williamsburgh, New York, challenged a redistricting plan that created a new black-majority district and, in order to meet the one-person, one-vote requirement, divided the Hasidic community between two districts. The Court upheld the redistricting plan, arguing the Hasidic community was virtually represented: they could expect to be represented by other white legislators in the state legislature, the Court concluded. For the same reason, the Court assumes that other elected Democrats will represent the stray Democrat in a majority Republican district.

In the redistricting cases, the Court focused on the problem of white filler people, whites added to black-majority districts to meet the equal-population mandate. Although the majority attacked the notion that racial groups have common political interests, the Court implicitly suggested that whites in black majority districts do have a common interest by assuming that they cannot be virtually represented by other whites. Put another way, the Court extends solicitude for white filler people without applying the same concern to black filler people. This appears to be what the Court means when it refers to "representational harms."[80] White privilege, we have argued, is invisible because whites, like the fish, cannot see the water. The redistricting cases, however, are an instance where the water is all too visible to the fish.

The Court also applied a double standard when it insisted, as Justice O'Connor did in her opinion in *Shaw,* that "traditional districting principles such as compactness, contiguity, and respect for political subdivisions" be used to judge whether race had been improperly considered in redistricting. These traditional principles could be used, O'Connor suggested, to rebut any claim of racial gerrymandering.[81] The Court's application of so-called traditional districting principles to racial gerrymanders, most observers agree, is inconsistent with its benign neglect of the shape or appearance of political gerrymanders. Compactness is certainly not a hallowed principle of redistricting—one can find numerous examples of weirdly shaped white-majority districts all over the country, an artifact (as Morgan Kousser's history of racial gerrymandering demonstrates) of the partisanship that drives all redistricting. Nor can one say that compactness is particularly relevant to representation. After all, why should one presume residents of a compact, contiguous area spanning parts of a city and its adjacent suburbs would amount to a more coherent political community than the bizarrely shaped twelfth district in North Carolina? Compactness did not become an issue until the redistricting process favored blacks and Latinos. Then the Court systematically treated black-majority districts differently than white-majority districts.[82]

Applying color-blind logic to redistricting has little to do with racial neutrality. Nor does it do anything to diminish racial conflict or racial stereotyping. The issues that divide blacks and whites will not disappear because of the Court's misguided effort to expunge race from redistricting. What it does do is treat African Americans and other racial minorities unequally. Karlan and Levinson write that "an equal protection principle that treats racially-affiliated voters differently than voters who affiliate along other shared characteristics and makes it more difficult for black voters than for other groups to enact favorable apportionment legislation inverts the constitutional commitments of the Fourteenth and Fifteenth Amendments."[83]

REPRESENTATION AND RACE

Majority-minority districts may not have a future, and some people, including Democratic Party officials, think this is just as well since they believe these districts diminish black political influence rather than augment it. Creating black-majority districts, in this view, only results in electing more Republicans who cannot be said to represent the interests of most African Americans or Latinos. This, at least, is the conclusion of a number of writers and analysts who believe that the 1990 redistricting cost the Democrats the House of Representatives in 1994. The alternative to black-majority districts, they think, is that blacks should cultivate alliances with white Democrats who will represent their interests.[84]

The Republican Party consciously supported racial gerrymanders in the South on the well-founded belief that white southern Democrats— and, they hoped, the Democratic Party as well—would be the real losers. Aggregating black voters (upwards of 65 percent) into one congressional district, they figured, would create additional almost entirely white Republican majority districts. The best available evidence shows the strategy worked in the South—both black Democrats and white Republicans prospered—but not in the North where there was no increase in the number of Republican districts. That is because displaced white northern voters were more likely to be registered Democrats than in the South. Although the creation of black-majority districts in the South helped white Republicans, redistricting did not cost the Democrats the House in 1994. Voters repudiated the Democrats across the country, not just in the South, and without the 1994 Republican tide, white Democrats who lost black voters due to redistricting would likely have survived.[85]

Blacks are clearly better off with Democratic majorities in Congress. But that does not settle the question of whether white Democrats adequately represent the interests of black voters. The Thernstroms, among others, insist that white Democrats, particularly those in districts with a sizable share of black voters, have ample incentive to meet the demands of their black constituents. This assumes race does not matter to representation. Black voters sharply disagree; almost two-thirds believe that white elected officials will not adequately represent their interests as well as an African American politician.[86] The available evidence suggests that black voters' skepticism of white Democrats is well founded.

In an analysis of roll-call voting among North Carolina Democrats, Morgan Kousser found dramatic differences between the voting behavior of the two black Democrats elected from the new districts and all other white Democrats. The white Democrats were far more conservative. Just as one would surmise from studies of white Democratic voters, their votes were more like their Republican colleagues' than black Democrats' were. White Democratic representatives from North Carolina, Kousser notes, consider "their 'primary obligations' to be to whites, while they have largely ignored the opinions of the black members of their constituencies."[87]

The best evidence that an elected official's race is crucial to the kind of representation blacks receive comes from a recent study of congressional representation. David T. Canon found that white members of Congress in districts 25 to 50 percent African American paid less attention to their black constituents' interests than black members of Congress. "African-American members of the House," Canon writes, "are more attentive to the distinctive needs of the black constituents than are their white counterparts who represent substantial numbers of blacks."[88] In an analysis of roll-call votes on racial issues, Canon found that black legislators were more responsive to African American constituents than white legislators were. He also found that white legislators were much less likely than black legislators to make speeches on racial issues or sponsor bills that focused on racial policy issues, matters their black constituents care about.[89] Ironically, Canon discovered that blacks elected from the South because of the 1990 redistricting did a much better job representing their white constituents than white legislators did representing blacks. Justice O'Connor's fear that blacks would represent only blacks turns out to be untrue. She should have worried more about the kind of representation blacks would receive in white-majority districts.

Just as white legislators are more responsive to their white constituents, it is doubtful that a majority-white political party would adequately represent the interests of black or Latino minorities. The reason for this, political scientist Paul Frymer recently suggested, is that a competitive two-party system in a racially divided society will "legitimate an agenda reflecting the preferences of white voters," and ignore black voters.[90] In a political system with single-member districts and plurality elections, political leaders have powerful incentives to appeal to the median voter, one of the large group of swing voters in the middle of the liberal-conservative continuum. Voters on either end of the continuum are typically dissatisfied with the moderate center. But in a competitive two-party system if they are to win elections, politicians must aim for the middle, where most voters reside.

It is commonly assumed that the political interests of black people will be adequately represented in a competitive party system because politicians will appeal to black voters like any other voter. The addition of black or Latino voters to the electorate merely shifts the median voter toward a political party's positions. Thus, there is a powerful incentive for party politicians to respond to minority demands. But this is only true, Frymer argues, when race is not a politically divisive issue. When race matters to political and social life, and when there are sharp divisions of opinion between the white majority and the black-Latino minority, politicians appeal to the white median voter rather than all median voters.[91] The logic of party competition in a racially divided society leads party leaders to ignore black voters' interests because it costs them white swing votes. Black voters, therefore, become a captured minority in one party, unable to switch parties and ignored by their own. Thus, party competition is not a viable alternative to race-conscious redistricting. So long as whites adamantly insist on defending their racial interests, politicians will mainly represent the median white voter's desires.

There is a perverse irony to the controversy over redistricting. The Court's attack on racial gerrymandering, its concern for the plight of white filler people, and its abandonment of virtual representation in the case of whites, raises the question of whether single-member districts can adequately represent the multitude of interests in a diverse society. The very problems that bothered the Court about racial gerrymandering are intrinsic to redistricting. Indeed the Court cannot clearly distinguish between racial gerrymandering, which is unconstitutional, and political gerrymandering, which is legal.[92]

This leaves us with the question of alternatives to single-member districts, whether the options are cumulative voting or more direct forms of proportional representation. It is debatable whether proportional representation is a solution or even a realistic possibility. What is not debatable is that political rights do not begin and end with the right to vote.

The issue is not whether a certain number of African Americans hold public office but whether African Americans and other racial minorities can acquire sufficient political leverage to influence public policy. Without a radical, and unlikely, change in the American system of territorial-based representation, majority-minority districts may be the only way to do this.

Without a crystal ball, it is difficult to know how these issues will evolve. But one thing is certain: the conservative case against black or Latino majority districts does not hold up. There is no evidence for their assertions, and their fears have not materialized. Rather than Balkanizing politics, black-majority districts have improved representation for *both* blacks and whites. They have also undermined white stereotypes of how black elected officials act. In sharp contrast, the color-blind logic espoused by racial conservatives, including the Supreme Court majority, is pernicious. It denies African Americans and Latinos adequate representation. The assumption that only individual representation matters and that racial groups cannot have common political interests relegates blacks and Latinos to the margins. It treats them as filler people instead of citizens. Color-blind redistricting denies the power of race in American politics and treats blacks and Latinos fundamentally different from whites. While whites suffer "representational injury" when they are a minority in a legislative district, blacks are immune to this injury when they are the minority. This recipe protects white dominance and undermines the promise of political equality contained in the Fourteenth and Fifteenth Amendments to the Constitution and the Voting Rights Act.

FACING UP TO RACE

Those of us who came of age in the 1960s grew up in a society where racism was overt. It was difficult to ignore or deny; the evidence of segregation was often as stark as the lettering on a "whites only" sign. The visibility of racial discrimination, together with the moral power of the civil rights movement, mobilized people of all races against Jim Crow laws and ushered in landmark civil rights legislation to end it. Divided into black and white, the world was relatively uncomplicated, and the options were straightforward. One favored either integration or segregation.

The majority of Americans alive today, however, were not even born when the Civil Rights Act was passed in 1964. In a very real sense, they are a post–civil rights generation. They have grown up in a world where de jure discrimination and segregation have been illegal for nearly forty years, the longest period that this has been true in American history. Because of the civil rights revolution, overt prejudice is at an all-time low, a significant African American middle and professional class has emerged, and at least some people of color can be found at the highest levels of every institution in American life, from the mayor's office to the State Department.

At the same time, the post–civil rights era is also a world of high crime rates and joblessness in black communities, with such deep enervating poverty that young, poor African Americans are sometimes called the "throwaway generation." Many in the post–civil rights generation see black students failing to graduate from high schools and colleges at the same rate as white students, homeless black men and women begging on the streets, jails full of young black men, and "broken" black families. Most believe these problems persist despite a rich assortment of programs and laws offering special opportunities and assistance to minorities. Consequently, an increasing number of white Americans think that the problems of many blacks cannot be attributed to discrimination—if anything, they believe discrimination today works in the opposite direction. It tilts the playing field against whites who are not beneficiaries of special programs.

White Americans, and African Americans and Latinos, are sharply divided over the successes and failures of the civil rights movement. African Americans are deeply disillusioned about the future. At the turn of the millennium, 71 percent of African Americans believed racial equality would not be achieved in their lifetimes or would not be achieved at all.[1] Seventy-three percent of African Americans believed they were economically worse off than whites. White Americans, on the other hand, are unduly sanguine about the state of black America. According to a recent survey, a majority of whites think blacks are worse off than whites themselves are, but 38 percent think blacks' economic status is about the same as their own (see table 3). Fifty percent of whites think America has achieved racial equality in access to health care, and 44 percent think African Americans have jobs that are about the same as those of whites.

As we have documented, however, white Americans are seriously misinformed. Blacks and Latinos are less likely to have access to health care, and blacks' and Latinos' income and occupational status lag substantially behind whites'.[2] In contrast to whites' perceptions, African Americans see a future of cramped economic opportunities. The difference of opinion could not be deeper: almost three-quarters of African Americans think they have less opportunity than whites, while almost three-fifths of whites think blacks have the same opportunities as they have. (The discrepancy in perceptions between Latinos and whites is almost as great as that between blacks and whites, though whites think Latinos are worse off than blacks.)

White Americans' failure to see durable racial inequality is hardly surprising. Racial realists have been saying for years that there is no more color line, that racism is no longer a powerful force in American life. Some version of this view is now a staple in the discourse on race in America not only among a handful of conservative social scientists but also among most whites, though few can muster the same sorts of statistical arguments to support them. What we have called the "racial realist" perspective comes close to being a consensus among whites in the United States today; it crosses conventional political boundaries and encompasses a great many people of good will. Increasingly, it drives our social and legal policies toward racial issues.

TABLE 3. ATTITUDES TOWARD BLACK
AND LATINO ECONOMIC PROGRESS BY RACE

	Attitudes Regarding African Americans		Attitudes Regarding Latino Americans	
	According to		*According to*	
	Blacks	*Whites*	*Latinos*	*Whites*
Oportunities available:				
more than whites	1%	13%	6%	11%
less than whites	74	27	61	32
about the same	23	58	28	54
Discrimination faced:				
a lot	48	20	28	15
some	39	51	59	49
little	9	17	16	24
none	2	8	5	9
Income:				
better off than whites	9	4	11	5
worse off than whites	73	57	60	68
about the same	15	38	27	26
Access to health care:				
better off than whites	9	11	15	6
worse off than whites	61	35	50	46
about the same	26	50	33	42
Types of jobs:				
better off than whites	9	6	12	6
worse off than whites	67	49	61	65
about the same	23	44	27	27

SOURCE: "Washington Post/Kaiser Foundation/Harvard University Racial Attitudes Survey," *Washington Post,* July 11, 2001.

Racial realists insist that the troubling and stubborn gaps in life-chances between black and white Americans no longer have much, if anything, to do with racism; they are not the result of discrimination in any meaningful sense. The way racial realists account for these disparities, however, is not so clearly stated, as earlier chapters indicate. At one extreme, the end-of-racism talk has helped fuel a resurgence of biological or genetic explanations for racial inferiority—arguments that are never far from the surface when race is discussed in America.[3] Closer to the mainstream, racial realists argue that some—usually vaguely defined—cultural and behavioral deficits are mainly to blame for the continued troubles of blacks in the United States.

Compared to the pre–civil rights era, racial discrimination today is often relatively invisible—at least to those who do not experience it. But just because racism is often harder to see, we should not conclude that it is gone. As we have shown repeatedly, the color of one's skin still determines success or failure, poverty or affluence, illness or health, prison or college. Race matters for two reasons—reasons that are separable in theory but closely intertwined in everyday life.

First, there is still substantial direct racial discrimination in many areas of American life. It is true, as the racial realists say, that things are not what they were during Jim Crow. It is emphatically *not* true, however, that overt discriminatory practices have largely disappeared from American life. Perhaps the most striking evidence that overt discrimination is still practiced is employers' widespread use of derogatory preconceptions to judge the qualifications of young black men. Evidence from other realms of social life is also abundant and compelling. In the criminal justice system, for example, it is now hard to avoid the mounting evidence of racial stereotyping and targeting at every stage of the process. Virtually all studies of racial disparities in incarceration, moreover, now show a significant residue of discrimination, even when potentially relevant social and legal factors are controlled. Residential discrimination persists despite Herculean efforts during the past thirty years to undo it. The hard fact is that all too many employers, apartment owners, lenders, prosecutors, and police use derogatory racial images in their routine dealings with people of color that hardly differ from the ones that flourished a hundred years ago. There can be no serious encounter with problems produced by race in America today that avoids the pervasiveness and destructive impact of plain old-fashioned racism.

Looking beyond plain old-fashioned racism, however, the second reason race matters is that the most important source of continuing racial disparities in modern America is still the legacy of past patterns of discrimination and racially coded patterns of disinvestment. Disaccumulation, as we have called it, persists today in good part because the people of the United States never moved with sufficient seriousness to remedy it. This is both the most crucial reality to understand in comprehending the problem of durable racial inequality in the twenty-first century, and the one that seems hardest for many Americans to fully grasp—because this kind of racism is largely invisible.

Much of the debate about race in America today still revolves around the question of whether ongoing racial disparities in schooling, jobs, income, incarceration, and other realms are mainly the result of current overt discrimination *or* the result of flawed culture and behavior of people of color. As we have demonstrated throughout this book, the correct answer is *neither*. Most of the current gap in life-chances and various measures of performance between blacks and whites reflects the legacy of past decisions—decisions that cumulatively resulted in a profound imbalance in the most fundamental structures of opportunity and support in America. In housing, in education, in transportation, in employment policy, and in income support/social insurance policy, the choices that systematically disadvantaged black Americans were also ones that, by design or otherwise, benefited white Americans. These policies, in combination and over generations, have had enormous and pervasive consequences.

There is no way the consequence of these deeply embedded patterns of racial discrimination and racially biased policies could have been realistically expected to disappear with the passage of civil rights legislation in the 1960s. That legislation helped, and helped mightily, to clear a legal path for African Americans, Latinos, and other groups to begin to overcome the legacy of discrimination. And it is crucial to preserve those gains against encroachment. But the removal of formal legal barriers to opportunity could not, by itself, rectify the effects of generations of systematic institutional disadvantage. A far deeper commitment on a variety of fronts was needed to reverse the crippling legacy of racial disaccumulation—what the Kerner Commission in the 1960s, a body that clearly recognized this imperative, called a "massive, compassionate, and sustained" assault on the crisis of the inner cities. That commitment never materialized, and that default of vision and policy bears a good part of the responsibility for the state of black America today.

Many whites see the *effects* of that legacy of disaccumulation—high crime rates, low educational attainment, poverty, and family breakdown—and, confusing symptoms with causes, conclude that these effects demonstrate the depth of cultural and behavioral deficits among blacks. This phenomenon of selective perception is understandable in a sense, because the causes—the fundamental social processes that led to the symptoms—tend to be relatively invisible in the present, while the symptoms are all too visible. To fully grasp the causes requires looking back into history and digging, as we have, through the voluminous research literature. The causes do not jump out in the way the symptoms often do. So it is not terribly surprising that the murky and temporally distant root causes of racial disadvantage get short shrift in the public consciousness, while the immediate symptoms drive much of our public debate about race.

The majority of white Americans today do not comprehend the multiple ways in which their lives are enhanced by a legacy of unequal advantage. They are unaware because their racial position is so much a part of their accepted surroundings that they do not even recognize it. They take it for granted. They consider it normal. All too many white Americans ascribe their well-being and hard-earned success to their own efforts, while believing that African American poverty is the result of character flaws or just plain laziness.

If we are to face up to race instead of whitewashing it, we must begin by acknowledging a fundamental reality: race is a relationship, not a set of characteristics that one can ascribe to one group or another. Racial inequality stems from a system of power and exclusion in which whites accumulate economic opportunities and advantages while disaccumulation of economic opportunity disempowers black and Latino communities. Therefore, the first task in challenging America's color line is to change the terms of discourse. It is time to move beyond the debate over color-blind versus color-conscious policies and to begin to discuss how we can change the devastating dynamics of accumulation and disaccumulation between black and white communities.

ATTACKING DURABLE RACIAL INEQUALITY

Now that segregation is illegal but racial inequality and discrimination persist, what can we do to challenge durable racial inequality? What kinds of policy strategies make sense? A vigorous political debate has erupted around these questions, and at least three political responses have emerged. One, forcibly articulated by law professor Derrick Bell, is that racism is a permanent feature of American society and cannot be eradicated.[4] The second strategy addresses racial inequality by attacking class inequality. Advocates of this position assume that social class is more fundamental to contemporary inequality than race. William Julius Wilson has believed for a long time that African Americans need to realize that black poverty is mainly caused by "*nonracial* economic forces"—wage stagnation among workers, collapsing demand for unskilled labor, and widening wealth inequality.[5] A third strategy calls for transforming American culture and identity. Proponents of this approach argue that white identity must be abolished or rearticulated as a positive identity.[6]

We agree with Derrick Bell that racial inequality is a fundamental feature of American society, but we are not sure it is permanent and incapable of being altered. It would be a mistake, however, to ignore Bell's powerful statement or to ascribe it to some idiosyncratic pessimism on his part. Bell's views reflect those of many African Americans who believe the civil rights revolution has not delivered on its promise. A recent survey of participants in the Million-Man March discovered that African American men today are far more racially conscious than integrationists in the pre-1965 era. They are "far more concerned with reforming the economic, political, and social order and removing racial impediments to their progress than with mere racial integration per se."[7] There is more support today for some form of black independence and autonomy than anytime since the late 1960s. The current racial consciousness among African Americans cuts across divisions between the black middle class and the black poor, and it has a powerful impact on black public opinion.[8] Historically, support for black nationalism and demands for racial solidarity have coincided with white opposition to racial equality. Today resurgent black nationalism reflects the corrosion of the 1960s egalitarian civil rights agenda into formal equality and white opposition to color-conscious policies.

Even if Derrick Bell is correct in his prognosis that durable racial inequality is permanent, it must be challenged. It cannot be ignored. And while we celebrate diversity and applaud cultural pluralism, we do not think that changing identities will eliminate or minimize the harsh realities of the durable racial inequality we have described in this book. Nor do we think that remedies for class inequality by themselves will overcome persistent racial stratification. In fact, if our analysis of U.S. social policies since the New Deal reveals anything, it is the folly of assuming class-specific policies will benefit all racial groups equally.

How then, can we undo racial inequality in America? We do not pretend to offer a detailed comprehensive blueprint for antiracist policies in the twenty-first century. Instead, we offer a set of principles for social action derived from our analysis, and examples of specific policies that address the constituent elements of contemporary racial inequality. Throughout this book we have distinguished between the historical legacy of racial discrimination and the current sources of contemporary racial disparities such as labor market discrimination and other institutionally generated inequalities. In actual experience, however, they are so closely intertwined that the consequences are difficult to disentangle. For example, the legacy of systematic public and private disinvestment in minority communities has led to the wholesale destruction of jobs and a constellation of social conditions that, most criminologists would agree, tend to increase the risks of violent crime and make street drug dealing relatively attractive despite its many perils to minority youth. The absence of significant investment in public employment and training programs creates a situation in which many younger black men have little experience with the world of socially acceptable work. At the same time, the reality of high levels of criminal violence and widespread open-air drug sales is in turn used by authorities to justify racial profiling that explicitly and overtly focuses police resources on minority communities, saddling young black men with arrest records. When they make hiring decisions, employers then use these realities to justify screening out young black men on the grounds that they are less reliable, more costly, and more troublesome employees.

Because the contemporary situation of African Americans and Latinos reflects both the persistence of overt discrimination and the enduring legacy of racially targeted disaccumulation, any effective long-term strategy to reduce racial disparities must tackle both at once. Strategies that address only the biased treatment of blacks will not touch the deep structural ills that hobble many blacks in the community, the economy, and the schools. Conversely, strategies confined to universal structural remedies will not confront the special barriers discrimination places in the path of people of color.

It should also be clear from earlier chapters that the central problem of disaccumulation in minority communities is a product of both private actions and public policies, and sometimes of both in concert. Accordingly, any effective assault on racial inequality must operate simultaneously on private and public institutions. Within the public sector, moreover, disaccumulation reflects not only the many ways in which the government is too *little* present in minority communities but also the ways in which it is too *much* present. Developing better and fairer social policies means not just providing more public investment in communities of color; it also requires changing the way public investment is now deployed in those communities. There is too little public investment in health care or job creation in the black community and too much public investment in corrections. There is too much public investment in the punitive response to drug abuse and too little public investment in high-quality drug treatment. There is too much public investment in tax breaks to lure large businesses to the ghetto, and too little public investment in the salaries of schoolteachers and day-care workers.

With these considerations in mind, we propose two kinds of policies that engage the sources of contemporary racial inequality. The first are policies that confront the legacy of disaccumulation in black and Latino communities. These policies are likely to be expensive, at least in the short run. They do, however, have the advantage of benefiting not just African Americans and Latinos but also a wide cross section of Americans. The second set of policies is aimed at diminishing current discrimination, both direct and indirect, intentional and unintentional, and encourages diversity in educational institutions. Like the problems they are designed to address, these strategies are often closely intertwined in everyday life, but they are analytically separable. Remedies for racial inequality require both redistribution of *resources* and *rules* capable of regulating the practices that generate racial inequality. Sometimes that means changing the rules of the game so that the playing field is less tilted toward whites; sometimes it means maintaining or strengthening rules that are already in place to counter discriminatory practices.

REVERSING DISACCUMULATION, INCREASING ACCUMULATION

Because the foundational source of much racial disparity today lies in historically embedded disaccumulation in black and Latino communities—not just in jobs and income but also in education, health, crime, and other realms—the search for solutions should focus on policies that allow individuals and communities to accumulate economic resources. This is not the same as simply increasing individuals' "human capital," which has been the main economic strategy to dismantle racial disadvantage up to the present. Efforts to boost minority skills should be one part of a larger attack on racial inequality, but only one part. The overarching goal should be to replace long-standing patterns of disinvestment in minority communities with investment in those communities. This means, among other things, reversing the common use of public policy to augment the income and wealth of whites at the expense of blacks and other groups.

Any effective policy to combat racial inequality today must be sensitive to the complex relationships between race and class in America. Many of the policies we propose are universalistic in that they benefit disadvantaged people of all races. However, we obviously do not think that universalistic or class-based policies alone will remedy the racial disparities described throughout this book. At the same time, we see no point in proposing universalistic policies that reinforce racial inequalities. The best policies mitigate racial inequality while also, if possible, lifting all boats. The minimum wage is an example, since it benefits low-income workers of all races.

In recent years a number of policies have been widely promoted to substitute market mechanisms for concerted public sector commitment. Although market-oriented solutions are ideologically and politically popular today, they may do more harm than good. The privatization of social security, for example, would virtually eliminate the redistributive features of the program as it now operates, leading to yet another form of upward income redistribution. Similarly, we think that tax incentives such as enterprise zones have limited use in rebuilding inner-city communities. Enterprise zones are enormously popular today, but their usefulness for combating racial disparities is minimal at best. These strategies typically entail large subsidies to the private sector that are generally much larger than up-front budgetary expenditures on economic or neighborhood development. Moreover, enterprise zones are subject to manipulation by businesses and politicians in ways that rarely benefit low-income people. Some cities have used enterprise zone subsidies to subsidize sports stadiums, convention centers, and other projects that have little or no benefit for poor inner-city workers and their families. In general, we think policies that erode the public sector (which has historically been critical to black economic advancement) will intensify racial inequality, especially as enforcement of civil rights in the private sector is reduced.

This does not mean, however, that we see no role for the private sector in reconstructing inner-city communities. Our point is rather that support for private sector initiatives needs to be assessed in the light of whether these initiatives can actually deliver tangible economic and social development benefits to residents. We believe, for example, that public-private partnerships to grow small businesses in inner-city communities offer some promise.

Given these criteria, we focus on three kinds of policies that are especially urgent today: (1) stepped-up public investment in schools, jobs, and critical services; (2) strategies that will create wealth in minority communities; and (3) policies to increase what economists call the "social wage"—the social and economic benefits that supplement earned income.

PUBLIC INVESTMENT IN SCHOOLS, JOBS, AND SERVICES There can be no enduring reversal of the legacy of disaccumulation without accumulation, that is, without increased investment in inner-city communities. Unless these investments are made, piecemeal reform of inner-city schools or welfare reform programs will fail. There is overwhelming evidence that the physical and economic deterioration of inner-city communities impedes the ability to alleviate deep poverty in these neighborhoods. Public investment should be designed to reduce social and physical isolation and to provide access to jobs, better schools, and needed services. While policies devised to transport poor African Americans from their neighborhoods to suburban jobs might help in the short run, they are no substitute for robust investment in those neighborhoods.

Improved education has become everyone's favorite remedy for racial inequality. We have argued that vouchers or programs that just shift African Americans into private (Catholic) schools are not likely to yield substantial improvement in test scores and performance. The problem is that most black children go to schools with fewer resources, lower-quality teachers, and lower expectations, even though many of them come from home and community environments that beg for *more*, not less, investment in their schooling. Voucher programs will do little to help the majority of poor black children.

The nation's priorities for allocating current educational resources are backward. Schools in low-income minority communities, which present the most difficult problems and most challenging needs, tend to get the fewest resources in terms of money, qualified personnel, or special programs. Thus in California, nearly forty thousand teachers, 14 percent of the teaching force overall, are presently working with emergency credentials in the state's public schools. Only half of the teachers hired in New York City in 2001 were certified.[9] As a report in the *Los Angeles Times* noted, "Novices tend to be concentrated in the lowest-performing schools—those in neighborhoods of stubborn poverty. These teachers are victims of an absurd pecking order that values seniority over need and typically consigns the greenest teachers to the toughest jobs."[10]

In order to improve preparation for school and college, we should provide free, high-quality preschool education to all low-income pupils beginning at age two, as is done in France and Scandinavia. We should also provide the resources for lower-income schools to reduce class size, recruit better teachers, and provide the richness in course offerings taken for granted in affluent school districts. (Proposed national legislation providing $6 billion through 2008 for training teachers who serve disadvantaged students is a step in the right direction.)

Similarly, it is critical to reverse the sources of disaccumulation put in motion by the criminal justice system. The massive increases in incarceration of blacks and Latinos during the past twenty years have resulted in an unprecedented economic and social disaster for these communities, and at the same time have radically changed the practice of criminal justice for the worse. Perversely, the enormous sums we now spend on imprisonment cut deeply into monies for programs that would prevent crime in the first place and would turn some offenders into productive citizens. Few things are more important to the future of black and brown America than reversing this destructive trend. Doing so will require challenging the discriminatory practices that continue to fuel the explosion of minority incarceration (we discuss this below). But it also requires increased investment in alternatives to incarceration that could help break the vicious cycle of over-criminalization, mass incarceration, and the resulting depletion of opportunity and human capital in minority communities.

For example, a criminal justice strategy more heedful of our collective future should strive to greatly enhance the quantity and, as important, the *quality* of drug treatment available in minority communities. Doing so will not only improve the prospects for many people now disabled by substance abuse but will simultaneously reduce the drug dealing and associated violence that undermines community stability, deters productive investment, and justifies the aggressive antidrug enforcement that now swells the jails and prisons with people of color. Effective drug treatment does not come cheaply: it requires considerable up-front investment, but, as has been repeatedly demonstrated, it generates substantial savings in the long run.

Investment should also be expanded in community-based programs that divert youth from the juvenile and adult justice systems and intensively treat their underlying problems in the community, not behind bars. At the same time, the primacy of rehabilitation in the juvenile justice system should be reasserted, and that commitment backed up with greatly increased investment in programs offering literacy training, education, and other strategies that integrate young offenders into the community. Both strategies would help end the revolving-door practices of the current juvenile justice system and instead harness the productive capacities of many young people who are now progressively discarded and handicapped because of their entanglement in the justice system. As with good drug treatment, there is strong evidence that the best alternative programs for youth in trouble not only effectively reduce crime and incarceration but are also cost-effective.

These are only a few areas that cry out for increased public investment. We could point to many others: public investment in inner-city infrastructure—construction, renovation, and expansion of schools, health clinics, day care, and housing; expansion of neighborhood development banks with substantial infusions of public cash; and combining redevelopment with public jobs programs for inner-city residents. Each of these strategies is intended to enhance the resources and capacities of those groups that have been most adversely impacted by generations of disaccumulation. They are explicitly redistributive, but they are not giveaways. They are strategic investments in the future. So is the second kind of policies we propose: strategies to create wealth in minority communities.

WEALTH CREATION It is popular today to propose redistributing assets rather than income as a strategy to reduce entrenched economic inequality. A coalition of private charities and philanthropies in Northern California, for example, Assets for All, has established a program to augment the savings of low-income workers. For every dollar that eligible workers save, Assets for All contributes two dollars. These savings accounts can be used for getting an education, starting a small business, buying or repairing a home, or going into retirement. Such programs point in the right direction, but we think bolder proposals are in order. As we have shown, the present distribution of wealth has multiple and pervasive negative consequences for blacks and Latinos. We know, for example, that college graduation rates are highly dependent on wealth, notably home ownership. To be successful, programs for increasing education and training need to be backed by substantial subsidies. Wealth creation is one way to address this problem.

Some proposed schemes involve broad redistribution of wealth, such as providing every citizen a trust fund at birth based on stocks or bonds. The debate over reparations for slavery and Jim Crow usually envisions distributing a lump sum to every African American, much like the reparations policy for the internment of Japanese Americans during World War II. We are inclined to support more tailored schemes in which assets could be used for education (college as well as specific skills training) or for start-up funds for a business. One of the main goals of this program would be to ensure that poor children of color are educated to the fullest extent possible. The appropriate analogy in this regard is the retraining programs for World War II veterans, which were instrumental in generating upward mobility for returning soldiers, many from poor backgrounds.

Where would the money be found for these programs? One possibility is a tax on wealth, whose proceeds would then be dedicated to financing various asset schemes for low-income blacks, Latinos, and whites.

This is especially attractive since the recent elimination of the estate tax is likely to dry up charitable contributions that might have helped fund wealth creation. The repeal of the estate tax will cost the federal government an estimated $1 trillion over the next twenty years.[11] Instead of tax relief for the offspring of the wealthiest 1 percent of the population, these funds could be used for a trust fund like the social security trust, with grants available for education and job training, small business capital, and down payments on home ownership.

There is also a civil rights component to reducing minority disaccumulation. Because home ownership is the main source of wealth for most people, housing discrimination against African Africans must be eliminated. So tough enforcement of laws against redlining and other forms of mortgage discrimination are clearly needed. But we think it is necessary to go further. One approach would be to create a source of public funding to repay the losses from residential segregation and other forms of indirect discrimination. This could be a way to recognize and remedy losses from discrimination without necessarily blaming individual or institutional defendants who may be convinced they have done nothing wrong. The quantity of compensatory funds could be linked to demonstrated levels of discriminatory impact in different arenas such as education, housing, or city services. Such a strategy would make it possible to repair the devastating impacts of racial inequality and would help to tackle the overarching problem of disaccumulation.

EXPANSION OF THE SOCIAL WAGE The relative absence of public entitlements often taken for granted in other industrial nations greatly exacerbates the difficulties American minorities experience in the labor market. Inequality in family disposable income is much higher in the United States than in societies with more extensive safety nets. Moreover, as we have shown, racial inequities operate within America's relatively meager safety net. The place to start is with a policy that makes sure every person in the country has access to health insurance. Universal access to health care is a prerequisite to equal opportunity in education, employment, or continuation of life itself. That goal requires a single-payer plan, universal health insurance, expanded public health programs, or something equivalent. In addition, public sector health facilities and safety net provider institutions should be significantly expanded, particularly in communities devastated by the disaccumulation of health care sites and practitioners. Tax incentives or subsidies to private sector hospitals might bring some of them back to inner cities from the suburbs. At the least, private hospitals should be encouraged to retain or initiate outpatient clinics in cities and unserved rural areas and to provide subsidized transportation and video connections, telemedicine connections, or both to more distant acute care facilities.

At the same time, we should greatly expand the Earned Income Tax Credit (EITC) and housing subsidies. The latter could be expanded by developer subsidies to build affordable and low-income housing and rent supplements or homeowner subsidies. Since some of these policies are dependent on employment, we also need policies that can help single mothers and others who are out of the labor force, or only intermittently in it, by including a child or mother allowance or both, funded through an expansion of survivors' benefits and a revamped unemployment compensation system. The current unemployment system covers far fewer people than it did twenty years ago, partly because of policy changes and partly because of the growth of temporary employment. Historically, eligibility for unemployment compensation was pegged to permanent, full-time work. As the character of work has changed, fewer workers are eligible. Ironically, today all workers are treated much like women (or minority men) have always been treated: women have always been more likely to move in and out of the labor force and are therefore disproportionately excluded from unemployment benefits. We should imagine ways in which the unemployment compensation system might become part of an all-purpose safety net geared to the realities of today's labor markets. Such a safety net would go far toward eliminating the racial disparities that have been characteristic of the U.S. welfare state.

ATTACKING PERSISTENT DISCRIMINATION

The measures we have just outlined are intended to counter the legacy of past discrimination by providing the critical investments that would help build the capacities of individuals, stabilize and strengthen communities, and reverse the effects of generations of neglect. These investments would help minorities to compete, but that competition would still be fundamentally unequal unless we also do our utmost to tackle the sources of *current* discrimination. Because, as we have shown, current discrimination can be both direct and indirect, intentional and unintentional, any strategy to combat it must be multifaceted. We think three kinds of policies need to be emphasized: (1) strengthening and augmenting antidiscrimination laws, (2) promoting diversity, and (3) challenging ostensibly neutral institutional practices that routinely generate inequality.

INVIGORATING ANTIDISCRIMINATION LAWS Today nothing is more contentious in the debate over racial inequality than the use of antidiscrimination laws that began with the Civil Rights Act of 1964. Conservatives have argued that the array of laws designed to prevent racial discrimination in employment, housing, and other realms, however well intended, have been a disaster—bringing unwarranted government intervention, giving unfair advantages to the less qualified, and undermining economic efficiency and productivity. But, as we have shown in earlier chapters, the notion that these laws have done more harm than good is simply wrong. It is certainly true that antidiscrimination measures did not eliminate racial inequality. But, for reasons we have made clear, no one should have expected them to. Instead, antidiscrimination laws have been an important, if limited, part of the story of black economic and social advancement in the years since World War II. They did help to narrow racial inequalities in jobs, income, and schooling. And they did so without the dire consequences for productivity and fairness that many predicted and some still fear.

But if the conservative view is empirically wrong, it has nevertheless dominated the public and legal debate about antidiscrimination policies. Court decisions like *Croson, Adarand,* and *Sandoval* have eroded the legal underpinnings of active civil rights measures; at the same time, cuts in enforcement agencies have weakened their capacity to combat even the most egregious forms of current discrimination. Clearly, in order to tackle contemporary discrimination, the dismantling of these laws and the agencies that enforce them must be resisted. Beyond that, however, the antidiscrimination legal arsenal should be strengthened and enhanced to not only maintain but also extend the gains already made.

The focus of antidiscrimination law should be shifted so that it more directly addresses the pervasive problem of "unintentional" discrimination. The standard applied in disparate treatment cases brought under Title VII of the 1964 Civil Rights Act needs to be changed. The current standard usually requires proof that an employer consciously intended to discriminate against a person of color. This requirement that employers know they are discriminating should be changed to a negligence standard that requires employers to take reasonable steps to avoid discrimination. Employers should be legally responsible when they apply racial stereotypes in making decisions or when they act carelessly or inattentively and, as a consequence, African American employees or applicants are treated differently than they would have been otherwise. Under this approach, courts could become more responsive to the harmful *effects* of employers' actions if they recognized negligent (careless, reckless) discrimination as a basis for action and remedy.[12]

Another approach to antidiscrimination law might be a policy of strict liability where the actor's fault is irrelevant and attention is focused on results. Strict liability evolved in the law to ensure that "externalities" (costs or harms occurring outside the traditional focus of legal action) would be incorporated within the costs of doing a particular business or activity. The paradigm is product liability law, which requires manufacturers of goods to internalize the costs of all injuries associated with the products they make, regardless of whether the injured party can prove that a particular blameworthy action caused the harm. This legal approach would also make producers (of products or discriminatory effects) far more careful about what they do.

A number of other steps would supplement these approaches to antidiscrimination law. Monitoring of firms, particularly small suburban firms, should be improved.[13] The federal government (through the EEOC) and private advocates (with foundation assistance) should conduct many more race discrimination tests, which could be used to pressure employers to change their employment practices or, if the results indicate systematic discrimination, to sue employers, unions, and employment agencies. These could be coupled with a program of self-monitoring by private and public employers. For example, private employers should be encouraged to conduct employment self-studies, examining whether they have a manifest imbalance in traditionally racially segregated job categories. Where they do, they should be encouraged to give preferences to black and Latino job applicants to the extent permitted by the Supreme Court's decision in *United Steelworkers v. Weber.*[14]

Given the expense and difficulty of successfully prosecuting employment discrimination cases, incentives to lawyers and public interest organizations that take on employment discrimination cases should be expanded. This can be accomplished by doubling or tripling attorneys' fees and awards for prevailing plaintiffs in Title VII cases. Moreover, the Equal Employment Opportunity Commission should be required to substantially expand its docket of impact litigation. This will require a significant increase in the agency's funding. Although the EEOC receives an average of 59,000 Title VII complaints each year, it files an average of less than 250 lawsuits annually. In other words, less than 0.5 percent of Title VII complaints lead to EEOC federal lawsuits. The decision to litigate substantially affects the amount of money the complainant recovers. During the agency's best year for nonlitigation recoveries, 8,170 cases (14.3 percent) were successfully conciliated, settled, or ended (because plaintiffs dropped the charge with a financial recovery). In these cases, the average recovery was $18,237 per complaint. By contrast, in the small number of cases actually litigated, the agency recovered an average of $105,263.[15]

Many white Americans are wary of tougher antidiscrimination measures, thinking that they give preferential treatment to minorities. Some believe that such treatment is not only unfair but also ultimately demeaning, since it suggests that minorities cannot compete with whites unless they have extra help. But, as we demonstrated in chapter 5, this is a common misperception about what antidiscrimination laws actually do—and have done. They are not, for the most part, about giving some people unearned preferential treatment; they are about ending unequal treatment. They are not about establishing quotas for representation of various groups; they are about removing obstacles that hinder the opportunity for people of color and for women to compete fairly.

PROMOTING DIVERSITY In our view, considering race in university admissions is necessary and justifiable in the pursuit of educational diversity. We also think that maintaining diversity is crucial to an effective assault on racial inequality. In this respect, we agree with a 2002 ruling of the federal court of appeals for the sixth circuit, which upheld the constitutionality of the use of race as a "plus" in admissions policy by the University of Michigan Law School.[16] The sixth circuit majority held that educational institutions have a compelling interest in maintaining a racially and ethnically diverse student body in order to achieve the legitimate educational goal of exposing students to a variety of backgrounds and views. Formal racial quotas, having been banned by the 1978 *Bakke* decision, would not pass the constitutional test. But using race as one among many possible "plus" factors to assure that the institution achieved a "critical mass" of minority students was a policy that did not rely on quotas, especially since all of the students in question met the same qualifications for admission.

This approach is both logical and principled. It does not, as the court's majority pointed out, establish a separate track for minority applicants that insulates them from competition with whites, and it does not create an academic subclass of the unqualified. Instead it affirms the intrinsic educational value of a diversity of perspectives and the importance of creating an environment in which, as one commentator put it, "people from the different groups in American society learn to live and work with one another."[17] This goal is important in itself. But it is also crucial to a larger battle against racial inequality. Increasing the numbers of minority students in graduate and professional schools not only diversifies those particular institutions and professions, it also helps to counteract the dominant perspective of whites. When more blacks and Latinos enter professional and graduate schools, they have the potential to broaden fundamental ideas and perspectives as well as to diversify personnel.

For both these reasons, it is time to reexamine conventional ideas of qualification and merit. When selection systems simply repave the traditional routes of entry for those who already have access, qualified individuals whose merit goes unrecognized under conventional admissions criteria are excluded. The gates to cultural, economic, and political power must be opened to racial minorities. But the points of entry themselves may also need to be reconstructed in rational ways that disentangle principle from the generation and perpetuation of racial privilege. A step in the right direction is the recent proposal to shift admissions criteria at the University of California, Berkeley away from strict reliance on test scores and grades alone and toward more "holistic" criteria (for example, success in overcoming economic adversity as an indicator of merit).

CHALLENGING THE ROUTINE GENERATION OF RACIAL INEQUALITY Durable racial inequality is both generated and sustained, as we have shown, by routine organizational rules and practices that on the surface may appear to have nothing to do with race. These policies and practices range from universities' treatment of students to rules governing the distribution of voting machines—a crucial matter for exercising the franchise, as Americans learned during the Florida recount of the 2000 presidential election. African American ballots were disproportionately rejected in Florida, and the reason, according to a study by the U.S. Civil Rights Commission, was "the greater propensity of black registered voters to live in counties with technologies that produce the greatest rates of rejected ballots."[18] Antiquated punch card machines, precisely the kind most likely to malfunction, were typically placed in African American precincts, with predictable results.

Similar considerations apply to other institutions, especially the justice system and the educational system, where these subtle sources of discrimination are pervasive. Changes in the routine practices of law enforcement agencies and courts are crucial to any effective long-term strategy for reducing racial disparities in the criminal justice system. As we have shown, while discrimination cannot explain the entire gap in arrest and imprisonment rates between blacks and whites, it does explain part of it. Accordingly, we must both tackle existing discriminatory practices in and around the justice system and take steps to minimize the legacy of past discrimination that spawns high crime rates and overly aggressive law enforcement. To deny that systemic discrimination is still practiced by the police and courts is, as we have clearly demonstrated, foolish. So is denying that the high levels of crime and violence bred by a legacy of adverse structural conditions represents a substantial obstacle to community well-being and individual advancement in minority communities. The reality of high crime rates also serves to justify racially targeted law enforcement practices and tough sentencing for minority offenders on the grounds that these policies serve the needs of law-abiding minorities in communities disproportionately ravaged by violence and drugs.

Several kinds of changes in the criminal justice system are necessary to reduce racial discrimination in arrest, sentencing, and incarceration. One of the most important is to reduce the use of racially coded police practices. It is clear that racial profiling and other aggressive police strategies are not only divisive but also represent the first step in a complex chain through which blacks and Latinos wind up in the criminal justice system in disproportionate numbers, contributing to a downward spiral among both individuals and communities. Several related steps would limit these practices. First, the collection of reliable data on different experiences of racial and ethnic groups with the justice system in police encounters, juvenile justice processing, adult sentencing, and incarceration should be continued and expanded. Although we recognize the justified sensitivities over the perils of collecting data by race, we also believe that without gathering and widely disseminating facts about the racial breakdown of police stops, we will have no basis on which to even measure the extent and location of discrimination, much less to combat it. North Carolina, Missouri, and Washington State have ordered police to gather statistics on whom they stop, and why; other states should do the same.

A second step is to make federal and state funding for local police agencies contingent on the development and implementation of strong plans to combat the practices that tend to disproportionately funnel minorities into the criminal justice process—including racial profiling and the overly broad use of antigang measures. Existing federal and state laws (as in California, Oklahoma, and Oregon) against racial profiling by police should also be vigorously enforced.

Another step to reduce racial disparities in the justice system is to challenge criminal laws that appear on the surface to be race-neutral but that disproportionately affect blacks and Latinos. The unreflective push to get tough on crime and drugs in recent years has resulted in sweeping penalties and harsher sentencing that have a disproportionate impact on minority communities. Those measures have created a climate of fear, resentment, and division in many areas and help to channel black and Latino Americans into swollen institutions of custody and control. We do not question the need for a vigorous attack on serious crime, but these measures have proven to be counterproductive and ill conceived. We need to restore a sense of balance to federal, state, and local justice systems in which the goals of crime control and social justice work together. To that end, we should reverse recent legislative provisions that, although promoted to help restore order in minority communities, actually fuel the extra surveillance and consequent over-incarceration of minorities, especially minority youth. These provisions include enhanced penalties for drug possession or sales near public housing and the spate of anti-gang initiatives like California's ill-conceived Proposition 21 that justify sweeping large numbers of minority youth and young adults into custody on slender pretexts.

Finally, the recent trend toward the increased use of mandatory sentences, especially for drug- or gang-related offenses, should also be reversed; the severity of sentences for low-level offenders should also be reduced. And incarceration ought to be replaced with treatment outside prison walls for minor drug offenders, as pioneered in Arizona and recently enacted by California's Proposition 36. Among other things, these changes would help to reverse the trend toward the increasing incarceration of women—who are disproportionately minority, disproportionately mothers, and disproportionately incarcerated for minor drug and property offenses.

In the educational system, we need to challenge the more subtle forms of organizational discrimination by opposing a variety of active policies that disadvantage minority students and the passive, laissez-faire approach to educational careers that characterizes too many schools from the earliest grades to graduate school.

First, the spate of self-consciously "tough" policies that mandate quicker and more frequent use of suspension and expulsion in elementary and secondary schools in the name of improving discipline and enhancing school climates needs to be reconsidered. There is abundant evidence that these policies—often promoted under the slogan of "zero tolerance" of deviant or disruptive behavior—have a disproportionate impact on black and Latino students, with no evidence that they significantly improve the quality of education.

Confronting the destructive effects of an ostensibly race-neutral laissez-faire regime in the schools and colleges is complicated, but even more crucial. One way that schools (and other institutions) perpetuate inequality is through inaction—often through the encouragement of a hands-off, sink-or-swim climate in which the likelihood of failure becomes higher for everyone, but especially for minorities.

At the level of higher education, for example, policies need to recognize that colleges and universities vary widely in their ability to teach, and to graduate, minority students. Stanford has a graduation rate for its African American students that is 20 points higher than the rate at the University of California, Berkeley.[19] A good part of the variation is linked to different levels of resources that the colleges provide for their students. It is also connected to a less tangible difference in the overall atmosphere and attitude toward minority students (and perhaps whites as well) that a university communicates. Stanford provides a broad and rich array of support services for entering students; UC Berkeley offers a brief one-time counseling session and little else.

The UC Berkeley–Stanford comparison has intriguing policy implications. Though Stanford is a private institution, it does not subject its students to the laissez-faire, competitive treatment conservatives suggest is so effective in producing high graduation rates. Indeed, it is extraordinarily nurturing and uses its impressive endowment to put services in place that make it very difficult for its students—black or white—to fail. Stanford's support services play an important role in its students' lives. Students are not forced to sink or swim. UC Berkeley, on the other hand, a public, state-supported university treats its students to laissez-faire practices and rewards its most competitive survivors. Yet Berkeley's graduation rate (for blacks and whites) is lower than Stanford's. This suggests that high graduation rates are less a matter of SAT scores and are more likely related to a supportive, nurturing educational environment.

The same principle applies to efforts to increase the number and proportion of minority students who enter college in the first place. As it now stands, many never even apply because they do not think they could make it into a good college or handle the work if they did, and that is often a consequence of the failure of too many high schools to put in the effort to prepare their students academically and emotionally. But there is evidence to suggest that, if they try, schools can provide intensive college preparation help for high school students in low-income minority communities who might otherwise never consider attending a high-quality college or university. One intriguing example is the Neighborhood Academic Initiative launched in South Central Los Angeles by the University of Southern California (USC) in 1990. The program was unique because it focused its energies on average students, not on the small stratum of the brightest students in the neighborhood. The aim was to "boost them to USC standards with rigorous courses, intensive oversight, and cultural opportunities," with the promise of full scholarships to USC if they succeeded. Not all of the inner-city students made it, but many did; of those who entered USC, the four-year graduation rate, though somewhat lower than the university's average, was expected to pull even within five years. That encouraging graduation rate reflects continued mentoring and attention for these students once in college.[20]

More generally, enforcing clearly defined state standards organized to achieve learning levels necessary for black students to attend four-year colleges should raise expectations in low-income schools. Financial rewards for teachers and schools that meet these standards should be provided. For the most part, these changes must take place in public education, where most black students will be for the near future. These schools will require additional resources; and they will need mechanisms of public accountability.

THE PROSPECT FOR CHANGE

We do not pretend that this is either a complete list or a wholly new one. On the contrary, what is striking about a number of our proposals is how closely they echo ones made more than thirty-five years ago in response to the urban disorders of the 1960s, when white Americans faced up to the consequences of long-festering racial inequalities and, for a while, vowed to respond on a scale that matched the magnitude of the problem.

In the more passive climate of the early twenty-first century, the boldness of proposals launched from even the mainstream of American political culture in those years is remarkable. In 1968, for example, the bipartisan Kerner Commission called for the creation of "one million new jobs in the public sector" in response to the employment problems of black Americans. A year earlier, the decidedly mainstream *Newsweek* magazine called for a tripling of the federal investment in job-training programs in a single year and argued that the government should immediately step in as the "employer of last resort" in the inner cities. It suggested putting unemployed and underemployed ghetto residents to work reconstructing their communities and training them in job skills as they did so. *Newsweek*'s editors justified this and other far-reaching proposals on the sensible grounds that the urgency of the situation required bold thinking and a reordering of priorities: the country needed "to give the plight of the disadvantaged at home the same urgency it affords the foreign obligations it has assumed." Yet they worried that America would not be able to act swiftly enough or seriously enough. Their words are well worth pondering today.

> Why can't history's most affluent, technologically advanced society act to make the black man a full participant in American life? The answer is a meld of ignorance and indifference, bigotry and callousness, escapism and sincere confusion. But the inescapable truth is that so far America hasn't wanted to. On that point there is, indeed, an American consensus—spelled out rather clearly in the way a democratic society allocates its resources. America spends . . . $17.4 billion for tobacco and liquor but only $1.6 billion for the war on poverty, $3.2 billion for cosmetics and toiletries but only $400 million a year for the training of adult unemployed.[21]

Making a serious movement to shift those priorities "while there is still time," they concluded, "is the heart of the problem." It remains so. Most of the bolder proposals that *Newsweek*, the Kerner Commission, and others put forward then never materialized—casualties of the stubbornness of that "consensus," exacerbated by the fiscal impact of the Vietnam War. The myth persists that America bent over backward during the 1960s to remedy past wrongs in the cities; those who were around at the time know better. The indifference and inertia that many keen observers worried would prevail did so, and the result was the deepening of the legacy of disaccumulation that, as we have shown, continues to shape the lives of blacks, Latinos, and whites alike today.

But did we not simply "throw money at the problem" in the 1960s, and are we not just proposing the same failed strategy today? No—we did not, and we are not. Many of the things we are proposing do indeed cost money, but others do not. Moreover, it is critical to keep in mind that racial inequality is expensive too. We pay for it in lost productivity, in lower tax revenues, in the massive and self-perpetuating costs of social pathology and incarceration.

Still, it is also important to be tougher-minded about these interventions than reformers often were in the past. Since the 1970s, the public has often believed that social programs do not work, that we tried more generous measures of this kind and they failed massively. That belief, in turn, justifies doing nothing at all or relying on the kinds of private or market solutions to social problems championed by racial conservatives. This view carries a superficial plausibility because it rests on—and then greatly exaggerates—a kernel of truth: some social programs designed to address the ills of minority communities really *did not* work. Sometimes it was because they were poorly conceived, and more often it was because the level of their resources, and consequently the intensity of their intervention, was never sufficient to meet the challenge. Rather predictably, therefore, the programs failed to produce immediate results.

One of the reasons activist approaches to the ills of urban minority communities in the 1960s and beyond collapsed is that too many liberals thought they could solve the tough and entrenched problems of generations of systematic disaccumulation with a handful of minimally funded and sometimes weakly conceived programs. This was a prescription for backlash, and it helps explain the pervasive skepticism about government solutions to these ills today and the automatic preference for market solutions. Those who wish to challenge this drift and to reestablish the idea of concerted public sector action as a central part of a strategy for social change in America need to be among those most vigilant in insisting that public interventions are theoretically sound, carefully implemented, and honestly evaluated.

We need to renew the American commitment to equality once more and combine it with the same sense of urgency that drove the best movements of a generation ago. But this time we need a much longer time horizon, a much deeper political and personal will, and a much more savvy appreciation of how deeply race continues to shape our experience, our language, and our destiny. We are aware that there are many people of good will in America who are uncomfortable with that kind of appreciation, who wish to downplay the public discussion of race in the interest of achieving a truly color-blind society. We are sympathetic to that desire. Yet we think the only way to achieve a society in which the color of people's skin *really* matters less than the content of their character is by forthrightly acknowledging the role that race still plays in American life, by facing up to the consequences, and by moving forward with a new seriousness to address the historical and contemporary sources of racial inequalities.

It is one thing to call for policies based on a set of principles about the role of race in America today. It is quite another to get them translated into social and political action. We fully expect some readers to object, arguing that white Americans will not support these principles, much less the specific policies we suggest. White Americans, they will point out, are not ready or willing to give up their generations-old privileges, or even to acknowledge that those privileges exist, especially in a political climate that is undeniably conservative and in which many significant political and legal decisions about race are going in the opposite direction.

No one but a Pollyanna would deny that powerful cultural and political obstacles exist, and we are well aware that the task at hand is a difficult and long-term proposition. This book, after all, is a chronicle of the stubbornness of the resistance to real racial equality. The blend of "ignorance and indifference, bigotry and callousness, escapism and sincere confusion" that *Newsweek*'s editors noted a generation ago is still very much with us. Yet we are equally aware that political change is about imagining future possibilities. What is considered impossible today may be possible tomorrow. It is well to remember that in the 1950s few Americans believed that a revolution in civil rights was just around the corner. Jim Crow seemed too deeply entrenched, racial prejudice too formidable a presence in the minds of white Americans. Yet many people of all races vigorously opposed segregation anyway, not because they knew they would prevail, but because they believed that doing so was morally necessary. And in the end they did prevail.

We believe the potential for constructive change in the present social and political climate may be greater than many assume. For one thing, Americans—including white Americans—generally favor many of the principles we have suggested. They also support, sometimes by large majorities, a variety of policies and programs that are designed to bring all citizens, of whatever color, up to full and productive participation in American social and economic life. More investment in job creation and training, early childhood education, accessible health care for all—every one of these is supported today by the majority of Americans, according to opinion polls. And this is true despite the absence of any concerted effort on the part of political leaders to educate the public about the sources of racial inequality or to mobilize public support behind active policies to counter it. It is true that many of these ideas—especially those that call for more public investment—have virtually disappeared from mainstream political discussion. That is due, in part, to a failure of political leadership, and part of our task is to put those ideas back on the nation's agenda—and keep them there.

But why should whites give up their gains from our country's historic pattern of unequal investment and accumulation? We have wrestled with this issue among ourselves, and we think that the answer is a complicated one. It is certainly true that the advantages whites have gained through accumulation and from the disaccumulation experienced by blacks and Latinos are very real. In the short term, this arrangement has often made whites, in many respects, better off than they would be otherwise. The more we look at our own evidence, however, the more we realize that this is not the whole story. There are also many ways in which whites lose as a result of racial inequality, and those ways become increasingly important—and increasingly troubling—over the long term. White Americans may win better jobs, better housing in better neighborhoods, a better shot at a high-quality education for their children. But they must also pay, and pay handsomely, for the prisons, police, mopping-up health care services, and other reactive measures predictably required by the maintenance of drastically unequal social conditions. They must live with the fear of violence, volatility, and social disruption that are among the most visible costs of the legacy of disaccumulation. They must, in a less direct but very crucial sense, pay for the economic losses that come with the exclusion of large numbers of non-white Americans from a productive place in the national economy. If they are working people, they will suffer economically in the long term because a low-wage pool of minority workers and potential workers depresses the overall wage structure and tilts economic power toward employers. If they are businesspeople, these losses are likely to be even more pressing. Without sufficient investment in quality education, from preschool through college, to enable a broad rise in educational and job skills among minority young people, white businesses will not have a workforce fit for the demands of the twenty-first century economy.

Even on the most basic economic terms, in short, the idea that whites uniformly and consistently gain from the continuation of black disadvantage is far too simplistic. The great racial disparities in social conditions and opportunities do not simply represent a win-lose situation that favors whites. They also represent a lose-lose situation in which citizens of all races are denied their full rights as citizens. No one has had a deeper appreciation of this than Martin Luther King Jr. In one of his last essays, he wrote,

> The black revolution is much more than a struggle for the rights of Negroes. It is forcing America to face all its interrelated flaws—racism, poverty, militarism and materialism. It is exposing evils that are rooted deeply in the whole structure of our society. It reveals systemic rather than superficial

flaws and suggests that radical reconstruction of society itself is the real issue to be faced. . . . To this day, black Americans have not life, liberty nor the privilege of pursuing happiness, and millions of poor white Americans are in economic bondage that is scarcely less oppressive. Americans who genuinely treasure our national ideals, who know they are still elusive dreams for all too many, should welcome the stirring of Negro demands. They are shattering the complacency that allowed a multitude of social evils to accumulate. Negro agitation is requiring America to reexamine its comforting myths and may yet catalyze the drastic reforms that will save us from social catastrophe.[22]

Will these considerations be enough to move white Americans to support the broad shifts in vision and policy that we propose? We cannot say in the abstract because the answer will depend on the seriousness and energy with which we pursue those changes and work to mobilize Americans of all races behind them. What we can say with certainty is that the opposite direction—which is too often the road we are taking today—is fraught with peril and potential tragedy.

Back in the 1950s and 1960s Martin Luther King Jr. and others often warned of the potentially dire consequences if the movement toward what the Kerner Commission in 1968 called "two societies" was allowed to continue. It is sobering to realize that to some extent, what they feared has already come to pass; the disorders of the 1960s became the permanent crisis of individualized violence and widespread social deterioration that persists today. It can be argued, however, that far worse tragedies were averted because of the efforts we *did* make to tackle the roots of minority disadvantage during the highly visible crises of the 1960s. A combination of public sector spending and moderately aggressive civil rights legislation strongly expanded black access to quality education and to the burgeoning public sector jobs that formed the economic backbone for a growing black middle class. The same legislation, coupled with modestly reformist administrations, pushed through at least moderate changes in the behavior of police toward minorities, one of the most sensitive and fateful areas of discontent before and during the 1960s. For a while, things did indeed improve for black people in America. They improved to a different degree, and for different reasons, than conservatives suggest. But they did improve.

Today even those modest steps toward racial equality are threatened. Recent Supreme Court decisions hampering civil remedies for discrimination under Title VI of the 1964 Civil Rights Act are among the most potentially far-reaching reversals we have seen in a generation. The courts' increasing preference for formal color-blindness over racial reality prevents most voluntary efforts to diminish racial disparities. Judicial recognition of discrimination only where individual animus is proven eliminates most public or private accountability for the kind of accumulated disadvantage we have described. The current climate of hostility toward public expenditure and the reprivatization of many public functions erodes the most important source of upward economic mobility for blacks in the postwar period. It also threatens to gut the educational, health, and social service agencies that helped so many blacks and Latinos make that upward climb in the past generation. Most of the historic sources of black advancement, in short, are under unprecedented attack. At the same time, social policies that have demonstrably failed in the past are being boosted or resurrected.

We think these developments are a recipe for disaster and call into question fundamental American values and ideas. We do not wish to seem alarmist, nor do we pretend to have a crystal ball, but we cannot help noting the many similarities between the current period and that of the 1960s. Then as now we had a long, uneven economic boom that left some people—especially those with dark skins—behind, while giving unprecedented material gains to those better situated. Then as now we had widespread anger and disaffection among black and Latino communities with police forces that often behaved more like armies of occupation than protectors of the peace. Then as now we had a stark juxtaposition of private affluence and public squalor—in John Kenneth Galbraith's words—in which the most basic institutions of care, support, and socialization have been gutted by long neglect. Then as now we had a good part of an entire generation of young people systematically blocked from achieving the status and dignity that others expect as a matter of course. The choice was clear then: in James Baldwin's words, to "make America what America must become," or face the coarsening and deterioration of our social fabric and our most dearly held values.

It remains so now.

Notes

PREFACE

1. Lani Guinier and Gerald Torres, *The Miner's Canary* (Cambridge, Mass.: Harvard University Press, 2002), p. 224.

2. See Lawrence Bobo and Camile L. Zubrinksy, "Attitudes on Residential Integration," *Social Forces* 74 (1996): 883–909.

3. Guinier and Torres refer to this as racial bribery. For a discussion see Guinier and Torres, *The Miner's Canary*, pp. 224–29.

INTRODUCTION

1. Donald R. Kinder and Tali Mendelberg, "Individualism Reconsidered: Principles and Prejudice in Contemporary American Opinion," in David O. Sears, Jim Sidanius, and Lawrence Bobo, eds., *Racialized Politics: The Debate about Racism in America* (Chicago: University of Chicago Press, 2000), p. 61.

2. Jim Sleeper, *Liberal Racism* (New York: Penguin Books, 1997), pp. 7, 175.

3. Tamar Jacoby, *Someone Else's House: America's Unfinished Struggle for Integration* (New York: The Free Press, 1998), pp. 4–5, 9.

4. Whether opposition to color-conscious policies is motivated by adherence to political principles or reflects a new manifestation of white racism is the subject of many of the essays in Sears, Sidanius, and Bobo, eds., *Racialized Politics: The Debate about Racism in America*. The wages of full-time male workers have risen only 1.3 percent since 1989. Alexander Stille, "Grounded by an Income Gap: Inequality Just Keeps Growing in the U.S.," *New York Times*, December 15, 2001, p. A15.

5. Southern Democrats and conservative Republicans from the Southwest, including Barry Goldwater and George H. W. Bush, the latter representing a conservative Texas constituency in Congress at the time, voted against the 1964 Civil Rights Act.

6. David Garrow, *Bearing the Cross: Martin Luther King, Jr., and the Southern Christian Leadership Conference* (New York: Vintage Books, 1988), p. 439.

7. Martin Luther King Jr., "A Testament of Hope," in James M. Washington, ed., *A Testament of Hope: The Essential Writings of Martin Luther King, Jr.* (New York: Harper and Row, 1986), p. 316.

8. Robert L. Carter, "A Reassessment of *Brown v. Board*," in Derrick Bell, ed., *Shades of Brown: New Perspectives on School Desegregation* (New York: Teacher's College, Columbia University, 1980), pp. 23–24. *Brown I* declared "separate but equal" unconstitutional in 1954. In *Brown II*, decided in 1955, the Court ruled that local jurisdictions should desegregate with "all deliberate speed."

9. Jim Sleeper, *The Closest of Strangers: Liberalism and the Politics of Race in America* (New York: W. W. Norton, 1990), p. 160.

10. Sleeper, *Liberal Racism*, pp. 9, 77–78.

11. Paul M. Sniderman and Thomas Piazza, *The Scar of Race* (Cambridge, Mass.: Harvard University Press, 1993), p. 103.

12. For recent examples, see, among others, Terry Eastland, "Endgame for Affirmative Action," *Wall Street Journal,* March 28, 1996; Todd Gaziano, "The New 'Massive Resistance,'" *Policy Review* 89 (1998): 22–29; John H. McWhorter, *Losing the Race: Self-Sabotage in Black America* (New York: Free Press, 2000).

13. Dinesh D'Souza, *The End of Racism: Principles for a Multiracial Society* (New York: The Free Press, 1995), chapter 12.

14. Jacoby, *Someone Else's House*, p. 10.

15. Sleeper, *Liberal Racism*, p. 4.

16. Stephen Thernstrom and Abigail Thernstrom, *America in Black and White: One Nation, Indivisible* (New York: Simon and Schuster, 1997), pp. 495, 498, 505; Jacoby, *Someone Else's House*, pp. 9, 539–40.

17. Alan Wolfe, "Enough Blame to Go Around," *New York Times Book Review*, June 21, 1998, p. 12.

18. Thernstrom and Thernstrom, *America in Black and White*, pp. 299–300; D'Souza, *End of Racism*, chapter 6.

19. Sleeper, *Liberal Racism,* p. 178.

20. Dr. Martin Luther King Jr., "I Have a Dream," in James Washington, ed., *A Testament of Hope*, p. 219; Sleeper, *Liberal Racism*, p. 178.

21. Conservative writers and think tanks have been in the forefront of the fight against affirmative action and other color-conscious policies. The D'Souza and Thernstrom books in particular are typical of conservative criticism of liberal policies. The research for *America in Black and White* was underwritten by many of the most influential conservative foundations, including the John M. Olin Foundation, the Smith Richardson Foundation, the Earhart Foundation, and the Carthage Foundation. Jacoby's research was sponsored by many of the same foundations. Both Jacoby and Abigail Thernstrom have been affiliated with the Manhattan Institute, an influential conservative think tank in New York City.

22. Thernstrom and Thernstrom, *America in Black and White*, pp. 189–94; see also James Smith and Finis Welch, *Closing the Gap: Forty Years of Economic Progress for Blacks* (Santa Monica, Calif.: Rand Corporation, 1986). The Thernstroms' interpretation of black economic progress assumes that labor market dis-

crimination was not a serious obstacle to good jobs and high wages for black workers after World War II. If this version of history is wrong and labor market discrimination was the cause of low wages and high unemployment, it would make little difference if blacks acquired more education. The Thernstroms' argument is implausible, and there is little evidence to support it. It rests on their assertion that the black unemployment rate was only slightly higher than the white unemployment rate in 1940 but twice as many blacks in the North were employed as in the South. This, the Thernstroms say, is "exactly the opposite of what we would expect if unemployment had been mainly the result of discrimination" since one would expect Mississippi employers to treat blacks less fairly than employers in the North (Thernstrom and Thernstrom, *America in Black and White*, p. 245). The Thernstroms are wrong to presume that labor market discrimination was unimportant in the North. In the late 1930s, black unemployment rates in northern cities were two to four times higher than white unemployment rates, mainly because of the virulent labor market discrimination unleashed during the depression when white workers displaced blacks. See Michael K. Brown, *Race, Money, and the American Welfare State* (Ithaca, N.Y.: Cornell University Press, 1999), pp. 68–70; W. A. Sundstrom, "Last Hired, First Fired? Unemployment and Black Workers during the Great Depression," *The Journal of Economic History*, 52 (1992): 415–29. Moreover, unemployment figures for blacks in the South are misleading because seasonal workers (mainly farm workers) were excluded and many of those reported as employed were unpaid family workers, which is "often little better than a make-shift activity for sons and daughters of farmers [and sharecroppers] when they cannot find other employment." U.S. Bureau of the Census, *Sixteenth Census of the United States: 1940, Population*, vol. 3, *The Labor Force*, part 1: *U.S. Summary* (Washington, D.C.: U. S. Government Printing Office, 1943), pp. 5, 7. There is no reason to presume that the difference in unemployment rates reflects a lack of discrimination in the South.

23. For a clear statement of this argument, see James A. Heckman, "Detecting Discrimination," *Journal of Economic Perspectives* 12 (1998): 101–16; for a critique, see William A. Darity Jr. and Patrick L. Mason, "Evidence on Discrimination in Employment: Codes of Color, Codes of Gender," *Journal of Economic Perspectives* 12 (1998): 63–90.

24. Richard Epstein, *Forbidden Grounds: The Case against Employment Discrimination Laws* (Cambridge, Mass.: Harvard University Press, 1992), p. 32. It should be noted that in his original statement of the economic theory of discrimination, Gary Becker acknowledged labor market discrimination and set out to explain why it occurred in specific circumstances. See Gary Becker, *The Economics of Discrimination*, 2nd ed. (Chicago: University of Chicago Press, 1971).

25. Epstein, *Forbidden Grounds*, p. 46. Epstein does not assume that segregation leads to wage differences. Wage discrimination and segregation are separate phenomena.

26. Lawrence D. Bobo and Ryan A. Smith, "From Jim Crow Racism to Laissez-Faire Racism: The Transformation of Racial Attitudes," in Wendy F. Katkin, Ned Landsman, and Andrea Tyree, eds., *Beyond Pluralism: The Conception of Groups and Identities in America* (Urbana: University of Illinois Press, 1998), p. 212.

27. Thernstrom and Thernstrom, *America in Black and White*, p. 183.

28. U.S. Bureau of the Census, "Race and Hispanic Origin of Householder—Families by Median and Mean Income: 1947 to 2001," (Table F-5), *Historical Income Tables — Families*, <http://www.census.gov/hhes/income/histinc/fo5.html> (accessed October 9, 2002).

29. Ibid. See also Sheldon Danziger and Peter Gottschalk, *America Unequal* (New York: Russell Sage Foundation, 1995), pp. 71–73. Using a measure of income that adjusts for family size and unrelated individuals, Danziger and Gottschalk show that in 1991 the real median income of black families was 1.85 times the poverty line, compared to 3.54 times for white families. Not until 1991 did black family income reach a level comparable to 1959 family income for the total population. Among nonelderly, two-parent families the ratio rose from 44 percent to 71 percent in 1991, still a large gap. In 2001, after the economic expansion, black married couples' income was 80 percent of white married couples'. However, this measure is not comparable to Danziger and Gottschalk's and may overstate the ratio.

30. U.S. Bureau of the Census, "Race and Hispanic Origin of People by Median Income and Sex: 1947 to 2001" (Table P-2), *Historical Income Tables — People*, <http://www.census.gov/hhes/income/histinc/po2.html> (accessed October 9, 2002).

31. Council of Economic Advisers, *Changing America* (Washington D.C.: U.S. Government Printing Office, 1998), p. 28. Many economists point out that it makes no sense to exclude unemployed or part-time black workers from these comparisons. Doing so inflates the relative income gain of black workers because low-income black workers (who have higher unemployment rates) and high-income white workers (who presumably retire early) are excluded from the calculations. This biases estimates of black-white earnings ratios upward. See William Darity Jr. and Samuel Myers Jr., *Persistent Disparity: Race and Economic Inequality in the United States since 1945* (Northhampton, Mass.: Edward Elgar Publishing, 1998), pp. 46–47.

32. Douglas Massey and Nancy Denton, *American Apartheid: Segregation and the Making of the Underclass* (Cambridge, Mass.: Harvard University Press, 1993), pp. 77, 87–88.

33. Preliminary studies conducted by the National Fair Housing Alliance reveal how this gap is created. The Alliance found that when creditworthy whites approach subprime lenders, they are systematically referred to prime lenders, who make loans on more favorable terms, with lower interest rates and less predatory foreclosure practices.

34. The ratio of black-white infant mortality rate rose from 1.94 in 1980 to 2.35 in 1998. National Center for Health Statistics, "Infant Mortality Rates, Fetal Mortality Rates, and Perinatal Mortality Rates, according to Race: United States, Selected Years 1950–99" (Table 23), *Centers for Disease Control*, <http://www.cdc.gov/nchs/products/pubs/pubd/hus/tables/2001/01hus023.pdf> (accessed October 9, 2002).

35. David Barton Smith, *Health Care Divided: Race and Healing a Nation* (Ann Arbor: University of Michigan Press, 1999), p. 210. Smith notes that the National Center for Health Statistics' 1996–97 report documents that blacks'

mortality rates are twice as high as those of whites for years of life lost before the age of seventy-five per 100,000 in population.

36. In 1986, for example, among males under 65, those with the highest educational attainment showed the largest relative racial discrepancies in mortality rates. For adult females, the largest relative racial disparity in mortality rates is found in the highest income category. Gregory Pappas et al., "The Increasing Disparity in Mortality between Socioeconomic Groups in the United States, 1960 and 1986," *New England Journal of Medicine* 329 (1987): 103–9.

37. Testimony of Ed Mendoza, Assistant Director, Special Initiatives and Program Evaluation, Office of Statewide Health Planning and Development, before Joint Hearing of the California Senate Committee on Business and Professions and the California Senate Committee on Health and Human Services, March 31, 1997, Handout #4, pp. 1, 11 (unpublished document on file with authors).

38. Smith, *Health Care Divided*, p. 201.

39. Elizabeth White, "Special Report: Public Health Racial and Ethnic Disparities," *Health Care Policy Report* 9 (2001): 315; "40% Rise Reported in Asthma and Asthma Deaths," *New York Times*, January 7, 1995, section 2, p. 10; "Asthma Toll Is Up Sharply, US Reports," *New York Times*, May 3, 1996, C18.

40. Smith, *Health Care Divided*, p. 208, table 6.8. We explore the reasons for these disparities in more detail in chapters 1 and 2.

41. Charles Tilly, *Durable Inequality* (Berkeley and Los Angeles: University of California Press, 1998), p. 17.

42. This is misleading because the small decline in residential segregation occurred largely in cities with very small black populations. See Massey and Denton, *American Apartheid*, pp. 66, 221–23.

43. Thernstrom and Thernstrom, *America in Black and White*, pp. 219–30.

44. Sally Satel, *PC, M.D.: How Political Correctness Is Corrupting Medicine* (New York: Basic Books, Inc., 2000), pp. 2, 23.

45. Ruth Milkman and Eleanor Townsend, "Gender and the Economy," in Neil J. Smelser and Richard Swedberg, eds., *Handbook of Economic Sociology* (Princeton, N.J.: Princeton University Press, 1994), p. 611; cited in Tilly, *Durable Inequality*, p. 31.

46. William Darity Jr., "What's Left of the Economic Theory of Discrimination," in Steven Shulman and William Darity Jr., eds., *The Question of Discrimination* (Middletown, Conn.: Wesleyan University Press, 1989), pp. 335–74. Economists have advanced a variety of ingenious explanations for the persistence of racial discrimination; all of these assume (at least implicitly) that discrimination is temporary and all are based on individual-level explanations. See Darity and Mason, "Evidence of Discrimination in Employment," pp. 81–87 for a summary. However, James Heckman points out that a bigoted employer can "indulge that taste so long as income is received from entrepreneurial activity" — so long, that is, as there is a willingness to pay the price. See Heckman, "Detecting Discrimination," p. 112.

47. Peter V. Marsden, "The Hiring Process: Recruitment Methods," *American Behavioral Scientist* 7 (1994): 979–91; Shazia R. Miller and James E. Rosenbaum, "Hiring in a Hobbesian World," *Work and Occupations* 24 (1997): 498–523.

48. Philip Kasinitz and Jay Rosenberg, "Missing the Connection: Social Iso-

lation and Employment on the Brooklyn Waterfront," *Social Problems* 43 (1996): 180–96; for a description see Thomas Sugrue, *The Origins of the Urban Crisis* (Princeton, N.J.: Princeton University Press, 1996), chapter 4.

49. Tilly, *Durable Inequality*, p. 91.

50. Economists have developed a very similar theory to Tilly's idea of opportunity hoarding; see Derek Leslie, *An Investigation of Racial Disadvantage* (Manchester, England: Manchester University Press, 1998), pp. 33–37.

51. Darity and Myers, *Persistent Disparity*, p. 58.

52. See Reynolds Farley and Walter Allen, *The Color Line and the Quality of Life in America* (New York: Oxford University Press, 1989), p. 247; Stanley Lieberson, *A Piece of the Pie: Blacks and White Immigrants since 1880* (Berkeley and Los Angeles: University of California Press, 1980), pp. 294–313. Epstein assumes that at least one employer will be motivated by the bottom line and not by negative stereotypes. But this neglects the pressure that white workers may bring to bear on employers to exclude blacks.

53. Pennsylvania nursing homes have a segregation index of .68, which means that 68 percent of nursing home residents would have to move in order to equalize the distribution of blacks and whites across all homes. The 1990 average segregation index for northern cities was .78. Some of the segregation in nursing homes is an artifact of residential segregation, but not all of it—the segregation index for Philadelphia nursing homes is .63. Smith, *Health Care Divided*, pp. 264–65, 267; Massey and Denton, *American Apartheid*, p. 222.

54. Smith, *Health Care Divided*, p. 267.

55. Ibid., pp. 319–20.

56. William Julius Wilson, *The Truly Disadvantaged* (Chicago: University of Chicago Press, 1987), p. 11.

57. Conley, *Being Black, Living in the Red* (Berkeley: University of California Press, 1999), p. 152.

58. Thernstrom and Thernstrom, *America in Black and White*, pp. 197–98.

59. Blacks save 11 percent of their income; whites save 10 percent. Conley, *Being Black, Living in the Red*, p. 29.

60. Todd Lewan and Dolores Barclay, "Torn from the Land: AP Documents Land Taken from Blacks through Trickery, Violence and Murder," *Associated Press,* December 2001, <http://wire.ap.org/APpackages/torn/> (accessed January 2, 2002).

61. Conley, *Being Black, Living in the Red*, pp. 38–39; Massey & Denton, *American Apartheid,* pp. 54–55.

62. Black babies are one and one-third times as likely as whites to suffer from low birth weight and more than three times as likely to suffer very low birth weight. See W. Michael Byrd and Linda A. Clayton, *An American Health Dilemma*, vol. 1, *A Medical History of African Americans and the Problem of Race: Beginnings to 1900* (New York: Routledge, 2000), p. 30.

63. Among black children one to six years of age, 11.5 percent had elevated blood lead levels in 1991–94, compared to 2.6 percent of white children of the same age. U.S. Department of Health and Human Services, *Healthy People 2010: Understanding and Improving Health*, 2nd ed. (Washington, D.C.: U.S. Government Printing Office, 2000), pp. 8–21.

64. Marianne Means, "Refocus Racism Conference Agenda," *San Francisco Chronicle*, August 13, 2001, p. A17.

65. Ian Haney-Lopez, *White by Law: The Legal Construction of Race* (New York: New York University Press, 1996), p. 1; see also Mary Francis Berry, *Black Resistance, White Law* (New York: Penguin Books, 1995).

66. See George Fredrickson, *The Arrogance of Race* (Middletown, Conn.: Wesleyan University Press, 1988), and *White Supremacy* (New York: Oxford University Press, 1981); and Leon A. Higginbotham, *In the Matter of Color: Race and the American Legal Process* (New York: Oxford University Press, 1978).

67. *Dred Scott v. Sanford*, 19 How. (60 U.S.) 393 (1857).

68. Vincent Harding, *There Is a River: The Black Struggle for Freedom in America* (New York: Oxford University Press, 1983), p. 201.

69. Stephen Steinberg, *Turning Back: The Retreat from Racial Justice in American Thought and Policy* (Boston: Beacon Press, 1995).

70. Jill Quadagno, *The Color of Welfare* (New York: Oxford University Press, 1994), pp. 19–24.

71. Brown, *Race, Money, and the American Welfare State*, p. 71.

72. Ibid, p. 82; U.S. Congress, Senate, Committee on Finance, *Economic Security Act Hearings on S. 1130*, 74th Congress, 1st Session, 1935, p. 641.

73. Brown, *Race, Money, and the American Welfare State*, p. 82.

74. Quadagno, *The Color of Welfare*, pp. 160–61.

75. Robert Lieberman, *Shifting the Color Line: Race and the American Welfare State* (Cambridge, Mass.: Harvard University Press, 1998), pp. 198–99, 210.

76. Brown, *Race, Money, and the American Welfare State*, chapters 2 and 5.

77. Herbert Hill, *Black Labor and the American Legal System* (Madison: University of Wisconsin Press, 1985), p. 105; Quadagno, *The Color of Welfare*, p. 23; Brown, *Race, Money, and the American Welfare State*, p. 68.

78. Irving Bernstein, *Promises Kept: John F. Kennedy's New Frontier* (New York: Oxford University Press, 1991), pp. 165–67.

79. George Lipsitz, *The Possessive Investment in Whiteness: How White People Profit from Identity Politics* (Philadelphia: Temple University Press, 1998).

80. Andrew Hacker, *Two Nations* (New York: Ballantine Books, 1992), p. 32.

81. Reva B. Siegel, "The Racial Rhetorics of Color-Blind Constitutionalism: The Case of *Hopwood v. Texas*," in Robert Post and Michael Rogin, eds., *Race and Representation: Affirmative Action* (New York: Zone Books, 1998), pp. 49–50.

82. Alexis de Tocqueville, *Democracy in America* (1835; reprint, New York: Anchor Books, 1969), p. 344.

CHAPTER ONE

1. Barbara Flagg makes this point in an illuminating and cogent way in "Was Blind, but Now I See: White Race Consciousness and the Requirement of Discriminatory Intent," *Michigan Law Review* 91 (1993): 953.

2. A recent study of racially and sexually harassing speech in public places

found that 63 percent of African Americans reported hearing comments about their race every day, or "often." Only 5 percent of whites reported such comments. See Laura Beth Nielsen, "Situating Legal Consciousness: Experiences and Attitudes of Ordinary Citizens about Law and Street Harassment," *Law and Society Review* 34 (2000): 1068.

3. Thomas Nagel, *The View from Nowhere* (New York: Oxford University Press, 1986).

4. Richard Morin, "Misperceptions Cloud Whites' View of Blacks," *Washington Post*, July 11, 2001, p. A1. Three-fifths of whites think blacks have access to health care equal to or better than that of whites; in reality more than twice as many blacks lack health insurance. The study was conducted by the *Washington Post*, Harvard University, and the Kaiser Family Foundation.

5. Thernstrom and Thernstrom, *America in Black and White*, p. 177.

6. "Refocus Racism Conference Agenda," *San Francisco Chronicle*, August 13, 2001, p. A17.

7. Thernstrom and Thernstrom, *America in Black and White*, p. 500.

8. Thernstrom and Thernstrom, *America in Black and White*, p. 177; Dinesh D'Souza, *The End of Racism* (New York: The Free Press, 1995), pp. 253–54.

9. Thernstrom and Thernstrom, *America in Black and White*, p. 141. For example, the Thernstroms report survey data that show 83 percent of whites in 1963 agreed with the statement "Negroes should have as good a chance as white people to get any kind of job."

10. Paul Sniderman and Thomas Piazza, *The Scar of Race* (Cambridge, Mass.: Harvard University Press, 1993), p. 46. Sniderman and Piazza asked whites whether they agreed with six common stereotypes of African Americans, for example, "Blacks need to try harder." Only 2 percent agreed with all six stereotypes.

11. We do not imply that everyone who uses this conception of race accepts the new orthodoxy on race.

12. Sniderman and Piazza, *Scar of Race,* p. 89.

13. Angela Harris, "Equality Trouble: Sameness and Difference in Twentieth Century Race Law," *California Law Review* 88 (2000): 1923, 2003.

14. See *Regents of the Univ. of Calif. v. Bakke*, 438 U.S. 265, 288 (1978); *Adarand v. Pena*, 515 U.S. 200, 217 (1995).

15. Alan D. Freeman, "Legitimating Racial Discrimination through Anti-discrimination Law: A Critical Review of Supreme Court Decisions," *Minnesota Law Review* 62 (1978): 1049.

16. See, for example, Paul Brest, "Foreword: In Defense of the Antidiscrimination Principle," *Harvard Law Review* 90 (1976): 1, 12–14; Owen M. Fiss, "Groups and the Equal Protection Clause," *Philosophy and Public Affairs* 5 (1976): 107–77; see especially pp. 118–29.

17. Reva B. Siegel, "Why Equal Protection No Longer Protects: The Evolving Forms of Status-Enforcing State Action," *Stanford Law Review* 49 (1997): 1131–35.

18. Ibid., p. 1137.

19. See *Griggs v. Duke Power,* 401 U.S 424 (1971). The Court retreated from this standard in a 1989 case, *Ward's Cove Packing v. Atonio* 490 U.S. 642, but

Congress reinstated the disparate impact theory in the Civil Rights Act of 1991. Despite the pervasive racial disparities in employment and federal contracting, very few disparate impact claims succeed in today's courts.

20. Linda Hamilton Krieger, "The Content of Our Categories," *Stanford Law Review* 47 (1995): 1161, 1168, 1248.

21. *Alexander v. Sandoval* 532 U.S. 275 (2001).

22. Krieger, "Content of Our Categories," p.1171.

23. David B. Oppenheimer, "Negligent Discrimination," *University of Pennsylvania Law Review* 141 (1993): 899–972.

24. Hans Morgenthau, *Politics among Nations*, 4th ed. (New York: Alfred A. Knopf, 1966), pp. 225, 249.

25. Determining the state of mind of a defendant is vital to the assessment of culpability for most crimes. See *Model Penal Code and Commentaries: Official Draft and Revised Comments*, § 2.02 (Philadelphia: American Law Institute, 1985); Wayne R. La Fave and Austin W. Scott Jr., *Criminal Law*, 2d ed., §§ 3.4–3.7 (St. Paul, Minn.: West Publishing, 1982).

26. The exception is criminal cases charging a hate crime where specific intent is properly required.

27. Orlando Patterson, *The Ordeal of Integration* (Washington, D.C.: Civitas/Counterpoint, 1997), p. 61.

28. Donald R. Kinder and Lynn M. Sanders, *Divided by Color: Racial Politics and Democratic Ideals* (Chicago: University of Chicago Press, 1996), pp. 105–6. See also Donald R. Kinder and Tali Mendelberg, "Individualism Reconsidered," in David Sears, Jim Sidanius, and Lawrence Bobo, eds., *Racialized Politics* (Chicago: University of Chicago Press, 2000), pp. 44–74; and Lawrence Bobo and Ryan A. Smith, "From Jim Crow Racism to Laissez-Faire Racism," in Wendy Katkin, Ned Landsman, and Andrea Tyree, eds., *Beyond Pluralism* (Urbana: University of Illinois Press, 1998), pp. 182–220.

29. Reynolds Farley et al., "Stereotypes and Segregation: Neighborhoods in the Detroit Area," *American Journal of Sociology* 100 (1994): 756, fig. 3.

30. Camille Zubrinsky Charles, "Processes of Racial Residential Segregation," in Alice O'Connor, Chris Tilly, and Lawrence D. Bobo, eds., *Urban Inequality: Evidence from Four Cities* (New York: Russell Sage Foundation, 2001), pp. 233–37, 257–58.

31. Tom W. Smith, "Ethnic Images," *GSS Technical Report No. 19*, (Chicago: National Opinion Research Center, January 1991). Sniderman and Piazza claim that blacks express equally invidious stereotypes of other African Americans; see *The Scar of Race*, p. 45. It is not clear what conclusions one can draw from this evidence, however.

32. Howard Schuman, Charlotte Steeh, and Lawrence Bobo, *Racial Attitudes in America: Trends and Interpretations* (Cambridge, Mass.: Harvard University Press, 1985), pp. 74–75. See also Gerald D. Jaynes and Robin M. Williams Jr., eds., *A Common Destiny: Blacks and American Society* (Washington, D.C.: National Academy Press, 1989), pp. 137–38.

33. Paul Sheatsley, "White Attitudes toward the Negro," in Talcott Parsons and Kenneth Clark, eds., *The Negro American* (Boston: Beacon Press, 1966), p. 312.

34. Schuman, Steeh, and Bobo, *Racial Attitudes in America,* pp. 74–75, 106–7. See also Howard Schuman and Lawrence Bobo, "Survey-Based Experiments on White Racial Attitudes toward Residential Integration," *American Journal of Sociology* 2 (1988): 273–99.

35. Schuman, Steeh, and Bobo, *Racial Attitudes in America,* pp. 74–75.

36. Douglas Massey and Nancy Denton, *American Apartheid: Segregation and the Making of the Underclass* (Cambridge, Mass.: Harvard University Press, 1993), p. 63.

37. Ibid., pp. 77, 222, table 8.1. See also Reynolds Farley et al., "Stereotypes and Segregation: Neighborhoods in the Detroit Area," pp. 750–80.

38. Thernstrom and Thernstrom, *America in Black and White,* p. 217.

39. Kinder and Sanders, *Divided by Color,* p. 63.

40. Herbert Blumer, "Race Prejudice as a Sense of Group Position," *Pacific Sociological Review* 1 (1958): 3–7. See also, among other works, Harold Baron, "The Web of Urban Racism," in L. Knowles and K. Prewitt, eds., *Institutional Racism* (Englewood Cliffs, N.J.: Prentice-Hall, 1969), pp. 134–77; Robert Blauner, *Racial Oppression in America* (New York: Harper and Row, 1972); Thomas Pettigrew, ed., *Racial Discrimination in the United States* (New York: Harper and Row, 1975); Charles R. Lawrence III, "The Id, the Ego, and Equal Protection: Reckoning with Unconscious Racism," *Stanford Law Review* 39 (January 1987): 317–23; Alexander Aleinikoff, "The Case for Race-Consciousness," *Columbia Law Review* 91 (June 1991): 1060–80; David Roediger, *The Wages of Whiteness* (New York: Verso, 1991); David Wellman, *Portraits of White Racism,* 2nd ed., rev. (New York: Cambridge University Press, 1993).

41. George Lipsitz, *The Possessive Investment in Whiteness: How White People Profit from Identity Politics* (Philadelphia: Temple University Press, 1998), p. viii.

42. Cheryl I. Harris, "Whiteness as Property," in Kimberle Crenshaw et al., eds., *Critical Race Theory* (New York: The New Press, 1995), p. 288.

43. See Stephanie M. Wildman, *Privilege Revealed: How Invisible Preference Undermines America* (New York: New York University Press, 1996).

44. Michael Quint, "Racial Disparity in Mortgages Shown in U.S. Data," *New York Times,* October 14, 1991, p. A1; Michael Quint, "Racial Gap Found in Mortgages," *New York Times,* October 21, 1991, p. C1.

45. Ian Ayres, "Fair Driving: Gender and Race Discrimination in Retail Car Negotiations," *Harvard Law Review* 104 (1991): 817.

46. Diana B. Henriques, "Review of Nissan Car Loans Finds That Blacks Pay More," *New York Times,* July 4, 2001, p. A1.

47. Lena Williams, "When Blacks Shop, Bias Often Accompanies Sale," *New York Times,* April 30, 1991, p. A1.

48. Joe R. Feagin and Melvin P. Sikes, *Living with Racism: The Black Middle-Class Experience* (Boston: Beacon Press, 1994), p. 34.

49. Marian E. Gornick, Paul W. Eggers, and Gerald F. Riley, "Understanding Disparities in the Use of Medicare Services," *Yale Journal of Health Policy, Law, and Ethics* 1 (2001): 135; Lorna Scott McBarnette, "African American Women," in Marcia Bayne-Smith, ed., *Race, Gender and Health* (Thousand Oaks, Calif.: Sage Publications, 1996), pp. 51–52.

50. Sally Squires, "Cancer Death Rate Higher for Blacks," *San Francisco Chronicle*, January 17, 1990, p. A5.

51. T. J. Powell, "Prostate Cancer and African American Men," *Oncology* 11 (1997): 599–605. Although in the period 1990–95 the rate of prostate cancer among white men was 24 per 100,000 people, the rate for black men was double, 55 per 100,000. For breast cancer, there were 26 cases per 100,000 for white women and 31.5 cases for African American women. Among whites of both sexes the figures for lung cancer were 49 per 100,000 for whites and 60 cases per 100,000 for blacks. See Phyllis Wingo et al., "Cancer Incidence and Mortality, 1973–1995: A Report Card for the U.S.," *Cancer* 82 (1998): 1197–1207.

52. Richard Cooper and Brian E. Simmons, "Cigarette Smoking and Ill Health among Black Americans," *New York State Journal of Medicine* 85 (1985): 344–49.

53. M. U. Yood et al., "Race and Differences in Breast Cancer Survival in a Managed Care Population," *Journal of the National Cancer Institute* 91 (1999): 1487–91. Even when access to health care is comparable, African Americans are diagnosed at a later stage and are 1.2 times more likely to die of breast cancer as whites.

54. Peter B. Bach et al., "Racial Differences in the Treatment of Early State Lung Cancer," *New England Journal of Medicine* 341 (Oct. 14, 1999): 1198.

55. McBarnette, "African American Women," p. 51.

56. Elizabeth White, "Special Report: Public Health Racial and Ethnic Disparities," *Health Care Policy Report* 9 (February 26, 2001), p. 315.

57. Michael Klag et al., "The Association of Skin Color with Blood Pressure in U.S. Blacks with Low Socioeconomic Status," *Journal of the American Medical Association* 265 (February 6, 1991): 599–602. See also David Perlman, "High Blood Pressure in Blacks Blamed on Economic Stress," *San Francisco Chronicle*, February 6, 1991, p. A4.

58. M. B. Wenneker and A. M. Epstein, "Racial Inequalities in the Use of Procedures for Patients with Ischemic Heart Disease in Massachusetts," *Journal of the American Medical Association* 261 (1989): 253–57.

59. Shimon Weitzman et al., "Gender, Racial, and Geographic Differences in the Performance of Cardiac Diagnostic and Therapeutic Procedures for Hospitalized Acute Myocardial Infarction in Four States," *American Journal of Cardiology* 79 (1997): 722–26. See also Eric Peterson et al., "Racial Variation in the Use of Coronary-Revascularization Procedures: Are the Differences Real? Do They Matter?" *New England Journal of Medicine* 336 (1997): 480–86. After controlling for age, gender, disease severity, comorbidity, smoking status, insurance, type of admitting medical services, and year of procedure, Peterson and his colleagues found that blacks were 32 percent less likely to have had coronary bypass surgery and 35 percent less likely to have had any revascularization procedure. Peterson's study was conducted in a major university medical center.

60. Eugene Oddone et al., "Race, Presenting Signs and Symptoms, Use of Carotid Artery Imaging, and Appropriateness of Carotid Endarterectomy," *Stroke* 30 (1999): 1350, 1353–54. The study controlled for factors such as age and other medical conditions.

61. Marian E. Gornick et al., "Effects of Race and Income on Mortality and Use of Services among Medicare Beneficiaries," *New England Journal of Medicine* 335 (1996): 791–99. (Blacks have lower-limb amputations almost four times as often as whites.)

62. Marian E. Gornick, Paul Eggers, and Gerald Riley, "Understanding Disparities in the Use of Medicare Services," *Yale Journal of Health Policy, Ethics and Law* 1 (2001): 138.

63. Angus Deaton and Darren Lubotsky, *Mortality, Inequality and Race in American Cities and States,* National Bureau of Economic Research Working Paper 8370 (Cambridge, Mass.: National Bureau of Economic Research, July 2001), p. 9.

64. We address this issue in detail in chapter 2.

65. "Minority Physicians' Experiences Obtaining Referrals to Specialists and Hospital Admissions," *Medscape General Medicine,* August 9, 2001, <http://www.medscape.com/view article/408160> (accessed February 27, 2002). The study also found that 12 percent of black and 15 percent of Latino physicians reported difficulty in obtaining specialty referrals compared to 8 percent of white doctors.

66. See *Crystal M. Ferguson et al. v. City of Charleston et al.,* 532 U.S. 67 (2001) (procedure for hospital screening and reporting to criminal authorities regarding population of largely minority women held unconstitutional). See also Dorothy Roberts, *Killing the Black Body: Race, Reproduction, and the Meaning of Liberty* (New York: Pantheon Books, 1997); Dorothy Roberts, "Punishing Drug Addicts Who Have Babies: Women of Color, Equality, and the Right of Privacy," *Harvard Law Review* 104 (1991): 1419–82; Marjorie M. Shultz, "Charleston, Cocaine, and Consent," *Journal of Gender Specific Medicine* 4 (2001): 14–16.

67. Janet Rich-Edwards et al., "Maternal Experiences of Racism and Violence as Predictors of Preterm Birth: Rationale and Study Design," *Paediatric and Perinatal Epidemiology* 15 (2000, Suppl. 2): 125.

68. K. Schulman et al., "The Effect of Race and Sex on Physicians' Recommendations for Cardiac Catheterization," *New England Journal of Medicine* 340 (1999): 618–26. The finding of racial disparities in this study was controversial. See Lisa M. Schwartz, Steven Woloshin, H. Gilbert Welch, "Misunderstandings about the Effects of Race and Sex on Physicians' Referrals for Cardiac Catheterization," *New England Journal of Medicine* 341 (1999): 279–83. All agreed, however, that blacks, particularly black women, were less often referred for aggressive treatment of cardiac symptoms than whites with identical symptoms and history. Schulman et al. reported an odds ratio of 40 percent less for blacks, p. 618; Schwartz et al. reported a probability of 7 percent less, p. 280.

69. Schwartz, Woloshin, and Welch, "Misunderstandings about the Effects of Race and Sex." On other traits, blacks and whites scored more similarly, or the differences ran in the opposite direction. For example, black males and females were judged to be happier, friendlier, and less likely to sue than their white counterparts.

70. Linda J. Krieger, "The Content of Our Categories," p. 1161.

71. Lawrence, "The Id, the Ego, and Equal Protection," p. 317.

72. M. Gregg Bloche, "Race and Discretion in American Medicine," *Yale Journal of Health Policy, Law and Ethics,* 1 (2001): 95.

73. Richard Lapchick and Kevin Matthews, *Racial Report Card: A Comprehensive Analysis of the Hiring Practices of Women and People of Color in the National Basketball Association, the National Football League, Major League Baseball, the NCCA and Its Member Institutions* (Boston: Northeastern University, Center for the Study of Sport in Society, 1997).

74. *Racial and Gender Report Card* (Boston: Center for the Study of Sport in Society, Northeastern University, 2001).

75. Ibid.; Lapchick and Matthews, *Racial Report Card.*

76. Sarah Nelson, "Racial Discrimination in the NFL" (unpublished paper written for Department of Community Studies, Saint Cloud State College, 2001, photocopy).

77. Janice Rule, "Black Coaches in the NFL: Superior Performance, Inferior Opportunities," (Department of Economics, University of Pennsylvania); quoted in Thomas George, "NFL Pressured on Black Coaches," *New York Times,* October 6, 2002.

78. Quoted in George, "NFL Pressured on Black Coaches." Lewis was hired as a head coach after the 2002 season.

79. Cited by Brent Staples, "When a Law Firm Is Like a Baseball Team," *New York Times,* November 27, 1998, p. A42.

80. Ibid.

81. Jennifer Hochschild, "Race, Class, Power and the American Welfare State," in Amy Gutmann, ed., *Democracy and the Welfare State* (Princeton: Princeton University Press, 1988), p. 178. Kinder and Sanders found that whites who believed their children's admission to colleges and universities was jeopardized by racial preferences were strongly opposed to race-conscious policies. See Kinder and Sanders, *Divided by Color,* pp. 62–63.

82. Kinder and Sanders, *Divided by Color,* p. 85.

83. David Barton Smith, *Health Care Divided* (Ann Arbor: University of Michigan Press, 1999), p. 138.

84. Richard Muth, "The Causes of Housing Segregation," in *Issues in Housing Discrimination: A Consultation/Hearings of the United States Commission on Civil Rights,* vol. 1 (Washington, D.C. The Commission, November 12–13, 1985), pp. 3–13; quoted in Lawrence Bobo and Camille L. Zubrinksy, "Attitudes on Residential Integration: Perceived Status Differences, Mere In-Group Preference, or Racial Prejudice?" *Social Forces* 74 (1996): 887.

85. Reynolds Farley, Susanne Bianchi, and Diane Colasanto, "Barriers to the Racial Integration of Neighborhoods: The Detroit Case," *Annals of the American Academy of Political and Social Science* 441 (1979): 97–113.

86. Massey and Denton, *American Apartheid,* p. 94

87. Stanley B. Greenberg, *Report on Democratic Defection* (Washington, D.C.: Analysis Group 35, 1985), pp. 13–18. Cited in Massey and Denton, *American Apartheid,* p. 94.

88. Bobo and Zubrinsky, "Attitudes on Residential Integration," pp. 892, 887.

89. Thernstrom and Thernstrom, *America in Black and White,* p. 503.

90. Kinder and Sanders, *Divided by Color,* p. 17.

91. Sniderman and Piazza, *Scar of Race,* p. 26.

92. Bob Herbert, "Mr. Lott's 'Big Mistake,'" *New York Times,* January 7, 1999.

93. Quoted by Adam Clymer, "Republican Party's 40 Years of Juggling on Race," *New York Times,* December 13, 2002.

94. Quoted by Bob Herbert, "Weirder and Weirder," *New York Times,* December 19, 2002.

95. Neil A. Lewis, "Senate Committee Back Bush Choice for Justice Dept.," *New York Times,* January 31, 2001, p. A14. The Republican party has used implicit racial appeals to attract white voters for the last thirty years. For a compelling account of this, see Tali Mendelberg, *The Race Card: Campaign Strategy, Implicit Messages, and the Norm of Equality* (Princeton: Princeton University Press, 2001).

96. Melanie Kaye-Kantrowitz, "Jews in the U.S.: The Rising Costs of Whiteness," in Becky Thompson and Sangeeta Tyagi, eds., *Names We Call Home* (New York: Routledge, 1996), p. 124.

97. From 1790 to 1952, only a "white person" could become a naturalized citizen. See Ian Haney-Lopez, *White by Law: The Legal Construction of Race* (New York: New York University Press, 1996), p. 1.

98. Kinder and Sanders, *Divided by Color,* pp. 106–9, 263. See also Lawrence Bobo and James R. Kluegel, "Opposition to Race-Targeting: Self Interest, Stratification Ideology, or Racial Attitudes," *American Sociological Review* 58 (1993): 443–64; Jim Sidanius, Felicia Pratto, and Lawrence Bobo, "Racism, Conservatism, Affirmative Action, and Intellectual Sophistication: A Matter of Principled Conservatism or Group Dominance?" *Journal of Personality and Social Psychology* 70 (1996): 476–90.

99. Harris, "Equality Trouble," pp. 2003, 2011.

100. In theory, affirmative action is still possible but under highly restrictive conditions. For example, to be permitted under Title VII, an affirmative action plan "must not unduly trammel the rights of non-beneficiaries." *United Steelworkers v. Weber,* 463 U.S. 193, 208 (1979). In effect, this means the plan must not interfere with the legitimate settled expectations (including seniority rights) of incumbent majority members, typically existing white male employees. It would be hard to find a better illustration of the thesis that current law maintains the existing distribution of advantage.

101. Siegel, "Why Equal Protection No Longer Protects," p. 1143.

102. Harris, "Equality Trouble," p. 2002.

103. Siegel, "Why Equal Protection No Longer Protects," p. 1143. Angela Harris describes a similar outcome, showing that the Court currently emphasizes discrimination as "differentiation" (classification) rather than discrimination as "disadvantage." Harris, "Equality Trouble," p. 2003.

104. Reva B. Siegel, "The Racial Rhetorics of Colorblind Constitutionalism: The Case of *Hopwood v. Texas,*" in Robert Post and Michael Rogin, eds., *Race and Representation: Affirmative Action* (New York: Zone Books, 1998), pp. 44–45.

105. *City of Richmond v. J. A. Croson Co.,* 488 U.S. 469 (1989).

106. The literature discussing the pitfalls of color-blind ideology is large. See

generally Neil Gotanda, "A Critique of 'Our Constitution Is Color-Blind,'" *Stanford Law Review* 44 (1991): 1; Kimberle Crenshaw, "Race, Reform and Retrenchment: Transformation and Legitimation in Anti-Discrimination Law," *Harvard Law Review* 101 (1988): 1331; Lawrence, "The Id, the Ego, and Equal Protection."

107. One of the authors' personal conversation with a voter during a 1994 judicial campaign.

108. Ian Haney-Lopez, "Institutional Racism: Judicial Conduct and a New Theory of Racial Discrimination," *Yale Law Journal* 190 (2000): 1728.

109. Ibid., p. 1736.

110. Ibid., p. 1742.

111. Ibid., pp. 1756–57.

112. Patricia Williams, *The Alchemy of Race and Rights: Diary of a Law Professor* (Cambridge, Mass.: Harvard University Press, 1991), pp 45–51.

113. In 1997, the legal profession was 2.7 percent black and 3.8 percent Hispanic. *Statistical Abstract of U.S.* (Washington, D.C.: U.S. Government Printing Office, 1998), p. 417. More significant, perhaps, for the development of legal perspectives, only one of the Supreme Court's law clerks was African American in the fall of 2001. None was Hispanic or Native American. Four were Asian. Tony Mauro, "Number of Minority Law Clerks for Supreme Court Justices Declines," *American Lawyer Media*, October 29, 2001. Supreme Court clerks play crucial roles in the discussion and drafting of Supreme Court opinions.

114. We address this question in chapter 6.

115. *McCleskey v. Kemp*, 481 U.S. 279 (1987); David C. Baldus, Charles A. Pulaski, and George Woodworth, *Equal Justice and the Death Penalty: A Legal and Empirical Analysis* (Boston: Northeastern University Press, 1991). In chapter 4 we examine the argument that there are no serious racial disparities in the administration of the death penalty.

116. Charles R. Lawrence III, "If He Hollers Let Him Go: Regulating Racist Speech on Campus," *Duke Law Journal* (1990): 431; Charles R. Lawrence III and Mari J. Matsuda, *Words That Wound: Critical Race Theory, Assaultive Speech, and the First Amendment* (Boulder, Colo.: Westview Press, 1993).

117. Mari J. Matsuda, "Voices of America: Accent, Anti-Discrimination Law and a Jurisprudence for the Last Reconstruction," *Yale Law Journal* 100 (1991): 1329.

118. Cheryl Harris; "Whiteness as Property," in Kimberle Crenshaw et al., eds., *Critical Race Theory* (New York: The New Press, 1995); Haney-Lopez, *White by Law*.

119. *Florida v. Bostick*, 501 U.S. 429, 437 (1991). The U.S. Supreme Court reversed a Florida Supreme Court ruling that a specific police search had been coercive. Quoting from *Michigan v. Chesternut*, 486 U.S. 567 (1988), the justices ruled that coerciveness depends on whether a "reasonable person [would have felt that] he was not at liberty to ignore the police presence and go about his business." The court held that under this reasonable person test, several black youths confronted by police at the back of a crowded bus should have had no trouble in believing they could terminate the encounter without consenting to the requested search. Therefore, their consent was voluntary. David Cole calls the Bostick test

"patently fictional." See *Equal Justice: Race and Class in the American Criminal Justice System* (New York: New Press, 1999), pp. 17–22

120. We draw the themes in this paragraph and the next from Dirk Tollotson, "Constitutional Eracism," Boalt Hall School of Law and the Center for the Study of Jurisprudence and Social Policy, University of California, Berkeley (photocopy available from authors).

121. Rogers Smith, *Civic Ideals: Conflicting Visions of Citizenship in U.S. History* (New Haven: Yale University Press, 1997), p. 101.

122. John T. Noonan Jr., "Comment on R. Kent Newmyer, 'John Marshall, Political Parties, and the Origins of Modern Federalism,'" in Harry N. Scheiber, ed., *Federalism: Studies in History, Law, and Policy: Papers from the Second Berkeley Seminar on Federalism* (Berkeley: University of California, Institute of Government Studies, 1988), p. 25.

123. Admissions decisions, particularly in public law schools, are not simply scholastic contests. They involve distributional equity, the allocation of scarce, tax-supported opportunities, access to a historic avenue of upward mobility, and opportunities for leadership in government. Consequently, admissions policies affect racial equity.

124. The correlation is moderate but greater than other indices that have been evaluated. Phil Shelton, president of the Law School Admission Council, acknowledged the narrow focus of the LSAT, saying, "All the LSAT was ever intended to predict was performance on property, contracts and torts essay questions. That's all. Period." See Michael Rooke-Ley, "Correction on Law School Admissions," *SALT Equalizer*, December 2001, <http://www.saltlaw.org> (accessed January 27, 2003). In focusing on correlates of first-year grades, admissions practice does not consider whether bias within law schools may influence law school grades. The first-year curriculum is still designed by overwhelmingly white law school faculties, and parallels what was taught nearly a century ago, when blacks were not even admitted. The greater alienation that students of color feel in law school has been widely documented and may affect their academic performance. See Kimberle Crenshaw, "Toward a Race-Conscious Pedagogy," *National Black Law Journal* 11 (1989): 1; Garner K. Weng, "Look at the Pretty Colors: Rethinking Promises of Diversity as Legally Binding," *La Raza Law Journal* 10 (1998): 753, 795–805; Claude M. Steele and Joshua Aronson, "Stereotype Threat and the Intellectual Test Performance of African-Americans," *Journal of Personality and Social Psychology* 69 (1995): 797.

125. In 1998, for applicants to Boalt Hall School of Law, UC Berkeley, who had GPAs of 3.75 or more, a 5-point difference in LSAT score cut the chance of admission from 89 to 44 percent; for the same year at UCLA, the chance of admission dropped from 66 to 10 percent. See William C. Kidder, "The Rise of the Testocracy: An Essay on the LSAT, Conventional Wisdom, and the Dismantling of Diversity," *Texas Journal of Women and the Law* 9 (2000): 193.

126. Because professional schools deal with enormous numbers of applicants, they are drawn to quantifiable indices that can be applied quickly and with apparent impartiality. Professional schools have traditionally been insecure about their intellectual credentials and legitimacy, perhaps tempting them to overemphasize test scores. Popular rankings of schools emphasize median scores of a

school's students. Finally, professors themselves did extremely well on conventional academic indicia and may be especially prone to believe in their validity.

127. When the University of California eliminated affirmative action from admissions decisions, reliance on traditional numerical indicators sharply reduced the number of minority students admitted to law schools. At three of California's public law schools (Boalt, UC Davis, and UCLA), white enrollments rose from 60 percent of all first-year students to 72 percent, while black and Latino enrollments plummeted and Asian American enrollments were largely unchanged. William C. Kidder, "Situating Asian Pacific Americans in the Law School Affirmative Action Debate," *Asian Law Journal* 7 (2000). The one study of how law school admissions would change nationally if affirmative action were eliminated estimated a 53 percent decline in the number of students of color admitted and a 90 percent decline in the number of black students admitted. See Linda F. Wightman, "The Threat to Diversity in Legal Education: An Empirical Analysis of the Consequences of Abandoning Race as a Factor," *New York University Law Review* 72 (1997): 1.

128. *Griggs v. Duke Power*, 401 U.S. 424 (1971), held that employers may use screening tests that yield racially disproportionate outcomes only if those tests are "reasonably necessary to job performance." Chapter 5 discusses conservative criticisms of the case.

129. Some courts have rejected efforts to apply *Griggs* to the bar exam. See, for example, *Tyler v. Vickery*, 517 F.2d 1089 (5th cir. 1975), cert denied 426 U.S. 940 (1976). Although the bar exam is a closer analogue to employment selection than school admissions decisions are, the few decisions may be anomalous; they are persuasively criticized in Cecil J. Hunt, "Guests in Another's House: An Analysis of Racially Disparate Bar Performance," *Florida State University Law Review* 23 (1996): 721.

130. Without a law school diploma, only a very few lawyers gain entry to the bar. Overwhelming majorities of graduates from the elite law schools, whose admissions practices are under discussion here, pass the bar exam, usually on the first try, and enter the profession.

131. See N. Schmidt et al., "Adverse Impact and Predictive Efficiency of Various Predictor Combinations," *Journal of Applied Psychology* 82 (1997): 719–30.

132. Christopher Jencks and Meredith Phillips, eds., *The Black-White Test Score Gap* (Washington, D.C.: The Brookings Institution Press, 1998), pp. 57–58.

133. Thernstrom and Thernstrom, *America in Black and White*, p. 544.

CHAPTER TWO

1. Stephen Thernstrom and Abigail Thernstrom, *America in Black and White* (New York: Simon and Schuster, 1997), p. 234.

2. Ibid., pp. 87, 187. James P. Smith and Finis R. Welch (in *Closing the Gap: Forty Years of Economic Progress for Blacks* [Santa Monica, Calif.: The Rand Corporation, 1986]) make a case for the importance of education to blacks' economic gains.

3. Thernstrom and Thernstrom, "The Real Story of Black Progress," *Wall*

Street Journal, September 3, 1997; cited in William A. Darity Jr. and Patrick L. Mason, "Evidence on Discrimination in Employment: Codes of Color, Codes of Gender," *Journal of Economic Perspectives* 12 (1998): 73. For arguments that labor market discrimination has all but disappeared, see James J. Heckman, "Detecting Discrimination," *Journal of Economic Perspectives* 12 (1998): 101–16; and Ronald F. Ferguson, "Shifting Challenges: Fifty Years of Economic Change toward Black-White Earnings Equality," in Obie Clayton Jr., ed., *An American Dilemma Revisited* (New York: Russell Sage Foundation, 1996), pp. 76–111. We evaluate this argument in chapter 3.

4. Besides Thernstrom and Thernstrom, *America in Black and White,* chapter 9, see Marvin Kosters, "Looking for Jobs in All the Wrong Places," *The Public Interest* (fall 1996): 125–31.

5. Sheldon Danziger and Peter Gottschalk, *America Unequal* (New York: Russell Sage Foundation, 1995).

6. Reynolds Farley and Walter R. Allen, *The Color Line and the Quality of Life in America* (New York: Oxford University Press, 1989), p. 225; Cordelia W. Reimers, "The Effect of Tighter Labor Markets on Unemployment of Hispanics and African Americans: The 1990s Experiences," in Robert Cherry and Williams Rodgers III, eds., *Prosperity for All? The Economic Boom and African Americans* (New York: Russell Sage Foundation, 2000), pp. 3–49.

7. William E. Spriggs and Rhonda M. Williams, "What Do We Need to Explain about African American Unemployment?" in Cherry and Rodgers, eds., *Prosperity for All?* pp. 195, 200.

8. Farley and Allen, *The Color Line and the Quality of Life in America,* p. 295.

9. Spriggs and Williams, "What Do We Need to Explain about African American Unemployment?" pp. 201–2. See also Darity and Mason, "Evidence on Discrimination in Employment," pp. 85–86; Steven Shulman, "Why Is the Black Unemployment Rate Always Twice as High as the White Unemployment Rate?" in Richard R. Cornwall and Phanindra V. Wunnava, eds., *New Approaches to Economic and Social Analyses of Discrimination* (New York: Prager, 1991), pp. 5–38.

10. Thomas N. Maloney, "Wage Compression and Wage Inequality between Black and White Males in the United States, 1940–1960," *Journal of Economic History* 54 (1994): 358–81.

11. Warren Whatley and Gavin Wright, "Race, Human Capital, and Labour Markets in American History," in George Grantham and Mary Mackinnon, eds., *Labour Market Evolution* (London: Routledge, 1994), p. 280.

12. Herbert R. Northrup, *Negro Employment in Basic Industry: A Study of Racial Policies in Six Industries* (Philadelphia: University of Pennsylvania Press, 1970), pp. 93, 404–5, 448. For an analysis of the role of the steelworkers union in creating and maintaining segregated seniority systems, see Robert J. Norell, "Caste in Steel: Jim Crow Careers in Birmingham, Alabama," *Journal of American History* 73 (1986): 669–94.

13. Northrup, *Negro Employment in Basic Industry,* p. 330; Thomas Sugrue, *The Origins of the Urban Crisis: Race and Inequality in Postwar Detroit* (Princeton, N.J.: Princeton University Press, 1996), pp. 101–5.

14. Harold Baron and Bennett Hymer, "The Negro Worker in the Chicago Labor Market," in Julius Jacobson, ed., *The Negro and the Labor Movement* (New York: Anchor Books, 1968), p. 261. Job ceilings imposed by white workers at the beginning of the twentieth century had very similar effects on black workers; see Stanley Lieberson, *A Piece of the Pie: Blacks and White Immigrants since 1880* (Berkeley and Los Angeles: University of California Press, 1980), pp. 294–320.

15. Farley and Allen, *The Color Line and the Quality of Life*, pp. 295, 298; Martin Carnoy, *Faded Dreams: The Politics and Economics of Race in America* (New York: Cambridge University Press, 1994), pp. 15–16; Baron and Hymer, "The Negro Worker in the Chicago Labor Market"; Maloney, "Wage Compression and Wage Inequality between Black and White Males."

16. Charles C. Killingsworth, "Negroes in a Changing Labor Market," in Arthur M. Ross and Herbert Hill, eds., *Employment, Race and Poverty* (New York: Harcourt, Brace and World, 1967), p. 60; Baron and Hymer, "The Negro Worker in the Chicago Labor Market," p. 255; Gerald David Jaynes and Robin M. Williams, eds., *A Common Destiny: Blacks and American Society* (Washington, D.C.: National Academy Press, 1989), p. 301.

17. Farley and Allen, *The Color Line and the Quality of Life*, p. 265.

18. Northrup, *Negro Employment in Basic Industry*, p. 26.

19. Ibid., p. 30; James J. Heckman, "The Central Role of the South in Accounting for the Economic Progress of Black Americans," *American Economic Review* 80 (May 1990): 245.

20. Michael K. Brown and Steven P. Erie, "Blacks and the Legacy of the Great Society: The Economic and Political Impact of Federal Social Policy," *Public Policy* 29 (1981): 299–330.

21. Carnoy, *Faded Dreams*, pp. 162–65.

22. Ibid., p. 185; Jaynes and Williams, *A Common Destiny*, pp. 316–18.

23. Jonathan Rieder, *Canarsie: The Jews and Italians of Brooklyn against Liberalism* (Cambridge, Mass.: Harvard University Press, 1985), p. 117.

24. Jaynes and Williams, eds., *A Common Destiny*, p. 278–79.

25. Farley and Allen, *The Color Line and the Quality of Life*, p. 298.

26. The President's Commission on Veterans' Pensions, *Readjustment Benefits: General Survey and Appraisal*, Staff Report No. 9, (Washington, D.C.: U.S. Government Printing Office, 1956), pp. 78, 111. The Bradley Commission's data comparing pre- and postservice occupations are striking. They found that 40 percent of preservice laborers using training and educational benefits made it into professional jobs compared to 23 percent who did not; and among preservice sales workers, 42 percent of those using training became professionals compared to 29 percent of those who did not. See pp. 96–97, table 12.

27. Ibid., p. 145.

28. Michael K. Brown, *Race, Money and the American Welfare State* (Ithaca, N.Y.: Cornell University Press, 1999), p. 191; Desmond King, *Separate and Unequal: Black Americans and the U.S. Federal Government* (New York: Oxford University Press, 1995), pp. 173–85.

29. Brown, *Race, Money, and the American Welfare State*, pp. 183.

30. David H. Onkst, "'First a Negro . . . incidentally a veteran': Black World

War Two Veterans and the G.I. Bill of Rights in the Deep South, 1944–1948," *Journal of Social History* (spring 1998): 4–5, 11, 14.

31. Brown, *Race, Money and the American Welfare State*, pp. 183–84.

32. Ibid., pp. 189–91; U.S. Bureau of the Census, *U.S. Census of Population: 1960, Final Report, Subject Reports, Veterans* (Washington, D.C.: U.S. Government Printing Office, 1961), table 16.

33. Jill Quadagno, *The Color of Welfare: How Racism Undermined the War on Poverty* (New York: Oxford University Press, 1994), p. 91.

34. Kenneth T. Jackson, *Crabgrass Frontier* (New York: Oxford University Press, 1985), p. 215; Henry Aaron, *Shelter and Subsidies: Who Benefits from Federal Housing Policies* (Washington, D.C.: The Brookings Institution, 1972), pp. 85–89.

35. Jackson, *Crabgrass Frontier*, pp. 208, 211.

36. U.S. Bureau of the Census, *Census of Housing, Residential Finance, 1960* (Washington, D.C.: U.S. Government Printing Office, 1961), vol. 5, part I, table 2; Brown, *Race, Money, and the American Welfare State*, p. 190.

37. Brown, *Race, Money and the American Welfare State*, pp. 132–33.

38. David Barton Smith, *Health Care Divided: Race and Healing a Nation* (Ann Arbor: University of Michigan Press, 1999), p. 103. *Simkins v. Moses H. Cone Memorial Hospital*, 323 F.2d 957 (C.A. 4, 1963); cert. denied, March 2, 1964. The *Simkins* case paved the way for Title VI of the 1964 Civil Rights Act, which prohibited discriminatory use of federal funds.

39. Douglas Massey and Nancy Denton, *American Apartheid: Segregation and the Making of the Underclass* (Cambridge, Mass.: Harvard University Press, 1993), pp. 54–55, 108; Dalton Conley, *Being Black, Living in the Red: Race, Wealth, and Social Policy in America* (Berkeley and Los Angeles: University of California Press, 1999), pp. 38–39, 42. Conley reports that in 1996 the median monthly mortgage payment was $279 and the median monthly rental payment was $400.

40. Council of Economic Advisers, *Changing America: Indicators of Social and Economic Well-Being by Race and Hispanic Origin* (September 1998), p. 39; Melvin Oliver and Thomas Shapiro, *Black Wealth/White Wealth* (New York: Routledge, 1997), pp. 86–87, 101–2.

41. Conley, *Being Black, Living in the Red*, pp. 48–51; Oliver and Shapiro, *Black Wealth/White Wealth*, pp. 136–47.

42. Carnoy, *Faded Dreams*, pp. 82–83.

43. Council of Economic Advisers, *Economic Report of the President, 1998* (Washington, D.C.: U.S. Government Printing Office, 1998), p. 150.

44. Roger Waldinger and Thomas Bailey, "The Continuing Significance of Race: Racial Conflict and Racial Discrimination in Construction," *Politics and Society* 19 (1991): 293. This is a classic example of opportunity hoarding; see introduction, "Group Hoarding and the Economic Theory of Discrimination."

45. Deirdre Royster, *Race and the "Invisible Hand"* (Berkeley and Los Angeles: University of California Press, 2003).

46. William Darity Jr. and Samuel L. Myers Jr., *Persistent Disparity: Race and Economic Inequality in the United States since 1945* (Northhampton, Mass.: Edward Elgar Publishing, 1998), pp. 9, 65–67, 69.

47. Darity and Myers, *Persistent Disparity*, pp. 47–48. The salaries of black workers moving from jobs as operatives to sales workers declined from $16,220 to $14,114; the salaries of white workers increased from $18,526 to $25,292.

48. Jerome Culp and Bruce H. Dunson, "Brothers of a Different Color: A Preliminary Look at Employer Treatment of White and Black Youth," in Richard B. Freeman and Harry J. Holzer, eds., *The Black Youth Unemployment Crisis* (Chicago: University of Chicago Press, 1986), p. 241.

49. Harry J. Holzer and David Neumark, "Assessing Affirmative Action," *Journal of Economic Literature* 38 (2000): 496. For a summary of recent research on discrimination, see Darity and Mason, "Evidence on Discrimination in Employment," pp. 79–81. Audit studies have been criticized on both conceptual and empirical grounds, but Deirdre Royster's study of employment discrimination takes the matched-pairs analysis common to audit studies to a new level of sophistication and overcomes the limits of previous studies. See Royster, *Race and the "Invisible Hand."*

50. Darity and Myers, *Persistent Disparity*, pp. 29–30.

51. Carnoy, *Faded Dreams*, pp. 95–99.

52. Darity and Myers, *Persistent Disparity*, p. 51. For a description of the experience of black workers during the depression, see Arthur M. Ross, "The Negro Worker in the Depression," *Social Forces* 18 (1940): 550–59.

53. Philip Moss and Chris Tilly, "'Soft' Skills and Race: An Investigation of Black Men's Employment Problems," *Work and Occupations* 23 (1996): 252–76; Philip Moss and Chris Tilly, "Why Opportunity Isn't Knocking: Racial Inequality and the Demand for Labor," in Alice O'Connor, Chris Tilly, and Lawrence D. Bobo, eds., *Urban Inequality: Evidence from Four Cities* (New York: Russell Sage Foundation, 2001), pp. 444–95.

54. Philip Moss and Chris Tilly, *Stories Employers Tell: Race, Skill, and Hiring in America* (New York: Russell Sage Foundation, 2001), p. 106; Harry J. Holzer, "Employer Hiring Decisions and Antidiscrimination Policy," in Richard B. Freeman, ed., *Generating Jobs: How to Increase Demand for Less-Skilled Workers* (New York: Russell Sage Foundation, 1998), p. 241.

55. Moss and Tilly, "Why Isn't Opportunity Knocking?" pp. 482–83.

56. Kathryn M. Neckerman and Joleen Kirschenman, "Hiring Strategies, Racial Bias, and Inner-City Workers," *Social Problems* 38 (1991): 433–47.

57. Gordon Lafer, "Minority Employment, Labor Market Segmentation, and the Failure of Job-Training Policy in New York City," *Urban Affairs Quarterly* 28 (1992): 224.

58. "Discrimination and Affirmative Action," *California Opinion Index,* (San Francisco: The Field Institute, May 1995), p. 2.

59. Lawrence M. Mead, "Social Programs and Social Obligations," *The Public Interest* 69 (fall 1982): 19. See also Charles Murray, *Losing Ground: American Social Policy, 1950–1980* (New York: Basic Books, Inc., 1984).

60. Jaynes and Williams, eds., *A Common Destiny*, pp. 277–79. By 2001, the poverty rate for blacks had dropped to 22.7 percent; for Latinos the rate was 21.4 percent.

61. Sara McLanahan and Lynn Casper, "Growing Diversity and Inequality in

the American Family," in Reynolds Farley, ed., *State of the Union: America in the 1990s*, vol. 2 (New York: Russell Sage Foundation, 1995), p. 21.

62. Thernstrom and Thernstrom, *America in Black and White*, p. 244.

63. Ibid., pp. 256, 595n. 40.

64. Ibid., p. 254; Robert I. Lerman, "The Impact of the Changing U.S. Family Structure on Child Poverty and Income Inequality," *Economica* 63 (1996): S119–39. Some writers explicitly ascribe widening income inequality to the choices of women. See, for example, Daniel Patrick Moynihan, "Toward a Post-Industrial Social Policy," *The Public Interest* (summer 1989): 16–27.

65. Thernstrom and Thernstrom, *America in Black and White*, p. 243. The Bush administration has made marriage an official anti-poverty policy and proposes to devote $100 million to encourage poor women to marry. See Robin Toner, "Welfare Chief Is Hoping to Promote Marriage," *New York Times*, February 19, 2002, p. A1.

66. Kristin Luker, *Dubious Conceptions: The Politics of Teenage Pregnancy* (Cambridge, Mass.: Harvard University Press, 1996), pp. 107, 113, 116.

67. Darity and Myers, *Persistent Disparity*, pp. 85–89.

68. McLanahan and Casper, "Growing Diversity and Inequality in the American Family," p. 21.

69. Marjorie E. Starrels, Sally Bould, and Leon J. Nicholas, "The Feminization of Poverty in the United States: Gender, Race, Ethnicity, and Family Factors," *Journal of Family Issues* 15 (1994): 602.

70. *Economic Report of the President*, p. 133; Lerman, "The Impact of the Changing U.S. Family Structure on Child Poverty," S135–36. Lerman estimates poverty would have declined by one-third if there had been no change in family structure. The difference between the CEA's estimate and Lerman's is the time period; the CEA's data take in the economic boom of the 1990s. Lerman, it should be noted, measures the decline in child poverty rather than the black-white poverty gap. See also Jaynes and Williams, *A Common Destiny*, p. 281.

71. Danziger and Gottschalk, eds., *America Unequal*, pp. 105–6.

72. Ibid., pp. 41–43, 50–51.

73. Rebecca Blank estimates that in the 1960s a 1 percent increase in GDP decreased poverty by 2.53 percent, but in the 1980s, by only 1.69 percent. Rebecca M. Blank, "Why Were Poverty Rates So High in the 1980s?" in Dimitri B. Papadimitriou and Edward N. Wolff, eds., *Poverty and Prosperity in the U.S.A. in the Late Twentieth Century* (New York: St. Martin's Press, 1993), pp. 25–26.

74. Blank, "Why Were Poverty Rates So High?" p. 51; Rebecca Blank and David Card, *Poverty, Income Distribution and Growth: Are They Still Connected?* (Evanston, Ill.: Center for Urban Affairs and Policy Research, Northwestern University, 1993), p. 38; Danziger and Gottschalk, *America Unequal*, pp. 103–6.

75. Darity and Myers, *Persistent Disparity*, pp. 106–9.

76. Gary Orfield, "Race and the Liberal Agenda: The Loss of the Integrationist Dream, 1965–1974," in Margaret Weir, Ann Shola Orloff, and Theda Skocpol, eds., *The Politics of Social Policy in the United States* (Princeton, NJ: Princeton University Press, 1988), p. 313.

77. Brown, *Race, Money, and the American Welfare State*, pp. 164, 192–93; Sugrue, *The Origins of the Urban Crisis*, p. 144.

78. Mark J. Stern, "Poverty and Family Composition since 1940," in Michael B. Katz, ed., *The "Underclass" Debate: Views from History* (Princeton, N.J.: Princeton University Press, 1993), pp. 237–38; Baron and Hymer, "The Negro Worker in the Chicago Labor Market," p. 266; Brown, *Race, Money, and the American Welfare State*, pp. 284–90. Elliot Liebow's brilliant book is one of the best available studies of the effects of joblessness on black men; see *Tally's Corner: A Study of Negro Streetcorner Men* (Boston, Mass.: Little, Brown, 1967).

79. Northrup, *Negro Employment in Basic Industry*, p. 418; Sugrue, *The Origins of the Urban Crisis*, p. 144.

80. Elizabeth Sanders, "Electorate Expansion and Public Policy: A Decade of Political Change in the South" (Ph.D. dissertation, Cornell University, 1978), pp. 45, 76, 87. See also Bruce J. Schulman, *From Cottonbelt to Sunbelt* (New York: Oxford University Press, 1991), pp. 177–79. Schulman argues that blacks were at a disadvantage in the southern economic boom. Blacks were restricted to low-wage or economically declining jobs; industry located in areas populated mostly by whites (northern Alabama, coastal Mississippi) and recruited white labor, partly because they thought that blacks were more likely to join unions.

81. James Jacobs, *Black Workers and the New Technology: The Need for a New Urban Training* (Ann Arbor, Mich.: Industrial Technology Institute, 1987), p. 9.

82. Ann Markusen, Peter Hall, and Amy K. Glasmeier, *High Tech America: The What, How, Where, and Why of the Sunrise Industries* (Boston: Allen and Unwin, 1986), pp. 177–78. See also James H. Johnson Jr. and Melvin H. Oliver, "Structural Changes in the U.S. Economy and Black Male Joblessness: A Reassessment," in George E. Peterson and Wayne Vroman, eds., *Urban Labor Markets and Job Opportunity* (Washington, D.C.: The Urban Institute, 1992), pp. 116–18.

83. The thirty-city average in 1990 was 77.8 percent, a small 11-point change. Massey and Denton, *American Apartheid,* pp. 46–49, 221–23; John E. Farley, "Race Still Matters: The Minimal Role of Income and Housing Cost as Causes of Housing Segregation in St. Louis, 1990," *Urban Affairs Quarterly* 31 (1995): 244–54; Anne B. Shlay, "Not in That Neighborhood: The Effects of Population and Housing on the Distribution of Mortgage Finance within the Chicago SMSA," *Social Science Research* 17 (1988): 137–63. For a recent analysis of studies on discrimination in mortgages, see Helen F. Ladd, "Evidence on Discrimination in Mortgage Lending," *Journal of Economic Perspectives* 12 (1998): 41–62.

84. Harold Baron, *Building Babylon: A Case of Racial Controls in Public Housing* (Evanston, Ill.: Center for Urban Affairs, Northwestern University, 1971), pp. 2, 67–70.

85. Ibid., pp. 37–42; Arnold Hirsch, *Making the Second Ghetto: Race and Housing in Chicago, 1940–1960* (New York: Cambridge University Press, 1983); Sugrue, *Origins of the Urban Crisis*.

86. Frederick A. Lazin, "Federal Low-Income Housing Assistance Pro-

grams and Racial Segregation: Leased Public Housing," *Public Policy* 24 (1976): 337–60.

87. Dennis R. Judd, "Symbolic Politics and Urban Policies: Why African Americans Got So Little from the Democrats," in Adolph Reed Jr., ed., *Without Justice for All: The New Liberalism and Our Retreat from Racial Equality* (Boulder, Colo.: Westview Press, 1999), pp. 134–35.

88. Basil Zimmer, "The Small Businessman and Relocation," in James Q. Wilson, ed., *Urban Renewal: The Record and the Controversy* (Cambridge, Mass.: The MIT Press, 1966), pp. 382, 386–87, 403.

89. Smith, *Health Care Divided*, p. 176.

90. Alan Sager, "Urban Hospital Closings in the Face of Racial Change: A Statement on Hospital Financing Problems," in *Civil Rights Issues in Health Care Delivery* (Washington, D.C.: U.S. Commission on Civil Rights, 1980), p. 415, table 2; cited in Smith, *Health Care Divided*, p. 176.

91. Massey and Denton, *American Apartheid*, p. 118.

92. Johnson and Oliver, "Structural Changes in the U.S. Economy and Black Male Joblessness," pp. 136, 141–42.

93. Gary Orfield and Carole Ashkinaze, *The Closing Door: Conservative Policy and Black Opportunity* (Chicago: University of Chicago Press, 1991), pp. 48, 66–68.

94. Lawrence M. Mead, *The New Politics of Poverty: The Nonworking Poor in America* (New York: Basic Books, 1992), p. 142; Kosters, "Looking for Jobs in All the Wrong Places," pp. 25–31.

95. Stephen M. Petterson, "Are Young Black Men Really Less Willing to Work?" *American Sociological Review* 62 (1997): 609–11.

96. Chris Tilly et al., "Space as a Signal: How Employers Perceive Neighborhoods in Four Metropolitan Labor Markets," in O'Connor et al., *Urban Inequality*, pp. 304–38.

97. Moss and Tilly, *Stories Employers Tell*, pp. 96–105.

98. Moss and Tilly, "Why Opportunity Isn't Knocking," pp. 482–83.

99. Richard B. Freeman and William Rodgers III, "Area Economic Conditions and the Labor Market Outcomes of Young Men in the 1990s Expansion," in Cherry and Rodgers, eds., *Prosperity for All?* pp. 50–87; Philip Moss and Chris Tilly, "How Labor Market Tightness Affects Employer Attitudes and Actions toward Black Job Applicants: Evidence from Employer Surveys," in Cherry and Rodgers, eds., *Prosperity for All?* pp. 129–59.

100. There is good reason to believe these effects are exaggerated. Larry Bennett and Adolph Reed Jr.'s portrayal of the residents of the Cabrini-Green housing projects in Chicago calls into question the stereotypes of an isolated group of people prone to antisocial behavior. Larry Bennett and Adolph Reed Jr., "The New Face of Urban Renewal: The Near North Redevelopment Initiative and the Cabrini-Green Neighborhood," in Reed, ed., *Without Justice for All*, pp. 175–211.

101. Dianne M. Pinderhughes, *Race and Ethnicity in Chicago Politics* (Urbana: University of Illinois Press, 1987), pp. 12–38. Where blacks have come to power, they have formed alliances with middle-class liberals and business interests. See Raphael Sonenshein, *Politics in Black and White: Race and Power*

in Los Angeles (Princeton, N.J.: Princeton University Press, 1993); Richard A. Keiser, *Subordination or Empowerment? African-American Leadership and the Struggle for Power* (New York: Oxford University Press, 1997).

102. Massey and Denton, *American Apartheid*, pp. 158–59.

103. Brown, *Race, Money and the American Welfare State*, pp. 330–32.

104. Ibid., pp. 326–27, 352–53; Demetrios Caraley, "Washington Abandons the Cities," *Political Science Quarterly* 107 (1992): p. 9; Loic J. D. Wacquant, "The New Color Line: The State and Fate of Ghetto in PostFordist America," in Craig Calhoun, ed., *Social Theory and the Politics of Identity* (London: Blackwell Publishers, 1994), pp. 231–76.

105. Heywood Sanders, "Convention Center Follies," *The Public Interest* 132 (summer 1998): 58–72.

106. U.S. Bureau of the Census, *Current Population Reports, Measuring the Effect of Benefits and Taxes on Income and Poverty: 1990* (Washington, D.C.: U.S. Government Printing Office, 1991), p. 13.

107. U.S. Bureau of the Census, *Current Population Reports, Characteristics of Recipients and the Dynamics of Program Participation: 1987–1988* (Washington, D.C.: U.S. Government Printing Office, 1992), pp. 36–37. Means-tested benefits include Aid to Families with Dependent Children; Food Stamps; Supplemental Security Income; Women, Infants, and Childrens program; and means-tested veterans compensation or pension. Non-means-tested benefits include social security or railroad retirement income, unemployment compensation, and non-means-tested veterans compensation and pensions. These are the most recent data available.

108. Brown, *Race, Money, and the American Welfare State*, pp. 194–202; Kenneth J. Neubeck and Noel A. Czenave, *Welfare Racism: Playing the Race Card Against America's Poor* (New York: Routledge, 2001), chapter 4; Martin Gilens, *Why Americans Hate Welfare* (Chicago: University of Chicago Press, 1999), pp. 67–79.

109. U.S. Bureau of the Census, *Current Population Reports, Money Income of Households, Families, and Persons in the United States: 1987* (Washington, D.C.: U.S. Government Printing Office, 1989), table 25.

110. For a detailed elaboration of this argument see Brown, *Race, Money, and the American Welfare State*, especially chapter 10.

111. U.S. Bureau of the Census, *Measuring the Effect of Benefits and Taxes on Income and Poverty*, p. 13.

112. Brown, *Race, Money, and the American Welfare State*, pp. 337–40.

113. Joe Soss et al., "The Hard Line and the Color Line: Race, Welfare, and the Roots of Get-Tough Reform," in Sanford F. Schram, Joe Soss, and Richard C. Fording, eds., *Race and the Politics of Welfare Reform* (Ann Arbor: University of Michigan Press, 2003), pp. 225–253. For an analysis of the role of race in the adoption state waivers from federal law before 1996, one the precursors of welfare reform, see Richard C. Fording, "'Laboratories of Democracy' or Symbolic Politics? The Racial Origins of Welfare Reform," in Schram, Soss, and Fording, eds., *Race and the Politics of Welfare Reform*, pp. 72–97.

114. Neubeck and Cazenave, *Welfare Racism*, pp. 193-94. See also Susan Tinsely Gooden, "Contemporary Approaches to Enduring Challenges," in

Schram, Soss, and Fording, *Race and the Politics of Welfare Reform*, pp. 254–75.

115. Harry Holzer and Michael Stoll, "Employer Demand for Welfare Recipients by Race," Discussion Paper No. 1213-00 (Madison: Institute for Research on Poverty, University of Wisconsin, 2000) p. 16; Soss et al., "The Hard Line and the Color Line," p. 245.

116. For an analysis of this problem, see Michael K. Brown, "Ghettos, Fiscal Federalism, and Welfare Reform," in Schram, Soss, and Fording, eds., *Race and the Politics of Welfare Reform*, pp. 47–71

117. Michael K. Brown, *Race, Money, and the American Welfare State*, p. 370.

CHAPTER THREE

1. Ronald F. Ferguson, "Shifting Challenges: Fifty Years of Economic Change toward Black-White Earnings Equality," in Obie Clayton Jr., ed., *An American Dilemma Revisited* (New York: Russell Sage Foundation, 1996), p. 105. James Heckman argues that "ability as it crystallizes at an early age accounts for most of the measured gap in black and white labor market outcomes" ("Detecting Discrimination," *Journal of Economic Literature* 12 [1998]: 107).

2. Milton Friedman, "The Role of Government in Education," in Robert A. Solo, ed., *Economics and the Public Interest* (New Brunswick, N.J.: Rutgers University Press, 1955), pp. 123–44; Thomas Sowell, *Black Education: Myths and Tragedies* (New York: David McKay, 1972); Richard Herrnstein and Charles Murray, *The Bell Curve: Intelligence and Class Structure in American Life* (New York: The Free Press, 1994); Dinesh D'Souza, *Illiberal Education: The Politics of Race and Sex on Campus* (New York: Free Press, 1991); Shelby Steele, *The Content of Our Character: A New Vision of Race in America* (New York: St. Martin's Press, 1990); William J. Bennett, *The De-valuing of America: The Fight for Our Culture and Our Children* (New York: Summit Books, 1992); Terry Moe, ed., *A Primer on America's Schools* (Stanford, Calif.: Hoover Press, 2001).

3. For seventeen-year-olds, the gap in scores continued to increase to the end of the decade (see Kate Zernike, "Gap Widens Again on Tests Given to Blacks and Whites," *New York Times*, August 25, 2000, p. A14). This is also the case in some subjects for nine- and thirteen-year-olds. But the widening gap, as reported by the *New York Times*, fails to note that math scores continue to rise for these young blacks, just not as fast as for whites.

4. Thernstrom and Thernstrom, *America in Black and White*, p. 360. For a more general attack on "discovery learning," and the influence of "liberal educators" and teachers unions in supporting this type of education, see Williamson Evers, "Standards and Accountability," in Moe, *A Primer on America's Schools*, chapter 9.

5. See William Schmidt, *Why Schools Matter: Using TIMSS to Investigate Curriculum and Learning* (San Francisco: Jossey-Bass, 2001).

6. Thernstrom and Thernstrom, *America in Black and White*, pp. 384–85.

7. Christopher Jencks and Meredith Phillips, eds., *The Black-White Test Score Gap* (Washington, D.C.: The Brookings Institution, 1998).

8. David Grissmer, Ann Flanagan, and Stephanie Williamson, "Why Did the Black-White Test Score Gap Narrow in the 1970s and 1980s?" in Jencks and Phillips, eds., *Black-White Test Score Gap*, pp. 182–226.

9. Zernike, "Gap Widens Again on Tests."

10. James Coleman and Thomas Hoffer, *Public and Private High Schools: The Impact of Communities* (New York: Basic Books, 1987); Anthony Bryk, Valerie Lee, and Peter Holland, *Catholic Schools and the Common Good* (Cambridge, Mass.: Harvard University Press, 1993).

11. Willam Sander, "Catholic Grade Schools and Academic Achievement," *Journal of Human Resources* 31 (1996): 540–48; Christopher Jepson, "The Private Schooling Market and Its Effect on Student Achievement" (Ph.D. dissertation, Northwestern University, 2000).

12. This finding is based on a reanalysis of data collected by James Coleman in his seminal study of school quality in the 1960s. See John F. Witte, "Private School versus Public School Achievement: Are There Findings That Should Affect the Educational Choice Debate?" *Economics of Education Review* 11 (1992): 371–94. Witte's work suggests only small differences in achievement once one corrects for socioeconomic background.

13. W. N. Evans and R. M. Schwab, "Finishing High School and Starting College: Do Catholic Schools Make a Difference?" *Quarterly Journal of Economics* 10 (1995): 941–74. Evans and Schwab show that students attending Catholic high schools are more likely to graduate and go on to college, and this results from the emphasis that Catholic high schools put on college attendance. This better outcome is not directly related to higher test scores.

14. Steven G. Rivkin, Eric Hanushek, and John Kain, "Teachers, Schools, and Academic Achievement" (Amherst College, April 2000, photocopy).

15. Ron Ferguson, "Can Schools Narrow the Black-White Test Score Gap?" in Jencks and Phillips, eds., *Black-White Test Score Gap*, pp. 318–74.

16. Hamilton Lankford, Susanna Loeb, and James Wyckoff, "Teacher Sorting and the Plight of Urban Schools: A Descriptive Analysis," *Educational Evaluation and Policy Analysis* 24 (2000): 37–62.

17. See Richard Rothstein, Martin Carnoy, and Luis Benveniste, *Can Public Schools Learn from Private Schools?* (Washington, D.C.: Economic Policy Institute, 1999); and Luis Benveniste, Martin Carnoy, and Richard Rothstein, *All Else Equal* (New York: Routledge, 2002).

18. Susanna Loeb and Marianne Page, "Examining the Link between Wages and Quality in the Teacher Workforce: The Role of Alternative Labor Market Opportunities and Non-Pecuniary Variation" (Department of Economics, University of California, Davis, 1998, photocopy). One recent study showing no relation is Dale Ballou and Michael Podgursky, *Teacher Pay and Teacher Quality* (Kalamazoo, Mich.: WE Upjohn Institute for Employment Research, 1997).

19. David Grissmer et al., *Improving Student Achievement: What State NAEP Test Scores Tell Us* (Santa Monica, Calif.: The Rand Corporation, 2000).

20. Julian Bond, foreword to Walter Feinberg, *On Higher Ground: Education and the Case for Affirmative Action* (New York: Teacher's College Press, 1998), p. ix.

21. Bowen and Bok argue that only 25 percent of the nation's colleges and

universities employ affirmative action in admissions, and that the other 75 percent do not have applicant pools large enough to be selective, accepting all qualified candidates regardless of race. See William Bowen and Derek Bok, *The Shape of the River* (Princeton, N.J.: Princeton University Press, 1998).

22. Thomas Kane, "Racial and Ethnic Preferences in College Admissions," in Jencks and Phillips, eds., *Black-White Test Score Gap,* pp. 431–56.

23. Dominic J. Brewer, Eric R. Eide, and Dan D. Goldhaber, *An Examination of the Role of Student Race and Ethnicity in Higher Education since 1972* (Washington, D.C.: The Rand Corporation, 1999).

24. Brian Pusser has done an extensive analysis of the UC regents' decision. See "The Contest over Affirmative Action at the University of California: Theory and Politics of Contemporary Higher Education Policy" (Ph.D. dissertation, Stanford University, 1999).

25. Thernstrom and Thernstrom, *America in Black and White,* p. 411.

26. Ibid., p. 388.

27. Ibid., p. 407.

28. Bowen and Bok, *Shape of the River,* p. 55.

29. Linda D. Loury and David Garman, "College Selectivity and Earnings," *Journal of Labor Economics* 13 (1995): 289–308.

30. Kane, "Racial and Ethnic Preferences in College Admissions," pp. 444–45. The Thernstroms claim that one such offsetting advantage is that elite colleges inflate grades. Yet if that were the case, it is hard to imagine why employers pay more to black, Latino, and white graduates of such colleges than to graduates of less prestigious institutions.

31. Nor is this picture typical of Berkeley even a few years later. Recent data suggest that graduation rates are much higher for black (71 percent) and white students than the 1980s rates reported by the Thernstroms. And SAT scores are not correlated with black graduation rates. See Gregg Thomson, "Is the SAT a 'Good Predictor' of Graduation Rates?" (Office of Student Research, University of California, Berkeley, photocopy, 1999).

32. Thernstrom and Thernstrom, *America in Black and White,* p. 409.

33. Ibid.

34. Frederick Vars and William Bowen, "Scholastic Aptitude Test Scores, Race, and Academic Performance in Selective Colleges and Universities," in Jencks and Phillips, eds., *Black-White Test Score Gap*, pp. 457–79.

35. Thomson, "Is the SAT a 'Good Predictor' of Graduation Rates?" p. 7. Thomson argues that SAT scores are not particularly good predicators of graduation rates. SAT scores for the 1988 cohort of Berkeley students, he writes, explain "almost none of the variation in graduation rates" (p. 6).

36. Vars and Bowen, "Scholastic Aptitude Test Scores, Race, and Academic Performance," figure 13-2. For example, men with 550–600 math SAT scores graduate at an 83 percent rate, and women, at a 90 percent rate.

37. Dalton Conley, *Being Black, Living in the Red* (Berkeley and Los Angeles: University of California Press, 1999), pp. 72–73.

38. Data provided to one of the authors by the UC Berkeley admissions office during the debate over Proposition 209.

39. Pell Grants declined by 13 percent in the 1980s, while the cost of tuition

at public four-year colleges rose by almost half in real terms. Thomas Kane suggests this may have accounted for about one-third of the decline in black college attendance during the decade. See Thomas Kane, "College Entry by Blacks since 1970: The Role of College Costs, Family and Background, and the Returns to Education," *The Journal of Political Economy* 102 (1994): 879.

40. Thernstrom and Thernstrom, *America in Black and White*, p. 447.

41. Karen DeAngelis and Martin Carnoy estimate that for male college graduates, one standard deviation higher on a math test score taken as seniors in high school in 1982 translated into 8 percent higher earnings at age 27 (1991). Since blacks scored about 0.75 of a standard deviation lower than whites on this test, their estimate for black-white earnings differences among college graduates is about 6 percent. Since Kane's estimate also includes the differences in earnings from differences in graduation rate, it is reasonable to assume that blacks who attend four-year colleges end up earning about 10 percent less than whites. See "Does Ability Increase Earnings, and, If So, by How Much?" (Stanford University School of Education, 2000, photocopy).

42. See, for example, Richard Murnane, John Willett, and Frank Levy, "The Growing Importance of Cognitive Skills in Wage Determination," *Review of Economics and Statistics* (1995): 251–65; Carnoy and DeAngelis, "Does Ability Increase Earnings, and, If So, by How Much?"

43. For example, see Richard Murnane et al., "The Role of Cognitive Skills in Explaining Inequality in the Earnings of American Workers: Evidence from 1985 and 1991" (National Center for Postsecondary Improvement, Stanford, Calif., 1998, photocopy). Using earnings, they estimate no increase in the payoff to cognitive ability for the 1982 cohort of college seniors compared to the 1972 cohort. Similarly, Carnoy and DeAngelis show no clear increase in the payoff to ability among cohorts, except among female college graduates. That result may be an artifact of the greater likelihood of full-time work among women in the later cohort.

44. Carnoy and DeAngelis, "Does Ability Increase Earnings?"

45. Martin Carnoy, *Faded Dreams: The Politics and Economics of Race in America* (New York: Cambridge University Press, 1994), pp. 84–85.

46. The problem with the Thernstroms' explanation is not simply that it is contradicted by the Asian American experience. The very study the Thernstroms cite to demonstrate why blacks earn less than whites estimated that reading scores had no impact on wages when education and work experience were held constant. Only math scores made a difference. See Murnane, Willett, and Levy, "The Growing Importance of Cognitive Skills in Wage Determination."

47. This argument closely parallels arguments the Chicago School of Economics has long made about markets and public policy. The conservative case against affirmative action in universities is directly related to these promarket arguments. The Chicago School claims that markets are generally efficient and correct themselves if left alone. Any attempt by public bureaucracies to interfere in markets will only make outcomes worse because interference in one part of the market only produces aberrations somewhere else. Since profit-maximization is the end-all of the market and profit-seekers are rational, public interference such as affirmative action perversely affects the ultimate outcomes for blacks.

48. Kane shows this result for the 1982 high school class.

49. Thernstrom and Thernstrom, *America in Black and White*, p. 411.

50. Ibid., p. 412.

51. Black freshmen's mean SAT score at Berkeley in 1992 was 947, and 58 percent of blacks graduated compared to 84 percent of whites. At the University of Virginia, black freshmen averaged 979 on the combined SAT, 241 points less than white entering freshmen, and 84 percent graduated, compared to 93 percent of whites. See Thernstrom and Thernstrom, *America in Black and White,* chapter 14, table 9.

52. The Thernstroms rely on a study by Linda Datcheı Loury and David Garman ("College Selectivity and Earnings," *Journal of Labor Economics* 13 [1995]: 304) that used data from the National Longitudinal Survey of the high school class of 1972 to show that, holding test score constant, attending more selective institutions has a negative effect on blacks but a positive one on whites. But Loury and Garman failed to adjust their data for the fact that many blacks attend historically black institutions, where average test scores are lower and graduation rates higher. Had they done so, the relation between selectivity and graduation rates would probably be equally positive for blacks and whites, as it is for the high school class of 1982 when that adjustment is made. *America in Black and White,* pp. 409–11.

53. Actually, there is solid evidence that even though students in Catholic secondary schools score only slightly higher on tests in public secondary schools than students from a similar socioeconomic background from other schools, high school graduation rates and college attendance rates are higher for students attending Catholic schools. See Evans and Schwab, "Finishing High School and Starting College."

54. The issue of institutional differences is important with respect to another aspect of educational performance. Besides the graduation gap, blacks also average lower grades than whites in college as a whole and in selective colleges. According to Kane, the GPAs of black and Latino students in the High School and Beyond Survey (of 1982 college seniors) is 0.3 points lower than those of white and Asian students—equivalent to a B instead of a B+ for example—without adjusting for SAT scores or high school grades. When SAT scores and high school grades are adjusted for, blacks and Latinos still get lower GPAs than whites, about 0.13 less. So, given the same admissions criteria, blacks and Latinos "underperform" in college relative to whites and Asians. Vars and Bowen found a similar effect in a sample of selective colleges. Without controlling for SAT scores, blacks scored about 0.5 grade point lower than whites; controlling for SAT score differences, blacks still score 0.33 grade point lower than whites. The GPA difference is larger when they compare black and white students with higher SAT scores. In contrast to the Thernstroms, who see the black-white grade differences as simply reflective of misguided college admissions policies, Vars and Bowen offer two explanations for this finding. The first is that apparently similar black and white students offered admission to these select colleges differ in ways that the colleges fail to measure. In essence, there is something about the family background of black students or the quality of their secondary schooling that makes them underperform in college relative to their test scores and high school grades. Vars and

Bowen analyze these possibilities but reject them in favor of the second explanation, mainly on the basis of large variation in GPA differences among selective colleges. This is analogous to widely varying graduation rate differences between whites and blacks at different colleges and universities. In both cases, some universities do much better in reducing black underperformance. Given other research findings by Claude Steele on black vulnerability to stereotypes, it is highly likely that practices at various institutions are an important variable in determining relative black GPA and graduation rates. Of course, this is the opposite of the Thernstroms' conclusion that the main reason blacks underperform is because they are underqualified. See Claude M. Steele and Joshua Aronson, "Stereotype Threat and the Test Performance of Academically Successful African Americans," in Jencks and Phillips, eds., *Black-White Test Score Gap*, pp. 401–27.

55. At least this was true until California's Governor Pete Wilson decided to run for the presidency and pushed through his anti–affirmative action measures.

56. Tamar Jacoby, "The Next Reconstruction," *The New Republic,* June 22, 1998, p. 21.

57. Manuel Castells, *The Power of Identity* (London: Blackwell, 1997), chapter 1.

58. Martin Carnoy, "Education in the Year 2010: Reflections on the Effects of Changing Labor Markets and Family Structure in a Globalized Environment" (Stanford University School of Education, October 1999, photocopy).

CHAPTER FOUR

1. James Q. Wilson, "The Facts," *Commentary* (January 1998); John DiIulio, "My Black Crime Problem and Ours," *City Journal* 6 (spring 1996); John McWhorter, *Losing the Race: Self-sabotage in Black America* (New York: Free Press, 2000), chapter 1; Thernstrom and Thernstrom, *America in Black and White,* chapter 10.

2. McWhorter, *Losing the Race,* p. 13.

3. Jim Sleeper, *Liberal Racism* (New York: Penguin Books, 1997), p. 41.

4. It is noteworthy that very little of this recent social science research finds its way into the works of racial conservatives.

5. Arnold Rose, *The Negro in America* (New York: Harper and Row, 1944), pp. 180–81.

6. Alfred Blumstein, "On the Racial Disproportionality of United States Prison Populations," *Journal of Criminal Law and Criminology* 73 (1982): 1259–81.

7. See, for example, Patrick A. Langan, "Racism on Trial: New Evidence to Explain the Racial Composition of Prisons in the United States," *Journal of Criminal Law and Criminology* 76 (1984): 666–83; Gary Kleck, "Racial Discrimination in Criminal Sentencing: A Critical Evaluation of the Evidence," *American Sociological Review* 46 (1981): 783–805.

8. Michael Tonry, *Malign Neglect: Race, Crime, and Punishment in America* (New York: Oxford University Press, 1995), pp. 30–31.

9. The Thernstroms, for example, make use of a copious amount of research

in their book, including some from as late as 1996, but leave out almost all of the Wave 3 research from the 1990s.

9. See, for example, Robert D. Crutchfield, George S. Bridges, and Susan R. Pitchford, "Analytical and Aggregation Biases in Analyses of Imprisonment: Reconciling Discrepancies in Studies of Racial Disparity," *Journal of Research in Crime and Delinquency* 31 (1994): 177–79; Darlene J. Conley, "Adding Color to a Black and White Picture: Using Qualitative Data to Explain Racial Disproportionality in the Juvenile Justice System," *Journal of Research in Crime and Delinquency* 31 (1994): 135–48; Donna M. Bishop and Charles E. Frazier, "Race Effects in Juvenile Justice Decision-Making: Findings of a Statewide Analysis," *Journal of Criminal Law and Criminology* 86 (1996): 404–29.

10. Human Rights Watch, *Race and Drug Law Enforcement in the State of Georgia* (New York: Human Rights Watch, 1996), p. 20.

11. See Michael J. Leiber and Jayne M. Stairs, "Race, Contexts, and the Use of Intake Diversion," *Journal of Research in Crime and Delinquency* 36 (1996): 76–78.

12. Crutchfield et al., "Analytical and Aggregation Biases in Analyses of Imprisonment," pp. 177–79.

13. Roy L. Austin and Mark D. Allen, "Racial Disparity in Arrest Rates as an Explanation of Racial Disparity in Commitments to Pennsylvania's Prisons," *Journal of Research in Crime and Delinquency* 37 (May 2000): 200–220.

14. Eileen Poe-Yamagata and Michael A. Jones, *And Justice for Some: Differential Treatment of Minority Youth in the Justice System* (San Francisco: National Council on Crime and Delinquency, April 2000), p. 28.

15. Bishop and Frazier, "Race Effects in Juvenile Justice Decision-Making," pp. 404–9.

16. Madeline Wordes, Timothy S. Bynum, and Charles J. Corley, "Locking Up Youth: The Impact of Race on Detention Decisions," *Journal of Research in Crime and Delinquency* 31 (May 1994): 149–65.

17. George S. Bridges and Sara Steen, "Racial Disparities in Official Assessments of Juvenile Offenders: Attributional Stereotypes as Mediating Mechanisms," *American Sociological Review* 63 (August 1998): 554–70.

18. Lieber and Stairs, "Race, Contexts, and the Use of Intake Diversion," pp. 65–78.

19. Christopher Hebert, "Sentencing Outcomes of Black, Hispanic, and White Males Convicted under Federal Sentencing Guidelines," *Criminal Justice Review* 22 (autumn 1997): 133–56.

20. Human Rights Watch, *Race and Drug Law Enforcement,* pp. 17–19.

21. Charles Crawford, Ted Chiricos, and Gary Kleck, "Race, Racial Threat, and Sentencing of Habitual Offenders," *Criminology* 36 (1998): 481–509.

22. James F. Nelson, *Disparities in Processing Felony Arrests in New York State, 1990–1992* (Albany: New York State Division of Criminal Justice Services, 1995).

23. Darrell Steffensmier, Jeffrey Ulmer, and John Kramer, "The Interaction of Race, Gender, and Age in Criminal Sentencing: The Punishment Cost of Being Young, Black, and Male," *Criminology* 36 (1998): 78.

24. Ibid., pp. 786, 789.

25. David Baldus, Charles Pulaski, and George Woodworth, "Comparative

Review of Death Sentences," *Journal of Criminal Law and Criminology* 4 (1983): 661–753.

26. U.S. General Accounting Office, *Death Penalty Sentencing Research Indicates Pattern of Racial Disparities* (Washington, D.C.: General Accounting Office, 1990).

27. See Richard A. Dieter, *The Death Penalty in Black and White: Who Lives, Who Dies, Who Decides* (Washington, D.C.: Death Penalty Information Center, June 1998).

28. On increases in imprisonment, see Elliott Currie, *Crime and Punishment in America* (New York: Henry Holt, 1998), p. 13; for the 80 percent figure, Human Rights Watch data, cited in Steven A. Holmes, "Race Analysis Cites Disparity in Sentencing for Narcotics," *New York Times,* June 8, 2000.

29. Kevin Flynn, "State Cites Racial Inequality in New York Police Searches," *New York Times,* December 1, 1999.

30. Irving Piliavin and Scott Briar, "Police Encounters with Juveniles," *American Journal of Sociology* 70 (September 1964): 206–14.

31. Ibid., p. 210.

32. Ibid., p. 213. For other early evidence on this pattern, see Jerome H. Skolnick, *Justice without Trial* (New York: Wiley, 1966).

33. Conley, "Adding Color to a Black and White Picture"; Scot Worley, Ross Macmillan, and John Hagan, "Just Des(s)erts? The Racial Polarization of Perceptions of Criminal Injustice," *Law and Society Review* 31 (1997): 648. One careful recent study finds that, with other relevant factors controlled, police in Los Angeles are far more likely to deploy police dogs in minority communities; see Alec Campbell, Richard S. Berk, and James J. Fyfe, "Deployment of Violence; the Los Angeles Police Department's Use of Dogs," *Evaluation Review* 22 (1998): 535–61.

34. Human Rights Watch, *Race and Drug Law Enforcement,* pp. 11–12.

35. State of New Jersey, Office of the Attorney General, *Selected Highlights of the Interim Report of the State Police Review Team Regarding Allegations of Racial Profiling* (Trenton, N.J.: Office of the Attorney General, 1999).

36. Ibid., p. 6.

37. Elliot Currie, Dan Macallair, and Khaled Taqi-Eddin, *Quiet Crisis: Youth, Race, Violence and Justice in Four California Counties* (San Francisco: Center on Juvenile and Criminal Justice, 1999), p. 34.

38. California Department of Justice, *Ethnic Distribution of Arrests for Participating in Street Gangs, 1998* (Sacramento, Calif.: Criminal Justice Statistics Center, 1999).

39. James Q. Wilson, *Thinking about Crime* (New York: Random House, 1975), chapters 1, 3.

40. Gary LaFree and Kriss A. Drass, "The Effect of Changes in Intra-racial Economic Inequality and Educational Attainment on Changes in Arrest Rates of African-Americans and Whites, 1957 to 1990," *American Sociological Review* 61 (1996): 614–34.

41. Richard Fowles and Mary Merva, "Wage Inequality and Criminal Activity: An Extreme Bounds Analysis for the United States, 1975–1990," *Criminology* 34 (1996): 163–82.

42. Edward S. Shihadeh and Darrel Steffensmeier, "Economic Inequality, Family Disruption, and Urban Black Violence," *Social Forces* 73 (December 1994): 729–51; Robert Sampson and John Laub, "Urban Poverty and the Family Context of Delinquency," *Child Development* 65 (1994): 538–45. Interestingly, the Thernstroms mention some of Sampson's findings in their footnotes (p. 604 n. 125) but do not confront the implications in the text of their book.

43. Currie, *Crime and Punishment in America,* chapter 4.

44. Cf. Sampson and Laub, "Urban Poverty and the Family Context of Delinquency."

45. On economic downturn and rising violence, see, for example, Edward S. Shihadeh and Graham C. Ousey, "Industrial Restructuring and Violence: The Link between Entry-Level Jobs, Economic Deprivation, and Black and White Homicide," *Social Forces* 77 (September 1998): 185–206. On the beneficent effects of improvements in the labor market generally, see Currie, *Crime and Punishment in America,* pp. 187–88; Richard B. Freeman and William M. Rodgers III, "Area Economic Conditions and the Labor Market Outcomes of Young Men in the 1990s Expansion" (Robert Cherry and William M. Rodgers III, eds., *Prosperity for All* (New York: Russell Sage Foundation, 2000), pp. 50–87; Jared Bernstein and Ellen Houston, *Falling Crime Rates in the 1990s: The Role of the Low-Wage Labor Market* (Washington, D.C.: Economic Policy Institute, February 2000).

46. See Marc Mauer, *Race to Incarcerate* (New York: New Press, 1999).

47. See Dina Rose and Todd Clear, "Incarceration, Social Capital, and Crime: Implications for Social Disorganization Theory," *Criminology* 36 (1998): 441–72.

48. See Richard B. Freeman, *Crime and the Employment of Disadvantaged Youths,* NBER Working Paper No. 3875 (Cambridge, Mass.: National Bureau of Economic Research, 1991); Robert Sampson, "Urban Black Violence: The Effect of Male Joblessness and Family Disruption," *American Journal of Sociology* 93 (1987): 348–82.

49. Bruce Western, "Incarceration, Unemployment, and Inequality," *Focus* 21 (2001).

50. Sentencing Project/Human Rights Watch, *Losing the Vote: The Impact of Felony Disfranchisement Laws in the United States* (Washington, D.C.: Sentencing Project/Human Rights Watch, 1998).

CHAPTER FIVE

1. See Thernstrom and Thernstrom, *America in Black and White*, chapters 12, 15–16; Andrew Kull, *The Color-Blind Constitution* (Cambridge, Mass.: Harvard University Press, 1992), chapters 10, 11; Hugh Davis Graham, *The Civil Rights Era: Origins and Development of National Policy* (New York: Oxford University Press, 1990), chapter 15.

2. Thernstrom and Thernstrom, *America in Black and White*, pp. 319–22; Kull, *Color-Blind Constitution*, pp. 171–81.

3. *Briggs v. Elliot*, 132 F. Supp. 776, 777 (E.D.S.C. 1955).

4. Richard Kluger, *Simple Justice* (New York: Alfred A. Knopf, 1980), p. 365.

Kull denies that the opinion in *Briggs* was an "artificially narrow construction of the desegregation mandate" and claims that it correctly reflects the Supreme Court's decision in *Brown* (*Color-Blind Constitution*, p. 172). The Court, however, mentions changes in school district boundaries as only one of a number of remedies and refers to the goal as a "transition to a racially nondiscriminatory school system." If anything, the Court was quite vague about remedies, and intentionally so. *Brown v. Board of Education of Topeka, Kansas (Brown II)*, 349 U.S. 294, 75 St. Ct 753 (1955).

5. Kluger, *Simple Justice*, p. 752.

6. Thernstrom and Thernstrom, *America in Black and White*, p. 322.

7. Jack Balkin refers to these two views of civil rights laws as the anticlassification and antisubordination principles, and argues they shape contending views of the Supreme Court's decision in *Brown v. Board of Education*. See Jack M. Balkin, ed., *What* Brown v. Board of Education *Should Have Said: The Nation's Top Legal Experts Rewrite America's Landmark Civil Rights Decision* (New York: New York University Press, 2001), p. 55–56.

8. Robert H. Bork, "Civil Rights—a Challenge," *The New Republic* (August 31, 1963): 21–22.

9. Richard Epstein, *Forbidden Grounds: The Case against Employment Discrimination Laws* (Cambridge, Mass: Harvard University Press, 1992); Clint Bolick, *The Affirmative Action Fraud: Can We Restore the American Civil Rights Vision?* (Washington, D.C.: Cato Institute, 1996), pp. 40–42.

10. Epstein, *Forbidden Grounds*, p. 192; Thernstrom and Thernstrom, *America in Black and White*, p. 430.

11. *Griggs v. Duke Power,* 401 U.S. 424 (1971).

12. Thernstrom and Thernstrom, *America in Black and White*, pp. 425–27, 429–32, 459–60.

13. Ibid., p. 432.

14. *Congressional Record,* 88th Cong., 2nd sess., 1964, 110, pt. 6: 7419; quoted in Epstein, *Forbidden Grounds,* p. 186.

15. Thernstrom and Thernstrom, *America in Black and White*, p. 439.

16. Epstein, *Forbidden Grounds,* p. 181.

17. Gary Bryner, "Congress, Courts, and Agencies: Equal Employment and the Limits of Policy Implementation," *Political Science Quarterly* 96 (1981): 423. Bryner thinks the Court was concerned with the similarity between employment tests and literacy tests used to disenfranchise black voters. In *United States v. Gaston* the Court held literacy tests unlawful because of the discriminatory impact on black voters. See also Graham, *Civil Rights Era,* pp. 388–89.

18. *Civil Rights Act of 1964, Title VII, U.S. Code,* vol. 42, secs. 2000e–2 (1964).

19. Ibid.

20. See Ivar Berg, *Education and Jobs: The Great Training Robbery* (Boston: Beacon Press, 1971).

21. Berg, *Education and Jobs.*

22. Herbert R. Northrup, *Negro Employment in Basic Industry: A Study of Racial Policies in Six Industries* (Philadelphia: University of Pennsylvania Press, 1970), p. 669.

23. Ibid., p. 81.

24. Ibid., pp. 307, 328.

25. Ibid., pp. 428, 444–47.

26. *Civil Rights Act of 1964, Title VII,* Section 703(a)(2).

27. *Griggs v. Duke Power,* p. 429.

28. *Civil Rights Act of 1964, Title VII,* Section 706(g).

29. Graham, *Civil Rights Era,* p. 389.

30. United States Equal Employment Opportunity Commission, *Legislative History of Titles VII and XI of Civil Rights Act of 1964* (Washington, D.C.: U.S. Government Printing Office, 1968), pp. 3006, 3019.

31. Mack A. Player, *Employment Discrimination Law* (St. Paul, Minn.: West Publishing, 1988), p. 435. In *Albemarle Paper Co. v. Moody,* 422 U.S. 405, 95 S.Ct 2362, 45 L.Ed. 2nd 280 (1975), the Supreme Court ruled that the term *intentional* means "no more than that the act itself was volitional, as opposed to accidental."

32. As discussed herein, the Civil Rights Act also limits discrimination actions based on discriminatory test results when a professionally developed test was not designed, intended, or used to discriminate.

33. See *Congressional Record,* 88th Cong., 2nd sess., 1964, 110, pt. 6: 7218 (reply to questions of Senator Dirksen by Senator Case). See also Paul Burstein and Margo W. MacLeod, "Prohibiting Employment Discrimination: Ideas and Politics in the Congressional Debate over Equal Employment Opportunity Legislation," *American Journal of Sociology* 86 (1980): 512–33. Burstein and MacLeod show that Title VII was modeled on state laws.

34. The issue of unintentional discrimination was also the subject of extensive discussion in law journals. As early as 1949, in a discussion of the developing law of state fair employment practice commissions, a *University of Chicago Law Review* article asserted that "discrimination may exist independently of malice or intention to discriminate." This article also addressed the question of whether a claim of discrimination could be proven if it was based on a statistical analysis of a "disproportionate representation." See "An American Legal Dilemma—Proof of Discrimination," *University of Chicago Law Review* 17 (1949): 107, 109, 117. And a *Harvard Law Review* essay that addressed the problems of determining the meaning of the term *discrimination* commented, a "question has arisen as to whether percentage quotas can be used to prove the presence of discrimination—whether it is sufficient, as some commissions have found, that there be a showing that no minority-group members, or a disproportionately small number, work or live at a given location." See Michael A. Bamberger and Nathan Lewin, "The Right to Equal Treatment: Administrative Enforcement of Antidiscrimination Legislation," *Harvard Law Review* 74 (1961): 526, 558–60.

35. *Lefkowitz v. Farrell, 1964, Race Relations Reporter* 393 (spring 1964), affirmed, *State Commission for Human Rights v. Farrell,* 252 NY Supp.2d 649 (1964).

36. Sydney H. Schanberg, "State Says Union Barred Negroes for Last 76 Years," *New York Times,* March 5, 1964, p. 1; Sydney H. Schanberg, "Union Is Ordered to Open Its Rolls," *New York Times,* March 24, 1964, p. 1 (union

ordered to start a new apprenticeship waiting list "based on objective standards").

37. See E. W. Kenworthy, "Rights Bill Wins 2 Tests in Senate by Wide Margins," *New York Times*, March 27, 1964, p. 1 ("Since March 9 the Southern opponents of the bill have been talking to stall a vote on calling it up for formal debate").

38. The decision is reprinted at *Congressional Record*, 88th Cong., 2nd sess., 1964, 110, pt. 5: 5562–64.

39. *Civil Rights Act of 1964, Title VII*, Section 703(h).

40. U.S. Equal Employment Opportunity Commission, *Legislative History of Titles VII and XI*, pp. 3160, 3162. The amendment was defeated by a vote of 38-49. The coalition voting for the first version of the Tower amendment included seventeen southern Democrats, seven western Republicans, and five Republicans from plains states. One can see in this coalition the core of the Republican party today.

41. Ibid., p. 3163.

42. *Civil Rights Act of 1964, Title VII*, Section 703(a)(2).

43. The Court subsequently found that seniority systems were protected from Title VII unless they were designed to discriminate. In so holding, the Court distinguished the first clause of Section 703(h), which protects seniority systems absent an "intent to discriminate," from the second clause, which protects professionally developed tests unless they are "designed, intended or used to discriminate." *International Brotherhood of Teamsters v. United States*, 431 U.S. 324 (1977).

44. Epstein, *Forbidden Grounds*, p. 197. See also Thernstrom and Thernstrom, *America in Black and White*, pp. 429–30.

45. Herman Belz, *Equality Transformed* (Brunswick, N.J.: Transaction Publishers 1991), p. 21.

46. Epstein, *Forbidden Grounds*, p. 199.

47. Ibid.

48. *Griggs v. Duke Power*, p. 434.

49. *1964 Race Relations Reporter* 393 (spring 1964), affirmed, *State Commission for Human Rights v. Farrell*, 252 NY Supp.2d 649 (1964).

50. Neither Belz nor Epstein discusses nepotism. See Belz, *Equality Transformed*, pp. 268–69; Epstein, *Forbidden Grounds*, pp. 191–97.

51. *The Equal Employment Opportunity Act of 1972, Statutes of the United States* 86 (1972): 103.

52. *Wards Cove Packing Company v. Atonio*, 490 U.S. 642 (1989).

53. Ibid., p. 659.

54. *Civil Rights Act of 1964, Title VII*, Section 703(k)(1)(A)(i).

55. Justice Brennan did not take part in the decision on the case. The remaining eight justices were equally divided among Republican appointees (Burger, Blackmun, Harlan, and Stewart) and Democratic appointees (Black, Douglas, White, and Marshall). Three of these justices were then considered conservatives (Burger, Blackmun, and Harlan). Two were then considered moderates (Stewart and White), and three were regarded at the time as liberals (Black, Douglas, and

Marshall). See Kermit L. Hall, ed., *The Oxford Companion to the Supreme Court of the United States* (New York: Oxford University Press, 1992), p. 351.

56. Ibid., p. 366. Hall describes Harlan as "the most significant critic of Warren Court trends."

57. W. Page Keeton et al., *Prosser and Keeton on the Law of Torts*, 5th ed. (St. Paul, Minn.: West Publishing, 1984), p. 160; see also, David B. Oppenheimer, "Negligent Discrimination," *University of Pennsylvania Law Review* 141 (1993): 899.

58. The Court did not decide that unexplained statistical disparities were sufficient to establish the presumption of discrimination until 1977 in a case involving union seniority rules, *Teamsters v. United States* 431 US 324 (1977). The Court concluded that sufficient statistical proof in unintentional discrimination cases would require the employer to prove the discriminatory practice is job related and necessary to the operations of the business. In intentional discrimination cases, statistical proof, if sufficient, requires the employer to rebut the inference of discrimination by articulating a nondiscriminatory reason for its decisions.

59. Thernstrom and Thernstrom, *America in Black and White*, p. 432.

60. John Donohue III and Peter Siegelman, "The Changing Nature of Employment Discrimination Litigation," *Stanford Law Review* 43 (1991): 983, 998, 989, table 2.

61. Ibid., p. 998 n. 57.

62. Peter Siegelman and John Donohue III, "Studying the Iceberg from Its Tip: A Comparison of Published and Unpublished Employment Discrimination Cases," *Law & Society Review* 24 (1990): 1133, 1164 n. 58.

63. Ibid., p. 984.

64. George Rutherglen, "From Race to Age: The Expanding Scope of Employment Discrimination Law," *Journal of Legal Studies* 24 (1995): 491. Rutherglen's analysis is based on data collected by the American Bar Foundation.

65. Ibid., p. 495, table 2. Many cases involved multiple claims and thus included allegations of unequal pay, termination, and harassment. Each claim is counted separately in the study. In a recent survey of 389 reported jury verdicts in California employment law cases, David B. Oppenheimer found only 6 alleged failure to hire; most concerned termination or harassment of employees. See "Verdicts Matter: An Examination of California Employment Discrimination and Wrongful Discharge Jury Verdicts" (Golden Gate University, 2003, photocopy).

66. *St. Mary's Honor Society v. Hicks,* 509 U.S. 502 (1993).

67. This belief, while unfounded, is widely held among white Americans. See Mollyann Brodie, *The Four Americas: Government and Social Policy through the Eyes of America's Multi-Racial and Multi-Ethnic Society,* A Report of the Washington Post/Kaiser Family Foundation/Harvard Survery Project (Menlo Park, Calif.: Kaiser Family Foundation, 1995), p. 100.

68. Thernstrom and Thernstrom, *America in Black and White*, p. 431.

69. *McDonald v. Santa Fe Trail Transportation Co.,* 427 U.S. 273 (1976).

70. Ibid., p. 273 n. 8.

71. *United Steelworkers of America v. Weber,* 443 U.S. 193 (1979). See also, *Johnson v. Transportation Agency of Santa Clara County,* 480 U.S. 616 (1987).

72. *Wygant v. Jackson Board of Education,* 476 U.S. 267 (1986); *Local 93,*

International Association of Firefighters v. City of Cleveland, 478 U.S. 501 (1986).

73. Thernstrom and Thernstrom, *America in Black and White,* p. 431.

74. Donohue and Siegelman, "The Changing Nature of Employment Discrimination Litigation," p. 984; Oppenheimer, "Verdicts Matter."

75. Alfred Blumrosen, "Draft Report on Reverse Discrimination Commissioned by Labor Department," *Daily Labor Report* (BNA) 56 (1995): d22.

76. Rutherglen, "From Race to Age," pp. 492, table 1, 504 n. 67.

77. Ibid., pp. 505, table 5, 492, table 1, 504.

78. Barbara F. Reskin, *The Realities of Affirmative Action in Employment* (Washington, D.C.: American Sociological Association, 1998), p. 73.

79. Theodore Eisenberg, "Litigation Models and Trial Outcomes in Civil Rights and Prisoner Cases," *Georgetown Law Journal* 77 (1989): 1567, 1588, table 1, 1592, table 3.

80. Michael Selmi, "The Value of the EEOC: Reexamining the Agency's Role in Employment Discrimination Law," *Ohio State Law Review* 57 (1996): 1, 19, table 4.

81. *Connecticut v. Teal,* 457 U.S. 440 (1982); see Jonathan S. Leonard, "The Impact of Affirmative Action Regulation and Equal Employment Law on Black Employment," *The Journal of Economic Perspectives* 4 (1990): 61.

82. Jonathan S. Leonard, "Antidiscrimination or Reverse Discrimination: The Impact of Changing Demographics, Title VII, and Affirmative Action on Productivity," *Journal of Human Resources* 2 (1984): 145–74.

83. Executive Order 11246, 3 C.F.R. 169 202(1) (1974); cited in Leonard, "Impact of Affirmative Action Regulation," p. 48.

84. Leonard, "Impact of Affirmative Action Regulation," p. 58.

85. Bernard E. Anderson, "The Ebb and Flow of Enforcing Executive Order 11246," *American Economic Review* 86 (1996): 298–301.

86. Bolick, *Affirmative Action Fraud,* pp. 40–42.

87. Thernstrom and Thernstrom, *America in Black and White,* p. 439.

88. *Civil Rights Restoration Act of 1991, U.S. Code,* vol. 42, sec. 1981a (1991).

89. See chapter 2, in the section "The 1980s Racial Backlash."

90. Leonard, "Impact of Affirmative Action Regulation," pp. 50–51; Leonard, "Antidiscrimination or Reverse Discrimination," p. 151.

91. Peter Gottschalk, "Inequality, Income Growth, and Mobility: The Basic Facts," *Journal of Economic Perspectives* 11 (1997): 29.

92. Henry J. Holzer and David Neumark, "Assessing Affirmative Action," *Journal of Economic Literature* 38 (2000): 506; Leonard, "Impact of Affirmative Action Regulation," p. 55.

93. Jonathan S. Leonard, "Employment and Occupational Advance under Affirmative Action," *Review of Economics and Statistics* 66 (1984): 381–84; Leonard, "Antidiscimination or Reverse Discrimination," pp. 151–52.

94. Leonard, "Impact of Affirmative Action Regulation," p. 58.

95. Jonathan S. Leonard, "Wage Disparities and Affirmative Action in the 1980s," *American Economic Review* 86 (1996): 285–89.

96. Holzer and Neumark, "Assessing Affirmative Action," pp. 507, 559.

97. Jed Rubenfeld, "The Anti-Antidiscrimination Agenda," *Yale Law Journal* 111 (2002): 1141–78.

98. *Adarand Constructors v. Pena*, 515 U.S. 200 (1995), p. 237.

99. *Richmond v. J. A. Croson*, 488 U.S. 492 (1989).

100. Ibid.

101. See Charles R. Lawrence III and Mari J. Matsuda, *We Won't Go Back* (New York: Houghton Mifflin, 1997), p. 299 n. 9 (citing T. Bates, "Do Black-Owned Businesses Employ Minority Workers? New Evidence," *Review of Black Political Economy* 16 [1988]: 51).

102. Mitchell F. Rice, "State and Local Government Set-Aside Programs, Disparity Studies, and Minority Business Development in the Post-*Croson* Era," *Journal of Urban Affairs* 15 (1993): 534.

103. See, for example, *Associated General Contractors v. Coalition for Economic Equality*, 950 F.2d 1401 (9th Cir. 1991); cf., *Middleton v. City of Flint*, 810 F. Supp. 874 (1993).

104. Steven A. Holmes, "Administration Cuts Affirmative Action While Defending It," *New York Times*, March 16, 1998, A1.

105. See James J. Heckman, "Detecting Discrimination," *Journal of Economic Perspectives* 12 (1998): 101–2, 107 n. 3.

106. Darity and Mason refer to this as the noncompeting groups hypothesis, which "blurs the orthodox distinction between in-market and premarket discrimination by inserting matters of power and social control directly into the analysis." See "Evidence on Discrimination," p. 85. This is similar to the idea of opportunity hoarding, which we have adapted from Charles Tilly, *Durable Inequality* (Berkeley and Los Angeles: University of California Press, 1998).

CHAPTER SIX

1. James E. Alt, "The Impact of the Voting Rights Act on Black and White Voter Registration in the South," in Chandler Davidson and Bernard Grofman, eds., *Quiet Revolution in the South: The Impact of the Voting Rights Act, 1965–1990* (Princeton, N.J.: Princeton University Press, 1994), pp. 362–63.

2. Ibid., pp. 366–67.

3. *Shaw v. Reno*, 509 U.S. 647 (1993).

4. *Miller v. Johnson*, 515 U.S. 913 (1995).

5. Thernstrom and Thernstrom, *America in Black and White*, p. 479; Andrew Kull, *The Color-Blind Constitution* (Cambridge, Mass.: Harvard University Press, 1992), pp. 210–12.

6. *United States v. Carolene Products Co.*, 304 U.S. 153 (1938).

7. Pamela S. Karlan and D. J. Levinson, "Why Voting Is Different," *California Law Review* 84 (1996): 1202, 1207–8.

8. Samuel P. Hays, *American Political History as Social Analysis* (Knoxville: The University of Tennessee Press, 1980), pp. 205–32.

9. J. Morgan Kousser, *Colorblind Injustice: Minority Voting Rights and the Undoing of the Second Reconstruction* (Chapel Hill: University of North Carolina Press, 1999), p. 37; Samuel Issacharoff, "The Redistricting Morass," in

Anthony Peacock, ed., *Affirmative Action and Representation:* Shaw v. Reno *and the Future of Voting Rights* (Durham, N.C.: Carolina Academic Press, 1997), p. 214.

10. For a historical account of this conception of the Constitution, see Kull, *The Color-blind Constitution.*

11. U.S. House of Representatives, "Voting Rights Act of 1965," House Report 439, 89th Cong., 1st Sess. (Washington, D.C.: Government Printing Office, 1965), p. 3; cited in Kousser, *Colorblind Injustice,* p. 60.

12. Bernard Grofman, Lisa Handley, and Richard G. Niemi, *Minority Representation and the Quest for Voting Equality* (New York: Cambridge University Press, 1992), p. 25.

13. Kousser, *Colorblind Injustice,* p. 31.

14. Ibid., pp. 26–27.

15. *Allen v. State Board of Education,* 393 U.S. (1969), 565; Kousser, *Colorblind Injustice,* pp. 55–56.

16. Thernstrom and Thernstrom, *America in Black and White,* pp. 466, 476.

17. Ibid., p. 467–68.

18. Kousser, *Colorblind Injustice,* pp. 56–58, 61. The Thernstroms provide only a sketchy discussion of *Allen* or of any of the congressional decisions during the 1970s that reaffirmed the broad interpretation of Section 5 of the VRA.

19. Ibid., pp. 150–53, 164–69. Kousser documents similar efforts in Los Angeles and Texas to deny Latinos any representation. See chapters 2 and 6.

20. Grofman, Handley, and Niemi, *Minority Representation and the Quest for Voting Equality,* p. 39.

21. Evidence of intent is not required, but plaintiffs must meet a very complicated set of requirements to demonstrate vote dilution. For a useful discussion of efforts to measure and prove vote dilution, see Grofman, Handley, and Niemi, *Minority Representation and the Quest for Voting Equality.*

22. Thernstrom and Thernstrom, *America in Black and White,* pp. 289–90.

23. The thirty-nine black members of the 106th Congress represent only 38 percent of all African Americans.

24. Stephen R. Shalom, "Dubious Data: The Thernstroms on Race in America," *Race and Society* 1 (1998): 136. For a systematic attempt to develop a fair standard for redistricting, see Gary King, John Bruce, and Andrew Gelman, "Racial Fairness in Legislative Redistricting," in Paul E. Peterson, ed., *Classifying by Race* (Princeton, N.J.: Princeton University Press, 1995), pp. 85–110.

25. David T. Canon, *Race, Redistricting, and Representation: The Unintended Consequences of Black Majority Districts* (Chicago: University of Chicago Press, 1999), p. 10.

26. Chandler Davidson and Bernard Grofman, "The Effect of Municipal Election Structure on Black Representation in Eight Southern States," in Davidson and Grofman, eds., *Quiet Revolution in the South,* pp. 305–6.

27. *Holder v. Hall,* 512 U.S. 893, 903 (1994).

28. *Shaw v. Reno,* 647.

29. Abigail Thernstrom, "Black Republicans?" *The Public Interest* 120 (summer 1995): 109.

30. Michael C. Dawson, *Behind the Mule: Race and Class in African-Amer-*

ican Politics (Princeton, N.J.: Princeton University Press, 1994), pp. 183–84; David Lublin, *The Paradox of Representation: Racial Gerrymandering and Minority Interests in Congress* (Princeton, N.J.: Princeton University Press, 1997), pp. 73–76.

31. James R. Kluegel and Eliot R. Smith, *Beliefs about Inequality* (New York: Aldine de Gruyter, 1986), pp. 173–74, 261–63.

32. Dawson, *Behind the Mule*, pp. 193–94.

33. We are not asserting that there are no substantial political differences among African Americans or that these internal divisions do not matter to the formation of a black political agenda. Quite clearly they do. What we do assert is that there is strong empirical evidence for rejecting arguments that African Americans do not have common, racially defined, political interests they are prepared to act on. For a detailed analysis of the problem, see Adolph Reed Jr., *Stirrings in the Jug: Black Politics in the Post-Segregation Era* (Minneapolis: University of Minnesota Press, 1999), chapter 1.

34. Thernstrom and Thernstrom, *America in Black and White*, p. 301.

35. The Thernstroms are not the only ones who oppose black-majority districts for partisan reasons. Morgan Kousser suggests that many of the inconsistencies in the Supreme Court's redistricting decisions—approving Republican racial gerrymanders while striking down Democratic racial gerrymanders, for example—can only be explained by the partisan motivations of specific justices, notably Justice O'Connor (*Colorblind Injustice*, pp. 431–37).

36. Lublin, *The Paradox of Representation*, pp. 46–47.

37. Lisa Handley and Bernard Grofman, "The Impact of the Voting Rights Act on Minority Representation: Black Officeholding in Southern State Legislatures and Congressional Delegations," in Davidson and Grofman, eds., *Quiet Revolution in the South*, pp. 338, 345, 350.

38. Grofman, Handley, and Niemi, *Minority Representation and the Quest for Voting Equality*, p. 134.

39. Eric Arnesen, "Like Banquo's Ghost, It Will Not Down: The Race Question and the American Railroad Brotherhoods, 1880–1920," *American Historical Review* 99 (1994): 1629.

40. Robert Huckfeldt and Carol Weitzel Kohfeld, *Race and the Decline of Class in American Politics* (Urbana: University of Illinois Press, 1989), pp. 3–4, 49–52. The presence of blacks in the Democratic Party coalition explains 63 percent of the variation in the white vote.

41. Ibid., pp. 79–82.

42. Paul Kleppner, *Chicago Divided: The Making of a Black Mayor* (DeKalb: Northern Illinois University Press, 1985), pp. 218–21, 238.

43. Ibid., pp. 250–51.

44. David Ian Lublin and Katherine Tate, "Racial Group Competition in Urban Elections," in Paul E. Peterson, *Classifying by Race* (Princeton, N.J.: Princeton University Press, 1995), pp. 245–61.

45. Raphael J. Sonenshein, *Politics in Black and White: Race and Power in Los Angeles* (Princeton, N.J.: Princeton University Press, 1993), pp. 306–7.

46. With the mobilization of the Latino vote in the 1990s, the racial divide in

local elections may be changing. The 2001 mayoral election in Los Angeles split the black and Latino vote.

47. Huckfeldt and Kohfeld, *Race and the Decline of Class in American Politics,* pp. 88–89.

48. Keith Reeves, *Voting Hopes or Fears? White Voters, Black Candidates and Racial Politics in America* (New York: Oxford University Press, 1997), pp. 82–85, 89.

49. Susan Howell, "Racial Polarization, Reaction to Urban Conditions, and the Approval of Black Mayors," in Yvette M. Alex-Assensoh and Lawrence J. Hanks, eds., *Black and Multiracial Politics in America* (New York: New York University Press, 2001), pp. 60–83.

50. Pei-te Lien and M. Margaret Conway, "Comparing Support for Affirmative Action among Four Racial Groups," in Alex-Assensoh and Hanks, eds., *Black and Multiracial Politics in America,* pp. 286–311.

51. Al Gore received 90 percent of the black vote, 67 percent of the Latino vote, and 54 percent of the Asian American vote. Blacks and Latinos have split in some local elections recently, but these elections often turn on local issues, and one cannot draw any conclusions about racial polarization. For an analysis of patterns of conflict and cooperation between blacks and Latinos in a northeastern city, see Jose E. Cruz, "Interminority Relations in Urban Settings: Lessons from the Black–Puerto Rican Experience," in Alex-Assensoh and Hanks, eds., *Black and Multiracial Politics in America,* pp. 84–112.

52. Dan T. Carter, *The Politics of Rage: George Wallace, the Origins of the New Conservatism, and the Transformation of American Politics* (New York: Simon and Schuster, 1995); Donald Kinder and Lynn M. Sanders, *Divided by Color: Racial Politics and Democratic Ideals* (Chicago: University of Chicago Press, 1996), pp. 221–28; Tali Mendelberg, *The Race Card: Campaign Strategy, Implicit Messages, and the Norm of Equality* (Princeton, N.J.: Princeton University Press, 2001), pp. 95–98.

53. Edward G. Carmines and James A. Stimson, *Issue Evolution: Race and the Transformation of American Politics* (Princeton, N.J.: Princeton University Press, 1989), p. 131.

54. Ibid., pp. 103–5, 114.

55. Kinder and Sanders, *Divided by Color,* pp. 234–36, 240–47.

56. Mendelberg, *The Race Card,* pp. 177, 184. Mendelberg shows that the race card succeeds only when the message is implicit, as it was in the Horton ads. Indeed, Republican success depends on the ability of candidates to deny that an ad or slogan is about race when in fact it is. See pp. 134–44.

57. Jack Citrin, Donald P. Green, and David O. Sears, "White Reactions to Black Candidates: When Does Race Matter?" *Public Opinion Quarterly* 54 (1990): 84, 87, 91.

58. V. O. Key Jr., *Southern Politics in State and Nation* (Knoxville: University of Tennessee Press, 1984), pp. 5, 516, 652.

59. Samuel Issacharoff, Pamela S. Karlan, and Richard H. Pildes, *The Law of Democracy: Legal Structure of the Political Process* (Westbury, N.Y.: The Foundation Press, 1998), p. 602. As we noted in chapter 1, whites express greater reservations about living next door to African American families as the propor-

tion of African Americans in the neighborhood increases; see the section "Conceptions of Race and Racism after the Civil Rights Revolution."

60. David Bositis, *Party, Redistricting, and Minority Representation: The Southern States, 1992–2002* (Washington, D.C.: Joint Center for Political and Economic Studies, May 2002).

61. Canon, *Race, Redistricting, and Representation*, p. 191 n. 3.

62. *Regents of the University of California v. Bakke*, 438 U.S. 265 (1978).

63. *City of Richmond v. J. A. Croson*, 488 U.S. 469 (1989).

64. Bernard Grofman, "The Supreme Court, the Voting Rights Act, and Minority Representation," in Peacock, ed., *Affirmative Action and Representation*, p. 183.

65. Issacharoff, "The Redistricting Morass," p. 207.

66. Karlan and Levinson, "Why Voting Is Different," p. 1202.

67. *Shaw v. Reno*, p. 679.

68. Kousser, *Colorblind Injustice*, p. 369. However, Karlan and Levinson point out that the "predominant motive" criterion is actually more restrictive than the standard criterion for triggering an equal protection case. See Karlan and Levinson, "Why Voting Is Different," p. 1215.

69. Kousser, *Colorblind Injustice*, pp. 412–13. We are indebted to Kousser's detailed history and analysis for our interpretation of the redistricting cases.

70. The distinction we are drawing here is similar to Reva Siegel's distinction between a "thin" and "thick" conception of race. Siegel argues the Supreme Court assumes that because race has no meaning as social category, it is a "morphological accident" and cannot be used to justify color-conscious remedies. The justices also assume that race is relevant to one's social and economic status, yet they seem to think that the Constitution does not permit government to do anything about it. See Siegel, "The Racial Rhetorics of Colorblind Constitutionalism: The Case of *Hopwood v. Texas*," in Robert Post and Michael Rogin, eds., *Race and Representation* (New York: Zone Books, 1998), pp. 42–43.

71. Kousser, *Colorblind Injustice*, pp. 380–82.

72. *Shaw v. Reno*, pp. 647–48.

73. Karlan and Levinson, "Why Voting Is Different," p. 1212; Kousser, *Colorblind Injustice*, p. 387.

74. Kousser, *Colorblind Injustice*, p. 395.

75. Karlan and Levinson, "Why Voting Is Different," pp. 1212–13, 1215.

76. Ibid., p. 1214.

77. Ibid.

78. Issacharoff, "The Redistricting Morass," pp. 210–11.

79. *United Jewish Organizations v. Carey*, 430 U.S. 144 (1977).

80. Kousser, *Colorblind Injustice*, p. 408. We are not arguing that the Court used the idea of "white filler people" as the basis for finding standing in *Shaw v. Reno*. We are suggesting that the Court's preoccupation with the status of white filler people can be interpreted as equating color-blind redistricting with the creation of white-majority districts. This is a plausible and compelling explanation of the Court's behavior. For an analysis of the legal questions regarding standing in the voting rights cases, see Samuel Issacharoff and Pamela S. Karlan, "Stand-

ing and Misunderstanding in Voting Rights Law," *Harvard Law Review* 111 (1998): 2276–92.

81. *Shaw v. Reno*, p. 647.

82. Kousser, *Colorblind Injustice*, chapter 8; Issacharoff, "The Redistricting Morass," p. 220.

83. Karlan and Levinson, "Why Voting Is Different," p. 1220.

84. See, for example, Carol M. Swain, "The Future of Black Representation," *The American Prospect* 23 (fall 1995): 78–83.

85. John R. Petrocik and Scott W. Desposato, "The Partisan Consequences of Majority-Minority Redistricting in the South, 1992 and 1994," *Journal of Politics* 60 (1998): 613–33.

86. Michael Dawson, *Black Visions: The Roots of Contemporary African-American Political Ideologies* (Chicago: University of Chicago Press, 2001), p. 328.

87. Kousser, *Colorblind Injustice*, p. 276.

88. Canon, *Race, Redistricting, and Representation*, p. 244.

89. Ibid., pp. 189, 193.

90. Paul Frymer, *Uneasy Alliances: Race and Party Competition in America* (Princeton, N.J.: Princeton University Press, 1999), p. 28.

91. Ibid., pp. 32–33.

92. The Court's inability to draw a clear distinction between racial and political gerrymandering is on full display in *Hunt v. Cromartie et al.* 532 U.S., 121 St. Ct 1452 (April 18, 2000). For an analysis of the problems of redistricting and representation, see Lani Guinier and Gerald Torres, *The Miner's Canary* (Cambridge, Mass.: Harvard University Press, 2002), chapter 5.

CONCLUSION

1. Michael Dawson, *Black Visions: The Roots of Contemporary African-American Political Ideologies* (Chicago: University of Chicago Press, 2001), p. 318. African Americans actually became more pessimistic during the economic boom of the 1990s. In 1994, about 65 percent thought that racial equality would never be achieved.

2. For a commentary on the survey, which was undertaken in the spring of 2001, see Richard Morin, "Misperceptions Cloud Whites' View of Blacks," *Washington Post*, July 11, 2001, p. A1.

3. One of the most popular nonfiction books of the past decade was Richard Herrnstein and Charles Murray, *The Bell Curve: Intelligence and Class Structure in American Life* (New York: The Free Press, 1994). Herrnstein and Murray claimed that genetics explains about 60 percent of intelligence and is behind the continuing gap in IQ tests between whites and blacks. The book has been thoroughly discredited. For a devastating critique, see Claude S. Fischer et al., *Inequality by Design: Cracking the Bell Curve Myth* (Princeton, N.J.: Princeton University Press, 1996).

4. Derrick Bell, *Faces at the Bottom of the Well: The Permanence of Racism* (New York: Basic Books, 1992).

5. William Julius Wilson, *The Bridge over the Racial Divide: Rising Inequality and Coalition Politics* (Berkeley and Los Angeles: University of California Press, 1999). See also Todd Gitlin, *The Twilight of Common Dreams* (New York: Metropolitan Books, 1995); Michael Tomasky, *Left for Dead: The Life, Death, and Possible Resurrection of Progressive Politics in America* (New York: The Free Press, 1996).

6. Proponents of abolishing white identity include Noel Ignatiev and John Garvey, eds., *Race Traitor* (New York: Routledge, 1996); David Roediger, *Colored White: Transcending the Racial Past* (Berkeley and Los Angeles: University of California Press, 2002); Paul Gilroy, *Against Race: Imagining Political Culture beyond the Color Line* (Cambridge, Mass.: Harvard University Press, Belknap Press, 2000). The authors of *White Reign* believe that white identity can be transformed into something positive (Joe L. Kincheloe et al., eds., *White Reign* [New York: St. Martin's Press, 1998]).

7. Joseph McCormick 2nd and Sekou Franklin, "Expressions of Racial Consciousness in the African American Community: Data from the Million Man March," in Yvette M. Alex-Assensoh and Lawrence J. Hanks, eds., *Black and Multiracial Politics in America* (New York: New York University Press, 2001), p. 331.

8. Dawson, *Black Visions*, pp. 126, 132–34.

9. Abby Goodnough, "With New Rules and Higher Pay, New York Gets Certified Teachers," *New York Times*, August 23, 2002, p. A1.

10. Duke Helfand, "Disruptive Students Test Many Novice Teachers," *Los Angeles Times*, May 23, 2001, p. B2.

11. Iris J. Law and Joel Friedman, "Estate Tax Repeal, a Costly Windfall for the Wealthiest Americans," *Center on Budget and Policy Priorities*, 2001, <http://www. cbpp.org>.

12. The Supreme Court's 2001 decision in *Alexander v. Sandoval* represents a giant step backward in this regard. The Court required that plaintiffs demonstrate intent in those cases in which private parties filed Title VI discrimination suits against the recipients of federal funds. As one observer put it, "Given the subtle and even unconscious nature of much discrimination, plaintiffs forced to prove the intent behind discriminatory acts do not last long in the courthouse." See David Troutt, "The Nation: Behind the Court's Civil Rights Ruling," *New York Times*, April 29, 2001.

13. See Henry J. Holzer, "Employment Hiring Decisions and Antidiscrimination Policy," in Richard B. Freeman, ed., *Generating Jobs: How to Increase Demand for Less-Skilled Workers* (New York: Russell Sage Foundation, 1998), pp. 242–43.

14. *United Steelworkers v. Weber*, 443 U.S. 193 (1979). Similarly, when public employers uncover strong evidence of discrimination, they should be required to give preference to black job applicants to the extent permitted by the Supreme Court's decisions in *Croson* and *Adarand*.

15. "Title VII of the Civil Rights Act of 1964 Charges," *Equal Employment Opportunity Commission*, <http://www.eeoc.gov/stats/enforcement.html> (accessed February 4, 2003).

16. *Grutter v. Bollinger*, 288 F. 3d 732 (6th cir. 2002).

17. Jack Balkin, "Diversity Offers Everyone a Stake," *Los Angeles Times*, May 17, 2002.

18. Allan J. Lichtman, *Report on the Racial Impact of the Rejection of Ballots Cast in the 2000 Presidential Election in the State of Florida* (Washington, D.C.: U.S. Civil Rights Commission, June 2001), <http://www.usccr.gov/vote2000/stdraft1/> (accessed July 3, 2001).

19. The black graduation rate at UC Berkeley after six years is about 60 percent compared to 80 percent at Stanford. The data on UC Berkeley graduation rates were provided by Gregg Thomson, director, Office of Student Research, Division of Undergraduate Affairs, University of California, Berkeley.

20. Rebecca Trounson, "Dream, Hard Work Pay Off at College," *Los Angeles Times*, May 11, 2001, p. A13.

21. "The Negro in America: What Must Be Done," *Newsweek*, November 20, 1967, p. 34.

22. Martin Luther King Jr., "A Testament of Hope," in James M. Washington, ed., *A Testament of Hope: The Essential Writings of Martin Luther King, Jr.* (New York: Harper and Row, 1986), p. 315.

Bibliography

Aaron, Henry. *Shelter and Subsidies: Who Benefits from Federal Housing Policies.* Washington, D.C.: The Brookings Institution, 1972.

Aleinikoff, Alexander. "The Case for Race-Consciousness." *Columbia Law Review* 91 (1991): 1060–80.

Alex-Assensoh, Yvette M., and Lawrence J. Hanks., eds. *Black and Multiracial Politics in America.* New York: New York University Press, 2001.

Alt, James E. "The Impact of the Voting Rights Act on Black and White Voter Registration in the South." In Chandler Davidson and Bernard Grofman, eds., *Quiet Revolution in the South: The Impact of the Voting Rights Act, 1965–1990.* Princeton, N.J.: Princeton University Press, 1994.

"An American Legal Dilemma—Proof of Discrimination." *University of Chicago Law Review* 17 (1949): 107–25.

Anderson, Bernard E. "The Ebb and Flow of Enforcing Executive Order 11246." *American Economic Review* 86 (1996): 298–301.

Appiah, K. Anthony, and Amy Gutmann. *Color Conscious: The Political Morality of Race.* Princeton. N.J.: Princeton University Press, 1996.

Arnesen, Eric. "Like Banquo's Ghost, It Will Not Down: The Race Question and the American Railroad Brotherhoods, 1880–1920." *American Historical Review* 99 (1994): 1601–33.

Austin, Roy L., and Mark D. Allen. "Racial Disparity in Arrest Rates as an Explanation of Racial Disparity in Commitments to Pennsylvania's Prisons." *Journal of Research in Crime and Delinquency* 37 (May 2000): 200–220.

Ayres, Ian. "Fair Driving: Gender and Race Discrimination in Retail Car Negotiations." *Harvard Law Review* 104 (1991): 817–72.

Bach, Peter B., et al. "Racial Differences in the Treatment of Early Stage Lung Cancer." *New England Journal of Medicine* 341 (1999): 1198–1205.

Baldus, David, Charles Pulaski, and George Woodworth. "Comparative Review of Death Sentences." *Journal of Criminal Law and Criminology* 4 (1983): 661–753.

————. *Equal Justice and the Death Penalty: A Legal and Empirical Analysis.* Boston: Northeastern University Press, 1991.

Balkin, Jack M., ed. *What* Brown v. Board of Education *Should Have Said: The Nation's Top Legal Experts Rewrite America's Landmark Civil Rights Decision.* New York: New York University Press, 2001.

Ballou, Dale, and Michael Podgursky. *Teacher Pay and Teacher Quality.* Kalamazoo, Mich.: WE Upjohn Institute for Employment Research, 1997.

Bamberger, Michael A., and Nathan Lewin. "The Right to Equal Treatment: Administrative Enforcement of Antidiscrimination Legislation." *Harvard Law Review* 74 (1961).

Baron, Harold. "The Web of Urban Racism." In L. Knowles and K. Prewitt, eds., *Institutional Racism.* Englewood Cliffs, N.J.: Prentice-Hall, 1969.

————. *Building Babylon: A Case of Racial Controls in Public Housing.* Evanston, Ill.: Center for Urban Affairs, Northwestern University, 1971.

Baron, Harold, and Bennett Hymer. "The Negro Worker in the Chicago Labor Market." In Julius Jacobson, ed., *The Negro and the Labor Movement.* New York: Anchor Books, 1968.

Bates, T. "Do Black-Owned Businesses Employ Minority Workers? New Evidence." *Review of Black Political Economy* 16 (1988).

Becker, Gary. *The Economics of Discrimination.* 2nd ed. Chicago: University of Chicago Press, 1971.

Bell, Derrick. *Faces at the Bottom of the Well: The Permanence of Racism.* New York: Basic Books, 1992.

Belz, Herman. *Equality Transformed.* Brunswick, N.J.: Transaction Publishers, 1991.

Bennett, Larry, and Adolph Reed Jr. "The New Face of Urban Renewal: The Near North Redevelopment Initiative and the Cabrini-Green Neighborhood." In Adolph Reed Jr., ed., *Without Justice for All: The New Liberalism and Our Retreat from Racial Equality.* Boulder, Colo.: Westview Press, 1999.

Bennett, William J. *The De-valuing of America: The Fight for Our Culture and Our Children.* New York: Summitt Books, 1992.

Benveniste Luis, Martin Carnoy, and Richard Rothstein. *All Else Equal.* New York: Routledge, 2002.

Berg, Ivar. *Education and Jobs: The Great Training Robbery.* Boston: Beacon Press, 1971.

Bernstein, Irving. *Promises Kept: John F. Kennedy's New Frontier.* New York: Oxford University Press, 1991.

Bernstein, Jared, and Ellen Houston. *Falling Crime Rates in the 1990s: The Role of the Low-Wage Labor Market.* Washington, D.C.: Economic Policy Institute, February 2000.

Berry, Mary Francis. *Black Resistance, White Law.* New York: Penguin Books, 1995.

Bishop, Donna M., and Charles E. Frazier. "Race Effects in Juvenile Justice Decision-Making: Findings of a Statewide Analysis." *Journal of Criminal Law and Criminology* 86 (1996): 404–29.

Blank, Rebecca M. "Why Were Poverty Rates So High in the 1980s?" In Dimitri

B. Papadimitriou and Edward N. Wolff, eds. *Poverty and Prosperity in the U.S.A. in the Late Twentieth Century*. New York: St. Martin's Press, 1993.

Blank, Rebecca, and David Card. *Poverty, Income Distribution and Growth: Are They Still Connected?* Evanston, Ill.: Center for Urban Affairs and Policy Research, Northwestern University, 1993.

Blauner, Robert. *Racial Oppression in America*. New York: Harper and Row, 1972.

Bloche, M. Gregg. "Race and Discretion in American Medicine." *Yale Journal of Health Policy, Law, and Ethics* 1 (2001): 95–121.

Blumer, Herbert. "Race Prejudice as a Sense of Group Position." *Pacific Sociological Review* 1 (1958): 3–7.

Blumrosen, Alfred. "Draft Report on Reverse Discrimination Commissioned by Labor Department: How the Courts Are Handling Reverse Discrimination Claims." *Daily Labor Report* (BNA) 56 (1995).

Blumstein, Alfred. "On the Racial Disproportionality of United States Prison Populations." *Journal of Criminal Law and Criminology* 73 (1982): 1259–81.

Bobo, Lawrence, and Vincent L. Hutchings. "Perceptions of Racial Group Competition: Extending Blumer's Theory of Group Position to a Mulitracial Context." *American Sociological Review* 61 (1996): 951–72.

Bobo, Lawrence, and James R. Kluegel. "Opposition to Race-Targeting: Self Interest, Stratification Ideology, or Racial Attitudes." *American Sociological Review* 58 (1993): 443–64.

Bobo, Lawrence, and Ryan A. Smith. "From Jim Crow Racism to Laissez-Faire Racism: The Transformation of Racial Attitudes." In Wendy Katkin, Ned Landsman, and Andrea Tyree, eds., *Beyond Pluralism: The Conception of Groups and Group Identities in America*. Urbana: University of Illinois Press, 1998.

Bobo, Lawrence, and Camille L. Zubrinksy. "Attitudes on Residential Integration: Perceived Status Differences, Mere In-Group Preference, or Racial Prejudice?" *Social Forces* 74 (1996): 883–909.

Bolick, Clint. *The Affirmative Action Fraud: Can We Restore the American Civil Rights Vision?* Washington, D.C.: Cato Institute, 1996.

Bond, Julian. Foreword to Walter Feinberg, *On Higher Ground: Education and the Case for Affirmative Action*. New York: Teacher's College Press, 1998.

Bork, Robert H. "Civil Rights—a Challenge." *The New Republic* (August 31, 1963): 21–22.

Bositis, David. *Party, Redistricting, and Minority Representation: The Southern States, 1992–2002*. Washington, D.C.: Joint Center for Political and Economic Studies, May 2002.

Bowen, William, and Derek Bok. *The Shape of the River*. Princeton, N.J.: Princeton University Press, 1998.

Brest, Paul. "Foreword: In Defense of the Antidiscrimination Principle." *Harvard Law Review* 90 (1976).

Brewer, Dominic J., Eric R. Eide, and Dan D. Goldhaber. *An Examination of the Role of Student Race and Ethnicity in Higher Education since 1972*. Washington, D.C.: The Rand Corporation, 1999.

Bridges, George S., and Sara Steen. "Racial Disparities in Official Assessments of Juvenile Offenders: Attributional Stereotypes as Mediating Mechanisms." *American Sociological Review* 63 (August 1998): 554–70.

Brodie, Mollyann. *The Four Americas: Government and Social Policy through the Eyes of America's Multi-Racial and Multi-Ethnic Society.* A Report of the Washington Post/Kaiser Family Foundation/Harvard Study Project. Menlo Park: Kaiser Family Foundation, 1995.

Brown, Michael K. *Race, Money, and the American Welfare State.* Ithaca, N.Y.: Cornell University Press, 1999.

———. "Race in the American Welfare State: The Ambiguities of 'Universalistic' Social Policy since the New Deal." In Adolph Reed Jr., ed., *Without Justice for All: The New Liberalism and Our Retreat from Racial Equality.* Boulder, Colo.: Westview Press, 1999.

———. "Ghettos, Fiscal Federalism, and Welfare Reform." In Richard Fording, Joe Soss, and Sanford Schram, eds., *Race, Welfare and the Politics of Reform.* Ann Arbor: University of Michigan Press, 2003.

Brown, Michael K., and Steven P. Erie. "Blacks and the Legacy of the Great Society: The Economic and Political Impact of Federal Social Policy." *Public Policy* 29 (1981): 299–330.

Bryk, Anthony, Valerie Lee, and Peter Holland. *Catholic Schools and the Common Good.* Cambridge, Mass.: Harvard University Press, 1993.

Bryner, Gary. "Congress, Courts, and Agencies: Equal Employment and the Limits of Policy Implementation." *Political Science Quarterly* 96 (1981): 411–30.

Burstein, Paul, and Margo W. MacLeod. "Prohibiting Employment Discrimination: Ideas and Politics in the Congressional Debate over Equal Employment Opportunity Legislation." *American Journal of Sociology* 86 (1980): 512–33.

Byrd, W. Michael, and Linda A. Clayton. *An American Health Dilemma.* Vol. 1, *A Medical History of African Americans and the Problem of Race: Beginnings to 1900.* New York: Routledge, 2000.

California Department of Justice. *Ethnic Distribution of Arrests for Participating in Street Gangs, 1998.* Sacramento, Calif.: Criminal Justice Statistics Center, 1999.

Campbell, Alec, Richard S. Berk, and James J. Fyfe. "Deployment of Violence; the Los Angeles Police Department's Use of Dogs." *Evaluation Review* 22 (1998): 535–61.

Canon, David T. *Race, Redistricting, and Representation: The Unintended Consequences of Black Majority Districts.* Chicago: University of Chicago Press, 1999.

Caraley, Demetrios. "Washington Abandons the Cities." *Political Science Quarterly* 107 (1992): 1–30.

Carmines, Edward G., and James A. Stimson. *Issue Evolution: Race and the Transformation of American Politics.* Princeton, N.J.: Princeton University Press, 1989.

Carnoy, Martin. *Faded Dreams: The Politics and Economics of Race in America.* New York: Cambridge University Press, 1994.

———. "Education in the Year 2010: Reflections on the Effects of Changing

Labor Markets and Family Structure in a Globalized Environment." Stanford University School of Education, October 1999. Photocopy.

Carter, Dan T. *The Politics of Rage: George Wallace, the Origins of the New Conservatism, and the Transformation of American Politics.* New York: Simon and Schuster, 1995.

Carter, Robert L. "A Reassessment of *Brown v. Board.*" In Derrick Bell, ed., *Shades of Brown: New Perspectives on School Desegregation.* New York: Teacher's College, Columbia University, 1980.

Castells, Manuel. *The Power of Identity.* London: Blackwell, 1997.

Charles, Camille Zubrinsky. "Processes of Racial Residential Segregation." In Alice O'Connor, Chris Tilly, and Lawrence D. Bobo, eds., *Urban Inequality: Evidence from Four Cities.* New York: Russell Sage Foundation, 2001.

Cherry, Robert, and William M. Rodgers III, eds. *Prosperity for All? The Economic Boom and African Americans.* New York: Russell Sage Foundation, 2001.

Citrin, Jack, Donald P. Green, and David O. Sears. "White Reactions to Black Candidates: When Does Race Matter?" *Public Opinion Quarterly* 54 (1990): 74–96.

Clayton, Obie Jr., ed. *An American Dilemma Revisited: Race Relations in a Changing World.* New York: Russell Sage Foundation, 1996.

Cole, David. *Equal Justice: Race and Class in the American Criminal Justice System.* New York: New Press, 1999.

Coleman, James, and Thomas Hoffer. *Public and Private High Schools: The Impact of Communities.* New York: Basic Books, 1987.

Congressional Record. 1964. Washington, D.C.

Conley, Dalton. *Being Black, Living in the Red: Race, Wealth, and Social Policy in America.* Berkeley and Los Angeles: University of California Press, 1999.

Conley, Darlene J. "Adding Color to a Black and White Picture: Using Qualitative Data to Explain Racial Disproportionality in the Juvenile Justice System." *Journal of Research in Crime and Delinquency* 31 (1994): 135–48.

Cooper, Richard, and Brian E. Simmons. "Cigarette Smoking and Ill Health among Black Americans." *New York State Journal of Medicine* 85 (1985): 344–49.

Council of Economic Advisers. *Changing America: Indicators of Social and Economic Well-Being by Race and Hispanic Origin.* Washington D.C.: U.S. Government Printing Office, September 1998.

———. *Economic Report of the President,* 1998. Washington, D.C.: U.S. Government Printing Office, 1998.

Crawford, Charles, Ted Chiricos, and Gary Kleck. "Race, Racial Threat, and Sentencing of Habitual Offenders." *Criminology* 36 (1998): 481–509.

Crenshaw, Kimberle. "Race, Reform and Retrenchment: Transformation and Legitimation in Anti-Discrimination Law." *Harvard Law Review* 101 (1988): 1331–87.

———. "Toward a Race-Conscious Pedagogy." *National Black Law Journal* 11 (1989): 1–14.

Crenshaw, Kimberle et al., eds. *Critical Race Theory.* New York: The New Press, 1995.

Crutchfield, Robert D., George S. Bridges, and Susan R. Pitchford. "Analytical and Aggregation Biases in Analyses of Imprisonment: Reconciling Discrepancies in Studies of Racial Disparity." *Journal of Research in Crime and Delinquency* 31 (1994): 177–79.

Cruz, Jose E. "Interminority Relations in Urban Settings: Lessons from the Black–Puerto Rican Experience." In Yvette M. Alex-Assensohm and Lawrence J. Hanks, eds., *Black and Multiracial Politics in America*. New York: New York University Press, 2001, pp. 84–112.

Culp, Jerome, and Bruce H. Dunson. "Brothers of a Different Color: A Preliminary Look at Employer Treatment of White and Black Youth." In Richard B. Freeman and Harry J. Holzer, eds., *The Black Youth Unemployment Crisis*. Chicago: University of Chicago Press, 1986.

Currie, Elliott. *Crime and Punishment in America*. New York: Henry Holt, 1998.

Currie, Elliot, Dan Macallair, and Khaled Taqi-Eddin. *Quiet Crisis: Youth, Race, Violence and Justice in Four California Counties*. San Francisco: Center on Juvenile and Criminal Justice, 1999.

D'Souza, Dinesh. *Illiberal Education: The Politics of Race and Sex on Campus*. New York: The Free Press, 1991.

———. *The End of Racism: Principles for a Multiracial Society*. New York: The Free Press, 1995.

Danziger, Sheldon, and Peter Gottschalk. *America Unequal*. New York: Russell Sage Foundation, 1995.

Darity, William Jr. "What's Left of the Economic Theory of Discrimination." In Steven Shulman and William Darity Jr., eds., *The Question of Discrimination*. Middletown, Conn.: Wesleyan University Press, 1989.

Darity, William A. Jr., and Patrick L. Mason. "Evidence on Discrimination in Employment: Codes of Color, Codes of Gender." *Journal of Economic Perspectives* 12 (1998): 63–90.

Darity, William Jr., and Samuel L. Myers Jr. *Persistent Disparity: Race and Economic Inequality in the United States since 1945*. Northhampton, Mass.: Edward Elgar Publishing, 1998.

Davidson, Chandler, and Bernard Grofman. "The Effect of Municipal Election Structure on Black Representation in Eight Southern States." In Chandler Davidson and Bernard Grofman, eds., *Quiet Revolution in the South: The Impact of the Voting Rights Act, 1965–1990*. Princeton, N.J.: Princeton University Press, 1994.

Dawson, Michael C. *Behind the Mule: Race and Class in African-American Politics*. Princeton, N.J.: Princeton University Press, 1994.

———. *Black Visions: The Roots of Contemporary African-American Political Ideologies*. Chicago: University of Chicago Press, 2001.

de Tocqueville, Alexis. *Democracy in America*. 1835. Reprint, New York: Anchor Books, 1969.

DeAngelis, Karen, and Martin Carnoy. "Does Ability Increase Earnings, and, If So, by How Much?" Stanford University School of Education, 2000. Photocopy.

Deaton, Angus, and Darren Lubotsky. *Mortality, Inequality and Race in American Cities and States*. National Bureau of Economic Research, Working

Paper 8370. Cambridge, Mass.: National Bureau of Economic Research, July 2001.

Dieter, Richard A. *The Death Penalty in Black and White: Who Lives, Who Dies, Who Decides.* Washington, D.C.: Death Penalty Information Center, June 1998.

Dilulio, John. "My Black Crime Problem and Ours." *City Journal* 6 (spring 1996).

"Discrimination and Affirmative Action." *California Opinion Index.* San Francisco: The Field Institute, May 1995.

Donohue, John III, and Peter Siegelman. "The Changing Nature of Employment Discrimination Litigation." *Stanford Law Review* 43 (1991): 983–1033.

Donohue, John III, and James Heckman. "Continuous versus Episodic Change: The Impact of Civil Rights on the Economic Status of Blacks." *Journal of Economic Literature* 29 (1991): 1603–43.

Eisenberg, Theodore. "Litigation Models and Trial Outcomes in Civil Rights and Prisoner Cases." *Georgetown Law Journal* 77 (1989): 1567–1602.

Epstein, Richard. *Forbidden Grounds: The Case against Employment Discrimination Laws.* Cambridge, Mass.: Harvard University Press, 1992.

Evans, W. N., and R. M. Schwab. "Finishing High School and Starting College: Do Catholic Schools Make a Difference?" *Quarterly Journal of Economics* 10 (1995): 941–74.

Evers, Williamson. "Standards and Accountability." In Terry M. Moe, ed., *A Primer on America's Schools.* Stanford, Calif.: Hoover Institution Press, 2001.

Farley, John E. "Race Still Matters: The Minimal Role of Income and Housing Cost as Causes of Housing Segregation in St. Louis, 1990." *Urban Affairs Quarterly* 31 (1995): 244–54.

Farley, Reynolds. "Blacks, Hispanics, and White Ethnic Groups: Are Blacks Uniquely Disadvantaged?" *American Economic Review* 80 (1990): 237–41.

Farley, Reynolds, and Walter Allen. *The Color Line and the Quality of Life in America.* New York: Oxford University Press, 1989.

Farley, Reynolds, Susanne Bianchi, and Diane Colasanto. "Barriers to the Racial Integration of Neighborhoods: The Detroit Case." *Annals of the American Academy of Political and Social Science* 441 (1979): 97–113.

Farley, Reynolds, et al. "Stereotypes and Segregation: Neighborhoods in the Detroit Area." *American Journal of Sociology* 100 (1994).

Feagin, Joe R., and Melvin P. Sikes. *Living with Racism: The Black Middle-Class Experience.* Boston: Beacon Press, 1994.

Ferguson, Ronald F. "Shifting Challenges: Fifty Years of Economic Change toward Black-White Earnings Equality." In Obie Clayton Jr., ed., *An American Dilemma Revisited.* New York: Russell Sage Foundation, 1996.

———. "Can Schools Narrow the Black-White Test Score Gap?" In Christopher Jencks and Meredith Phillips, eds., *The Black-White Test Score Gap.* Washington, D.C.: Brookings Institution Press, 1998.

Fischer, Claude S., et al. *Inequality by Design: Cracking the Bell Curve Myth.* Princeton, N.J.: Princeton University Press, 1996.

Fiss, Owen M. "Groups and the Equal Protection Clause." *Philosophy and Public Affairs* 5 (1976): 107–77.

Flagg, Barbara. "Was Blind, but Now I See: White Race Consciousness and the Requirement of Discriminatory Intent." *Michigan Law Review* 91 (1993): 953–1017.

Fording, Richard C. "'Laboratories of Democracy' or Symbolic Politics? The Racial Origins of Welfare Reform." In Schram, Soss, and Fording, eds. *Race and the Politics of Welfare Reform.* Ann Arbor: University of Michigan Press, 2003.

Fowles, Richard, and Mary Merva. "Wage Inequality and Criminal Activity: An Extreme Bounds Analysis for the United States, 1975–1990." *Criminology* 34 (1996): 163–82.

Fredrickson, George. *White Supremacy.* New York: Oxford University Press, 1981.

———. *The Arrogance of Race.* Middletown, Conn.: Wesleyan University Press, 1988.

———. *Racism: A Short History.* Princeton: Princeton University Press, 2002.

Freeman, Alan D. "Legitimating Racial Discrimination through Anti-discrimination Law: A Critical Review of Supreme Court Decisions." *Minnesota Law Review* 62 (1978).

Freeman, Richard B. *Crime and the Employment of Disadvantaged Youths.* National Bureau of Economic Research Working Paper No. 3875. Cambridge, Mass.: National Bureau of Economic Research, 1991.

Freeman, Richard B., and William Rodgers III. "Area Economic Conditions and the Labor Market Outcomes of Young Men in the 1990s Expansion." In Robert Cherry and William M. Rodgers III, eds. *Prosperity for All? The Economic Boom and African Americans.* New York: Russell Sage Foundation, 2001.

Friedman, Milton. "The Role of Government in Education." In Robert A. Solo, ed., *Economics and the Public Interest.* New Brunswick, N.J.: Rutgers University Press, 1955.

Frymer, Paul. *Uneasy Alliances: Race and Party Competition in America.* Princeton, N.J.: Princeton University Press, 1999.

Garrow, David. *Bearing the Cross: Martin Luther King, Jr., and the Southern Christian Leadership Conference.* New York: Vintage Books, 1988.

Gaziano, Todd. "The New 'Massive Resistance.'" *Policy Review* 89 (1998): 22–29.

Gilens, Martin. *Why Americans Hate Welfare: Race, Media, and the Politics of Antipoverty Policy.* Chicago: University of Chicago Press, 1999.

Gilroy, Paul. *Against Race: Imagining Political Culture beyond the Color Line.* Cambridge, Mass.: Harvard University Press, Belknap Press, 2000.

Gitlin, Todd. *The Twilight of Common Dreams.* New York: Metropolitan Books, 1995.

Gornick, Marian E., Paul Eggers, and Gerald Riley. "Understanding Disparities in the Use of Medicare Services." *Yale Journal of Health Policy, Law, and Ethics* 1 (2001): 133–58.

Gornick, Marian E., et al. "Effects of Race and Income on Mortality and Use of

Services among Medicare Beneficiaries." *New England Journal of Medicine* 335 (1996): 791–99.

Gotanda, Neil. "A Critique of 'Our Constitution Is Color-Blind.'" *Stanford Law Review* 44 (1991): 1–68.

Gottschalk, Peter. "Inequality, Income Growth, and Mobility: The Basic Facts." *Journal of Economic Perspectives* 11 (1997): 21–40.

Graham, Hugh Davis. *The Civil Rights Era: Origins and Development of National Policy.* New York: Oxford University Press, 1990.

Greenberg, Stanley B. *Report on Democratic Defection.* Washington, D.C.: Analysis Group 35, 1985.

Grissmer, David, Ann Flanagan, and Stephanie Williamson. "Why Did the Black-White Test Score Gap Narrow in the 1970s and 1980s?" In Christopher Jencks and Meredith Phillips, eds., *The Black-White Test Score Gap.* Washington, D.C.: Brookings Institution Press, 1998.

Grissmer, David, et al. *Improving Student Achievement: What State NAEP Test Scores Tell Us.* Santa Monica, Calif.: The Rand Corporation, 2000.

Grofman, Bernard. "The Supreme Court, the Voting Rights Act, and Minority Representation." In Anthony Peacock, ed., *Affirmative Action and Representation.* Durham, N.C.: Carolina Academic Press, 1997.

Grofman, Bernard, Lisa Handley, and Richard G. Niemi. *Minority Representation and the Quest for Voting Equality.* New York: Cambridge University Press, 1992.

Guinier, Lani. *The Tyranny of the Majority: Fundamental Fairness in Representative Democracy.* New York: The Free Press, 1994.

Guinier, Lani, and Gerald Torres. *The Miner's Canary.* Cambridge, Mass.: Harvard University Press, 2002.

Hacker, Andrew. *Two Nations.* New York: Ballantine Books, 1992.

Hall, Kermit L., ed. *The Oxford Companion to the Supreme Court of the United States.* New York: Oxford University Press, 1992.

Hamilton, Dona C., and Charles V. Hamilton. *The Dual Agenda: Race and Social Welfare Policies of Civil Rights Organizations.* New York: Columbia University Press, 1997.

Handley, Lisa, and Bernard Grofman. "The Impact of the Voting Rights Act on Minority Representation: Black Officeholding in Southern State Legislatures and Congressional Delegations." In Chandler Davidson and Bernard Grofman, eds., *Quiet Revolution in the South: The Impact of the Voting Rights Act, 1965–1990.* Princeton, N.J.: Princeton University Press, 1994.

Haney-Lopez, Ian. *White by Law: The Legal Construction of Race.* New York: New York University Press, 1996.

Haney-Lopez, Ian. "Institutional Racism: Judicial Conduct and a New Theory of Racial Discrimination." *Yale Law Journal* 190 (2000): 1717–92.

Harding, Vincent. *There Is a River: The Black Struggle for Freedom in America.* New York: Oxford University Press, 1983.

Harris, Angela. "Equality Trouble: Sameness and Difference in Twentieth Century Race Law." *California Law Review* 88 (2000): 1923–93.

Harris, Cheryl I. "Whiteness as Property." In Kimberle Crenshaw et al., eds., *Critical Race Theory.* New York: The New Press, 1995.

Hays, Samuel P. *American Political History as Social Analysis*. Knoxville: The University of Tennessee Press, 1980.

Hebert, Christopher. "Sentencing Outcomes of Black, Hispanic, and White Males Convicted under Federal Sentencing Guidelines." *Criminal Justice Review* 22 (Autumn 1997): 133–56.

Heckman, James J. "The Central Role of the South in Accounting for the Economic Progress of Black Americans." *American Economic Review* 80 (May 1990): 242–46.

———. "Detecting Discrimination." *Journal of Economic Perspectives* 12 (1998): 101–16.

Herrnstein, Richard, and Charles Murray. *The Bell Curve: Intelligence and Class Structure in American Life*. New York: The Free Press, 1994.

Higginbotham, Leon A. *In the Matter of Color: Race and the American Legal Process*. New York: Oxford University Press, 1978.

Hill, Herbert. *Black Labor and the American Legal System*. Madison: University of Wisconsin Press, 1985.

Hirsch, Arnold. *Making the Second Ghetto: Race and Housing in Chicago, 1940–1960*. New York: Cambridge University Press, 1983.

Hochschild, Jennifer L. "Race, Class, Power and the American Welfare State." In Amy Gutmann, ed., *Democracy and the Welfare State*. Princeton, N.J.: Princeton University Press, 1988.

———. *Facing Up to the American Dream: Race, Class and the Soul of the Nation*. Princeton, N.J.: Princeton University Press, 1995.

Holzer, Harry J. "Employer Hiring Decisions and Antidiscrimination Policy." In Richard B. Freeman, ed., *Generating Jobs: How to Increase Demand for Less-Skilled Workers*. New York: Russell Sage Foundation, 1998.

Holzer, Harry J., and David Neumark. "Assessing Affirmative Action." *Journal of Economic Literature* 38 (2000): 483–568.

Howell, Susan. "Racial Polarization, Reaction to Urban Conditions, and the Approval of Black Mayors." In Yvette M. Alex-Assensoh and Lawrence J. Hanks, eds., *Black and Multiracial Politics in America*. New York: New York University Press, 2001.

Huckfeldt, Robert, and Carol Weitzel Kohfeld. *Race and the Decline of Class in American Politics*. Urbana: University of Illinois Press, 1989.

Human Rights Watch. *Race and Drug Law Enforcement in the State of Georgia*. New York: Human Rights Watch, 1996.

Hunt, Cecil J. "Guests in Another's House: An Analysis of Racially Disparate Bar Performance." *Florida State University Law Review* 23 (1996): 721–93.

Ignatiev, Noel, and John Garvey, eds. *Race Traitor*. New York: Routledge, 1996.

Issacharoff, Samuel. "The Redistricting Morass." In Anthony Peacock, ed., *Affirmative Action and Representation: Shaw v. Reno and the Future of Voting Rights*. Durham, N.C.: Carolina Academic Press, 1997.

Issacharoff, Samuel, and Pamela S. Karlan. "Standing and Misunderstanding in Voting Rights Law." *Harvard Law Review* 111 (1998): 2276–92.

Issacharoff, Samuel, Pamela S. Karlan, and Richard H. Pildes. *The Law of Democracy: Legal Structure of the Political Process*. Westbury, N.Y.: The Foundation Press, 1998.

Jackson, Kenneth T. *Crabgrass Frontier*. New York: Oxford University Press, 1985.

Jacobs, James. *Black Workers and the New Technology: The Need for a New Urban Training*. Ann Arbor, Mich.: Industrial Technology Institute, 1987.

Jacoby, Tamar. *Someone Else's House: America's Unfinished Struggle for Integration*. New York: The Free Press, 1998.

Jaynes, Gerald D., and Robin M. Williams Jr., eds. *A Common Destiny: Blacks and American Society*. Washington, D.C.: National Academy Press, 1989.

Jencks, Christopher, and Meredith Phillips, eds. *The Black-White Test Score Gap*. Washington, D.C.: Brookings Institution Press, 1998.

Jepson, Christopher. "The Private Schooling Market and Its Effect on Student Achievement." Ph.D. dissertation, Northwestern University, 2000.

Johnson, James H. Jr., and Melvin H. Oliver. "Structural Changes in the U.S. Economy and Black Male Joblessness: A Reassessment." In George E. Peterson and Wayne Vroman, eds., *Urban Labor Markets and Job Opportunity*. Washington, D.C.: The Urban Institute, 1992.

Judd, Dennis R. "Symbolic Politics and Urban Policies: Why African Americans Got So Little from the Democrats." In Adolph Reed Jr., ed., *Without Justice for All: The New Liberalism and Our Retreat from Racial Equality*. Boulder, Colo.: Westview Press, 1999.

Kane, Thomas. "College Entry by Blacks since 1970: The Role of College Costs, Family and Background, and the Returns to Education." *The Journal of Political Economy* 102 (1994): 878–911.

———. "Racial and Ethnic Preferences in College Admissions." In Christopher Jencks and Meredith Phillips, eds., *The Black-White Test Score Gap*. Washington, D.C.: Brookings Institution Press, 1998.

Karlan, Pamela S., and D. J. Levinson. "Why Voting Is Different." *California Law Review* 84 (1996): 1201–32.

Kasinitz, Philip, and Jay Rosenberg. "Missing the Connection: Social Isolation and Employment on the Brooklyn Waterfront." *Social Problems* 43 (1996): 180–96.

Katkin, Wendy F., Ned Landsman, and Andrea Tyree, eds. *Beyond Pluralism: The Conception of Groups and Identities in America*. Urbana: University of Illinois Press, 1998.

Katz, Michael B., ed. *The "Underclass" Debate: Views from History*. Princeton, N.J.: Princeton University Press, 1993.

Kaye-Kantrowitz, Melanie. "Jews in the U.S.: The Rising Costs of Whiteness." In Becky Thompson and Sangeeta Tyagi, eds., *Names We Call Home*. New York: Routledge, 1996.

Keeton, W. Page, et al. *Prosser and Keeton on the Law of Torts*. 5th ed. St. Paul, Minn.: West Publishing, 1984.

Keiser, Richard A. *Subordination or Empowerment? African-American Leadership and the Struggle for Power*. New York: Oxford University Press, 1997.

Key, V. O. Jr. *Southern Politics in State and Nation*. Knoxville: University of Tennessee Press, 1984.

Kidder, William C. "Situating Asian Pacific Americans in the Law School Affirmative Action Debate." *Asian Law Journal* 7 (2000): 29–68.

———. "The Rise of the Testocracy: An Essay on the LSAT, Conventional Wisdom, and the Dismantling of Diversity." *Texas Journal of Women and the Law* 9 (2000): 167–218.

Killingsworth, Charles C. "Negroes in a Changing Labor Market." In Arthur M. Ross and Herbert Hill, eds., *Employment, Race and Poverty*. New York: Harcourt, Brace and World, 1967.

Kincheloe, Joe L., et al., eds. *White Reign*. New York: St. Martin's Press, 1998.

Kinder, Donald R., and Tali Mendelberg. "Individualism Reconsidered: Principles and Prejudice in Contemporary American Opinion." In David O. Sears, Jim Sidanius, and Lawrence Bobo, eds., *Racialized Politics: The Debate about Racism in America*. Chicago: University of Chicago Press, 2000.

Kinder, Donald R., and Lynn M. Sanders. *Divided by Color: Racial Politics and Democratic Ideals*. Chicago: University of Chicago Press, 1996.

King, Desmond. *Separate and Unequal: Black Americans and the U.S. Federal Government*. New York: Oxford University Press, 1995.

King, Gary, John Bruce, and Andrew Gelman. "Racial Fairness in Legislative Redistricting." In Paul E. Peterson, ed., *Classifying by Race*. Princeton, N.J.: Princeton University Press, 1995, pp. 85–110.

King, Martin Luther Jr. "A Testament of Hope." In James M. Washington, ed., *A Testament of Hope: The Essential Writings of Martin Luther King, Jr.* New York: Harper and Row, 1986.

Klag, Michael, et al. "The Association of Skin Color with Blood Pressure in U.S. Blacks with Low Socioeconomic Status." *Journal of the American Medical Association* 265 (1991): 599–602.

Kleck, Gary. "Racial Discrimination in Criminal Sentencing: A Critical Evaluation of the Evidence." *American Sociological Review* 46 (1981): 783–805.

Kleppner, Paul. *Chicago Divided: The Making of a Black Mayor*. DeKalb: Northern Illinois University Press, 1985.

Kluegel, James R., and Eliot R. Smith. "Whites' Beliefs about Blacks' Opportunity." *American Sociological Review* 47 (1982): 518–32.

———. *Beliefs about Inequality*. New York: Aldine de Gruyter, 1986.

Kluger, Richard. *Simple Justice*. New York: Alfred A. Knopf, 1980.

Kosters, Marvin. "Looking for Jobs in all the Wrong Places." *The Public Interest* (fall 1996): 125–31.

Kousser, J. Morgan. *Colorblind Injustice: Minority Voting Rights and the Undoing of the Second Reconstruction*. Chapel Hill: University of North Carolina Press, 1999.

Krieger, Linda Hamilton. "The Content of Our Categories." *Stanford Law Review* 47 (1995): 1161–223.

Kull, Andrew. *The Color-Blind Constitution*. Cambridge, Mass.: Harvard University Press, 1992.

La Fave, Wayne R., and Austin W. Scott Jr. *Criminal Law*. 2d ed. St. Paul, Minn.: West Publishing, 1982.

Ladd, Helen F. "Evidence on Discrimination in Mortgage Lending." *Journal of Economic Perspectives* 12 (1998): 41–62.

Lafer, Gordon. "Minority Employment, Labor Market Segmentation, and the

Failure of Job-Training Policy in New York City." *Urban Affairs Quarterly* 28 (1992): 206–35.

LaFree, Gary, and Kriss A. Drass. "The Effect of Changes in Intra-racial Economic Inequality and Educational Attainment on Changes in Arrest Rates of African-Americans and Whites, 1957 to 1990." *American Sociological Review* 61 (1996): 614–34.

Langan, Patrick A. "Racism on Trial: New Evidence to Explain the Racial Composition of Prisons in the United States." *Journal of Criminal Law and Criminology* 76 (1984): 666–83.

Lankford, Hamilton, Susanna Loeb, and James Wyckoff. "Teacher Sorting and the Plight of Urban Schools: A Descriptive Analysis." *Educational Evaluation and Policy Analysis* 24 (2000): 37–62.

Lapchick, Richard, and Kevin Matthews. *Racial Report Card: A Comprehensive Analysis of the Hiring Practices of Women and People of Color in the National Basketball Association, the National Football League, Major League Baseball, the NCCA and Its Member Institutions.* Boston: Northeastern University, Center for the Study of Sport in Society, 1997.

Law, Iris J., and Joel Friedman. "Estate Tax Repeal, a Costly Windfall for the Wealthiest Americans." *Center on Budget and Policy Priorities,* 2001. <http://www. cbpp.org>.

Lawrence, Charles R. III. "The Id, the Ego, and Equal Protection: Reckoning with Unconscious Racism." *Stanford Law Review* 39 (1987): 317–88.

———. "If He Hollers Let Him Go: Regulating Racist Speech on Campus." *Duke Law Journal* (1990): 431–83.

Lawrence, Charles R. III, and Mari J. Matsuda. *Words That Wound: Critical Race Theory, Assaultive Speech, and the First Amendment.* Boulder, Colo.: Westview Press, 1993.

———. *We Won't Go Back.* New York: Houghton Mifflin, 1997.

Lazin, Frederick A. "Federal Low-Income Housing Assistance Programs and Racial Segregation: Leased Public Housing." *Public Policy* 24 (1976): 337–60.

Leiber, Michael J., and Jayne M. Stairs. "Race, Contexts, and the Use of Intake Diversion." *Journal of Research in Crime and Delinquency* 36 (1996): 76–78.

Leonard, Jonathan S. "Antidiscrimination or Reverse Discrimination: The Impact of Changing Demographics, Title VII, and Affirmative Action on Productivity." *Journal of Human Resources* 2 (1984): 145–74.

———. "Employment and Occupational Advance under Affirmative Action." *Review of Economics and Statistics* 66 (1984): 381–84.

———. "The Impact of Affirmative Action Regulation and Equal Employment Law on Black Employment." *The Journal of Economic Perspectives* 4 (1990): 47–63.

———. "Wage Disparities and Affirmative Action in the 1980s." *American Economic Review* 86 (1996): 285–89.

Lerman, Robert I. "The Impact of the Changing U.S. Family Structure on Child Poverty and Income Inequality." *Economica* 63 (1996): S119–39.

Leslie, Derek. *An Investigation of Racial Disadvantage.* Manchester, England: Manchester University Press, 1998.

Lewan, Todd, and Delores Barcaly. "Torn from the Land: AP Documents Land Taken from Blacks through Trickery, Violence and Murder." *Associated Press,* December 2001. <http://wire.ap.org/APpackages/torn/> (accessed January 2, 2002).

Lichtman, Allan J. *Report on the Racial Impact of the Rejection of Ballots Cast in the 2000 Presidential Election in the State of Florida.* Washington, D.C.: U.S. Civil Rights Commission, June 2001. <http://www.usccr.gov/vote2000/stdraft1/> (accessed July 3, 2001).

Lieberman, Robert. *Shifting the Color Line: Race and the American Welfare State.* Cambridge, Mass. Harvard University Press, 1998.

Lieberson, Stanley. *A Piece of the Pie: Blacks and White Immigrants since 1880.* Berkeley and Los Angeles: University of California Press, 1980.

Liebow, Elliot. *Tally's Corner: A Study of Negro Streetcorner Men.* Boston: Little, Brown, 1967.

Lien, Pei-te, and M. Margaret Conway. "Comparing Support for Affirmative Action among Four Racial Groups." In Yvette M. Alex-Assensoh and Lawrence J. Hanks., eds., *Black and Multiracial Politics in America.* New York: New York University Press, 2001.

Lipsitz, George. *The Possessive Investment in Whiteness: How White People Profit from Identity Politics.* Philadelphia: Temple University Press, 1998.

Loeb, Susanna, and Marianne Page. "Examining the Link between Wages and Quality in the Teacher Workforce: The Role of Alternative Labor Market Opportunities and Non-pecuniary Variation." Department of Economics, University of California, Davis, 1998. Photocopy.

Loury, Glenn C. *The Anatomy of Racial Inequality.* Cambridge, Mass.: Harvard University Press, 2000.

Loury, Linda Datcher, and David Garman. "College Selectivity and Earnings." *Journal of Labor Economics* 13 (1995): 289–308.

Lublin, David. *The Paradox of Representation: Racial Gerrymandering and Minority Interests in Congress.* Princeton, N.J.: Princeton University Press, 1997.

Lublin, David Ian, and Katherine Tate. "Racial Group Competition in Urban Elections." In Paul E. Peterson, ed., *Classifying by Race.* Princeton, N.J.: Princeton University Press, 1995.

Luker, Kristin. *Dubious Conceptions: The Politics of Teenage Pregnancy.* Cambridge, Mass.: Harvard University Press, 1996.

Maloney, Thomas N. "Wage Compression and Wage Inequality between Black and White Males in the United States, 1940–1960." *Journal of Economic History* 54 (1994): 358–81.

Markusen, Ann, Peter Hall, and Amy K. Glasmeier. *High Tech America: The What, How, Where, and Why of the Sunrise Industries.* Boston: Allen and Unwin, 1986.

Marsden, Peter V. "The Hiring Process: Recruitment Methods." *American Behavioral Scientist* 7 (1994): 979–91.

Massey, Douglas, and Nancy Denton. *American Apartheid: Segregation and the*

Making of the Underclass. Cambridge, Mass.: Harvard University Press, 1993.

Matsuda, Mari J. "Voices of America: Accent, Anti-Discrimination Law and a Jurisprudence for the Last Reconstruction." *Yale Law Journal* 100 (1991): 1329–99.

Mauer, Marc. *Race to Incarcerate.* New York: New Press, 1999.

Mauro, Tony. "Number of Minority Law Clerks for Supreme Court Justices Declines." *American Lawyer Media*, October 29, 2001.

McBarnette, Lorna Scott. "African American Women." In Marcia Bayne-Smith, ed., *Race, Gender and Health.* Thousand Oaks, Calif.: Sage Publications, 1996.

McCormick, Joseph 2nd, and Sekou Franklin. "Expressions of Racial Consciousness in the African American Community: Data from the Million Man March." In Yvette M. Alex-Assensoh and Lawrence J. Hanks, eds., *Black and Multiracial Politics in America.* New York: New York University Press, 2001.

McLanahan, Sara, and Lynn Casper. "Growing Diversity and Inequality in the American Family." In Reynolds Farley, ed., *State of the Union: America in the 1990s.* Vol. 2. New York: Russell Sage Foundation, 1995.

McWhorter John H. *Losing the Race: Self-Sabotage in Black America.* New York: The Free Press, 2000.

Mead, Lawrence M. "Social Programs and Social Obligations." *The Public Interest* 69 (fall 1982): 17–33.

———. *The New Politics of Poverty: The Nonworking Poor in America.* New York: Basic Books, 1992.

Mendelberg, Tali. *The Race Card: Campaign Strategy, Implicit Messages, and the Norm of Equality.* Princeton, N.J.: Princeton University Press, 2001.

Milkman, Ruth, and Eleanor Townsend. "Gender and the Economy." In Neil J. Smelser and Richard Swedberg, eds., *Handbook of Economic Sociology.* Princeton, N.J.: Princeton University Press, 1994.

Miller, Shazia R., and James E. Rosenbaum. "Hiring in a Hobbesian World." *Work and Occupations* 24 (1997): 498–523.

Mink, Gwendolyn. *Welfare's End.* Ithaca, N.Y.: Cornell University Press, 1998.

"Minority Physicians' Experiences Obtaining Referrals to Specialists and Hospital Admissions." *Medscape General Medicine* (August 9, 2001). <http://www.medscape.com/view article/408160> (accessed February 27, 2002).

Model Penal Code and Commentaries: Official Draft and Revised Comments. Philadelphia: American Law Institute, 1985.

Moe, Terry, ed. *A Primer on America's Schools.* Stanford, Calif.: Hoover Press, 2001.

Moss, Philip, and Chris Tilly. "'Soft' Skills and Race: An Investigation of Black Men's Employment Problems." *Work and Occupations* 23 (1996): 252–76.

———. "How Labor Market Tightness Affects Employer Attitudes and Actions toward Black Job Applicants: Evidence from Employer Surveys." In Robert Cherry and William M. Rodgers III, *Prosperity for All? The Economic Boom and African Americans.* New York: Russell Sage Foundation, 2000.

———. "Why Opportunity Isn't Knocking: Racial Inequality and the Demand for Labor." In Alice O'Connor, Chris Tilly, and Lawrence D. Bobo, eds., *Urban Inequality: Evidence from Four Cities*. New York: Russell Sage Foundation, 2001.

———. *Stories Employers Tell: Race, Skill, and Hiring in America*. New York: Russell Sage Foundation, 2001.

Moynihan, Daniel Patrick. "Toward a Post-Industrial Social Policy." *The Public Interest* (summer 1989): 16–27.

Murnane, Richard, John Willett, and Frank Levy. "The Growing Importance of Cognitive Skills in Wage Determination." *Review of Economics and Statistics* (1995): 251–65.

Murnane, Richard, et al. "The Role of Cognitive Skills in Explaining Inequality in the Earnings of American Workers: Evidence from 1985 and 1991." National Center for Postsecondary Improvement, Stanford, Calif., 1998. Photocopy.

Murray, Charles. *Losing Ground: American Social Policy, 1950–1980*. New York: Basic Books, 1984.

Muth, Richard. "The Causes of Housing Segregation." In *Issues in Housing Discrimination: A Consultation/Hearings of the United States Commission on Civil Rights*. Vol. 1. Washington, D.C.: The Commission, November 12–13, 1985.

Nagel, Thomas. *The View from Nowhere*. New York: Oxford University Press, 1986.

National Center for Health Statistics. "Infant Mortality Rates, Fetal Mortality Rates, and Perinatal Mortality Rates, according to Race: United States, Selected Years 1950–99," (Table 23). *Centers for Disease Control*. <http://www.cdc.gov/nchs/products/pubs/pubd/hus/tables/2001/01hus023 .pdf>. Accessed March 9, 2003.

Neckerman, Kathryn M., and Joleen Kirschenman. "Hiring Strategies, Racial Bias, and Inner-City Workers." *Social Problems* 38 (1991): 433–47.

"The Negro in America: What Must Be Done." *Newsweek*, November 20, 1967, p. 34.

Neibuhr, Reinhold. *The Irony of American History*. New York: Scribner, 1962.

Nelson, James F. *Disparities in Processing Felony Arrests in New York State, 1990–1992*. Albany: New York State Division of Criminal Justice Services, 1995.

Nelson, Sarah. "Racial Discrimination in the NFL." Unpublished paper written for Department of Community Studies, Saint Cloud State College, 2001. Photocopy.

Neubeck, Kenneth J., and Noel A. Czenave. *Welfare Racism: Playing the Race Card Against America's Poor*. New York: Routledge, 2001.

Nielsen, Laura Beth. "Situating Legal Consciousness: Experiences and Attitudes of Ordinary Citizens about Law and Street Harassment." *Law and Society Review* 34 (2000): 1068–90.

Noonan, John T. Jr. "Comment on R. Kent Newmyer, 'John Marshall, Political Parties, and the Origins of Modern Federalism.'" In Harry N. Scheiber, ed., *Federalism: Studies in History, Law, and Policy: Papers from the Second*

Berkeley Seminar on Federalism. Berkeley: University of California, Institute of Government Studies, 1988.

Norell, Robert J. "Caste in Steel: Jim Crow Careers in Birmingham, Alabama." *Journal of American History* 73 (1986): 669–94.

Northrup, Herbert R. *Negro Employment in Basic Industry: A Study of Racial Policies in Six Industries.* Philadelphia: University of Pennsylvania Press, 1970.

O'Connor, Alice, Chris Tilly, and Lawrence D. Bobo, eds., *Urban Inequality: Evidence from Four Cities.* New York: Russell Sage Foundation, 2001.

Oddone, Eugene, et al. "Race, Presenting Signs and Symptoms, Use of Carotid Artery Imaging, and Appropriateness of Carotid Endarterectomy." *Stroke* 30 (1999).

Oliver, Melvin, and Thomas Shapiro. *Black Wealth/White Wealth.* New York: Routledge, 1997.

Onkst, David H. "'First a Negro . . . incidentally a veteran': Black World War Two Veterans and the G.I. Bill of Rights in the Deep South, 1944–1948." *Journal of Social History* (spring 1998).

Oppenheimer, David B. "Negligent Discrimination." *University of Pennsylvania Law Review* 141 (1993): 899–972.

———. "Verdicts Matter: An Examination of California Employment Discrimination and Wrongful Discharge Jury Verdicts." Golden Gate University, 2003. Photocopy.

Orfield, Gary. "Race and the Liberal Agenda: The Loss of the Integrationist Dream, 1965–1974." In Margaret Weir, Ann Shola Orloff, and Theda Skocpol, eds., *The Politics of Social Policy in the United States.* Princeton, N.J.: Princeton University Press, 1988.

Orfield, Gary, and Carole Ashkinaze. *The Closing Door: Conservative Policy and Black Opportunity.* Chicago: University of Chicago Press, 1991.

Orfield, Gary, and Susan E. Eaton. *Dismantling Desegregation: The Quiet Reversal of* Brown v. Board of Education. New York: The New Press, 1996.

Pappas, Gregory, et al. "The Increasing Disparity in Mortality between Socioeconomic Groups in the United States, 1960 and 1986." *New England Journal of Medicine* 329 (1987): 103–9.

Patterson, Orlando. *The Ordeal of Integration.* Washington, D.C.: Civitas/Counterpoint, 1997.

Peterson, Eric, et al. "Racial Variation in the Use of Coronary-Revascularization Procedures: Are the Differences Real? Do They Matter?" *New England Journal of Medicine* 336 (1997): 480–86.

Petrocik, John R., and Scott W. Desposato. "The Partisan Consequences of Majority-Minority Redistricting in the South, 1992 and 1994." *Journal of Politics* 60 (1998): 613–33.

Petterson, Stephen M. "Are Young Black Men Really Less Willing to Work?" *American Sociological Review* 62 (1997): 609–11.

Pettigrew, Thomas, ed. *Racial Discrimination in the United States.* New York: Harper and Row, 1975.

Piliavin, Irving, and Scott Briar. "Police Encounters with Juveniles." *American Journal of Sociology* 70 (September 1964): 206–14.

Pinderhughes, Dianne M. *Race and Ethnicity in Chicago Politics.* Urbana: University of Illinois Press, 1987.

Player, Mack A. *Employment Discrimination Law.* St. Paul, Minn.: West Publishing, 1988.

Poe-Yamagata, Eileen, and Michael A. Jones. *And Justice for Some: Differential Treatment of Minority Youth in the Justice System.* San Francisco: National Council on Crime and Delinquency, April 2000.

Powell, T. J. "Prostate Cancer and African American Men." *Oncology* 11 (1997): 599–605.

The President's Commission on Veterans' Pensions. *Readjustment Benefits: General Survey and Appraisal.* Staff Report No. 9. Washington, D.C.: U.S. Government Printing Office, 1956.

Pusser, Brian. "The Contest over Affirmative Action at the University of California: Theory and Politics of Contemporary Higher Education Policy." Ph.D. dissertation, Stanford University, 1999.

Quadagno, Jill. *The Color of Welfare: How Racism Undermined the War on Poverty.* New York: Oxford University Press, 1994.

Racial and Gender Report Card. Boston: Center for the Study of Sport in Society, Northeastern University, 2001.

Reed, Adolph Jr. *Stirrings in the Jug: Black Politics in the Post-Segregation Era.* Minneapolis: University of Minnesota Press, 1999.

Reed, Adolph Jr., ed. *Without Justice for All: The New Liberalism and Our Retreat from Racial Equality.* Boulder, Colo.: Westview Press, 1999.

Reeves, Keith. *Voting Hopes or Fears? White Voters, Black Candidates and Racial Politics in America.* New York: Oxford University Press, 1997.

Reimers, Cordelia W. "The Effect of Tighter Labor Markets on Unemployment of Hispanics and African Americans: The 1990s Experiences." In Robert Cherry and Williams Rodgers III, eds., *Prosperity for All? The Economic Boom and African Americans.* New York: Russell Sage Foundation, 2000.

Reskin, Barbara F. *The Realities of Affirmative Action in Employment.* Washington, D.C.: American Sociological Association, 1998.

Rice, Mitchell F. "State and Local Government Set-Aside Programs, Disparity Studies, and Minority Business Development in the Post-*Croson* Era." *Journal of Urban Affairs* 15 (1993).

Rich-Edwards, Janet, et al. "Maternal Experiences of Racism and Violence as Predictors of Preterm Birth: Rationale and Study Design." *Paediatric and Perinatal Epidemiology* 15 (2000, Suppl. 2).

Rieder, Jonathan. *Canarsie: The Jews and Italians of Brooklyn against Liberalism.* Cambridge, Mass.: Harvard University Press, 1985.

Rivkin, Steven G., Eric Hanushek, and John Kain. "Teachers, Schools, and Academic Achievement." Amherst College April 2000. Photocopy.

Roberts, Dorothy. "Punishing Drug Addicts Who Have Babies: Women of Color, Equality, and the Right of Privacy." *Harvard Law Review* 104 (1991): 1419–82.

———. *Killing the Black Body: Race, Reproduction, and the Meaning of Liberty.* New York: Pantheon Books, 1997.

Rodgers, William M. III, and William E. Spriggs. "The Effect of Federal Contractor Status on Racial Differences in Establishment-Level Employment Shares: 1979–1992." *American Economic Review* 86 (1996): 290–93.

Roediger, David. *The Wages of Whiteness.* New York: Verso, 1991.

————. *Colored White: Transcending the Racial Past.* Berkeley and Los Angeles: University of California Press, 2002.

Rooke-Ley, Michael. "Correction on Law School Admissions." *SALT Equalizer*, December 2001. <http://www.saltlaw.org> (accessed January 27, 2003).

Rose, Arnold. *The Negro in America.* New York: Harper and Row, 1944.

Rose, Dina, and Todd Clear. "Incarceration, Social Capital, and Crime: Implications for Social Disorganization Theory." *Criminology* 36 (1998): 441–72.

Ross, Arthur M. "The Negro Worker in the Depression." *Social Forces* 18 (1940): 550–59.

Royster, Deirdre. *Race and the "Invisible Hand."* Berkeley: University of California Press, 2003.

Rothstein, Richard, Martin Carnoy, and Luis Benveniste. *Can Public Schools Learn from Private Schools?* Washington, D.C.: Economic Policy Institute, 1999.

Rubenfeld, Jed. "The Anti-Antidiscrimination Agenda." *Yale Law Journal* 111 (2002): 1141–78.

Rutherglen, George. "From Race to Age: The Expanding Scope of Employment Discrimination Law." *Journal of Legal Studies* 24 (1995): 491–521.

Sager, Alan. "Urban Hospital Closings in the Face of Racial Change: A Statement on Hospital Financing Problems." In *Civil Rights Issues in Health Care Delivery.* Washington, D.C.: U.S. Commission on Civil Rights, 1980.

Sampson, Robert. "Urban Black Violence: The Effect of Male Joblessness and Family Disruption." *American Journal of Sociology* 93 (1987): 348–82.

Sampson, Robert, and John Laub. "Urban Poverty and the Family Context of Delinquency." *Child Development* 65 (1994): 538–45.

Sander, Willam. "Catholic Grade Schools and Academic Achievement." *Journal of Human Resources* 31 (1996): 540–48.

Sanders, Elizabeth. "Electorate Expansion and Public Policy: A Decade of Political Change in the South." Ph.D. dissertation, Cornell University, 1978.

Sanders, Heywood. "Convention Center Follies." *The Public Interest* 132 (summer 1998): 58–72.

Satel, Sally, M.D. *How Political Correctness Is Corrupting Medicine.* New York: Basic Books, 2000.

Schmidt, N., et al. "Adverse Impact and Predictive Efficiency of Various Predictor Combinations." *Journal of Applied Psychology* 82 (1997): 719–30.

Schmidt, William. *Why Schools Matter: A Cross-National Comparison of Curriculum and Learning.* San Francisco: Jossey-Bass, 2001.

Schram, Sanford F., Joe Soss, and Richard C. Fording, eds. *Race and the Politics of Welfare Reform.* Ann Arbor: University of Michigan Press, 2003.

Schulman, Bruce J. *From Cottonbelt to Sunbelt.* New York: Oxford University Press, 1991.

Schulman, K., et al. "The Effect of Race and Sex on Physicians' Recommendations for Cardiac Catheterization." *New England Journal of Medicine* 340 (1999): 618–26.

Schuman, Howard, and Lawrence Bobo. "Survey-Based Experiments on White Racial Attitudes toward Residential Integration." *American Journal of Sociology* 2 (1988): 273–99.

Schuman, Howard, Charlotte Steeh, and Lawrence Bobo. *Racial Attitudes in America: Trends and Interpretations.* Cambridge, Mass.: Harvard University Press, 1985.

Schwartz, Lisa M., Steven Woloshin, and H. Gilbert Welch. "Misunderstandings about the Effects of Race and Sex on Physicians' Referrals for Cardiac Catheterization." *New England Journal of Medicine* 341 (1999): 279–83.

Sears, David O., Jim Sidanius, and Lawrence Bobo, eds. *Racialized Politics: The Debate about Racism in America.* Chicago: University of Chicago Press, 2000.

Selmi, Michael. "The Value of the EEOC: Reexamining the Agency's Role in Employment Discrimination Law." *Ohio State Law Review* 57 (1996): 1–64.

Sentencing Project/Human Rights Watch. *Losing the Vote: The Impact of Felony Disfranchisement Laws in the United States.* Washington, D.C.: Sentencing Project/Human Rights Watch, 1998.

Shalom, Stephen R. "Dubious Data: The Thernstroms on Race in America." *Race and Society* 1 (1998): 125–57.

Sheatsley, Paul. "White Attitudes toward the Negro." In Talcott Parsons and Kenneth Clark, eds., *The Negro American.* Boston: Beacon Press, 1966.

Shihadeh, Edward S., and Graham C. Ousey. "Industrial Restructuring and Violence: The Link between Entry-Level Jobs, Economic Deprivation, and Black and White Homicide." *Social Forces* 77 (September 1998): 185–206.

Shihadeh, Edward S., and Darrel Steffensmeier. "Economic Inequality, Family Disruption, and Urban Black Violence." *Social Forces* 73 (December 1994): 729–51.

Shlay, Anne B. "Not in That Neighborhood: The Effects of Population and Housing on the Distribution of Mortgage Finance within the Chicago SMSA." *Social Science Research* 17 (1988): 137–63.

Shulman, Steven. "Why Is the Black Unemployment Rate Always Twice as High as the White Unemployment Rate?" In Richard R. Cornwall and Phanindra V. Wunnava, eds., *New Approaches to Economic and Social Analyses of Discrimination.* New York: Prager, 1991.

Shultz, Marjorie M. "Charleston, Cocaine, and Consent." *Journal of Gender Specific Medicine* 4 (2001): 14–17.

Sidanius, Jim, Felicia Pratto, and Lawrence Bobo. "Racism, Conservatism, Affirmative Action, and Intellectual Sophistication: A Matter of Principled Conservatism or Group Dominance?" *Journal of Personality and Social Psychology* 70 (1996): 476–90.

Siegel, Reva B. "Why Equal Protection No Longer Protects: The Evolving Forms of Status-Enforcing State Action." *Stanford Law Review* 49 (1997): 1111–48.

———. "The Racial Rhetorics of Colorblind Constitutionalism: The Case of *Hopwood v. Texas.*" In Robert Post and Michael Rogin, eds., *Race and Representation: Affirmative Action.* New York: Zone Books, 1998.

Siegelman, Peter, and John Donohue III. "Studying the Iceberg from Its Tip: A

Comparison of Published and Unpublished Employment Discrimination Cases." *Law and Society Review* 24 (1990): 1132–70.

Skolnick, Jerome H. *Justice without Trial.* New York: Wiley, 1966.

Sleeper, Jim. *The Closest of Strangers: Liberalism and the Politics of Race in America.* New York: W. W. Norton, 1990.

———. *Liberal Racism.* New York: Penguin Books, 1997.

Smith, David Barton. *Health Care Divided: Race and Healing a Nation.* Ann Arbor: University of Michigan Press, 1999.

Smith, James P., and Finis R. Welch. *Closing the Gap: Forty Years of Economic Progress for Blacks.* Santa Monica, Calif.: The Rand Corporation, 1986.

Smith, Rogers. *Civic Ideals: Conflicting Visions of Citizenship in U.S. History.* New Haven: Yale University Press, 1997.

Smith, Tom W. "Ethnic Images." *GSS Technical Report No. 19.* Chicago: National Opinion Research Center, January 1991.

Sniderman, Paul, and Thomas Piazza. *The Scar of Race.* Cambridge, Mass.: Harvard University Press, 1993.

Sniderman, Paul, and Edward G. Carmines. *Reaching beyond Race.* Cambridge, Mass.: Harvard University Press, 1997.

Sonenshein, Raphael J. *Politics in Black and White: Race and Power in Los Angeles.* Princeton, N.J.: Princeton University Press, 1993.

Soss, Joe, et al. "The Hard Line and the Color Line: Race, Welfare, and the Roots of Get-Tough Reform." In Sanford F. Schram, Joe Soss, and Richard C. Fording, eds., *Race and the Politics of Welfare Reform.* Ann Arbor: University of Michigan Press, 2003.

Sowell, Thomas. *Black Education: Myths and Tragedies.* New York: David McKay, 1972.

Spriggs, William E., and Rhonda M. Williams. "What Do We Need to Explain about African American Unemployment?" In Robert Cherry and Williams Rodgers III, eds., *Prosperity for All? The Economic Boom and African Americans.* New York: Russell Sage Foundation, 2000.

Starrels, Marjorie E., Sally Bould, and Leon J. Nicholas. "The Feminization of Poverty in the United States: Gender, Race, Ethnicity, and Family Factors." *Journal of Family Issues* 15 (1994).

State of New Jersey, Office of the Attorney General. *Selected Highlights of the Interim Report of the State Police Review Team Regarding Allegations of Racial Profiling.* Trenton, N.J.: Office of the Attorney General, 1999.

Steeh, Charlotte, and Maria Krysan. "Trends: Affirmative Action and the Public, 1970–1995." *Public Opinion Quarterly* 60 (1996): 128–58.

Steele, Claude M., and Joshua Anderson. "Stereotype Threat and the Test Performance of Academically Successful African Americans." In Christopher Jencks and Meredith Phillips, eds. *The Black-White Test Score Gap.* Washington, D.C.: Brookings Institution, 1998.

Steele, Shelby. *The Content of Our Character: A New Vision of Race in America.* New York: St. Martin's Press, 1990.

Steffensmier, Darrell, Jeffrey Ulmer, and John Kramer. "The Interaction of Race, Gender, and Age in Criminal Sentencing: The Punishment Cost of Being Young, Black, and Male." *Criminology* 36 (1998).

Steinberg, Stephen. *Turning Back: The Retreat from Racial Justice in American Thought and Policy.* Boston: Beacon Press, 1995.

Stern, Mark J. "Poverty and Family Composition since 1940." In Michael B. Katz, ed., *The "Underclass" Debate: Views from History.* Princeton, N.J.: Princeton University Press, 1993.

Sugrue, Thomas. *The Origins of the Urban Crisis: Race and Inequality in Postwar Detroit.* Princeton, N.J.: Princeton University Press, 1996.

Sundstrom, W. A. "Last Hired, First Fired? Unemployment and Black Workers during the Great Depression." *The Journal of Economic History* 52 (1992): 415–29.

Swain, Carol M. "The Future of Black Representation." *The American Prospect* 23 (fall 1995): 78–83.

Tate, Katherine. *From Protest to Politics: The New Black Voters in American Elections.* Cambridge, Mass.: Harvard University Press; New York: Russell Sage Foundation, 1994.

Thernstrom, Abigail. "Black Republicans?" *The Public Interest* 120 (summer 1995).

Thernstrom, Stephen, and Abigail Thernstrom. *America in Black and White: One Nation, Indivisible.* New York: Simon and Schuster, 1997.

Thomson, Gregg. "Is the SAT a 'Good Predictor' of Graduation Rates?" Office of Student Research, University of California, Berkeley, 1999. Photocopy.

Tillotson Dirk. "Constitutional Eracism." Boalt Hall School of Law and the Center for the Study of Jurisprudence and Social Policy, University of California, Berkeley. Photocopy available from authors.

Tilly, Charles. *Durable Inequality.* Berkeley and Los Angeles: University of California Press, 1998.

Tilly, Chris, et al. "Space as a Signal: How Employers Perceive Neighborhoods in Four Metropolitan Labor Markers." In Alice O'Connor, Chris Tilly, and Lawrence D. Bobo, eds., *Urban Inequality: Evidence from Four Cities.* New York: Russell Sage Foundation, 2001.

"Title VII of the Civil Rights Act of 1964 Charges." *Equal Employment Opportunity Commission.* <http://www.eeoc.gov/stats/enforcement.html> (accessed February 4, 2003).

Tomasky, Michael. *Left for Dead: The Life, Death, and Possible Resurrection of Progressive Politics in America.* New York: The Free Press, 1996.

Tonry, Michael. *Malign Neglect: Race, Crime, and Punishment in America.* New York: Oxford University Press, 1995, pp. 30–31.

United States Equal Employment Opportunity Commission. *Legislative History of Titles VII and XI of Civil Rights Act of 1964.* Washington, D.C.: U.S. Government Printing Office, 1968.

U.S. Bureau of the Census. *Census of Population, 1940.* Vol. 3, *The Labor Force.* Washington, D.C.: U.S. Government Printing Office, 1943.

———. *Census of Housing, Residential Finance, 1960.* Washington, D.C.: U.S. Government Printing Office, 1961.

———. *Census of Population: 1960. Final Report, Subject Reports, Veterans.* Washington, D.C.: U.S. Government Printing Office, 1961.

———. *Current Population Reports, Money Income of Households, Families, and Persons in the United States: 1987.* Washington, D.C.: U.S. Government Printing Office, 1989.

———. *Current Population Reports, Measuring the Effect of Benefits and Taxes on Income and Poverty: 1990.* Washington, D.C.: U.S. Government Printing Office, 1991.

———. *Current Population Reports, Characteristics of Recipients and the Dynamics of Program Participation.* Washington, D.C.: U.S. Government Printing Office, 1992.

———. "Race and Hispanic Origin of Householder—Families by Median and Mean Income: 1947 to 2001." Historical Income Tables—Families. *U.S. Census Bureau.* <http://www.census.gov/hhes/income/histinc/f05.html> (accessed October 9, 2002).

———. "Race and Hispanic Origin of People by Median Income and Sex: 1947 to 2001." Historical Income Tables—People. *U.S. Census Bureau.* <http://www.census.gov/hhes/income/histinc/p02.html> (accessed October 9, 2002).

U.S. Department of Health and Human Services. *Healthy People 2010: Understanding and Improving Health.* 2nd ed. Washington, D.C.: U.S. Government Printing Office, 2000.

U.S. General Accounting Office, *Death Penalty Sentencing Research Indicates Pattern of Racial Disparities* (Washington, D.C.: General Accounting Office, 1990).

Vars, Frederick, and William Bowen. "Scholastic Aptitude Test Scores, Race, and Academic Performance in Selective Colleges and Universities." In Christopher Jencks and Meredith Phillips, eds. *The Black-White Test Score Gap.* Washington, D.C.: Brookings Institution Press, 1998.

Wacquant, Loic J. D. "Redrawing the Urban Color Line: The State and Fate of Ghetto in PostFordist America." In Craig Calhoun, ed., *Social Theory and the Politics of Identity.* London: Blackwell Publishers, 1994.

Waldinger, Roger, and Thomas Bailey. "The Continuing Significance of Race: Racial Conflict and Racial Discrimination in Construction." *Politics and Society* 19 (1991).

Walton, Hanes Jr. *African American Power and Politics: The Political Context Variable.* New York: Columbia University Press, 1997.

Washington, James M., ed. *A Testament of Hope: The Essential Writings of Martin Luther King, Jr.* New York: Harper and Row, 1986.

Weitzman, Shimon, et al. "Gender, Racial, and Geographic Differences in the Performance of Cardiac Diagnostic and Therapeutic Procedures for Hospitalized Acute Myocardial Infarction in Four States." *American Journal of Cardiology* 79 (1997): 722–26.

Wellman, David. *Portraits of White Racism.* 2nd ed., rev. New York: Cambridge University Press, 1993.

Weng, Garner K. "Look at the Pretty Colors: Rethinking Promises of Diversity as Legally Binding." *La Raza Law Journal* 10 (1998).

Wenneker, M. B., and A. M. Epstein. "Racial Inequalities in the Use of Procedures for Patients with Ischemic Heart Disease in Massachusetts." *Journal of the American Medical Association* 261 (1989): 253–57.

Western, Bruce. "Incarceration, Unemployment, and Inequality." *Focus* 21 (2001).

Whatley, Warren, and Gavin Wright. "Race, Human Capital, and Labour Markets in American History." In George Grantham and Mary Mackinnon, eds., *Labour Market Evolution.* London: Routledge, 1994.

White, Elizabeth. "Special Report: Public Health Racial and Ethnic Disparities." *Health Care Policy Report* 9 (2001).

Wightman, Linda F. "The Threat to Diversity in Legal Education: An Empirical Analysis of the Consequences of Abandoning Race as a Factor." *New York University Law Review* 72 (1997): 1–53.

Wildman, Stephanie M. *Privilege Revealed: How Invisible Preference Undermines America.* New York: New York University Press, 1996.

Williams, Patricia. *The Alchemy of Race and Rights: Diary of a Law Professor.* Cambridge, Mass.: Harvard University Press, 1991.

Wilson, James Q. *Thinking about Crime.* New York: Random House, 1975.

———. "The Facts." *Commentary* (January 1998).

Wilson, William Julius. *The Truly Disadvantaged.* Chicago: University of Chicago Press, 1987.

———. *When Work Disappears: The World of the New Urban Poor.* New York: Random House, 1996.

———. *The Bridge over the Racial Divide: Rising Inequality and Coalition Politics.* Berkeley and Los Angeles: University of California Press, 1999.

Wingo, Phyllis, et al. "Cancer Incidence and Mortality, 1973–1995: A Report Card for the U.S." *Cancer* 82 (1998): 1197–1207.

Witte, John F. "Private School versus Public School Achievement: Are There Findings That Should Affect the Educational Choice Debate?" *Economics of Education Review* 11 (1992): 371–94.

Wordes, Madeline, Timothy S. Bynum, and Charles J. Corley. "Locking Up Youth: The Impact of Race on Detention Decisions." *Journal of Research in Crime and Delinquency* 31 (May 1994): 149–65.

Worley, Scot, Ross Macmillan, and John Hagan. "Just Des(s)erts? The Racial Polarization of Perceptions of Criminal Injustice." *Law and Society Review* 31 (1997): 637–76.

Yood, M. U., et al. "Race and Differences in Breast Cancer Survival in a Managed Care Population." *Journal of the National Cancer Institute* 91 (1999): 1487–91.

Zimmer, Basil. "The Small Businessman and Relocation." In James Q. Wilson, ed., *Urban Renewal: The Record and the Controversy.* Cambridge, Mass.: The MIT Press, 1966.

About the Authors

MICHAEL K. BROWN is professor and chair of the Department of Politics at the University of California, Santa Cruz. He is author of *Working the Street: Police Discretion and the Dilemmas of Reform* (Russell Sage Foundation, 1988) and numerous articles on race, politics, and welfare reform. His most recent book is *Race, Money, and the American Welfare State* (Cornell University Press, 1999).

MARTIN CARNOY is professor of education and economics at Stanford University. Among his books are *The State and Political Theory* (Princeton University Press, 1984); *Education and Work in the Democratic State,* with Henry Levin (Stanford University Press, 1985); *Faded Dreams: The Economics and Politics of Race in America* (Cambridge University Press, 1994); and *Sustaining the New Economy: Work, Family and Community in the Information Age* (Harvard University Press and Russell Sage, 2000).

ELLIOTT CURRIE is author of *Confronting Crime: An American Challenge* (Pantheon, 1985); *Reckoning: Drugs, the Cities and the American Future* (Hill and Wang, 1993); and *Crime and Punishment in America* (Metropolitan Books, 1998). He is currently lecturer in legal studies at the University of California, Berkeley, and visiting professor in the School of Criminology and Criminal Justice, Florida State University.

TROY DUSTER is professor of sociology and senior fellow at the Institute for the History of the Production of Knowledge at New York University. He also holds an appointment as chancellor's professor at the University of California, Berkeley. He is author of *The Legislation of Morality* (The Free Press, 1970); *Cultural Perspectives on Biological Knowledge* (Ablex, 1984) with Karen Garrett; and numerous articles on youth unemployment and postindustrialism, diversity, and higher education. His most recent book is *Backdoor to Eugenics* (Routledge, 1990).

DAVID B. OPPENHEIMER is professor of law and associate dean for academic affairs at Golden Gate University. He has contributed articles on discrimination law and affirmative action to the *University of Pennsylvania Law Review,* the *Cornell Law Review,* the *Columbia Human Rights Law Review,* the *Berkeley Journal of Employment and Labor Law,* the *Berkeley Women's Law Journal,* the *UC Davis Law Review,* the *Hastings Constitutional Law Quarterly,* and numerous other law journals.

MARJORIE M. SHULTZ is professor of law at Boalt Hall School of Law, University of California, Berkeley. She is the author of numerous articles on race, gender, family issues, and health care. Her articles have appeared in the *Yale Law Journal,* and the California, Wisconsin, Stanford, and Iowa Law reviews, as well as in medical and scientific anthologies and journals.

DAVID WELLMAN is professor of community studies at the University of California, Santa Cruz, and research sociologist at the Institute for the Study of Social Change at the University of California, Berkeley. He has written extensively on race and racism in American society. He is the author of *Portraits of White Racism* (Cambridge University Press, 1977); a second edition was published in 1993. His most recent book is *The Union Makes Us Strong* (Cambridge University Press, 1997).

Index

Abrams, Charles, 77
acculturation gap, 7
accumulation: disaccumulation vs., 22–25; efforts to increase, 231–32; examples of, 22–23, 24
ACT (American College Test), 106
Adarand Constructors v. Pena, 187–90
ADC (Aid to Dependent Children), 29
AFDC, 100
affirmative action policies: *Adarand* decision standards for, 189–90; aimed at minimizing white advantages, 186; anti-Affirmative Action ballot (Proposition 209 [California]) and, 85; color-blindness proponents on, 12; conservative opposition to, 161, 254n.21–255n.21; definition of, 25; historic origins of, 25–26; Ole Miss model as alternative to admissions, 124–29; permitted under Title VII, 266n.100; Reagan administration halting enforcement of, 187; Supreme Court ruling five criteria required of, 180–81; Supreme Court on third party burden imposed by, 37; symbols and realities of politics of, 190–92. *See also* Executive Order 10925; public policy; race-conscious admissions
African Americans: attitudes by race toward economic progress of, 225*t;* on civil rights movement successes/failures, 224; claims regarding progress of, 9–10; federal social welfare transfers received by, 98–99; health care insurance access by, 47; higher death rates

for, 45–46; impact of color-blind admissions on, 106–7; impact of cumulative inequalities on, 21–22; income/health care gap between whites and, 13–15; as proportion of prison population, 133; public disinvestment of, 96–102; racial awareness by, 34–36; racial realists view of current state of, 6–9; VRA and political representation of, 198–204; welfare reform (1996) and, 100–101. *See also* black workers
age discrimination, 178, 182, 183*t*
Albonetti, Celesta, 144
Alexander v. Sandoval, 298n.12
Allen, Mark D., 139
Allen v. State Board of Education, 199–200
America in Black and White: One Nation Indivisible (Thernstrom and Thernstrom), 1, 5, 6, 15, 105, 132, 153
American Apartheid (Massey and Denton), 42
An American Dilemma (Myrdal), 136
American Dream, 130
American Enterprise (magazine), 153
anti-Affirmative Action ballot (Proposition 209 [California]), 85
Ashcroft, John, 55
Asian Americans: attendance at UC Berkeley by, 117; test score gap and later earnings by, 121, 122
attitudes: gap between behavior and, 41–43; racial identity and public policy, 31; racial realists on inequality reduced

Designer: Jessica Grunwald
Typeface: 10/13 Sabon
Display: Akzidenz Grotesk Condensed
Compositor: BookMatters, Berkeley
Printer/Binder: Maple-Vail Manaufacturing Group